SELECTED PAPERS ON LEARNING DISABILITIES

Eighth Annual International Conference
of the
Association for Children with Learning Disabilities

March 18-19-20, 1971
Chicago, Illinois

THE CHILD WITH LEARNING DISABILITIES: HIS RIGHT TO LEARN

Edited by John I. Arena

ASSOCIATION FOR CHILDREN WITH LEARNING DISABILITIES
2200 Brownsville Road
Pittsburgh, Pennsylvania 15210

©
Copyright 1971

Association for Children with Learning Disabilities

*Library of Congress Catalogue Card Number 75-184174
ISBN Number: 0-87879-028-4*

All rights reserved. This book, or parts thereof, may not be reproduced in any form without permission from the publisher.

Printed in the United States of America.

Published and distributed by
Academic Therapy Publications
San Rafael, California 94901

ASSOCIATION FOR CHILDREN WITH LEARNING DISABILITIES

2200 BROWNSVILLE ROAD • PITTSBURGH, PA 15210 • AREA CODE 412 882-5201

July 1, 1971

Dear Friend of ACLD:

In 1971, the ACLD returned to hold its 8th Annual Conference in the city where the first meeting was held in 1964—Chicago, Illinois.

It was a thrilling return home for ACLD, and some 5,000 persons attended the three days of presentations.

The Conference theme, "Our Challenge: The Right to Learn," was selected by the Program Committee with great care and sincerity, and it was enforced by several important events. The ACLD Professional Advisory Board met to formulate new pathways for insuring LD Children their right to learn. For the first time a meeting was held with other national organizations who share our interests in helping children.

Through the use of audio and video taping volunteers, many highlights of the Conference were captured for future use.

The high quality of the 75 sessions featuring 277 speakers is reflected in the representative selections presented in this volume.

The ACLD proudly typifies the volunteer movement in America—dedicated people combining together to accomplish specific objectives. And these persons devote their time and energies while receiving no personal benefit except to see a worthy goal attained. ACLD is indeed fortunate to be able to harness and take advantage of these varied individual talents to help our children.

So—to the participants, the workers, the attendees of the 8th International Converence of the ACLD—thank you! Please continue to keep your eyes on the goal as you have so well in the past.

Sincerely,

W. Joseph Gartner
ACLD President
1971-1972

ACLD PARENT-ORGANIZED GROUPS CONCERNED WITH LEARNING DISABILITIES

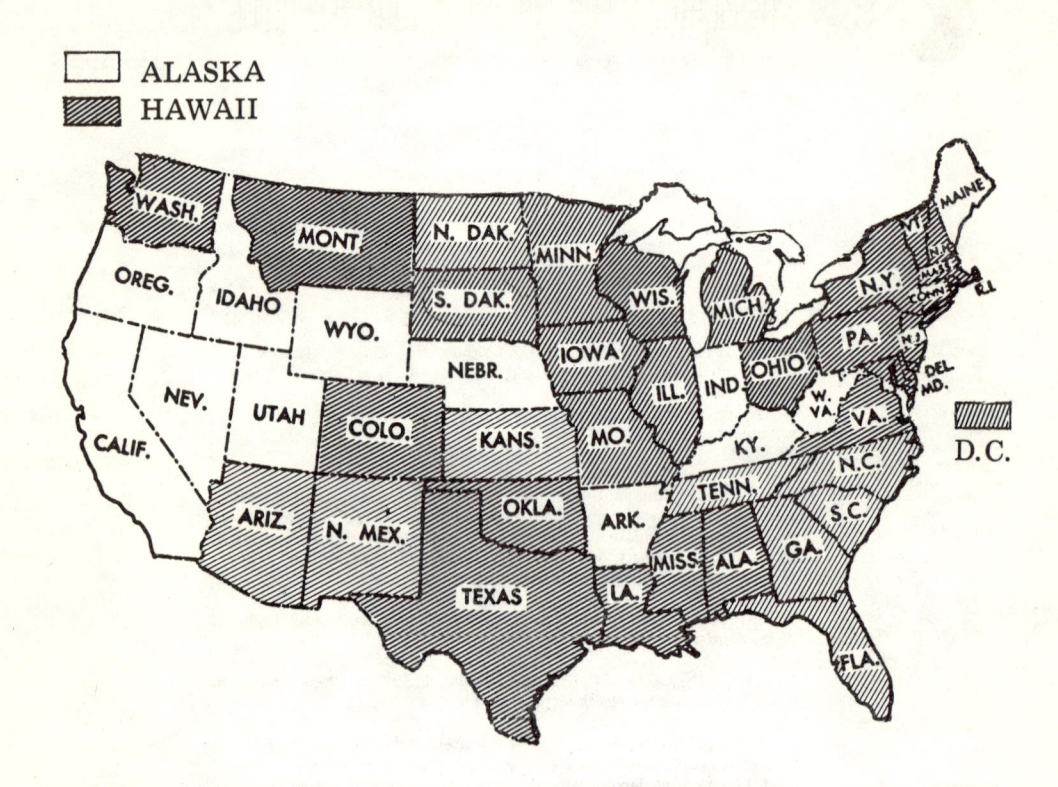

☐ ALASKA
▨ HAWAII

STATES WITH ONE OR MORE ACLD AFFILIATES IN EARLY 1971

Alabama	Illinois	Montana	Pennsylvania
Arizona	Iowa	New Hampshire	Rhode Island
Colorado	Kansas	New Jersey	South Carolina
Connecticut	Louisiana	New Mexico	South Dakota
Delaware	Maryland	New York	Tennessee
D. of Columbia	Massachusetts	North Carolina	Texas
Florida	Michigan	North Dakota	Vermont
Georgia	Minnesota	Ohio	Virginia
Hawaii	Mississippi	Oklahoma	Washington
	Missouri		Wisconsin

Awards

EACH YEAR, the outgoing ACLD president has the honor to present awards at the annual banquet. Of all the responsibilities, this one, by far, is the most pleasant. It is a wonderful feeling to stop, and instead of looking at what is not being done, to look at the many and varied accomplishments that have been achieved and that are continuing to take place. With these awards we honor five wonderful and great persons. The work of each of these has reached out and has brought light, hope, confidence, and a future to many children and parents, who, without their help, would be in despair.

JOHN E. FOGARTY AWARD

The John E. Fogarty Award is named in honor of the late Congressman, John E. Fogarty of Rhode Island, who was an outstanding advocate of special education legislation in the House of Representatives. The 1970 Fogarty Award is made in grateful appreciation for an individual's distinguished governmental service and for his concern for the welfare of children with learning disabilities. The recipient of this award served as coordinator of the Unit on Learning Disabilities with the Bureau of the Handicapped, United States Office of Education. He performed untiring efforts in pursuit of excellence with regard to teacher training and services for learning-disabled children. His efforts in bringing about growth in teacher training programs and for establishing communications among professionals involved in teacher training came at a time when they were critically needed. He is presently professor of special education at Southern Connecticut State College in New Haven. As this year's chairman of our conference program committee, he has spent endless hours planning and working to put together this outstanding conference.

It is a great honor for me to present the John E. Fogarty Award to Dr. J. Gerald Minskoff.

PIONEER AWARD

The ACLD Pioneer Award is given each year to a person from the state in which the Conference is held, upon the recommendation of the conference host affiliate. Our presentation this year is both unique and most appropriate. It is unique in that we are giving two Pioneer Awards, one to a professional and one to a nonprofessional. It is appropriate because our two award recipients are not only pioneers in the state of Illinois, but they are truly pioneers to the entire movement of learning disabilities in the United States.

Pioneer Award—Professional

We are recognizing our Professional Pioneer Award recipient for her long devoted professional services, which date back to the very beginnings of the learning-disabilities movement. While working primarily in fields of education and psychology, her writing, research, and practice at the Cove Schools have given enlightenment to members of all the disciplines involved in remediating children with learning disabilities. Through her knowledge and understanding, parents and professionals have discovered and learned to use the tools to train these young people for a better life. Besides her contribution to professional knowledge, she early realized the need for greater parent understanding and participation. Because of this perceptive outlook of the needs of these children and their families, she aided in the founding of the first parent organization, the Fund for Perceptually Handicapped Children. She was on ACLD's first professional advisory board. She has the unique gift of brilliant professional contribution coupled with compassion for these children and their families.

It is an honor to confer ACLD's Pioneer Award on Dr. Laura Lehtinen Rogan.

Pioneer Award—Nonprofessional

Our second Pioneer Award also has special meaning. Our award winner is neither a parent of a learning-disabled child, nor a professional. She is one of those rare individuals who early recognized a need and dedicated herself to that need. She is a founder of the Fund for Perceptually Handicapped Children, the group that was most instrumental in helping to organize our national Association for Children with Learning Disabilities. She served as president of the Fund from 1957 to 1960, and is presently a director. She also served as the first treasurer of ACLD in 1964 and 1965. She was a leading supporter of the bill that became Article XIV of the Illinois School Code, which has required all state school districts to provide special education programs as needed, since July 1, 1969. She was awarded the Illinois Council for Children with Learning Disabilities' Distinguished Service Award for 1970 and the Illinois Council for Exceptional Children's Distinguished Service Award for 1968. She is chairman of the Illinois State Advisory Council on the Education of Handicapped Children. ACLD and children with learning disabilities are deeply indebted to this true pioneer in learning disabilities.

We in ACLD are proud to confer the Pioneer Award upon Mrs. Gordon (Dolly) Hallstrom.

PRESIDENT'S AWARD

The President's Award is one which is given by the decision of the ACLD president alone. Usually this award is given to someone within the organization who has been outstanding not only in the performance of his responsibilities but in his overall efforts on behalf of learning-disabled children. This makes the decision a difficult one, because we are fortunate in ACLD to have so many fine workers. The winner of our President's Award this year has literally dedicated his life to ACLD and to the children we serve. For fifty-six consecutive months, without interruption, he has produced the ACLD *Items of Interest*. This month 31,000 copies are in print. The impact and usefulness of the excellent information circulated cannot be underestimated. The newsbriefs have far greater impact than most people realize. In addition to the newsbriefs, he originated the *ACLD Directory*. He has served faithfully and efficiently on ACLD's board of directors and on many committees. The Library of Congress has recently turned to him for help in preparing a brochure on *Talking Book Services for Learning Disabled Children*.

It is with great personal pleasure that I confer the President's Award on Randolph T. Snively.

LEARNING-DISABILITIES AWARD

ACLD's highest award, the Learning-Disabilities Award, is given each year to a person of professional status who has made outstanding contributions to children with learning disabilities.

In looking back, we see that in 1965 the Learning-Disabilities Award was given to Dr. Samuel Kirk; in 1966 it was presented to Dr. Helmer Myklebust; in 1967, to Dr. Marianne Frostig; in 1968, to Dr. Sylvia Richardson; and in 1969, to Dr. William Cruickshank.

For 1970, we continue in this great tradition and confer the ACLD Learning-Disabilities Award on a professional who has distinguished herself not only during the past year, but for many years.

She has offered a combination of academic proficiency plus common sense, power plus charm, as she has proceeded through every phase of the educational circuit on behalf of our children. She has held important positions, beginning with teaching at the University of Illinois and now directing diagnostic services at Schaumburg School District 54, Hoffman Estates, Illinois. She has served as a consultant to the United States Office of Education since 1967. The number of universities at which she has been a visiting teacher are too many to mention. We are particularly proud that she is public school oriented and has conducted many workshops for teachers throughout the country. She is currently president of the Council for Exceptional Children's Division of Learning Disabilities.

She has served on ACLD's professional advisory board since 1968 and responds instantly to any call. Just last week, with only a few days notice, she prepared testimony for an ACLD presentation to a congressional committee that is considering appropriations for learning-disabilities programs. She has served on ACLD conference planning committees for the last five conferences, including this one. Her generosity in writing and in giving her articles to parent groups for their resources has been unequaled. She seems to have an inexhaustible availability to travel and participate in local, regional, and national seminars and conferences. Through her participation in these meetings throughout the country, she has helped untold numbers of teachers and children.

We confer this award because of her many distinguished years of service and also because she is the one who, in our opinion, did more for learning disabilities in 1970 than any other person in the United States.

It is a privilege and honor to present ACLD's Learning-Disabilities Award to Dr. Jeanne McRae McCarthy.

Hyman J. Gardsbane
ACLD President
1970-1971

Jeanne McRae McCarthy

1971 EIGHTH ANNUAL INTERNATIONAL CONFERENCE
of the
ASSOCIATION FOR CHILDREN WITH LEARNING DISABILITIES

Conference Planning

Mrs. Bert P. Schloss, *Program Chairman*
J. Gerald Minskoff, Ed.D., *Committee Chairman*
W. Joseph Gartner, *Coordinator*
Mrs. Clifford Hullinger, *Recording Secretary*
Adam Silverstein, *Treasurer*
Joseph B. Hall, *National Liaison*
James C. Chalfant, Ed.D.
Doris Johnson
Jeanne M. McCarthy, Ph.D.
Harold J. McGrady, Ph.D.
Mrs. John Mueller
William C. Wilson, M.D.

Local Arrangements Committee

Mrs. Donald F. Foertsch, *Resources*
Mrs. W. Joseph Gartner, *Administration*
Mrs. Charles R. Goldstein, *Hospitality*
David Hedberg, *Printing*
Lester O. Johnson, *Exhibits*
Mrs. Bernard Kamin, *Personnel Recruitment*
Robert F. Kelly, *Public Relations*
Mrs. Ronald Lapin, *Film Theater*
Sawyer E. Smaller, *Audio Visual*
Randolph T. Snively, *Research*
Mrs. Ellis L. Stukenberg, *President's Dinner*
Mrs. Gilbert Tierney, *Registration*

NATIONAL OFFICERS, DIRECTORS, AND ADVISORS OF ACLD

OFFICERS

1970-71		1971-72
Hyman J. Gardsbane	**President**	W. Joseph Gartner
W. Joseph Gartner	**First Vice-President**	Val L. Schoenthal
Mrs. Willetta Silva	**Second Vice-President**	Mrs. Martha B. Bernard
Robert A. Jackson	**Third Vice-President**	Robert A. Jackson
Mrs. Robert M. Tillotson	**Secretary**	Mrs. Robert M. Tillotson
Mrs. B. Thompson	**Treasurer**	Mrs. B. Thompson
Robert W. Russell	**Past President**	Hyman J. Gardsbane

DIRECTORS

1970-71
- Mrs. Alfhild Akselsen, Ph.D.
- Mrs. F. D. Asher
- Mrs. Martha B. Bernard
- Joseph B. Hall
- Lee W. Haslinger
- Mrs. Hugh Lanier
- Mrs. B. F. McMahon
- John R. Moss
- Chester Poremba, Ph.D.
- Val L. Schoenthal
- Arthur S. Seidman
- Mrs. Keith Slettehaugh
- Randolph T. Snively
- Mrs. Yates Trotter, Jr.
- Sumner J. Zabriskie

1971-72
- Mrs. Alfhild Akselsen, Ph.D.
- Mrs. F. D. Asher
- Joseph B. Hall
- Lee W. Haslinger
- Albert Katzman
- John R. Moss
- Mrs. Everard Munsey
- Chester Poremba, Ph.D.
- Robert W. Russell
- Mrs. Bert P. Schloss
- Mrs. Keith Slettehaugh
- Eli Tash
- Mrs. Yates Trotter, Jr.
- Mrs. Gene Walker
- Sumner J. Zabriskie

PROFESSIONAL ADVISORS

1970-71
- Ray H. Barsch, Ph.D.
- Herbert G. Birch, M.D., Ph.D.
- William L. Byrne, Ph.D.
- James C. Chalfant, Ed.D.
- William M. Cruickshank, Ph.D.
- Leon Eisenberg, M.D.
- Elizabeth Freidus
- Edward C. Frierson, Ph.D.
- Marianne Frostig, Ph.D.
- Doris Johnson
- Samuel A. Kirk, Ph.D. (Chmn.)
- Jeanne M. McCarthy, Ph.D.
- Helmer R. Myklebust, Ph.D.
- Sylvia O. Richardson, M.D.
- Charles R. Strother, Ph.D.

1971-72
- Herbert G. Birch, M.D., Ph.D.
- William L. Byrne, Ph.D.
- James C. Chalfant, Ed.D.
- William M. Cruickshank, Ph.D.
- Leon Eisenberg, M.D.
- Elizabeth Freidus
- Edward C. Frierson, Ph.D.
- Marianne Frostig, Ph.D.
- Gerald Getman, O.D.
- Oliver Hurley, Ph.D.
- Doris Johnson
- Samuel A. Kirk, Ph.D. (Chmn.)
- Donald Mahler, Ph.D.
- Jeanne M. McCarthy, Ph.D.
- Helmer R. Myklebust, Ph.D.
- Angie Nall
- Sylvia O. Richardson, M.D.
- Julien Stein, Ed.D.

Other collections available in this series...

SELECTED PAPERS ON LEARNING DISABILITIES
from
Proceedings of Conferences
of the
Association for Children with Learning Disabilities

Third Annual Conference
1966 — Tulsa, Oklahoma
**International Approach to Learning Disabilities
of Children and Youth**

Fourth Annual Conference
1967 — New York City
**Management of the Child with Learning Disabilities:
An Interdisciplinary Challenge**

Fifth Annual Conference
1968 — Boston, Massachusetts
**Successful Programing:
Many Points of View**

Sixth Annual Conference
1969 — Fort Worth, Texas
**Progress in Parent Information,
Professional Growth, and Public Policy**

Seventh Annual Conference
1970 — Philadelphia, Pennsylvania
**Meeting Total Needs of Learning-Disabled Children:
A Forward Look**

Prices sent on request
by

Academic Therapy Publications
San Rafael, California 94901

Contents

Awards . . . . *Hyman J. Gardsbane* v

Foreword . . . . *Hyman J. Gardsbane* xvii

Preface . . . . *John I. Arena* xix

I. KEYNOTE ADDRESSES

Language Acquisition
   in Developmental Dyslexics . . . . *Macdonald Critchley* 3

The Right to Learn . . . . *Edwin W. Martin* 11

On the Morning of the Fifth Day . . . . *Walter W. Straley* 19

II. PARENTS

Parents Need to Know:
   Parents and Teachers
   Work Together . . . . *Leo F. Buscaglia* 27

The Parents Talk to Doctors . . . . . *Sylvia O. Richardson* 41
                                           Joseph L. Kloss
                                           Dean Timmons

III. EDUCATIONAL TRENDS

Computer Applications
   in the Field
   of Learning Disabilities . . . . *Janet W. Lerner* 59
                                           David Anderson

A Management Approach
   for Meeting the Needs
   of Children with Specific
   Learning Disabilities . . . . *Mary Ben McDorman* 65

Prescriptive Living . . . . *Angie Nall* 69

Formal Evaluation of the
Effectiveness of Performance
Contracting Programs
for Learning Disabilities . . . . *Lowell A. Seymore*   75
                                                  Barton B. Proger

Madison School Plan . . . . *Frank D. Taylor*   85

Success-Oriented Program:
Private Plus Public Schools . . . . *Ruth Tofanelli*   91
                                              Nancy Jo Telford

An Inner City Program for
Children with Learning Disabilities:
Problems and Solutions. . . . . *Lillie Pope*   97

IV. EDUCATIONAL TECHNIQUES

Typing Keys for Remediation
of Reading and Spelling . . . . *Maetta Davis*   105
                                       Mary Inez Brownlee

The Nonreading Parallel Curriculum
Part I: Philosophy . . . . *Douglas E. Wiseman*   111

The Nonreading Parallel Curriculum
Part II: Administration . . . . *Warren Panushka*   117

The Nonreading Parallel Curriculum
Part III: Classroom. . . . . *Aina McDaniel*   123

Teaching Visual and Auditory
Decoding Skills to
Learning-Handicapped Children
within a Reinforcement System . . . *A. Carol Hartman*   131
                                     Thomas M. Stephens

Judgment-Making Skills:
Can They be Developed? . . . . *Maurice Kubena*   137

Music in Special Education . . . . *Vera Moretti*   143

V. LANGUAGE PROGRAMS

Processes of
Language Development . . . . *Sandie Barrie*   151

Neurological Basis
of Language in Children . . . . *Clement E. Brooke*   157

Analysis of Syntax as a Method
of Determining the Linguistic
Facility of Individuals . . . . *Marvin D. Loflin*   163
                                     Nancy Barron

Syntactic Structures Used
by Learning-Disabled Children. . . . . *Patricia Goodding*   169

Complexity of Spoken Language
of Children with
Learning Disabilities:
Implications for Instruction . . . . . . *Veralee B. Hardin*   177

A Program for Teaching
Language to Aphasic Children . . . . *Kim Winston*   181

VI. EARLY IDENTIFICATION

Early Identification
of the Not-So-Specific
Learning-Disability Population . . . *Howard S. Adelman*   187

Learning-Disability Children
in the Public School Setting . . . . . *Philip A. Hansen*   191

Some Questions About
Early Identification . . . . *Barbara K. Keogh*   195

Early Identification:
A Diagnostic Dilemma . . . . *Annette Tessier*   197

VII. THE ADOLESCENT

Personality and Reading
Retardation in Junior
High School Students . . . . *D. Bruce Bell*   203
Franklin D. Lewis
Robert P. Anderson

Bridging the Achievement
Gap in Negative
Learning Adolescents . . . . *Kathleen McDonnell*   209

Learning-Disabled Children
at the Secondary Level:
Educational Programing
in Perspective . . . . *J. Gerald Minskoff*   213

VIII. TEACHER TRAINING

Teacher Certification
in Learning Disabilities . . . . *Harold J. McGrady*   219
Margaret Atchison

Description of a Secondary
SLD Teacher-Training
Program and its Clientele . . . . *Shirley Pearl*   225

Teacher Training
in the Public Schools . . . . *Carole Post* 233

IX. RESEARCH FROM ALLIED FIELDS

Vision and Learning
Disabilities: Part I . . . . *Curtis D. Benton, Jr.* 243

Vision and Learning
Disabilities: Part II . . . . *Irving J. Peiser* 247

Cerebral Stimulants for
Children with
Learning Disorders . . . . *Hunter H. Comly* 259

Reading Achievement as a
Function of Maturity, Diet,
and Manipulation of Chronic
States of High Arousal . . . . . . *George von Hilsheimer* 269

Making the Child Accessible
for Teaching-Learning:
The Role of the Internist and
Allergist in Learning Disabilities . . . . *S. D. Klotz* 283

Biobehavioral Psychiatry
and Learning Disabilities . . . . . . *William H. Philpott* 293

APPENDIX OF TESTS   311

Foreword

THE 8TH ANNUAL ACLD International Conference celebrates ACLD's seventh birthday. In these few years, ACLD has grown from affiliates in just a few states into a large, mature organization in thirty-seven states, the District of Columbia, and the Virgin Islands. From the theme of our first conference, "Conference on Exploration into the Problems of the Perceptually Handicapped Child" to our theme of this conference, "Our Challenge: The Right to Learn," we have witnessed far more than the maturing of a national voluntary organization. We have seen an explosion of interest, knowledge, and study into the problem of a learning-disabled child. In addition, we have seen new legislation on state and federal levels. But despite all of this interest and effort, we are also seeing more parents becoming disillusioned and discouraged, and their voices are growing louder. The "Challenge" in our theme today may very well become the "Demand" of tomorrow.

Hyman J. Gardsbane
ACLD President
1970—1971

Preface

IT WAS not too long ago that children with unique learning styles were unable to receive the special educational treatment they needed. There was simply not enough known about the ways in which they learned. The conferences of the Association for Children with Learning Disabilities have, year after year, brought together thinkers and doers for a mutual sharing of knowledge, and as a result, children have benefited.

This year's conference, appropriately titled, "Our Challenge: The Right to Learn," reiterates and reinforces succinctly, the proposition that children with learning disabilities can indeed profit from classroom programs when they are geared to their specific patterns of learning.

John I. Arena
Editor
Academic Therapy Publications

SECTION I

Keynote Addresses

Language Acquisition in Developmental Dyslexics

Macdonald Critchley*

THE ACQUISITION of language skills by the developing child is one of the most striking adventures within the field of perception. In the first place, there is the steady growth of an ability to communicate by way of articulated verbal symbols. This is a process of learning that is in many ways unusual—if not, indeed, unique—when compared with other accomplishments. Though a linguistic environment is obligatory, for no child can possibly attain language if reared in an acoustic vacuum, the learning takes place without the active intervention of a preceptor. From out of the booming, buzzing confusion of auditory signals that surround him, the child gradually derives meaning, and by an elaborate process of selection, reception, imitation, and exteriorization, he gradually succeeds in coding and decoding the auditory symbols.

Those who are interested in what is currently dubbed "psycholinguistics" are apt to take for granted the veritable miracle that goes on every day under our noses; namely, the facile and seemingly effortless acquirement of speech by a normal child. How often do we pause to consider the sheer magnitude of this learning process? This might be especially appreciated by those who experience the laborious acquisition of a second language later in life. In this connection, some pertinent questions have been put forward by Jesperson, the famous linguist of the last century who, though himself a Dane, wrote and spoke in the most perfect English:

> How did it happen that children, in general, learn their mother tongue so well? That this is a problem becomes clear when we contrast a child's first acquisition of its mother tongue with the later acquisition of any foreign language. The contrast is indeed striking and manifold. Here, we have quite a little child without experience or prepossessions. There, a bigger child, or it may

---

*Macdonald Critchley, M.D., is consulting physician, Institute of Neurology, London, England, and president of the World Federation of Neurology. Portions of this paper are based on Dr. Critchley's presentation, "Developmental Dyslexia: A Constitutional Disorder of Symbolic Perception," given at the symposium of the Association for Research in Nervous and Mental Diseases, entitled Perception and Its Disorders, December 6 and 7, 1968.

be a grown-up person with all sorts of knowledge and powers. Here, a haphazard method of procedure. There, the whole task laid out in a system, for even in the school books that don't follow the old grammatical system, there is a certain definite order of progress from more elementary to more difficult material. Here, no professional teachers, but the child's parents, brothers and sisters, nursery maids, and playmates. There, teachers trained for many years specially to teach language. Here, only oral instruction. There, not only that, but reading books, dictionaries, and other assistance. And yet, this is the result. Here, complete and exact command of the language as a native speaks it, however stupid the children. There, in most cases, even with people otherwise highly gifted, a defective and inexact command of language.[1]

The acquisition of language skills depends, as a matter of fact, upon a constellation of influences, some of them extrinsic, others intrinsic. Sociocultural factors are as important, perhaps, as questions of innate intellectual level and the degree of ego strength. G. A. Miller, a linguist, provides a concise summary of the factors that influence the acquisition of spoken speech: "If we tried to picture the most precocious child orator, we should think of a blind girl, the only daughter of wealthy parents. The child with the greatest handicap would be a hard-of-hearing boy, one of a pair of twins, born into a large family with poor parents who speak two or three languages."[2] These two formulae describe succinctly the diversity of the circumstances that influence the rate of speech acquirement. At a later age and by dint of a process of indoctrination and learning, a child ordinarily achieves mastery over the graphic symbols with which he is confronted so that he can not only discern meaning within the lines and shapes before him, but, in turn he can transmit his ideas into a set of graphic symbols that can be stored for an indefinite period. This aspect of the acquisition of language comprises, in plain terms, the art of reading and of writing.

Charles Dickens must have come across many, many children who had difficulties with learning and reading. In *Great Expectations* he wrote, "I struggled through the alphabet as if it had been a bramble bush, getting considerably worried and scratched by every letter. After that, I fell among thieves, the nine figures, who seemed every evening to do something new to disguise themselves and baffle recognition. But at last, I began, in a purblind, groping way to read, write, and cipher on the very smallest scale."

Neurologists and others are aware that this communicative faculty is highly sensitive and vulnerable. It can readily become impaired and even destroyed by dint of disease processes within the brain, particularly when the lesion is located within certain regions that seem to possess peculiar significance in the specialization of linguistic function. Nor is that all. The developing child does not always attain expertise in the facility that is common to the average child. In the acquisition of spoken speech, he may lag behind, not by dint of a congenital deafness, which is understandable, nor by reason of intellectual inadequacy. The problem may be essentially one of delayed development of articulate utterance, occurring in vacuo, as it were. We have no adequate term for this state of affairs, the usual expression, *congenital aphasia*, being wholly unacceptable to neuropsychological purists.

Pursuing this problem more deeply, we can also discern cases where the processes of decoding are at fault; that is, where the perception of linguistic information does not keep pace with the child's ability to transmit data. There are two chief examples of this kind of perceptual difficulty; one of them very rare, one comparatively common. The more unusual of these constitutional deficits comprises an inability on the part of the child to comprehend the meaning of auditory speech—in other words, congenital word deafness, or better, congenital auditory imperception. The current habit of referring to this syndrome as *childhood aphasia* cannot be too strongly deplored by neurologists.

THE MORE COMMON INSTANCE of an innate difficulty in the realm of language comprehension occurs in cases of specific reading retardation, a topic which I will consider in a little more detail. Reading skill, together with its allied faculty of correct writing, is less easily attained than articulate utterance and the correct interpretation of speech and sounds. Many circumstances may cause the school child to lag behind his age group in reading and writing. Some of these are intrinsic—others, environmental. There is, however, a condition whereby—and for constitutional and genetically determined reasons—the youngster falls behind others, not only in his own age group but also those in his intellectual bracket, when it comes to the task of mastering the mystery of verbal symbols in print or in script. This is not a psychologically occasioned difficulty, nor a consequence of inadequate teaching techniques, nor the outcome of intellectual insufficiency, nor the by-product of imperfect vision or hearing. This particular difficulty represents to neurologists an isolated entity, which is currently spoken of as *specific developmental dyslexia*. Somerset Maugham probably stumbled on this in his short story, "The Verger." He said, "The cook in my first place tried to teach me to read, but I didn't seem to get the knack of it. I couldn't seem able to get the letters in the head when I was a nipper."

Neurologists have often been criticized for neglecting to define clearly what they mean by the expression, *developmental dyslexia*. The definition that has been promulgated by the World Federation of Neurology is as follows: "A disorder manifested by difficulty in learning to read, despite conventional instruction, despite adequate intelligence, and despite socio-cultural opportunity. It is dependent upon fundamental cognitive disabilities which are frequently of constitutional origin." That is the agreed definition.

It is perhaps desirable to re-create the negative features of this particular type of difficulty in learning to read. The child with developmental dyslexia is not emotionally disturbed—primarily, at any rate—although, understandably, he may become frustrated later with ideas of inferiority or with reactive aggression, and it is important to note here that he has no disorders in the visual sphere. This includes such less obvious defects as occular-motor imbalance or incoordinate eye movements. It was concluded at a recent symposium in the United States that an increasing number of parents are being bilked out of large sums of money by charlatans who have made a travesty of the eye's role in reading. Much of this activity has centered around the phenomenon of eye dominance. The belief that this can be at the root of so profound and broad a human problem as a reading or learning disability is naive, simplistic, and unsupported by scientific data.

With these children, no impairment has been discovered in the auditory field, not even any confusion in the interpretation of phonemes of somewhat similar nature. The blame cannot be laid upon such pedagogic shortcomings as unduly frequent changes of schools, nor to either premature or belated attempts at teaching, nor even to inappropriate techniques of instruction. The grotesque illogicality of the spelling of the queen's English cannot be blamed either, for we now realize that dyslexia is encountered in children throughout the world, whatever the basic linguistic structure of the mother tongue.

This difficulty in learning to read is also not aligned with any obvious cerebral pathology. It is perhaps necessary to emphasize this side of the problem, for there has been a tendency in some circles to correlate developmental dyslexia with minimal brain damage. This latter, in itself, is an entity of dubious validity. Some physicians have laid stress upon the presence of subtle, tenuous, or miniscule neurological signs. Regrettably, they are spoken of as "soft" neurological signs. But, with greater experience with this problem, one realizes that these "soft" physical disabilities disappear as a child grows older, and one is tempted to look upon them as marks of an associated maturational lag, rather than of a structural lesion.

In the normal child, reading entails two separate, albeit coordinated, processes. The child not only learns to attach meaning to a graphic symbol, but also to associate the visual appearance of that symbol with its acoustic properties. In the Indo-European group of tongues, this double task is facilitated by the fact that each constituent word is phonetic, being made up of a combination of phonemic signs, that is to say, letters. Expressed differently, it can be said that such words can be spelled out and synthesized along phonetic pathways.

Japanese is different in that there is a combination of two types of script, neither of which is literal. One is syllabic, and the other is ideographic. Chinese, however, is an extreme example of a total linguistic dissociation between appearance, sound, and meaning. The task of aligning these three activities must be one of unusual difficulty, and it would not be surprising if we were to learn that reading retardation is unusually common in China. This, of course, would not have any real bearing upon the problem of developmental dyslexia, which we regard as independent of the inherent structure of the language concerned.

A child with developmental dyslexia has no problem when it comes to identifying and distinguishing straightforward signs and symbols and signals, even though they are instances of nonverbal communication. Thus, the developmental dyslexic has no trouble at all in understanding traffic signs. He can, like anyone else, pick out, sort, and name various makes of automobiles or aircraft, postage stamps, dogs, birds, butterflies, flowers—indeed anything except verbal symbols. Usually, he can identify numerals, and his powers of calculation are intact until his school grade brings him up against the task of interpreting mathematical problems as set out in writing or print. Musical notation may or may not be beyond the competency of a dyslexic. There is no rule here.

By way of specialized skill and intensive remedial training, the dyslexic gradually overcomes much of his predicament with reading. Indeed, some fortunate dyslexics, even without special tuition, learn eventually to read through a process of sheer intellectual effort, coupled with drive and assisted by sympathetic parental and scholastic encouragement. However, such "exdyslexics," as I like to call them, may confess that even after their school days are behind them, they do not read for pleasure. Or, if they do, they may read slowly. They skip long and unfamiliar words. Or, in an obsessional fashion, they endeavor to look up puzzling terms in the dictionary. These exdyslexics confess that they continue to feel embarrassed when called upon to read aloud, for they find particularly bothersome the duplex task of enunciation and interpretation. The former problem is well shown by the manner in which, confronted with a polysyllabic word, they may put the stress upon the wrong syllable. The performance of these ex-dyslexics is sensitive to stressful situations. Thus, called to the witness stand in a law court, an exdyslexic adult may experience unusual perplexity in reading aloud the letters and documents handed to him by the attorney. Such an individual may also undergo a temporary deterioration in reading skills as the result of an intercurrent anxiety state or a depressive illness.

DIFFICULTY IN WRITING is the natural consequence of difficulty in reading. Copying usually presents no burden, although the dyslexic child may have great difficulty in copying from a blackboard because the words are exposed for too short a time. The dyslexic who is an "uncertain speller, a seldom reader," as Harper Lee put it in her novel, *To Kill a Mocking-Bird*, or a reluctant reader, an erratic speller, as I prefer to say it, is unable to express himself freely and easily on paper, or even to take down a text that is dictated to him. The principal hardship, however, lies in the correct spelling of the words that he wishes to write. So extreme are the errors perpetrated by the dyslexic that it is possible to diagnose the nature of the disability from the mere perusal of the text. In other words, the dyslexic's mode of writing transcends that which one might ascribe to mere educational inadequacy, or intellectual subnormality, or sheer idiosyncratic poor spelling. It would take too long to do justice to the great diversity of defects that may be discerned in the spontaneous writing executed by a dyslexic. The following are a few, broad types of defects:

- Overall untidy penmanship, with badly formed letters. Indeed, some of the words are so distorted that they are barely identifiable. Not infrequently, one letter may fuse with the next so as to form an unorthodox scriptorial amalgam. Capital letters are often interpolated within the middle of the word, or one word may be linked with the next in an odd way by means of smooth or interlacing strokes.
- Rotations of letters. These are not infrequent, and confusion commonly occurs between such mirror-opposite letters as *d* and *b*, *h* and *y*.
- Reversal of syllables or words, for example, *was* instead of *saw*.

- Abnormal arrangement of the constituent letters of a word, the correct letters being used but in the wrong order. Thus, instead of *not*, the dyslexic may write *tno*, and instead of *evening*, he might write down something like *enevgni*.
- Gross errors of spelling, other than the above. Some are explicable as phonetic substitutions like *laf* for *laugh*. Others are quite bizarre in character to the extent that the word may be wholly unintelligible to the reader. On the whole, the dyslexic errs by putting down too few letters, resulting in a misspelled word that is shorter than it should be. Occasionally, the dyslexic puts in too many letters, and here again, Charles Dickens must have stumbled upon this phenomenon in the boys around him, because in *Bleak House* he says, "If he were not so anxious about his spelling and took less pains to make it clear, he'd do better, but he puts so many unnecessary letters into short words that they sometimes quite lose their English appearance."
- An overall impairment of a semantic rather than syntactic or orthographic character may at times be identified. The victim of dyslexia, particularly in adolescence or adulthood, may obviously find graphic exposition an uphill job. In other words, he cannot express himself on paper very well. The superficial impression is that of an acquired language disorder, though it would not be correct to speak of congenital dysgraphia in this context, as some have done.

Many of the foregoing spelling mistakes can be interpreted as resulting from an inherent disorder in the conception of serial arrangement. This is especially so when the dyslexic sets down on paper the right letters but in the wrong order. Older dyslexics often admit to considerable difficulty in checking their spelling when referring to a dictionary. Their automatic recall of the letters of the alphabet in their correct sequence is too vague. For the same reason, these dyslexics are perplexed when it comes to tracing a number in a telephone directory. This confusion as to serial order may well extend beyond the alphabet, for many dyslexics are somewhat confused as to the correct succession of the months of the year, or, occasionally, the days of the week. More understandably, they may be unable to correctly align historical events. For example, the dyslexic may be quite at a loss to say whether William McKinley preceded or followed James Abram Garfield as President of the United States and where in that same connection stood Chester Alan Arthur.

IN CONCLUSION, we should take a sympathetic view of the plight of the adolescent who is undiagnosed and untreated, the dyslexic in a contemporary sociological setting. He is in many ways an alien in a world where the written language is quite foreign to him. Although the vernacular is familiar, the environment is strange, almost hostile. Symbols surround him, but to him they are nonsymbolic, for they are devoid of reference, function, or meaning. And yet, they have menacing overtones. In his view, they are angry hieroglyphs. He does not know whether they indicate "In" or "Out," "This Way" or "Keep Off." Another quote from Dickens' *Bleak House* indicates the dilemma: "To shuffle through the streets in utter darkness, to see people read and not to have the least idea of all that language."

The crusade for the due recognition of learning disorders in general, and developmental dyslexia in particular, has been long and arduous. Many doubters have to be convinced, and many prejudices overcome. I believe the goal is in sight when these unfortunate and misunderstood children will soon be recognized for what they are, and soon they will be screened adequately and at an even earlier age. Fads and faddists claiming to cure reading retardation by strange techniques will be deservedly forgotten. It is a public responsibility to take in hand these appropriate scientific and rational remedial instructions so as to fit them into the community which their basic intelligence warrants. In the nineteenth century, the philosopher, Herbert Spencer, described the three phases through which human opinion passes—the unanimity of the ignorant, the disagreement of the inquiring, and then the unanimity of the wise. It is manifest that the second is the parent of the third, and this is the phase we are witnessing today.

NOTES

1. O. Jespersen, *Language, Its Nature, Development and Origin* (London: George Allen & Unwin, Ltd., 1934).
2. G. A. Miller, *Language and Communication* (New York, N.Y.: McGraw-Hill Book Company, 1951).

The Right to Learn

Edwin W. Martin*

I WANT TO BEGIN by congratulating you (ACLD) on your existence. This is something of an existential comment that is related to the concept that "being" is the ultimate reality.

I see your existence as being tremendously important for a number of reasons. First, as a parent's organization, you are dedicated to providing your children with the "right to learn." Secondly, from the earliest days of the Association for Children with Learning Disabilities, you have made your allegiances with professionals who are also dedicated to your goal, and so, today, you have an organization that combines into useful effort these two important segments of our population. The third reason, and perhaps this is the most important one, is that your existence and your successes exemplify a characteristic of our American system that is vital to our *survival* as people.

You are a minority group that has identified a need—equal educational opportunity for your children. You are now in the process of rearranging national, state, and local priorities towards the end of meeting this need. I think your progress has been exceptional.

The Congress of the United States has recognized this need and has created a special section under the Education of the Handicapped Act, which will develop increased educational opportunities for your children. The National Advisory Committee on Handicapped Children, stimulated by such men as Samuel Kirk, Charles Strothers, Jack Irwin, and others who have served on this committee, has attempted to provide a definition or description of children with learning disabilities, and this has facilitated the development of federal statutes and of federal programing. In many states and localities, the results have been even more impressive in terms of the number of children who are now being served and in the establishment of new priorities at the local governmental level.

With the assistance of the Bureau of Education for the Handicapped programs, a number of colleges and universities are developing new programs

---

Edwin W. Martin is associate commissioner, Bureau of Education for the Handicapped, U.S. Office of Education, Washington, D.C.

or modifying older programs so that the teachers who are being trained will be able to offer assistance to an even greater number of children with learning disabilities.

These are impressive accomplishments that are attested to by the thousands of people who attend this convention and by the tens of thousands of children who are now in special education programing. The forces that have caused the system to change and to modify in the past are the forces that must be multiplied and expanded in the future, if the "right to learn" is to become a reality rather than rhetoric.

Children with learning disabilities now find themselves included in a group of approximately six million school-age children and perhaps another million preschool-age children who are identified as educationally handicapped. All of these children require a special response from the schools if they are to succeed. Our estimate is that about 40 percent of these children are now receiving some special education services, although we know that in some cases, these services may not be of the highest quality. For example, only about 50 percent of the 120,000 teachers who are employed in the states are certified, and an estimated one-half of the noncertified teachers are no longer operating on valid temporary certificates. This does not automatically mean that the services to those children who are being taught by noncertified teachers are less adequate than the services offered by certified teachers. In fact, each of us knows of examples to the contrary. It does suggest, however, the magnitude of the problem that we have in relation to feeling some minimal assurance that our handicapped children will be reasonably well educated.

EACH DAY I RECEIVE letters from across the country. In addition to the letters that I receive and those that the bureau staff receives, 25,000 letters have come in to *Closer Look*, which is our computerized service that provides a list of schools that offer special education classes. These letters that I receive are important, and I want to share a few excerpts of some of them with you. Some of us do not know about such letters, and I believe that we should continue to keep them visible, and that we should continue to try and open ourselves to the feelings of these parents who write them so that our level of motivation toward responding to them is kept at a maximum high.

> A mother wrote that she had a young child who had a physical handicap in addition to being deaf. During the first years of the child's life, the mother had been able to get some services for her youngster by visiting the university hospital school in her state. When the child was older and required daily instruction, the hospital school could not provide this service because they had no teacher for deaf children. The state school for the deaf, which was located in another city, did not accept physically handicapped deaf children, and there was no place for her to turn.

Kurt Vonnegut presents a powerful statement on the destructiveness of mankind, particularly relating this destructiveness to the fire bombing of Dresden, in *Slaughterhouse Five, Or the Children's Crusade: A Duty Dance with Death.*[1] In an ironic refrain, each time death is mentioned in the book he adds the phrase, "so it goes," and I think that this is society's response to this lady who had no place to take her deaf and physically handicapped child for instruction . . . so it goes. I received the following letter this week:

> I am hoping you can direct my efforts in seeking education for my handicapped son, age sixteen. He is brain-damaged with some emotional problems stemming from the brain damage. First, he is excluded from public school education. Our state allows a parent $2,000 toward tuition in a private school. We purchased a privately published directory and wrote to every school in the U.S. which is listed as accepting this type of child. There is not one residential facility with a tuition of $2,000. Most cost at least $6,200 and one as much as $22,000 per year. If my son is to have a chance to live in society and not be institutionalized the rest of his life (can you imagine being doomed at sixteen years of age?) then he must be in a proper educational setting. I have written or gone to see many resources in the state in which I live, but none have any constructive advice.

So it goes

While both of these letters are from parents who have children with multiple handicaps, they probably represent our most critical need in terms of nonavailability of services. It is no less a fundamental violation for a child with a mild handicapping condition to be deprived of a full educational opportunity.

I have tried to understand what the reasons are for our present failure to provide special education for handicapped children. A number of possibilities come to mind. The most commonly verbalized problem is that there is not enough money, but an analysis of school budgeting suggests that this is probably not true. There are many items in the school budget that support parts of the educational program that may be desirable but which may not be critical; for example, my son receives instruction in such subjects as music, art, and physical education. I am happy that these courses of study are provided in our schools and that my children have a chance to participate in them. At the same time, it does not seem to me that extras for the normal child have a higher priority than reading, writing, and other basic educational essentials for the handicapped child. And what about the provision of transportation? We make transportation available to and from school for non-handicapped children, but not for handicapped children. The problem of not having enough money is really the problem of insufficient priorities. And this problem is probably not based on the fact that school officials, or school board members, are heartless and cruel. There must be other reasons.

The first possible reason is that most people in this nation do not understand that education for handicapped children really works, and that the overwhelming majority of the handicapped children can be educated. With appropriate vocational education and training, handicapped children can fit into the job stream as well as into society in general.

Patterns of isolating handicapped children from the majority of the citizenry have resulted, I think, in stereotypes of what handicapped people are. The picture that comes to mind is only of the most severely retarded, the most severely emotionally ill, the most severely physically disabled child. With this picture in mind, the average man probably sees education for the handicapped as being a "kind" thing to do, a kind of charitable babysitting, but not truly cost-beneficial to society, and this average man also imagines that there are very few handicapped children. I have had instances reported to me of school officials who honestly felt that there were no handicapped children in their areas, and that all handicapped children were being well served because there was a state school for the blind, deaf, and retarded.

Society's prejudices

It is also possible to speculate that there are deeper psychological barriers to the provision of services to handicapped children; and this includes not only education, but some of the other problems that handicapped people face, such as being denied job opportunities, access to public buildings, and access to transportation. The fact that people do have handicaps may suggest to us the fact that injury, crippling conditions, and ultimately death, are part of human life, and a part of our own experience. The desire to repress and not focus on this aspect of our finite human existence, causes us to hide our heads in the sand. When these feelings are strong enough, they may make us wish to deny the presence of handicapped children, to deny the reality of their circumstances, and to focus, instead, on areas that are more reassuring, and more comforting.

In discussing these issues, Robert Lewis Shayon of the *Saturday Review* has called them funds, fatalism, and fear, which helped us focus our attention upon them. I am sure that many of you can offer additional hypotheses concerning societal attitudes, or additional parameters of the problem—and we should strive to do just that so that we understand the nature of our opposition, and how to develop the best possible constructive answers to these problems.

Labeling learning disabilities

A number of years ago, Wendell Johnson, the great speech pathologist and semanticist at the University of Iowa, wrote a little piece called, "The Indians Have No Word for It."[2] Johnson's premise, as it was developed in that article and in other articles, was that the problem of stuttering was caused, in good part, by the actual labeling and identification of the disorder itself. He proposed that normal hesitations and disfluencies in speech for many children, at least, were received with an over-response from the parents and teachers in the child's environment. This over-reaction sets up a circular process in which the child, himself, begins to become fearful of hesitations, begins attempting to avoid them, and begins to struggle. This succession of self-conscious awareness creates the pattern of stuttering.

Whether one agrees fully with Johnson on the etiology of stuttering, it seems clear to me that he understood at least part of the process, and we recognize a phenomenon that is part of our everyday human experience as we struggle with self-consciousness with various kinds of fears.

There is a self-fulfilling prophecy dimension to much of human experience. In a conversely analogous way, Robert Rosenthal's studies, published in recent years, suggested that the positive prophecies of teachers with regard to the ability of children very much influenced not only their perceptions of these children, but the children's actual achievements in school.[3] Additional research is necessary to substantiate this theory, but for the sake of argument, let's accept the premise that behavior can be shaped, at least in part, by the label we give to it and by the assumptions we have about it.

I think we need to keep these principles in mind as we think about the future development of programing for children with learning disabilities, and for children with all kinds of handicapping conditions. Identifying and labeling the learning problems of children by their individual handicaps has been useful to us in a variety of ways. Labeling may help us to focus attention on the problems, to communicate the seriousness of the educational needs of our children, and it allows for the development of specific programs to meet those needs. We are a great society for categorizing and labeling, and to a certain point such methods of classification are useful.

A basic premise in the development of programing for learning-disabled children, however, has been an attempt to avoid strict etiological labels, such as brain injured and dyslexic. Instead, we have attempted to focus on the specific learning tasks that are necessary for the child to succeed in school. Extending this reasoning a little, I think all of us—you as an association interested in these children, and those of us in federal government interested in developing programing—should consider carefully what our future strategy will be as we approach the general education system on behalf of these children.

In what may be seen by some as a kind of Swiftian "modest proposal," I think that we should consider an amicable divorce of learning-disabled children from the ranks of the handicapped, and expand the ranks of the normal student to include many children with the kind of variations and learning styles that are displayed by the majority of children who are called learning disabled. I think this approach is worth considering for the following reasons:

- The question of the self-fulfilling prophecy of the label "handicapped," a premise we are accepting positively for the sake of argument, which is that behavior can be shaped by the label we give to it and by the assumptions we have about it.

- A careful analysis of the distribution of educational resources suggests that nowhere in the United States are handicapped children receiving full educational opportunities. While this pattern is changing and improving, I am dedicating myself to bringing about a full commitment across the nation, to equal educational opportunity for every handicapped child by the end of this decade. It is nevertheless true that in many instances special education is a separate and segregated school system, and that it suffers from the inequality that segregated systems are recognized to have.

A new direction for education

I think we should challenge the general educator with his own responsibility for increasing the flexibility within every school, as well as within every classroom, so that a broader segment of the normal population of children may be served. This is the direction of innovation in education. This is the direction of flexibility of programing and scheduling. This is the direction of individualization. It should not be necessary to separate the child, to identify him as handicapped, and to provide him with separate programing in order to meet his individual learning needs.

Do not misunderstand my meaning. A number of years ago I made a similar suggestion to the people who were then interested in the development of this association, and I think that some of them interpreted my remarks as an attempt to close them out of the handicapped camp. That is not what I am saying. We have a substantial commitment to learning-disabled children in the special education field and in the Bureau of Education for the Handicapped, and we will be expanding that commitment as rapidly as we are able.

Essentially, I see the development of programing for learning-disabled children moving down the paths of increased programing under special education laws. Here, the ultimate success of services for children depends on the development of new national attitudes and making a national commitment to each child that will afford him an appropriate educational opportunity. In many states, we are well along the way in this direction and this may be the best and fastest route to travel. In other states and localities we are just beginning. And here I think we ought to consider, carefully, whether our children's needs can be met through reform of the general education system.

Future plans

As most of you know, we now support programs for training teachers of children with learning disabilities, under our training authority. As this program develops, through our own authorities and through the authorities of the Bureau of Educational Personnel Development, we will be encouraging the training of specialists who can fit into either model. There will be teachers who are better able to help children with learning disabilities participate in regular educational programs and specialists who will work intensively with children for whom regular education is not the answer. Similarly, in our research program, we will continue to emphasize research in a variety of approaches towards solving this educational problem. One of the ways we propose to implement the learning-disabilities portion of the Education of the Handicapped Act is through a special institute of national leaders in the learning-disabilities field for the purpose of developing a careful plan for future research and training activities. With such a plan, we will then go about funding the kind of projects that will bring us the information that is critically needed in this field. At the same time, we will make grants available to a number of states in conjunction with local school systems, colleges, and universities, and private agencies for the expansion of the best current practices in the treatment of learning-disabled youngsters. Our efforts in this program will be directed towards having a maximum catalytic or multiplier effect on the use of federal funds by providing support to the agencies that are now established in several states, which can do the most to bring about the expansion of educational opportunity for learning-disabled children.

It seems to me that your program chairman, Gerald Minskoff, and the other officers who have selected "The Right to Learn" as the theme for this conference are exactly on target in identifying the critical issue in the education of learning-disabled children and in the education of all handicapped children.

We must move out of the charity era; we must move out of the era of just enough programing to ease the conscience of the citizenry and which does not offer full educational opportunities for the learning disabled and the handicapped. We must establish that the right to an education is an intrinsic right and that it is not something to be given by the "haves" to the "have nots" in the spirit of generosity. We are in an era in the United States in which there is a new sensitivity to the concept of equality, and we know that equality does not mean sameness. Instead, it means appropriateness, so that equality of opportunity for one child may be quite different from equality of opportunity for another child.

On many occasions I have said that this is an important work that we do, not just for the handicapped children that we serve, or their parents, and not just for the teachers who will participate in it. But it is an important work for all of the United States because, at least in part, it helps to promote this understanding of equality. It helps all citizens to understand the intrinsic nature of man and that his worth is not dependent on whether his arms and legs work the same as those of a nonhandicapped person, or whether he is able to grasp reading or arithmetic as quickly as a "normal" child, or whether his skin is black or white.

What is important is that he is a human being and that under our system it is his humanity to which we must respond. Your efforts to bring the right to learn to your children are the efforts that will strengthen the character of our nation. Do not hesitate to claim that right. Do not feel that your purposes are selfish. They serve every man. I pledge my support to you in your endeavors.

NOTES

1. Kurt Vonnegut, *Slaughterhouse Five, Or the Children's Crusade: A Duty Dance with Death* (Boston, Mass.: Delacorte Press, 1969).
2. Wendell Johnson, "The Indians Have No Word for It," *Quarterly Journal of Speech*, 30 (1944), 330-337.
3. Robert Rosenthal, *Pygmalion in the Classroom: Teachers' Expectations and Children's Intellectual Development* (New York, N.Y.: Holt, Rinehart, and Winston, Inc. 1968).

On the Morning of the Fifth Day

Walter W. Straley*

I AM NOT an expert in reading disabilities, but I would like to talk about the general reading problem, and say essentially what I said to a group of people in Los Angeles earlier this week who had gathered for the first city-wide seminar to make new attacks on reading disabilities in the Los Angeles area.

I call these musings by a strange sort of title, which may come clear with my remarks: "On the Morning of the Fifth Day." It seems to me that there is in our nation a decreasing faith in our institutions. Be it church or school, business corporation or government, there seems to be a gathering uncertainty that our institutions produce our personal views of progress or reflect the values that we suppose to be our own. I say we suppose that our institutions do not reflect our own values, for we are not altogether sure that we possess the higher moral values, which once we hoped to live by, and we seem only certain that the values of others are more suspect than our own. Thus, we build our frustration, based upon self-doubt and suspicion, and return increasingly to confrontation that takes many forms.

If you are grumbling aloud to your TV set, and many of us are doing more of that these days, I suppose it is a form of confrontation that is very satisfying; at least we can have the last word. More people are calling and writing presidents of corporations, universities, school superintendents, congressmen, bishops, and this is a form of increasing confrontation. More of us are looking for and joining groups and subgroups and splinter groups in which we can find a kind of matching indignation toward those idiots in other groups whose values and goals are obviously wrong. And sooner or later this grouping process, of course, leads to the physical confrontation, to the committee charged with seeking redress, to the mass march on city hall. Often we attack our own institutions for their lack of foresight, for their failure of initiative on our part, knowing at least subconsciously that the attack itself will produce a natural defensive stance of self-protection,

---

*Walter W. Straley is vice-president, American Telephone and Telegraph Company, and chairman, National Reading Council.

less risk, fewer inhibitions, and a retreat to the relative safety of the status quo.

WE REQUIRE CHANGE, chiefly a change from our own emptiness of spirit. We demand results, which, we assure ourselves, can only accrue from the efforts of others. We assume that at some distant place solutions will be found to the problems we create. I suppose we believe that a great and simple program finally will be devised if we scream hard enough, which will produce self-serenity and return to us our faith in each other. If we continue to use accusative confrontation to produce such a program, there is only one that is likely to emerge, I think, and that will be a program of hydrogen extinction, the logical ultimate in confrontation.

Now, you may think this is an ominous introduction to a few remarks about reading, and I suppose it is. I work down the street from city hall in New York and recall the day, just recently, when I got out of town early to escape the crush of a threatened quarter of a million people who had been scheduled to mass around the downtown area and around city hall to protest a prospective forty-million-dollar deficit in our school system's billion-and-a-half budget. Well, at the last minute the forty million dollars were found in the bookkeeping fiction of next year's budget. I was an intimate participant in the New York school crisis of 1968 and 1969, in which we battered each other over the helpless figures of many children, each of us claiming, often shouting, that only we could be trusted to serve the child. We all turned into villains. No heroes emerged from that fiasco.

Across the country, more than half of last year's school bond issues were defeated in confrontations of often angry voters. Taxpayers are striking against their schools. Teachers are striking against school boards. Administrators cut the staff and strike curricula. Many schools this year must close before normal terms are ended, and probably a million children will strike this year simply by dropping out of school, many to drugs and decay. Into this anger, this turmoil and sadness, I drop this matter of literacy.

The reason for this kind of an introduction is that I think of reading and of learning to read as one, but perhaps an important pact to a new kind of confrontation, a loving confrontation between a person who reads and one who does not read or does not read well enough.

Perhaps one of every four Americans cannot read well enough to get his full shout in our society. If this be so, there must be three Americans who can read pretty well. Now, suppose half of these reading people could teach somebody else who is not disabled how to do it. Now I hear the cries, "But they would have to be trained. They would need materials. They would interfere with school process." But will you lay all of that aside just a moment to bear in mind that there might be 75 million people who could teach a normal child or a nonreading adult how to read.

Let me make what I hope will not be a digression by quoting LaVerne Cunningham, Dean of the College of Education at Ohio State University, from his recent article, "Shut It Down":

> I am not advancing a namby-pamby approach to solving the nation's reading problem or any other for that matter. This is an

earnest, deadly serious proposal. I recommend that we use, unshackle, if you prefer, our total capacity in a massive assault and that we give our complete, undivided attention to the problem by shutting the nation down. Let us visualize a nation closed down in a maximum mass education effort that is not a holiday, but no one goes to school, no one goes to work, no one plays golf. We simply inform ourselves about this national deficiency, and we search for ways to eliminate it. Think of continuous radio and television programing on reading, newspapers carrying no news—I suppose they would have to carry the legal notices and obituaries—just stories on reading. Picture the supplementary role the schools could play. Visualize churches and thousands of other voluntary and civic associations turning their attention to the problem. All other news, problems, world events would be set aside, shelved, for this brief period, total attention zeroed in on reading. Can you imagine the nation closed down, total saturation programing on radio and television, all stations, all channels, for four days, newspapers and other printed materials devoting complete attention to the national reading problem. Just imagine, comprehensive in-depth, lending attention to the problems and issues of reading. Programing so rich that it would attract the interest of everyone, toddlers and teenagers, gurus and grandpas, potters and Ph.D.'s.

I wish LaVerne Cunningham well in his recommendation to shut the the country down for four days of concentration on the reading problem. I do not envision his success, mostly because I don't think he can get people to stop playing golf for four days. His plan, however, is speculative on the possible results of such single-mindedness.

ON THE MORNING OF THE FIFTH DAY, I think we would see the professional educator as a devoted, often overburdened, sometimes highly successful teacher of reading, puzzled as to why her successes do not seem to spread to other places and people of even greater need. I suppose we would all discover the millions of children, as many have already discovered, who need food or medicine or glasses or hearing aids to help with their handicap before they can read successfully. Perhaps mothers and fathers and older brothers and sisters might become interested in teaching the baby to read before he goes to school. We might come to pity, and through it determine to rescue the adult from illiteracy. We might even decide that in many and certain bilingual areas we would keep right on teaching Spanish all the way through high school, as well as teaching English. We might conclude that if television and radio and newspapers could teach us so much about reading in four days, that they should teach a little reading every day thereafter. Maybe we would ask whether every child who is learning to read shouldn't be allowed to have his very own books, and perhaps we would start to revolutionize the book distribution system.

We could decide, after four days of concentration, to make reading a national game, a simple "Scrabble" for everybody — reading lessons on cereal packages, peanut butter jars, pop bottles, candy wrappers. I suppose we would also think that business ought to really get down to the business of reading-teaching its reading-lame employees. There's one thing that is certain: from among those 75 million prospective reading teachers, there would, I know there would, appear on the morning of the fifth day many millions of Americans who had determined to engage in a new confrontation, not in groups, but straggling along or in couples into schools mostly, I suppose, or maybe community centers or child-care centers or churches. Children and aged, and mammas and clerks, and tycoons and the campus young. And when they got to where they were going, they would say, "I'd like to help teach someone to read. I'd like to help."

Now, this would not, I think, be a grand, federally directed super-program. It would be local and chaotic, confusing, distressing, and altogether a lovely outpouring of poor and rich people, villagers and farmers, commuters and high-rise dwellers, who at long last would say as they used to say, "This needs to be done. I'd better go and help do it." I think that teachers and parents and children and principals and superintendents and social agencies all would find ways to channel this person-to-person flood of good people into union with one child or one needful adult. I would guess that on the morning of the fifth day, a great loving confrontation of learning and life begins.

Now, what does all this have to do with our National Reading Council and its National Reading Center? Most importantly, the Council and the new Center that we are forming are a symbol of what may exist of a national determination to solve our reading problem. It is a place and partnership where the professional educator, the parent, the child, the communications expert, the businessman, and others may offer their contribution toward reading success. The Council exists because President Nixon and Secretary Richardson brought it into being. Upon its formation, the President said, "I hope the Council will serve as a catalyst for the nation in producing dramatic reading improvement, the improvement in reading ability for those who require it."

WE COUNT AS VALUED COLLEAGUES such people as ACLD president, Hyman J. Gardsbane, and Commissioner Sydney P. Marland of the U. S. Office of Education, and we acknowledge with great affection and respect the father of "Right to Read," former Commissioner of Education, James Allen. But this sponsorship we support gives us no license to overpromise nor to interfere with people and processes underway. We are small. We will have, under Donald Emery, who is the executive director of our new Center, a small but lively staff. It is not much bigger than a baseball team roster. At the outset, we will try to do these things, and most of these things will be done in conjunction with the Office of Education and many other people and other agencies. We will try to build, and we are now in the process of building an information service where people who want to gain can find out how they can fit into the production of reading progress. We will help spread national information, to build national determination to lick this problem. We will serve the people who are building community networks of volunteer tutors. We will help them with training and with training materials. We will stimulate the communications we need and work with them toward a greater effort to stress the importance of reading-teaching and to do more reading-teaching in their own mass media. We will assist librarians, publishers, distributors, and others to break through some of the roadblocks to book ownership by the reading student who can't own books now. We will encourage a coalition of cartoonists, games people, packagers, who can help to make reading-learning a national game that everybody can play. Excepting the building of this Information Center, it is important to note, I think, that every suggested accomplishment rests prospectively in the hands of others, millions of others. We will try, as the President has charged us, to be a small but visible working symbol of his and your and our determination to produce dramatic reading improvement in this decade.

Not long before her death, Marilyn Monroe was supposed to have said, "People say I'm a sex symbol, but when I see some of the things that other people are symbols of, I guess I don't mind." If, as LaVerne Cunningham suggests, we were to shut this country down for four days to sweat out the disgrace of our own illiteracy, I assume that we would begin on the morning of the fifth day to offer millions of personal symbols of a willingness to make real what we now rather grandly call "your right to read." If we of the National Reading Council can serve as one of today's symbols of the "right to read," it's all right with me. It would also be all right with me if you and I could learn without such a shutdown how to count the personal urgency, personal understanding, and personal determination, each to our morning of the fifth day.

SECTION II

Parents

Parents Need to Know: Parents and Teachers Work Together

Leo F. Buscaglia*

IT IS A TREMENDOUS, exciting thing for me to discuss some of my ideas about parent conferencing, about parents and teachers working together. My students always tell me that even though my classes have different labels, they all end up being Love 1A and Love 1B and Love 1C, and that's probably how this paper will end up. But I do have an enormous love for parents, and the sum of what I am going to say is this: as far as I am concerned, it is about time that professionals began to look at parents as warm, pulsating, beautiful, tender, fantastic, unbelievable, intelligent, incredible human beings. And then I want to discuss how parents and professionals can work together, for as long as parents are trapped with professionals, and professionals are trapped with parents, we are going to have to find a way to reach one another.

First, some ideas I have about things like change—and things like hope—and things like growth—because I believe fervently that counseling is education. When I am talking about counseling, I'm not talking about psychotherapy. It is of little or no interest to me to find out about parents' sex life. This won't help me to help their child. But there are ways in which the two of us can get together and really help the child. The focus will be on the child and the people who will be working around him. Counseling is education, growth, and change.

In connection with this, I recommend that readers become familiar with the work of Herbert Otto, who is one of the people involved in a wonderful thing called the Institute for the Development of the Human Person. I hope that some day I'll be there, and perhaps some of you will end up there, too. It's a place where they are trying to find out how to help people *Become*, and I can't think of a more wonderful undertaking. Herbert Otto says this: "Change and personal growth take place when a person has risked himself and dared to become involved in experimenting with his own life."[1] Isn't that fantastic? It's true—growth is a risk—and after risk, it is an experiment. You never know what is going to be happening next in this process of

---

Leo F. Buscaglia, Ph.D., is associate professor of education, University of Southern California, Los Angeles.

becoming. It's beautiful! Everything is new, everything is exciting. It's also fearful because you can't be certain about what is around the corner. I tell my students all the time that probably the greatest trip you take in the world is the trip you take in becoming you.

Change is inevitable. Everything is changing. It is going to occur with or without you. De Chardin, in *The Phenomenon of Man*, makes a wonderful statement: "Change is occuring so quickly today that you can no longer stand still, for if you are, you are moving backwards."[2] That's exactly what is happening, and we have got to keep up with change. One way to do this is to be curious about what is happening out there and to be wondrous about all the things that are in yourself that you haven't yet realized but that are waiting to be let out. That is what I believe to be the essence of counseling— a voyage, so to speak, into the world of you to find out about yourself, to discover yourself, the process of growth.

Saint Exupery, in a beautiful book called *Wind, Sand and Stars*, says, "Love is perhaps a process of my leading you gently back to yourself."[3] And maybe teaching is a process of my leading you gently back to yourself. And certainly counseling is a process of my leading you gently back to yourself. Not to *me* but to *who you are* because, of all things, you are the best you. One of the most beautiful things in the world—and probably the greatest hope I have—is that we can change you back to believing that you are the best you—and not try to make you anyone else. One of the things that I tell my students in love class all the time is that the game we don't want to play is "follow the guru." If you try to be me, you are always going to be like oleomargarine—the second-best spread. I'm the best spread if I'm the best me. But you are the best you. And so counseling is the process of leading you gently back to yourself, leading the children gently back to themselves, leading the parents back to themselves.

So I am talking about a process that I call educational counseling, which is not psychotherapy, which is not encounter groups. I am really kind of uptight about encounter groups. I recently saw the film, *Diary of a Mad Housewife*. That film really got to me, and I recommend it to you wholeheartedly. But I warn you, if you are the kind of person who attends a film and is up and halfway out the door the minute the last shot is on, you are going to miss the most significant part because the film ends with an encounter group. For two hours we've been face to face with the life of this incredible woman, a housewife, who runs around baking pies and taking her husband's shirts to the cleaners and taking care of two little kids and walking the dog in the park, and so on. We've been very intimate with this woman. We've been allowed to get into her head, and we feel—at least I feel—a tremendous empathy with her. I couldn't help but weep over her life, her beautiful, incredible life. There should have been more than just what she was having to experience here—walking the dog and cleaning the kids' noses. She was also an individual. The final shot, which occurs behind the credits for director, producer, writer, etc., is the face of this woman while you hear the people in her encounter group saying such things as, "You're lucky, you don't know how lucky you are, what are you sitting there crying about? You have a husband, and you live in a ten-room apartment . . . ." And you can just see on her face, "My God! Nobody sees me. Nobody knows really what I'm up against. Nobody knows really who I am. Nobody understands my real needs." But it is very easy for these people to sit there and attack her.

I have a very essential philosophy, very simple indeed, and that is that most of us are extremely vulnerable, most of us are very easily hurt, most of us are very close to tears. God knows there is enough of this kind of thing going on without having to sit around and attack each other. Now that may offend some people, and it may be that that's your bag—and if so, attack. But as far as I am concerned, people are very puncturable, I am really afraid to stick my fingers through them, to make interpretations of them. I don't know you. I don't know what loneliness you are feeling, what joy you are feeling, what makes you cry, what makes you happy. I don't know what will turn you on and what will turn you off. I can only see you as essentially a human being and identify with you as a human being. I know what I feel, for instance, when someone attacks me. And so I believe that counseling should be a very gentle process.

The counseling I am talking about is essentially a learning process. I believe that emotions are learned, and I believe that anything we have learned, we can unlearn, and we can relearn. It is a process of trying out your new learning behavior and seeing if it is right for you, not for the counselor, but for *you*, and then behaving accordingly. That's essentially it. So when I talk about educational counseling, I am talking about helping the counselee to desire to change and to have hope that change is possible, then to volitionally try out new behavior that will lead him to new adjustments.

FOR SIX YEARS of my life as director of special education in a large community in California, I did little more than sit down with parents of children who were exceptional, who had impairments, everything from severe cerebral palsy to one woman who had three blind children—and I rapped with them. There is nothing in the world that annoys me more than either a counselor or a teacher who says that a parent must accept his exceptional child. The best response I ever heard to that in my life was from a beautiful woman, and I almost burst through a one-way mirror and hugged her. A counselor said to her in a teaching situation, "You must accept your exceptional child or I can't help you." And she said, "Why the hell must I?" And I thought, "Good for you, honey!"

It becomes a process of education and reeducation; it becomes a process of becoming ready. Another thing that is always ludicrous to me is when professionals turn parents away, saying that they are uncooperative. You know what that usually means? "They don't see things the way I do. They're uncooperative. They don't accept their children. They don't really understand the problem. They are unrealistic." How many times have you heard that? Let's put ourselves in the place of this parent and let's look at the dynamics involved in being a parent of an exceptional child. In fact, let's look at the dynamics involved in being the parents of "normal" children.

The role of the individual within the family is a very unique and wondrous thing with an enormous responsibility, because it is essentially within the family that a person learns to love or hate, that a person learns how to accept or how to spend his life fearing, learns how to kill or create, learns how to live with life or live without life, how to relate or how to be lonely.

In the family you learn who you are, you learn what the world is all about, you learn what is expected of you and what you can expect. In other words, you learn how to perceive yourself and your world. These things all happen in the family, and that is why the early years of life are tremendously important. Many of us were raised in a time that told us once these years were set, there was nothing we could do about it, we were stuck with our hang-ups for the rest of our lives. I essentially do not believe this. I believe that there comes a time in your life when you can take your life in your hands, and you can do with it what you will. That is why if you wanted to put a philosophy around me, you would not only say I was a humanist, I hope, but an existential humanist because I truly believe that you make your own scene. I have said before that you write your own play, paint your backdrop, surround yourself with actors, play your background music, and if you don't like the show, then get the hell off the stage and write a new one. Don't sit there and wallow in your own loneliness. Ask yourself, "What can I do?"

I am always telling people who go around saying how lonely they are, that maybe if they removed the wall and let people in, they would be less lonely. Maybe if we expected less from people in terms of their coming to us and saying, "May I help you?"—it would be beautiful but that's not what life is all about—maybe we should reach the point where we can turn to people and say, "I need you." I had a beautiful girl in love class who, when someone asked, "What do you do if there is a wall around someone," said, "I ignore it." Think about that. "I ignore it."

Now let's look at the family that has an exceptional child. There is a very interesting study now going on at UCLA. Many of you are acquainted with the literature and are, as I am, following it eagerly. They are trying to find out what is the difference in the hospital atmosphere when an exceptional child is born. What happens when a child is born, let's say, without an arm, or when a child is born blind or with cerebral palsy? What happens in that hospital? They have found some very, very interesting things. First, there is a delay from the time that the child is born to the time that the child is taken to its mother. Mothers are human, too, and they sense this: "What's wrong? Is something wrong? How come everyone else has their child, and I don't have mine?" A delay in time. There is also a contest as to who will be the nurse that will bring this child, who will be the person who will tell this mother. What does this say to the mother right from the beginning? "My child is different, my child is unique, there is something not quite right with my child." Rejection.

We are also in a culture that stresses perfection. Our idea of perfection amuses me. It's the Rock Hudson-Doris Day perfection syndrome. It always amuses me that in this country we are in the Audrey Hepburn all-bone syndrome—and then I go to Italy where it is the Sophia Loren all-flesh syndrome. Notions of perfection change. We have this conflict about what is perfection, and we are a little bit afraid of what is imperfect. The whole phenomenon of birth is a miracle. You can't take it lightly. A child is a gift, and nobody wants to give an imperfect gift. And so immediately what happens? Different dynamics! You are dealing with a different kind of human being, not only with the hang-ups of every family—for no family is perfect and all have their essential loneliness and fears—but on top of this you have *new* dynamics at work.

First, there is fear, real honest-to-God fear. The parents wonder, "What's going to happen to this child? If he is different, will I be able to educate him? Is he going to be able to find work? What are my friends going to say?" Old wives' tales are conjured up. My beautiful mother used to tell my sisters when they were pregnant that they shouldn't go out during an eclipse, and she really believed it. I am sure that if my sisters had gone out—they were just as superstitious as Mama—and something had happened, they would have blamed it on the eclipse. There are real fears, fears that the child will be rejected later on. There are real guilt feelings—"What did I do?" I have never worked with the parents of an exceptional child who didn't wonder, "Was it something I did? Did I do something wrong? Did I not take care of myself? Did we not get the right doctors? Could I have done more?" What I am trying to do is create for you how unique these people are with whom we are working and how impossible it is to say to them, "You must accept your exceptional child. Rid yourself of all these things overnight." How unrealistic this is—we forget that we are still dealing with human beings.

And then there is shame. It wasn't too long ago that any kind of exceptionality was associated with filth, with disease, and we are not altogether through with this. When an exceptional child walks down the street, you still see people turn around and gawk and say, "Look, Mabel." You know that, and I know that. There is still fear. I require that every single one of my students who wants to do anything in terms of teaching children and understanding people must work in a situation with exceptional children. Every time we bring them into a hospital setting, an institutional setting, a school setting, they all admit how fearful they are until they get down to working with these kids. Then all of a sudden they recognize human beings, and the fear vanishes, and they even forget. One of my students who was working with blind children was horrified because one day she had said, "What's the matter with you, Johnny, can't you see?" And you know he giggled! He was human, too.

I have never sat down with a parent of an exceptional child without finding out that these poor people have been to 150 pediatricians, 150 neurologists, 150 educators, all with great hope in their hearts that they could find an answer, a miracle cure. These are the things we are going to have to deal with because parents don't just get over it. We are going to have to look at them. We are going to have to face them, and we are going to have to realize that they are not superhumans. They are only human beings, and of course, that is their greatest strength—as it is ours. But not only do they have all of the problems and handicaps that all families have, they have a special complex problem. We have to recognize their uniqueness and try to get into their heads and see the problem from their side of the fence. So no more talking about "you must accept your exceptional child."

THE FIRST STEP in educational counseling is to help the parent get over this period that Solnit and Stark call—and I like this—"a period of mourning,"[4] a period of loneliness, a period of isolation, a period of confusion, a period of fear, a period of misunderstanding, a period of guilt, a period of depreciation of self, a period even of shame. In doing so, several things can happen. One is that they can hide away in confusion or, secondly, they can overreact, and you get the very aggressive parent who breaks the door down and says, "This isn't enough; I've got to have more." We need this kind of parent, for they are the ones who keep us moving.

How can we help parents to get over these initial feelings? First of all, we have to have some empathy, we have to be able to relate to them as people. I always start this by saying that parents are people—just like you. It always amused me when I was working in the schools when open house came, and all the teachers were reacting, "My God! The parents are coming!" They overlooked the fact that they, too, were parents. On the other hand, I have a psychiatrist friend who is scared to death of teachers! He's got three kids, and when he goes to school for a conference, I am sure that the teacher looks at the records, sees that he is a psychiatrist, and is scared to death of him. So here comes a man scared to death of the teacher, and she's afraid to open her mouth because he might interpret it, and they are supposed to try to relate about his kids, and they don't get anywhere. It's hysterical! We must believe that parents are people, too, and give them credit for having intelligence. In California, before we passed laws, we never allowed parents to look at any of the children's records—*their kids*, yet all records were secret. We would only tell them what we thought they should know. That's absolutely brilliant. "It's your kid but I'm not going to tell you anything about him; I have secrets about him." We couldn't imagine that parents could possibly understand what we big teachers and psychologists understand! Anything you know, they can know, too, but you have to take the time to let them know it.

When I was director of special education, I decided that I would solve all the parent conferencing in one big fell swoop. This was my first or second year, and I had about 300 parents at a parent education seminar. Isn't that exciting? Poor things, they worked all day and then had to get dressed up and come to this damned seminar! I had neurologists and psychologists and fantastic teachers, and I was never so brilliant in my life—lectures that lasted two hours in which I told them everything they had to know! Then at the end I made an incredible mistake. I gave them an evaluation form which asked, "What is the one most important thing that you got from this seminar?" Of course, I was sure it would be something brilliant that I had said. Do you know what it was? More than 70 percent of them said, "The greatest value I got from this seminar was to find that there are other parents like me who have exceptional children." Boy, did that make me humble—and I stopped having mass meetings.

It is the same ludicrous kind of thing, for instance, that we assume when we take third graders and put them together in one room and believe we can teach them all in the same way. Every parent is unique, every parent is an individual. You are not and can never be me, and I can never be you.

I can never really understand you 100 percent, even though I might believe I can, nor can you ever understand me 100 percent, even though you might believe you can. All you have to do is read some of the things that psychologists write about parents, and you can see how far away they are. The same parent I interview is not the parent that she interviews nor the parent that you interview. Everybody perceives through their own eyes and their own hang-ups.

You can't ignore this frozen period of inability to go beyond the emotions. I know some programs, for instance, that start parents immediately when strong feelings still exist, and then they are wondering why parents are resisting. It is because they still have these very real feelings, and they have to deal with these first before they can become really involved in this process. That doesn't mean that they have to become self-actualized. They only have to become aware that those feelings are there, and then they can do something.

THE SECOND aspect of educational counseling is to help the parent to bring himself to the point where he can accept himself, love himself, be able to say, "I am not responsible. I am not guilty. There are things I can do. I am also alive. I have a responsibility to me as well as to my children, because as I grow, so can they grow. If I stand still in this frozen position, so will they be frozen in their position." Mama plays the largest role in adjustment and in learning in children. One of the professors at the University of Southern California has just finished a study of deprived children in which he showed that the attitude of the mother toward learning was the most important factor in the child's ability to learn, regardless of how poor they were, how deprived they were, and so mother's attitude is tremendously important.

Now we have to take parents in and let them become part of a team, and I don't mean a team in words but an actual team in the process of initiating change. The mother must be asked how much she can do in this process and then become really involved. *The Siege* is a beautiful book by a woman who had an emotionally disturbed child,[5] and her thoughts are highly pertinent here. She put her finger right on it. She took her little child to a neurologist and a psychologist and educators. Weeks and months and thousands of dollars later they sat this mother down, and she writes:

> This is what they had to say. It is not a summary of what they said. It is *all* they said, although the psychiatrist, a hesitant, rather inarticulate, elderly man took considerably more time to say it than it takes to write it here.
>
> 1. Ellie needs therapy.
>
> 2. She has performed above her age level on that part of the IQ test she could do. It was, therefore, believed that she had no mental deficiency.
>
> 3. She has many fears. That's it. That is what they had to say of all that information and of all our time, energies, and money.

Her reaction to this is not unfamiliar to many parents:

> We wanted information, we wanted techniques, we wanted

sympathy, not the soapy kind, we were grown up adults, but some evidence of feeling that ordinary doctors seem to have. Was it so unreasonable to ask for this? We wanted a little reassurance, a little recognition of our own needs, and a little praise. It never occurred to us that these expectations were naive, that the gulf between the parent and the professional must deliberately be kept unabridged by any ordinary techniques of interpersonal relationships.

Does this sound familiar?

It should have been easy, after all, to say, 'Look, you're a professional, I need references, I need to know how to do for Ellie. I need to know all I can do and all I can learn about my child because whoever else may or may not work with her, I, her parent, shall always be her main psychotherapist.'

So—parents need help, but not the current kind of idea of h-e-l-p. She continues:

I feel a breakdown or separation between the parents and professionals. At present it is common practice for a child to receive education or therapy for months and sometimes years without the mother or the father having any direct conversation with that child's therapist or teacher. This is especially true of the large clinic where the social worker acts as a sort of mediator or buffer between the therapist, teacher and the parent. It is thought best that the parents of a small child know nothing of what goes on in these privileged sessions, and the only way she may hear of what the therapist actually thinks of her child's case is if she happens to meet him accidentally in the hall, and he is nice enough to tell her a thing or two.

She ends up with this paragraph, and if I had any sense, I'd end this paper here— but I don't have any sense:

The answer must be in training parents as nonprofessionals unless there is to be no answer at all. Above all, we must train parents to do with skill and effectiveness what they have to do anyway. Mothers will make ready pupils as people do when they are learning what they have immediate need for.

HOW DO WE HELP people to change? This is something that recently I have questioned very, very strongly. I have read as much of the literature on change as I could possibly get my fingers on, and I think I have a few ideas. First of all, I think we have to help people see the dissonance between what they are seeing and what they are doing, and to see what is "reality," the reality of the situation. This is a very difficult thing to do because we don't see things actually as they are. We see them as we must see them. You know this is true. You see a tree uniquely your way, and this may not at all be the tree.

If you really want to go back and get some exciting mind trips, read the works of Virginia Woolf. Get her books—they are all in paperback—and sit down and read this remarkable woman, a woman who, like so many women today, was wasted—and it really freaks me when I see this happen. You know, intelligent women have a hard time surviving in our culture. I don't know how women do it—I mean, who wants an intelligent woman? Men seem to want some of the little freaky gigglers—that's the kind they marry. They have discussion groups with the others. Virginia Woolf struggled and struggled to communicate. Recently an incredible volume of her letters has been published. Read them, for they are unbelievable. She struck up a tremendous letter-writing situation with a minister who was inferior mentally to Virginia Woolf, but he was aware emotionally of her needs to be recognized and to be realized. Even though she sent him tremendously deep, profound, unbelievable letters, he would write to her about trout fishing and so forth. She kept exposing herself in these letters, and he really kept her alive longer even than he thought. Eventually she committed suicide, throwing herself into the Thames, drowning herself in that muddy river, which is again one of the great tragedies.

Sometimes when we look at the works of these great sensitive people, we find definitions that the great scientists can't give us. When I look for a a definition of *perception*, how we see things, I always turn to the works of Virginia Woolf, for here is a sensitive, beautiful woman talking about perception as I have never been able to read about it in any book. This is what she says simply in one of her letters:

> We are constantly endeavoring to give meaning and order to our lives, the past, the present, and in the future, meaning to our surroundings and the world we live in, with the result that our lives appear to be a total entity in our own conception which, to be sure, is constantly changing more or less radically, more or less rapidly depending on the extent to which we are obliged, inclined or able to assimilate the onrush of different experiences.[6]

That is an amazing thing to say about reality and the constant change of reality.

Like a teacher, the greatest counselor is a person who is aware. I cannot handle techniques of counseling—you know, for example, the ten rules of greeting people. "How do you do, Mrs. Jones," is number one. "Oh, hello, Mrs. Jones," is number two. "Please, Mrs. Jones, won't you sit down . . . ." That's nonsense! What I am trying to do is to help people return to themselves, and we are doing wonderful little things that I call renewing our awareness. Some people call it sensitivity. I don't care what you call it. We're learning to taste again, we're learning to smell again, we're learning to feel again, we're learning how little we do these things. I brought in fresh spinach, and I put a leaf of fresh spinach in front of each of the students, and I said, "Eat it." They picked it up and started munching like, "Oh, God, here goes Buscaglia again." They started eating it, and they started lighting up and saying, "Wow!" Do you know there were people there who had never tasted fresh spinach? One man said, "My God, why do we cook it to death and put vinegar on it when it tastes so good?" But we're learning again to taste, we're learning again to smell, we're learning to put linguistic structures around the things we are experiencing so that we can express ourselves to other people because, like it or not, the only things we have to deal with are symbols. Yet symbols don't serve us because those are the symbols that someone has taught us, not what we truly feel.

Recently Buckminster Fuller said an incredible thing: "I've gone through my life dealing with my environment in terms of words people have given me, and I found myself using other people's words to describe my experiences and my feelings, and they weren't adequate, and so I moved away to a little ghetto."[7] He did—for two years when he was twenty-two he lived in a little ghetto in Chicago. He got a tiny room, and he said, "In these years I spent my time clearing my mind of old concepts of words and finding out what words can mean. What did this word mean to me? Not what did it mean to all those people who had taught it to me . . . . I'm having a ball with language because every time I speak, I say what I mean and not what other people mean."

My students and I made a dictionary of what we called "bummer" words, and we made a long list of words we were not going to use—words that were prejudicial, words that were full of fear, words that were full of hate. In another dictionary with an enormous number of pages, we wrote down positive words, happy words, joyous words, and we decided that these were the words we were going to use just for an experiment for about a week. It changed people's lives! All of a sudden things really happened. They started looking at things in a more positive way. People were responding to them in a more positive way just because they had changed the words they were using.

I am very concerned about this process of change and this process of growth, and I think that all change involves a disintegration of where you are at and a reintegration of something new, a breaking down of what you are presently believing and a re-creation, an allowing in, of new things. And so we are doing things like tasting and touching and feeling. Another thing—I'm giving people mirrors, and I say, "Look at yourself, but I mean *really look* at yourself." For five minutes they stare into that mirror and, of course, there is an awful lot of giggling. People don't know how to look at themselves—so they titter and laugh. And then I say, "Put your mirror down and tell me what you saw." They start describing themselves, and it's amazing how little they see. Then I go round the group, and I say, "Let's add and tell them what else there is." And people start saying, "There are little lines by your eyes that are so beautiful . . . . I love the curve of your lips . . . . You have beautiful hands . . . ." All of a sudden you find out how little you do see. This is a growing process, a becoming process, and as you grow and become, then will those in your environment grow and become because you can give them all the things that you see and touch and feel and smell and know, the new world you have become aware of.

THE PHENOMENON OF CHANGE, then, occurs only when we get out of our mind, the way we are now, and move into raw experience. If I don't say anything else, that's the one thing I feel the most strongly about. Change will occur when we get out of our minds and into raw experience. You can talk about it forever; you can lie on the analyst's couch until you are blue in the face, but until you get out and *do* something, you will not know who you are. And so to be is to do, and that's one of the most important things. That may mean all kinds of things. It may mean, for instance, getting parents involved in a good course in learning theory. How does a child learn? Why not teach parents learning theory? If this is what you are going to be doing in the classroom, why not let the parent know what you are doing, how you are doing it, what are the best techniques, and then teach them what *they* should be doing—instead of this great gap, this mystery between school and the home. Teach the parent how to teach the child. I would love it if we could train parents as paraprofessional personnel and bring them into the schools. Let them see that they can do. Help them learn techniques and then work together really as a team. But this can only be done if we don't judge, if we recognize the need of all individuals, and if we remember that we are not gods. We are guides—we are not gods. And we must realize that even a maladjustment is an adjustment, so we don't condemn people for maladjustment. We help them. I remember one mother—and I shall never get her face out of my mind—who came into the office and said, "Now I know why I was given three blind children. That is because God was sure that I was the one who would be able to take it and help them. Of all the mothers in the world, God chose me to have three blind children because I would be able to help them." If she believed that and if she could function and bring up three beautiful healthy kids, get off it, man, if you have the urge to say to her, "What nonsense! God didn't choose you. Let's be realistic, Mrs. Jones." She did a damned good job with those three kids. All three of them are in a university right now.

We must act on our belief, then, that each person has dignity—and starting to treat parents as if they are human beings with dignity—and that each person has to find his own path. Your way is not my way, and there have never been two parents who have had exactly the same way to go. They must find their own way, and then you must guide them along that way. Give them reinforcement. Help them.

Castaneda's book, *Teachings According to Don Juan*, has a beautiful quotation about paths. The book is about an old Yaqui Indian of great wisdom who says:

> Each path is only one of a million paths. Therefore, you must always keep in mind that a path is only a path. If you feel that you must not follow it, you need not stay with it under any circumstances. Any path is only a path. There is no affront to yourself or others in dropping it if that is what your heart tells you to do. But your decision to keep on the path or leave it must be free of fear or ambition or hate. I warn you: look at every path closely and deliberately. Try it as many times as you think necessary. Then ask yourself and yourself alone one question. It is this: Does this path have heart? All paths are the same. They all lead nowhere. They are paths going through the brush or over the brush or under the brush. Does this path have a heart is the only question. If it does, then the path is good. If it doesn't, it is of no use. Both paths lead nowhere but one has heart and the other doesn't. One makes for a joyful, productive journey. As long as you follow it, you are one with it, but the other will make you curse your life and die of loneliness.[8]

Working with parents involves the following things: the cognitive, certainly, the head, and the manipulation of knowledge. Parents need facts, and we are the only ones who can give them. And, secondly, the psychomotor—they need to be put into action. They are productive, exciting, intelligent human beings, and we need to use them in this way. And, thirdly, we need to be concerned about the affective, and that is the emotional reaction all along the way.

I am ending this paper with another man's thoughts on changing our existence. Written by Joseph Zinker, it is one of those precious things I've found in the past few years. He is at the Gestalt Institute in Cleveland, and he ends his paper, "On Public Knowledge and Personal Relevance,"[9] in this way:

> If the man in the street were to pursue personal knowledge, what kind of guiding thoughts would he come up with about changing his existence? He would perhaps discover that his brain is not yet dead and that his body has not dried up and that no matter where he is right now, he is still the creator of his own destiny. And he can change this destiny by taking his one decision to change seriously, by fighting his petty resistance against change, by learning more about his mind, by trying out behavior which fits his real needs, by carrying out concrete acts rather than conceptualizing and talking about them, by practicing to hear and see and feel as if he has never known these senses before, by creating something with his own hands without demanding perfection, by picking out ways in which he behaves in a self-defeating manner, by listening to the words that he utters to his wife and his kids, by listening to the words and looking into the eyes of those who speak to him, by learning to respect the process of his own creative endeavors, and by having faith that they will get him there some day, and by engaging in collective activities with his neighbors and his friends which are designed to build both their mutual efforts. He must remind himself, however, that no change takes place without getting your hands dirty, and no change takes place without suffering, and no change takes place without some conflict. But he is not afraid. There are no formulae and no books to memorize for this process.
>
> I only know this. I exist. I am. I am here. I am becoming. I make my life, and nobody else makes it for me. I must face my own shortcomings, my own mistakes, and my own transgressions. No one can suffer my own non-being as I do. But tomorrow is another day, and I must decide to leave my bed and live again. And if I fail, I don't have the comfort of blaming you or life or God.

NOTES

1. Herbert Otto, *Explorations in Human Potentialities* (Springfield, Ill.: Charles C Thomas, 1966); Herbert Otto and John Mann (eds.), *Ways of Growth: Approaches to Expanding Awareness* (New York, N.Y.: The Viking Press, Inc., 1969); Herbert Otto, *Guide to Developing Your Potential* (New York, N.Y.: Charles Scribner's Sons, 1967).
2. Pierre Teilhard de Chardin, *The Phenomenon of Man* (New York, N.Y.: Harper & Row, Publishers, Inc., 1959).

3. Antoine de Saint Exupery, *Wind, Sand and Stars* (New York, N.Y.: Harcourt, Brace & World, Inc., 1940).
4. Albert J. Solnit and Mary H. Stark, "Learning with Teachers," *Children*, 14, No. 1 (January-February 1967), 19-24; Albert J. Solnit and Morris Green, "The Pediatric Management of the Dying Child, Part II: The Child's Reaction to the Fear of Dying," *Perspectives in Child Development*, eds. Albert J. Solnit and Sally Provence (New York, N.Y.: International Universities Press, Inc., 1963), 217-228; Albert J. Solnit, "Psychologic Considerations in the Management of Deaths in Pediatric Hospital Services, I. The Doctor and the Child's Family," *Pediatrics*, 24 (1959), 106-112.
5. Clara Claiborn Park, *The Siege* (New York, N.Y.: Harcourt, Brace & World, Inc., 1967).
6. Virginia Woolf, *Flush: A Biography* (New York, N.Y.: Harcourt, Brace, Johanovich, Inc., 1933).
7. Buckminster Fuller, *Ideas and Integrities* (New York, N.Y.: Prentice-Hall, Inc., 1963).
8. Carlos Castaneda, *Teachings of Don Juan: A Yaqui Way of Knowledge* (Berkeley, California: University of California Press, 1968).
9. Joseph Zinker, "On Public Knowledge and Personal Revelation," *Explorations* (April 1968).

The Parents Talk to Doctors

Sylvia O. Richardson*
Joseph L. Kloss
Dean Timmons

The following dialogue is a tape-recorded transcription of a unique panel that was held at the 1971 ACLD conference.

DR. RICHARDSON: It is often said about medical people that you can't ever talk to us or we don't ever listen to you, or some such thing. Now you have the opportunity to talk to some physicians who are also quite remarkable men because they are two of the rare breed that you usually don't see very often at meetings, since they are too busy seeing patients. They practice medicine. This group is probably the least represented at most meetings.

Dr. Joseph Kloss is a pediatrician who received his medical training at St. Louis University and trained in pediatrics at Children's Hospital in Akron, Ohio. Probably more important than the fact that he has been practicing pediatrics for ten years, is the fact that Dr. Kloss has five children, four boys and one girl.

Dr. Dean Timmons is a pediatric neurologist who is practicing in Akron. He received his medical training at Indiana Medical School and his subsequent training in pediatrics, pediatric neurology, and neurology in Indiana. Dr. Timmons is also a father. He has three girls.

Both of these men are certified members of their respective boards, which is a very important fact. Each man is going to speak, briefly, about his point of view, and then we are going to ask for questions from the floor.

There are a couple of ground rules we are going to ask you to observe: speakers from the floor are asked to limit their talks and questions to five minutes; otherwise things can get out of hand. Please try to keep the questions general and avoid personal case histories; it is very difficult to make a diagnosis on the telephone and most of us don't try to do this. You can direct the questions to whomever you like, and then we can argue up here and question each other if necessary. First, Dr. Kloss is going to tell us about

---

Sylvia O. Richardson, M.D., is an associate clinical professor of pediatrics and assistant director of the university affiliated program for children with severe learning disabilities at the University of Cincinnati, Ohio.

Joseph L. Kloss, M.D., is a pediatrician in Cuyahoga Falls, Ohio.

Dean Timmons, M.D., is a pediatric neurologist in Akron, Ohio.

some problems he sees in his office, and give us a general idea of how he looks at children with learning disabilities.

DR. KLOSS: I want to make some general comments on the role of the pedeatrician in handling learning-disabled children. There are two possible situations that should be considered. The first situation is one where you have taken care of this child from the time of birth. The second situation is one where you are seeing this child for an initial evaluation, although the child has already been diagnosed as having a problem. It is helpful if you have taken care of a family from the time the child was born. You have a knowledge of things that we might talk about later, what you would call high-risk children, or high-risk infants because of certain problems. As doctors, we like to see the children in the hospital after delivery for initial examination, if at all possible, and then we follow-up with regular visits. If you see the child in the hospital after delivery, you immediately have the information concerning the child's delivery, pregnancy, how the child acted at birth, and various things that might be significant. You then have the opportunity to follow the child with regular checkups, noting his developmental milestones, how he performs in relation to other children his age, and hopefully, to see if there are signs of problems or difficulties that will help the family, prewarn them, if possible, that something significant might be coming.

If you are performing an initial evaluation on an older child who is having problems already, then the situation and approach are a little different. You are familiar with the health background of the child whom you have followed regularly; you know his past medical history. But in the case of the child you are seeing initially, your first function is to perform a good physical examination to rule out the possibility that there might be anything physically wrong with the child that might impair his school performance. You might consider whether there are types of metabolic or glandular problems that would be significant. Is the child anemic? Is he malnourished? Does he have allergies? If you screen this child and find that, medically speaking, he is in good health, and there is no obvious reason why he should be having problems in this regard, then you will consider his school background, educational background, home environment, and so on. You consider the behavioral aspects of this child in the home setting versus what the child does in the school setting. When this type of evaluation is completed, then there are three possible considerations left for the practicing pediatrician: does the child qualify for and would he benefit from some type of drug therapy? Counsel the family regarding the child's problem, as much as possible. Refer the child to other qualified people for further evaluation and further testing, if you feel that more information is necessary to make a true evaluation. Some of the children you have problems with are then referred to a pediatric neurologist, such as Dr. Timmons.

DR. TIMMONS: The child, by the time he gets to me, has been diagnosed quite adequately in the general pediatric mode. At this point, there are several things that have to be considered. Most of the time, I see a child for one of two basic reasons—one is to give support to what the parent has already been told because the child may very well have been adequately diagnosed;

however, the diagnosis may not have been acceptable to the parent, and it may have to be reinforced by a second, sometimes a third, fourth, fifth, sixth, and seventh party. The other function is to find further diagnostic avenues of approach, and as a pediatric neurologist, obviously, I am interested in the functioning of the nervous system, and I am interested in the functioning of the nervous system in regard to the child's intellectual development, motor development, verbal development, and social development. Obviously, you are quite limited in a single hour as to how much you can do, so you try to define the primary aspects and from there consider further diagnostic avenues of approach. Further referral to the speech and language therapist may be indicated, or to the physical therapist, to an orthopedic surgeon, and so forth. The point is, though, that at this time, I attempt to define what appears to be the primary problem. I feel it is very important to emphasize the primary problem because the child may have a number of different problems, and if you attempted to attack all of them at once, you would overwhelm the youngster to such an extent that he would certainly not function. At this point, too, since we're talking about the school-age child, a high number of these children certainly have significant educational problems, which have to be identified in conjunction with the educator and the school psychologist, and then attempts must be made to get such a child into the correct educational program. As you are all aware, programs certainly vary from one school system to another and from one state to another, depending on what facilities are available, and what tag has to be placed on the child so that he can qualify for placement in a certain educational program.

PARENT: *I would like to know what exactly are "soft signs" in a neurological examination?*

DR. TIMMONS: This depends on the person with whom you are talking, but the most important thing is to recognize that this is a type of neurological sign, and that it is not one of the classical "hard signs" like the Babinski, or increased reflexes, paralysis of the limbs, and so forth. This may be a mild overflow of movement, such as opening the hand, back and forth, and not being able to check it correctly. You can have the same type of thing with the tongue, or it may be a mild difficulty in opposing the finger to the thumb. It may be mild difficulty in the development of motor criteria. The child may be four years old and not be able to perform three-year-old level motor tasks yet. These are within the realm of the "soft signs."

DR. RICHARDSON: (repeating a question from the audience) This question was very nicely and very politely put: *If only 40 percent of the children who are handicapped are getting special education services, couldn't we doctors provide, in addition to our practice in medicine, psychological and diagnostic services of other types?*

DR. KLOSS: One of the problems we have on something like this is, in a way, beyond our control. All of the children aren't in proper placement because there are not enough classes. There aren't enough classes because there are not enough qualified teachers to handle them, and there is not enough money in the budget to set up more classes. In Ohio, we use the term, *neurologically handicapped*. We have long waiting lists of children who need to get into neurologically handicapped classes. In the city of Akron alone, we probably could handle double the number of classes. Some of this backlog is taken up with part-time tutoring of some of these children for an hour or two a day, and there are some who could benefit from full-day special classes, but we are unable to do anything with them because of placement. This is frustrating to the physician, and it is even more frustrating to the parents when you tell them they have a child who has a problem and there is no place for them to go to solve it. I think this is an area in which the ACLD chapters and local lobbying in your state congress is helpful for initiating funds for more classes. Of course, we still have an inadequate number of teachers for the classes. There is not much that we can do about this right away, except hope that more and more teachers are being trained who can handle this type of problem.

DR. TIMMONS: As I heard the question, in essence, we are being asked if the physician could have some ancillary personnel working out of his office. Some do. As a matter of fact, in my office I have a girl with a master's degree in speech and hearing, and I have a part-time psychologist. We attempt to do this, but we are limited. You know it takes a lot of money to continually pay for private tutorial services and this type of thing, and I grant you that much more can be done along this line. I'm sure that many avenues can be investigated that we are not touching on at the present time. However, I think this is sort of a stop-gap solution; the real thing to do is to identify the problem where it exists and try to fund it so that all children in the community can benefit from the help they need, not just the ones whose parents can afford it.

DR. RICHARDSON: I think one of the most difficult things pertaining to what you are asking, is early identification of children with possible learning disabilities, which of all the problems is probably closest to home for the pediatricians because we see the child develop gradually. There have been many feelings about the effectiveness of early identification of children with possible problems. One approach has been suggested in some areas. We know that if an infant had a difficult birth, and had a little difficulty in the neonatal period, this may indicate a possible high risk. The question that arises is this: does the physician tell the mother at that time that the child may have a problem? Many of us don't like this idea because we know about something called a self-fulfilling prophecy. You know if you look for trouble you'll get it in any area. If you look for a "terrible two," you'll get one, no matter what else you have. Most professional people dislike the notion of warning that there may be a problem. On the other hand it is possible for the physician to put a star on the chart or have some way of noting to himself to closely watch the manner in which this child develops. Some of the areas that are the toughest for pediatricians are now gradually being overcome. For example, Dr. Kloss, Dr. Timmons, and I did not see any normal kids when we were in our medical training. We saw sick children, we saw problem children. We didn't really get to know about the normal child's growth and development sequence. This is changing. Today our pediatric students, residents, and interns are beginning to get this kind of training built into their program.

PARENT: *I would like to know who you recommend if you examine the child and he does not have brain damage but he is perceptually handicapped, but the psychologist hasn't been able to pinpoint the extent of the child's perceptual handicap.*

DR. TIMMONS: I think this opens up a whole bag of worms, really. In the first place, we get into our definitions of terms, and, unfortunately, the term *brain damage*, even when we put a qualifier of *minimal* in front of it, carries a connotation to a neurologist of a child who has had some anatomical destruction of the neuron. This means that those nerve cells are dead. As a consequence, this presents great problems, and even when we put qualifying terms and adjectives in front of it, *brain damage* runs parents right up the wall and makes them feel that there are great problems that this child is going to develop in the future. I don't know where you are from or what terms are used in your locale, but in the child that you are talking about, there may very definitely *not* be any true anatomical destruction or disruption of the nervous system. However, he may be quite impaired in his perceptual abilities. It makes no difference, really, whether this child is functioning well one day and poorly the next day. We know that some days he is going to be functioning poorly and, as a consequence, he has to get some type of special educational approach or program that is defined primarily for the days he is doing poorest. The training should build from that point. I care not what term you put on it, I care not where you are or who is the local "god" in your area. However, it is very important that this child's problems should be defined, and that some kind of program is outlined for him—one that is not dependent upon who you happen to be reading at the time, and one that is specifically suitable for the child.

DR. KLOSS: I would like to comment on the term. From a pediatric standpoint we would prefer, at least in our own usage, to either drop the aspect of of the brain altogether and just say "the child with learning disabilities," or if you need to bring the brain or nervous system into it, perhaps use the term *cerebral dysfunction*, which at least doesn't imply damage or specific anatomical problems. You're saying then that things don't function the way they should. This may be to some extent a maturational lag. We know that many of these children do improve with time. I am not advocating that you wait for this to occur because there are things that need to be done in the meantime. The idea that they'll grow out of it is partly true. I don't advocate relying on this exclusively because by the time they do outgrow it, they encounter so many educational and psychological problems that they may never catch up, but I think this term has a little less connotation as a definition of actual neurological problems.

PARENT: *As a parent, I find that in most areas pediatric neurologists are rare birds. They just don't exist. We have pediatricians who are very good. Even in a large town the size of Houston, if you can find this rare bird, he works only with diagnosticians. We have become so specialized in medicine that we are in a mess again. You take your child to a doctor because he walks funny, and the doctor prescribes special shoes because he has difficulty with his feet. He doesn't see too well, so you take him to an eye specialist, and you put glasses on him. He is so accident-prone that you decide he has crisp bones and take him to a bone specialist. How do we tie all of these things together?*

DR. RICHARDSON: The pediatrician, my lady in purple says, is paralyzed when he gets all these reports from all these different doctors and he has to correlate them. There are training centers to relate these findings. There is one at the University of Cincinnati. Its primary purpose is to provide interdisciplinary training using representatives from many different viewpoints. We have a department of pediatrics, a department of special education, social service, psychology, nursing, speech, and hearing. Each of the separate departments has its own trainees, but they all attend lectures in all the departments, and at the case conferences on the children when the trainees are present, they are uniquely able in each setting to say to any one of us, "What are you talking about?" Someone in education can say to a doctor, "I don't understand a word of what you just said. Rephrase it." We're beginning to learn the gobbledygook of the different disciplines. It's a place where people in training can learn about how other professional people think, and move, and have their meanings. This is good. Scholarships are being offered. There is a lot of post-graduate training available now. There are many medical schools that have post-graduate courses just like those offered in the field of education.

DR. KLOSS: Dr. Timmons and I are in separate practices, although we do work together quite a bit. I am sure the day is coming when there will be pediatricians who will do nothing but specialize in learning disabilities. I think that this is probably a coming thing. They may do this on their own, or they may work with a pediatric neurologist directly in the same office. There are enough fellowships now in developmental pediatrics and in learning disabilities, and handicapped children, in the medical schools that some of these fellows are going to filter out into practice. They are not all going to stay in the university, which unfortunately happens too often.

DR. TIMMONS: There is quite a bit being done, in addition to what Dr. Richardson said. In our Children's Hospital we have approximately ten to fifteen residents a year in pediatrics, and these boys all have to go through clinics, which are staffed by educators, speech and hearing people, psychologists, physical therapists, occupational therapists, and so forth. All of these children have been evaluated by separate people and then reports are given and then following this, the decision is made as to what the priorities are concerning the approach to each youngster. In addition to this, Ohio has recently recognized some of these problems. There is now a joint committee between the state medical association and the state's special education section. We are in the very first aspects of looking very hard at the qualifications for various special educational programs and we just started the first pilot program this month.

PARENT: *I would like to expand on that question a little bit. In our town, this multidisciplinary concept just hasn't worked at all. The parents may have the diagnosis of their child and have an idea what is there, but at a certain point they need a further prescription about what to do. How does a parent know where to turn, where to go, other than Cincinnati or something like that. Where do we get the straight talk on whom to see?*

DR. RICHARDSON: Medically, you should be getting this from your pediatrician, and educationally, you should be getting it from the school. One thing I would like to point out, too, is that the physician's primary responsibility is to determine the health or lack of health in a child. Our job is to keep people well, basically. The medical follow-up should be through your physician. He knows the child.

PARENT: *They don't do it, this is the point. Where in the profession can we get some straight answers on who is qualified to give answers, and if it isn't in your town then recommend some other town. This is what we're saying. Where do you get the straight answers on which person to see?*

PARENT: *Who's responsible? I'd like to talk further on this. When you go from place to place and you get an answer from this one and that one, and you finally go to one whom you think is the authority, your state medical school, or something else, then you may also get the statement that we got from a pediatric psychiatrist, "This child is the victim of a fat folder syndrome." He's been seen all over the place and nobody has given anybody any answers.*

DR. RICHARDSON: By one token, you may have an answer very early in the game from a physician whom you couldn't hear. Don't forget this: you will hear when you're ready to hear. In our setup and in most of the UAF (University Affiliated Facility for Children with Developmental Defects), when the child is seen by the different specialists that are required in conference, then you go back for counseling to the pediatrician who has been following this and who wraps up the whole thing for you, because we recognize that the parents can't put medical information together and come up with an understandable picture of what has been said. But when you ask who's responsible, the physician who is taking care of the child really holds that responsibility and I'll stop on that.

DR. KLOSS: You have to remember that doctors are people and they have different interests. There are some pediatricians who have no interest whatsoever in school problems or learning disabilities; they couldn't care less about it and they aren't about to change. There are others who do have some interest, and they try, but they also have a busy practice of pediatrics and can't do everything. I have a family at home, and to try to space out my time to do this and do that becomes increasingly difficult. If someone calls the office and has a child with a school problem, it might be a long wait before I am able to see him. This is a simple mechanical problem when you have a busy schedule. This is distressing to us, too. I'm sorry there is nothing you can do about it. You're going to encounter a number of people who have no interest in the problem whatsoever, and to get you out of their hair they send you to somebody else. You have to accept this for what it is. Hopefully, the people who are coming up, the so-called new breed, are being trained differently and will have different interests. Of course, this doesn't help your immediate problem.

PARENT: *Will you please tell me whether you have found an increase in adopted children with learning disabilities and what your feelings are about this?*

DR. TIMMONS: I will address myself to that, because I was very impressed with the number of adopted children who were coming to my office that were having problems. I was asked last spring to participate in a meeting at Ohio University, and since I have such interest in this, I thought I would use this as my address. Unfortunately, it is difficult to find the basic figures concerning adopted children in the general population, and the only good figures that I was able to find were from Canada. But for the United States or anywhere else, I haven't been able to find any good figures. What really surprised me and shocked me and almost panicked me, because it shot little pieces out of my address when I finally came up with it, was that the incidence of adopted children who were in the special educational program in the city of Akron, Ohio, was exactly the same as the number of adopted children in the general population of Canada.

PARENT: *What do you think accounts for this? Why?*

DR. KLOSS: There was an article published recently and I really can't remember if it was from Canada or not. This article stated that in a number of surveys, an increased number of adopted children were found to have learning disabilities of one type or another. Some of the hypotheses that were put forth were that all of these children were unwanted children in the first place. We see mothers of twelve, thirteen, and fourteen years of age not infrequently. You have a number of factors here. Many of these mothers have no prenatal care whatsoever. They show up in the hospital at the time of delivery and say, "I'm going to have a baby." No one has taken care of them during their whole pregnancy. A lot of them walk into a hospital with eclampsia or toxemia. They have had no care for this. A lot of them are very young and this is their first pregnancy. They often have difficult deliveries. The mother may or may not have an adequate pelvis for delivering children, and I think in general a fair number of these children probably have a more traumatic birth situation both prenatally and postnatally than the average population.

DR. RICHARDSON: We don't have any evidence, and I don't know of any way of getting any evidence as to how many of these young mothers try, but without success to abort themselves. This also is a factor that needs to be considered.

PARENT: *What do you feel about medication?*

DR. TIMMONS: You'll probably find three different opinions up here in that regard. I must admit that my experience has been that medication can be quite effective for modifying the behavior activities of these youngsters. The physician has to be willing to work with the family, with the school, and with the child. He must see to it that the dosage of medication is adequate for helping this youngster. I think that one of the big hang-ups we get, though, is people who expect that this pill is going to magically solve all their problems. This certainly is not the case. The only thing that I attempt to do is try to modify the behavior, to relate and structure the environment of this child. If you can take the edge off just a little bit, you get through to the parents much easier in regard to working with the child. For example, if Mama has a kiddy who is getting up at 3:00 AM every morning and wandering downstairs and taking all the pots and pans out and spilling flour and sugar around on the kitchen floor, she is not very nice to him the next morning when she gets up, and she is a little grouchy to Daddy and everyone else. If you can establish a good sleep pattern for this child through medication, then mother is in a much better situation to deal with the problem in a very structured program the next day. Likewise, if you can slow down the child so that his attention span, instead of being five seconds, becomes fifteen minutes, he can begin to be reached by the educator. It is awfully nice to be able to sit at least fifteen minutes at the dinner table without having this kid kick it over or jump up to run into the other room and so forth. I feel that you certainly can do a lot with behavior modification, but these are not magic answers. There are many other problems that have to be identified and worked with at the same time, and unless you do this you are going to fall flat on your face as far as the medication is concerned.

DR. KLOSS: I would rank with Dr. Timmons as a "pill pusher." I give medication frequently and have no hesitation about using it if I think it is indicated. I don't think there is any problem related to using it as far as habituation or addiction or anything like this. You may remember that there was a flurry last year out in Kansas, I believe, about all the children taking pills. There have been several reports recently, one by a study through the AMA and another report just last week through senator Gallager's committee, and there didn't appear to be any problems related to using medication with these children. Medication should be used if you think it is really needed. If you have a child who, in your opinion, really doesn't need medication, then don't use it. It should be individualized. There are various types of medication, and I don't know how deeply you want to get into this, but I can tell you the general types we use. The two most popular types would fall into what is called the stimulant or psychic-energizer group. First, there are the amphetamines, such as Dexedrine, which I use quite frequently, and which often is spectacular in its effect in the appropriate child. In one or two days, the mother will call my office and say that he is a completely different child. You have to remember that this is a trial-and-error type of thing. What works beautifully for one child may have no effect whatsoever on another. It may show just the opposite effect and set the child off even more, so the parents have to realize from the start that if we are going to use some kind of medication that we think is appropriate in a situation, we can't expect immediate results. We may have to adjust the dosage; we may have to stop it altogether and try different medications. Second to Dexedrine, another common type is Ritalin. After this, you go into a "tranquilizing" type of medication. In our area, the medication that we use most in this category is Mellaril. Children can tolerate quite large doses of this without any difficulty. We use Thorazine on some children, and Benadryl at time on others. These are some of the medications, and there are others that can be used also, but this is a representative amount. I have not encountered any problems up to the present time with the use of medication. It has been my finding, personally, that as these children get older, they don't want to take medication anymore, and they tell the parents, "I don't want these pills, I don't need them now." And I say, "Fine, if you don't need them, let's try it without them." I have not encountered children who wanted to stay on medication. To the contrary, most of them are more than happy to stop taking the pills as they approach adolescence. If we still encounter problems, we may want to start them again. I have no hesitation about using medication in appropriate circumstances.

DR. TIMMONS: Could I give a couple of personal biases about this? As a physician I feel very strongly that when you treat, you treat. You can't cast a broken leg on weekends and uncast it during the week. Likewise, you don't treat a little diabetes nor do you treat a little congestive heart failure. You decide on the appropriate program to follow, and then you treat it. You treat seven days a week, fifty-two weeks a year. The child does not cease learning just because he is not in a formal educational system. The fact of the matter is that he is learning more outside his formal educational system than he is learning in school. This is one of the things that disturbs me personally. I recognize that a number of patients whom I see have been counseled otherwise and that there are many others that feel quite differently about this. However, I still feel that once you have decided to treat, you should treat.

DR. RICHARDSON: I surely agree with that. One handicap that we face, if a child is on medication, is that we have to count on the reliability of the parent. If the doctor has prescribed medication seven days a week, then give it to him seven days a week. A mother called me two weeks ago and said, "Well, I just wanted to find out if that stuff was really needed, so we took her off it. Then we put her back on." When you try these home experiments, it really doesn't help anybody, and there is no way for the physician to gauge the accuracy of the treatment.

PARENT: *I am a physician in a family practice and I am interested in the problem because I have six children, two of whom have learning problems. In our area, we have encountered difficulties because of a number of reasons. We don't have any physicians who are interested in the problem; it's a new science to us—nobody trained us. I became interested only because my immediate family is involved. There aren't many physicians who have had formal training. Secondly, some of us have problems on the school district level. I think that ACLD chapters are a very good source for experts in all the disciplines, and by urging parents to go through ACLD, you can actually set up family protocols and projects.*

DR. RICHARDSON: That's very good and useful.

DR. KLOSS: I would like to comment on one thing that the doctor mentioned. I am sure you are aware of this yourself: just as there are differences in physicians who are interested in the problem, there are differences in school principals who are interested in the problem. I have had encounters with people who say, "Well, there is no such thing as a hyperactive child. They're all just spoiled brats. There is no such thing as a learning disability." You can't convince them otherwise.

PARENT: *I have always heard about medication for children who are hypoactive. Could you explain?*

DR. KLOSS: This depends. We treat children who are hyperactive because they don't function well in any setting. They can't sit still long enough to concentrate on anything or accomplish anything constructively, and to temper them down, we treat these children. We don't usually hear too much about the hypoactive children because they don't bother anybody, and the parents usually don't come to us because these children are so nice, quiet, and cooperative. Occasionally, we will get a situation where we may treat an extremely hypoactive child. The type of medication that works here is, again, difficult to say. If you were to just take a number of average people and put them on Dexedrine or Ritalin, they would be stimulated. For some reason hyperactive children get a paradoxial affect: they are calmed. If you want to treat hypoactive children, you might try this type of medication to see if you would get the normal, stimulated response.

DR. TIMMONS: This is the child, probably, that one has to feel the sorriest for, simply because this child goes the longest without being recognized either by the educator or the parent. One of the great problems we have here is that the child who is excessively hypoactive has given up many times, and although we occasionally can get some help with medication, the big secret here is to try to work with this child in successful reinforcement, and this is where the educator must really come in and dig in with this youngster. My experience in treating hypoactive children with any kind of medication has been dismal.

PARENT: *I have a comment and a question. If parents are having difficulty getting appropriate programs for their children, we have them go right to the very top state level because every state has mandatory legislation and does have somebody in charge. We suggest that if you get brushed off, you have your lawyer talk to them the next time.*

PARENT: *I think as parents we waste too much time running back and forth between doctors and school principals, and we must realize that our child's problem is really in the classroom and not in the doctor's office. My question is this: I am wondering what will be the future effect of drugs that are now being taken by our high school and college kids, and what effects do these drugs have on learning disabilities, and what effects will they have on future babies?*

DR. TIMMONS: I don't think that either Dr. Kloss or I tend to try to put ourselves forward as experts on drug ingestion, drug culture, and all of this. We do know that, particularly, LSD has shown some chromosomal breaks as such. Whether these other medications will also show some problems along this line, I don't know. One has to be impressed with what happens to a new-born infant whose mother is a heroin addict, as the infant is convulsing, coming out of the withdrawal situation after it is born. In essence, are these youngsters who are taking the various forms of medication at the present time going to harm their unborn babies, or perhaps their unfertilized babies at the present time? I don't know. The problem is, you see, that you name just a few drugs, and what some of these kids put into their veins is fantastic. Many times when you ask them, they really don't know. They will have a mixer party where they dump everything they have and stir it up and some of the problems that they get from it are fantastic!

DR. KLOSS: I would agree with Dr. Timmons. I have no comments, except that in some studies with the use of LSD there have been chromosome breaks in the infants, and this, of course, will increase the possibilities that there might be some difficulties. I think we should be concerned, also, with what happens to these children after they are born. This would be a significant thing to consider in caring for these children in a family type setting or whatever it might be: what happens to them then?

PARENT: *I found that by organizing small groups of parents, you might be able to talk things over with someone else who has the same problem that you have. I think that sometimes when you're able to talk with another parent this helps to generate your understanding as well as that of the group.*

DR. RICHARDSON: You mean groups like the ACLD chapters?

PARENT: *Yes, like breaking them down into smaller groups.*

DR. RICHARDSON: Small groups of ACLD chapters, groups of parents who have children with learning disabilities who could work together and study together and talk together about their various problems. And what do we do about that one?

DR. KLOSS: I think this would be an excellent idea because when you talk to parents who have children with these problems it is surprising to hear some of the solutions and answers that they come up with that you never thought of yourself. I think we could all benefit from each other's experiences, and this is really the best way, to sit down, and talk about it, and if you have an active ACLD group, there is no reason why you can't have a meeting, or several meetings a year when you have nothing but a gab session.

DR. RICHARDSON: If you do this you could bring in local people.

DR. KLOSS: You could decide on a certain facet of behavior that you are going to talk about and people could bring in their suggestions or comments.

DR. RICHARDSON: It's also nice to find out that somebody else has a kid that's worse than yours.

DR. TIMMONS: We have experienced this in such things as myelodysplasia, epilepsy, and so forth. We find that a parent can say to another parent the same thing that a physician has said to the parent, and the parent may not hear the physician but he will hear another parent. We also find that the psychological support that a subcategory group like this can give to one another is fantastic. It is much more than any medical individual can do.

PARENT: *What about the Doman-Delacato method?*

DR. TIMMONS: My experience has not been good with this. My personal bias is not in favor of it. I recognize that there is a lot of enthusiasm for this and that there are a lot of programs for this throughout. I think that they have done one very good thing, though. They have made everyone who works with handicapped children recognize the importance of involving the parents in the actual day-to-day handling of the child's problem, whether the handicap is a learning one or a physical one. My personal experience has been that many times the results are less than what the parents have been led to believe they would get from this. In addition, on many occasions it requires the localization of a rather large number of the adult population where you live to follow through with the total program. I recognize, as I said, that there is a lot of popular enthusiasm and that many people in this audience probably have their children in this program or a program based on this, but my personal bias is that I do not recommend it.

DR. KLOSS: I would agree. The few patients that I have had who were involved in such programs, have not at all been satisfactory as far as the way things have worked out. The thing you have to remember is that the Doman-Delacato method is a theory. There are lots of theories in the world, and this is an individual theory from the group in Philadelphia at The Institutes for the Achievement of Human Potential. There are many physicians and neurologists who do not support this whatsoever. They have found no basis for the theory that has been proposed. In fact, last year the American Academy of Pediatrics, The American Academy of Neurology and United Cerebral Palsy, and about eight other groups came out with a formal statement saying that they found this method to be of no proven value. One thing that I personally have noted is that it took an enormous amount of the parent's time to carry out the programs as recommended. Often this was to the detriment of the other people in the family. The other children, the father, and the mother are all relegated to a secondary position and everything is focused on this one child; getting the patterning done and getting this done and that done at the right time. On two different occasions I had families whom I knew well, and they had done their best to do things as recommended, and when they went back for reevaluation they were told that their child was not progressing well because they weren't doing their part. This was an enormous emotional problem for these families. They were devoting great amounts of time trying to do their part, and they were told that their children were not getting better because they were not working. This gave me a very bad opinion. Several studies have been done, one by Dr. Robbins, in which these same theories were tried in a formal program, and another was done on the Doman-Delacato method, with problem readers. These studies showed that the theory had no particular value as had been predicted.

DR. RICHARDSON: There are portions of the theory that are perfectly legitimate. If you look at some of the ideas of the Doman-Delacato method, you will see that we utilize a lot of the visual-motor techniques. Occupational therapists use some of these techniques, and other disciplines use many of the techniques. It's the packaging that is disturbing and very distractive to many. I have often thought that mothers should take some training in tutorial assistance for children and start working on their school systems, not as, you know, "Sit down and read with me Johnny" type of tutors, but as real tutors of various types, utilizing all different kinds of techniques. I would like to see these mothers do that kind of work instead of working as patterners and using so much of their time to pattern a patient of mine, while all the time I am thinking, "My golly, if I would have had those seventy-seven mothers tutoring kids in school." It would have been a greater blessing for a large number of children. I feel strongly about the use of time in this regard.

PARENT: *It took us ten years in New York to get the medical profession to recognize this, and it has only been within the last five years that some have accepted. This is a question of expecting and demanding clinical services, diagnostic services, and treatment. I must admire the strength of the three on the panel because here we are discussing the problem that you are undertaking and trying to solve, and no one has said one word about the obstetricians. The fact is that many of these children have prenatal and paranatal problems. Nothing has been said about practices of the obstetrician, the induced labor, the long labor, the medication or lack of medication, the overdoses of medication, whatever it may be. Now I know that this is a very touchy subject because I'm asking one field of medicine to be critical of another field of medicine. The only reason I'm mentioning this is because they deliver the child, walk away, and this is the end of it, and yet I think there is a lot to be added to and demanded of this particular field of medicine. I don't know how the other areas of medicine can help us in this, but we certainly do care.*

DR. KLOSS: This is a question that is difficult to generalize because there is no question that most of the obstetricians I'm familiar with are very conscientious, good physicians. As in any field, there are differences in individuals. Some things are done for convenience, some patients are over-medicated before delivery and they get a very sleepy baby, and we know we can expect this from certain obstetricians. You can tell them about it but there is not a whole lot else you can do to get them to change their practice. They say, "Well, my mothers love it because they are very comfortable and don't have any pain." And we say, "Well, the babies don't love it." But it isn't until they get involved in a serious problem situation where the baby doesn't breathe or doesn't survive that they then sometimes think twice about how things are approached. The comment on prenatal care isn't always the fault of an obstetrician; there are some mothers who just don't show up until just before delivery, and we can't blame the physicians for that.

DR. TIMMONS: I don't think this is a simple problem. We're talking about society. Where do you have the high incidence of prematurity? You have it around your poverty areas. Where do you have your high incidence of lack of prenatal care? Again, it is in your poverty areas. Where do you have your high incidence of young mothers much more so than in another place? Again, it is in your poverty areas. I grant you that not every obstetrician is a shining knight, and there is no question that mistakes are made. However, I think that there is much of the problem that they cannot always control, such as the dietary problems of the mother during the time of pregnancy, whether or not she lives in an area where the incidence of TB or other diseases is very high. Rather than just pointing a finger at obstetricians, we also have to point a finger back at ourselves and really ask if we are willing to extend the monies, and the time, and the effort to try to assure the right of every child to be born without complications. We haven't accepted this challenge yet, and until we get to the point that we are willing to accept this, we are going to continue to have a fantastic number of children who, by the time they are one hour old, are already predestined to have a significant number of problems.

PARENT: *Is there anything for the laymen to read so that they can understand the problem better?*

DR. RICHARDSON: I think that the nicest things for parents to read are good common-sense books on normal child growth and development. One thing that scares me about parents reading a lot of books is that we get an awful lot of parents that come in with a diagnosis. I have one father who literally came in and handed me a *Pageant Magazine* and said, "That's my son." It was a psychopathic child. It's very hard to differentiate when you read something whether it is real or it is not. I use the example that I had a brain tumor in medical school while my roommate had tuberculosis. So you have to watch what you read. There are some books written for parents that are good books, if you read them intelligently. There are quite a few books about things you can do. I think that one of the best books on the problem of learning disabilities is *Waysiders*, by R. Liston, a neurologist, and R. M. Crosby, a layman. I think that this is an excellent book to read about learning disabilities in children. There are many books, one of which is written by Joanne Beck, *How to Raise a Brighter Child*, which has all kinds of practical advice on what to do, what you can do, how a normal child grows up, and how to apply this kind of information in this particular setting. Then there are other nice books about how to avoid having your children run you around. Rudolf Dreikurs and Vici Stoltz wrote a book entitled *Children, the Challenge*, which is a very nice book to have and is helpful for parents who are interested in child management. You know, in times of stress, I think that there is one book that is better than any other that I know of on child care and that's the Bible, and I'm serious about that—the more you read it, the more you find out.

SECTION III

Educational Trends

Computer Applications in the Field of Learning Disabilities

Janet W. Lerner*
David Anderson

SINCE THE INTRODUCTION of the first large-scale commercial computer in 1951, electronic computers and the technology of data processing have permeated almost every phase of life in the United States. The activities to which this tool has been applied range from space flight to dating services, from inventory control to hospital management. The computer has made a tremendous impact upon the development of many fields of endeavor, including the physical sciences, engineering, linguistics, military science, medicine, and political science. Almost all areas of business have been touched by the electronic revolution. Thus, in a few short years a new technology has exploded, revolutionizing many areas of study. New ways to analyze data, new ways to develop models, new ways to study relationships, and new ways to simulate experiences are now possible.

The field of learning disabilities, however, has scarcely been touched by this powerful and adaptable new tool. There have been few applications of computer technology other than the use of statistical library programs to analyze data in research studies. Most students who are preparing to become learning disabilities specialists and researchers within college and university programs have not been exposed to computer technology. Consequently, the potential applications of computer science to this field have been largely uninvestigated.

With the rapid adoption of computer facilities within all institutions, learning disabilities specialists are more and more likely to find themselves in career positions in hospitals, schools, and clinics that will have unused computer capacity available. At present, such computer facilities are used largely for housekeeping functions—for attendance records, recording of grades and test scores, and scheduling of classes. The electronic facilities could well be used for investigating certain problems of learning disabilities—for research, diagnosis, treatment, and inservice education. Moreover, with a better understanding of the nature of computer capabilities, the learning disabilities spe-

---

*Janet W. Lerner, Ph.D., is associate professor in the Learning Disabilities Center at Northwestern University, Evanston, Illinois. David Anderson is a doctoral student at Northwestern University.

cialists could communicate with computer science specialists. As a consequence they could work together in tackling many problem areas in the field of learning disabilities.

A Pilot Study: Computer technology for learning-disabilities specialists

The learning-disabilities program at Northwestern University took an initial step in exploring and developing ways of applying computer technology to the field of learning disabilities and in training learning-disabilities specialists who are capable of utilizing computer technology.

During the winter quarter of the 1969-1970 academic year, graduate students in the learning-disabilities program were given the opportunity to learn the computer language, FORTRAN, to write programs, and to run these programs on the CDC 6400 computer at Northwestern University's Vogelback Computer Center. The students who availed themselves of this opportunity were given an option of developing a computer application to learning disabilities as part of the requirements for a course in the "Diagnosis of Learning Disabilities," in which they were enrolled.

In addition, all the students in this course were given additional exposure to the computer through the experience of diagnosing a simulated learning-disabilities case. Students were assigned to a diagnostic team, and each team made decisions concerning the case in a simulated clinic situation.

The major goal of our pilot project was to introduce the computer to learning-disabilities students and to alert these students to possible areas and problems in the field of learning disabilities that might be handled by this technology. Our immediate goal was not necessarily to develop a computer program that would make a diagnosis or one that would manage or plan a teaching program. Rather, the goal was to familiarize prospective learning-disabilities specialists with the power and adaptability of this new technology and to encourage them to begin to explore ways to use the electronic computer.

Several resulting programs are described in this paper. They are not presented as sophisticated, final solutions to diagnostic problems. Rather, they are presented to illustrate (1) the computer facility of students training to be learning-disabilities specialists after a few sessions in computer programing, and (2) ways that computer technology can be adapted to routine problems faced by learning-disabilities specialists.

Three areas for which programs were written are discussed in the balance of this paper:
- A simulated learning-disabilities diagnosis.
- Identification of children with learning disabilities: the learning-disabilities quotient.
- A program to analyze performance on the *Illinois Test of Psycholinguistic Abilities* (ITPA).[1]

A simulated learning-disabilities diagnosis

A primary aim of the learning-disabilities program in colleges and universities is to train prospective learning-disabilities specialists to make a diagnosis of a child with a suspected learning disability and to plan and implement remediation within a clinical teaching program. The process of diagnosing and teaching is ongoing and dynamic; it requires the intercorrelation of many elements and variables, including tests, observations, medical reports, and case histories. The selection of data, the functions to be tested, follow-up procedures, hypothesis formulation concerning the nature of the problem, recommendations and referrals, and the development of a teaching plan are among the decisions that must be made.

Typically, the diagnostic and teaching process is discussed in a theory course, and the student gains experience while working with children in a clinic or practicum course. Students generally find such clinic experiences to be extremely valuable. Unfortunately, this clinic practice is often limited within the training program because of the cost. For the following reasons, clinical experiences are frequently insufficient to adequately train the learning-disabilities specialists:

- Clinic space is often limited.
- College supervisory personnel are in short supply.
- Student time that can be devoted to clinic work is insufficient.
- Mistakes made in diagnosing and teaching may be detrimental for the child involved.

Computer simulation can provide one way to supplement and enrich training experiences for the learning-disabilities specialist. Thus, simulation is a way to bridge the gap between the theory course and clinical experiences. It is not intended to be a substitute for either, but it does provide additional experiences without the expense and difficulties involved in the clinical setting.

Simulation has been described as a procedure in which a model or an analog to a real-life situation is created for the purpose of testing or teaching. Simulation procedures have been increasingly recognized as an effective technique in education. In fact, in a recent report to Congress, the Commission on Instructional Technology forecasted that simulation "is likely to become the most important new educational development in the decade."[2] Although simulated computer games have been used extensively in the fields of business management, military science, and political science to promote efficient decision-making, little has been done with this new technology in the field of education in general or in learning disabilities in particular. Computer simulation of learning disabilities is a challenging area of application.

This project used a computer simulation game approach to enable the participants (students) to practice diagnostic decision-making. Information on a specific-learning-disabilities child was stored in computer memory. Students were organized into several diagnostic teams, and as teams they made decisions concerning the simulated case. Several staff conferences were held to choose diagnostic procedures and these data were requested from computer memory. The scarce resource was time; each request or decision came at a cost of time. Computer printouts reported the requested information to each diagnostic team—information such as case history, behavior symptoms, and medical reports.

At a final staffing, a number of diagnostic decisions and remediation recommendations were made. Specific remedial recommendations were decided upon and evaluated by the computer. A printout showing the diagnostic decisions of all teams was distributed to every member of the class. This information permitted a discussion of the case and team decisions by the class as a whole.

Student reaction to this simulation project has been enthusiastic. The students commented that:

- Simulation required them to make decisions concerning tests and time allotments.
- Simulation created a realistic face-to-face staffing situation.
- Simulation forced them to organize the data to develop hypotheses.
- Simulation permitted them to compare their decisions with decisions made by the other diagnostic teams.

Identification of children with learning disabilities: the learning-disabilities quotient

Two teams selected the task of writing a computer program for quick identification of the children within a school population who have learning disabilities. While each team, which consisted of two students, selected to write a FORTRAN program of the learning-disabilities quotient as their area of application, each team proceeded to attack the problem in a unique manner. There were, however, certain similarities in the two programs. In each program, the computer stored input data that consisted of each child's name, IQ score, chronological age, grade in school, and achievement scores in academic skills such as reading, arithmetic, and spelling. In addition, the computer calculated each child's learning quotient according to a programed formula, and determined whether the child had a learning disability and printed out pertinent information. The program permitted dozens of children to be analyzed in this manner within a few seconds of computer time.

These programs were written by graduate students in the learning-disabilities program after five weeks of instruction in the computer language, FORTRAN.

Computer analysis of the ITPA

Another illustration of the use of computers in the field of learning disabilities is a program designed by two students, after completion of the FORTRAN sessions, which analyzes a child's performance on the ITPA.

The program they developed performs the following operations:

- Takes and prints scaled scores for the ITPA.
- Calculates a mean scaled score.
- Determines which areas are significantly above the mean and which are significantly below the mean.
- Determines other tests to verify the areas of integrities or areas of deficits.

- Suggests teaching procedures to use for a child with the abilities or disabilities that have been measured.

The ITPA tests of ten children were analyzed in a period of a few seconds.

This program was created, formulated, and written in FORTRAN, then "debugged," and finally run by two prospective learning-disabilities specialists after a few weeks of instruction in FORTRAN programing. The students concluded that the two aspects of the computer, which seemed to offer the greatest potential for exploration, were (1) the storage of potentially relevant test results for a subsequent diagnostic teaching design, and (2) quick, efficient and accurate determination of significant and near significant strengths and weaknesses as determined by deviation from mean scores.

THE COMPUTER is a powerful and adaptable tool that has had a tremendous impact upon many phases of life. The field of learning disabilities, however, has scarcely been touched by this new technology. The program described in this paper suggests that learning-disabilities specialists can be readily trained in data processing techniques and that such training encourages and creates opportunities to find effective applications of computer use in this field.

The use of computers requires the user to convert his mode of thinking and analysis into terms that are objective, specific, and systematic. If the logic is not concise and consistent, the computer rejects the program, and the user is forced to rethink the problem. While in a field that deals with the human problems of a child's failure to learn, it is essential that we realize the importance of the human element, the child's feelings, the establishment of rapport, and the intuitive skills of the clinician, yet we must also take advantage of the available technological tools if optimum progress is to be made.

NOTES

1. For sources of tests mentioned in this article, see Appendix.
2. The Commission on Instructional Technology, *To Improve Learning: A Report to the President and Congress* (Washington, D.C., March, 1970).

A Management Approach for Meeting the Needs of Children with Specific Learning Disabilities

Mary Ben McDorman*

THE PRIMARY GOAL of the Specific Learning Disabilities (SLD) program is to meet the needs of as many children with learning disabilities as possible and return them to function successfully in the regular classroom as quickly as possible. In order to help the student succeed in the regular class, it is necessary to deal not only with his learning skills, but also with the social behaviors that are required by most classroom teachers. Instruction time in an SLD class is precious. The goal is to maximize this time. Even the master teacher cannot implement a prescriptive instructional program if behaviors are not conducive to learning.

The SLD program described in this paper has attracted an excellent staff of teachers. Although these teachers brought with them a wealth of experience and training, their backgrounds vary. This, therefore, presented the challenge of developing a uniform framework in which each person could function without sacrificing his unique qualities.

Despite the short life of this program, some important information has been learned about the academic, social, and emotional needs of the children served. The basic needs of SLD children are the same as the basic needs of all children. The difference lies in the fact that it may be more difficult to satisfy these needs. These children do not perceive as easily, their perceptions are not as dependable, and they do not generalize as well as average children; for these reasons they require more consistency, more time, and more varied approaches than normal children do. They need multisensory experiences in which they can see, hear, and touch in order to test and reinforce their perceptions.

Children come to the program exhibiting a wide range of academic and social behaviors. A child may be hyperactive, highly distractible, lacking in order or have any combination of the characteristics that are usually associated with the learning-disabled child. It is a certainty that he will:

---

*Mrs. Mary Ben McDorman is school psychologist for the SLD Program at the Robert Shaw Center in Scottdale, Georgia.

- View school as a hostile territory.
- See the teacher as an enemy.
- Expect to be unsuccessful.
- Have a poor self-concept.
- Be dependent on the external environment for his security and control.

He must be allowed to find from experience that positive growth is possible.

Very little has been accomplished by dwelling on the multiplicity of problems these children present. Although they are children to whom many labels and diagnoses have been applied, the focus in this program is not on etiology or diagnoses, but rather on a *developmental behavioral model*. The emphasis is placed on determining the adaptive behaviors that are necessary for learning to take place, and on deciding what each child needs to master first in order to be a successful student. In other words, the child's problems are considered as learning problems. This is the area in which we, as educators, are trained and function most competently.

IN CRITICALLY EVALUATING the program it was determined that the children who had profited most had received a prescriptive instructional program within a classroom that offered the security of a well-defined and dependable structure, and in which there was *positive* interaction between student and teacher. In order to help each teacher create a positive classroom environment in which prescriptive teaching could be implemented, two decisions were made. First, an inservice training program was planned, which presented a theoretical model as well as a practical, applicable model for classroom structure and management. Next, each teacher was assigned a teacher-assistant to help her in the classroom. Volunteers were recruited from the community with the help of the local chapter of ACLD. These women were required to attend the inservice program with the teachers.

The concept of the engineered classroom as proposed by Dr. Frank Hewett and implemented in the Santa Monica, California school system, was selected as the basic model. The participants were also asked to accept five basic premises:

- Children want to please; they want to do what is expected of them.
- Children fail because the expectations that are set for them are not appropriate.
- An individual behaves at any given time as well as he is able, considering the conditions surrounding him.
- Behavior IS; the terms good and bad are not appropriate; acceptable behaviors should be rewarding.
- Success begets success; success in any one area will foster success in other areas.

The training program was quite specific. A model classroom was set up and methods of positive reinforcement were suggested and demonstrated. The need for careful planning was stressed. Many instructional materials were provided and teachers were encouraged to incorporate as many nonverbal cues as possible. The stage was set for the child to *experience* something different in a classroom—success.

Evaluation of this plan after the first six months of operation produced the following conclusions:

• It has provided the teacher with an applicable theoretical framework in which to function.

• It promotes teachers' confidence and self-assurance to which children respond favorably.

• Teachers have been able to maximize their efforts at prescriptive teaching.

• It has provided a preestablished plan to help in emergencies.

• The child with unusual needs, that is, the one whose primary problem is emotional, comes vividly and quickly into focus. The supportive personnel (psychologist, curriculum specialist, and program coordinator) know what has been done, where the breakdown has occurred, and are better able to offer assistance.

• Within this framework, no child can be overlooked.

• It is a "teachable" model.

• Most important, this model has provided an environment that is *positive* and therefore, conducive to learning.

REFERENCES

Allyon, T., and Arzin, N. *The Token Economy*. New York, N.Y.: Appleton-Century-Crofts, 1968.

Becker, Wesley C., Don R. Douglas, and Douglas Carnine. *Reducing Behavior Problems: An Operant Conditioning Guide for Teachers*. Chicago, Ill.: Educational Resources Information Center, 1969.

Glasser, William. *Schools Without Failure*. New York, N.Y.: Harper and Row, 1969.

Gnagey, William J. *The Psychology of Discipline in the Classroom*. New York, N.Y.: The MacMillan Company, 1968.

Hewett, Frank S. *The Emotionally Disturbed Child in the Classroom*. Boston, Mass.: Allyn and Bacon, Inc., 1968.

Tharp, Roland G., and Ralph J. Wetzel. *Behavior Modification in the Natural Environment*. New York, N.Y.: Academic Press, 1969.

Prescriptive Living

Angie Nall*

IF WE COULD select two words to describe children with learning disabilities, they would probably be "more so." All children are complex; ours are more so. All children need individual teaching; these need it more so. All children need guidance in learning how to live happily and productively; these children need it more so. All children need to have their individual needs met, their individual problems studied and solved. They need individual understanding of their own needs and needs of others so that they may more easily grow into mature, mentally healthy adults. Children with learning disabilities just need it more so.

The adult who works and lives with these children must know how to provide all this "more so"; he must study in depth all that has been discovered about the child with learning disabilities. He must learn what methods are successful. He must be willing to try all methods until he finds one that is successful with each particular difficulty of each particular child. Then he must be constantly on the alert for more information about such children, causes not yet found and solutions not yet uncovered. He must never sit back and say, "Now we have found why these children do not learn. Now we know how to teach them." He probably can say, "Now we have found why *many* of these children have not learned and now we know how to meet the needs of *many* of them." We so often find something that causes learning disabilities and feel that we have found the cause of all disabilities. Sometimes one wonders if a lone disability can cause a child not to be able to do school work, or if his problems are more often related to a combination of difficulties.

FOUR OR FIVE YEARS AGO in a clinic where learning-disabled children were being successfully taught school subjects, a group of doctors wondered if the sugar level of the blood had anything to do with a child's classroom performance. They began taking a fasting sample of the blood of these children and found some children who had difficulty, but the number was

---

Miss Angie Nall is director of the Angie Nall School-Hospital, Beaumont, Texas.

not significant enough to get excited about. Then, about three years ago, glucose tolerance tests were ordered on all children who came to this school for diagnosis, and a pattern of difficulty started evolving. A study was made of 123 of these test results; it showed that 51 percent of the children had difficulty with the blood sugar level. This involved sixty-three children, twenty of whom were diagnosed as hyperglycemic. Of the sixty-three children, 52 percent had a very rapid drop in their sugar level within one-half hour after eating, and 38 percent had a rapid drop an hour and a half after eating.

Usually, a person's blood sugar level is within normal range before breakfast, rises when food is taken, slowly lowers each hour after eating, and rises again when more food is taken. The fasting level of the children in the study, (those who later showed drops in sugar level), was as often within the normal range as it was low. However, after taking glucose, there was a normal rise that was followed either one-half hour or an hour and a half later by a drop. This drains all of the energy from the child. He becomes droopy, fussy, and dull—and where is he at this particular time? In the classroom. Interestingly enough, the blood sugar level rises in many of these children as the hours go by. By the time four or five hours have passed, the sugar level is normal and the child feels fine. Then the child eats again, which makes for another drop, another period of irritability, dullness, and often open rebellion. And where is he again? In the classroom! Often these first thirty to sixty minutes in the classroom set the climate for the day. Such a child is doomed.

At the school-hospital we have discussed the problem of low blood sugar with the children who had this type of difficulty, because *they* must understand. They are the ones who must control their eating pattern so that this condition can be helped. They are the ones on a high protein, low carbohydrate diet. They are the ones who must eat again shortly after a meal, this time eating fruit—fresh fruit—or honey to supply the fructose needed for energy.

What is the cause of this hypoglycemic condition and how does it relate to a learning disability? Seeking the answer to these questions took us to the laboratory of biochemist Dr. Mary Maurice Allen. She is in the process of studying the cellular metabolism of the blood, tissue, and muscle of children with learning disabilities. Fifty percent of our children at the school-hospital are taking part in this study. We have no report to give at this time, but we can share what we have observed.

Several weeks ago I asked our staff if they had noticed any marked differences in any of the children in the last few weeks. Fifteen children were cited as having improved to a marked degree in behavior, attitude, and ability to learn. All fifteen were part of this metabolic study and were being treated with megavitamin therapy. Another interesting observation is that some of the children on this megavitamin therapy can have their other medication reduced by half after four to six months and still show improvement.

ANOTHER NEW and fascinating area is that of alpha-wave training, which opens many doors to possibilities and raises many questions in our minds. We have been conscious for many years of the problems confronting the child who has little or no alpha brain wave or who has a poorly organized alpha-wave pattern. These have been some of our hardest-to-work-with children. They are not always the hardest to teach, but they have been the hardest to help in gaining necessary controls. For example, there was a girl who came to us at the age of twelve. She had been in an excellent school where she had received good instruction. This school did not take anyone over twelve years of age, and this child was not ready to go into the classroom. She read well. She did math well. She wrote well. She just could not get along with others. She was too impulsive. What she thought, she said. She scratched where it itched. She went where she happened to look. When she was finally academically ready to enter high school, she could not be sent. She would not have lasted there a day. She is now in college as an art student. In the atmosphere of free speech and actions that surrounds many of our college students, she is having no trouble. She is comfortable being an odd ball. She had little or no alpha wave.

Now what have we found? A little Tumin Alpha Pacer, no bigger than a transistor radio. It is connected to a plastic band that goes around the head and is easy to put on and wear. This Tumin Pacer records the alpha wave of the person in an audible pattern. When the Pacer is silent, this indicates that there is no alpha wave. Squealing and sputtering indicates tension artifact. When the person reaches the alpha level, a steady, low beeping sound is heard. He is told then to keep "that feeling" or "those thoughts" so that the alpha will continue.

We have a pilot study in progress in this area. We cannot tell you if behavior modification can truly be achieved by the control and development of the alpha wave, but we hope so. We hope some day, for some children, that it might be substituted for medication. We do know that we are getting some excellent results with some children. One little boy stopped stuttering for the first time. Another boy has been living at my home, because he is too hyperkinetic and excitable to live at his home and go to public school. He is reported to have been rebellious, uncontrollable, and "bad" at his home. He never sat still. When he went to bed he rolled, he tumbled, he sang, and he took hours to go to sleep. The Alpha Pacer training is the only change in teaching or management that he has had. His movements are now more controlled, and he gets along well with his family when he visits home; he is no longer rebellious. Believe it or not, when he goes to bed I can say, "Turn on your Alpha," and he is asleep within a very few minutes.

THERE IS ONE more point that I want to stress. It relates to what Dr. John A. Schindler, in his book, *How to Live 365 Days a Year*, calls "emotional stasis." He says that "Many of us lack emotional stasis because many leave to chance a quality that must be learned."[1] According to Dr. Schindler, the only way a person can develop emotional stasis is through the right kind of education. He feels that the right kind of education does not exist, that there is no place to learn emotional stasis. I disagree. At the school-hospital we teach it, but we call it SCADQUIC.

We have become convinced over the years that children with learning disabilities do not have to stay different from other people. Just as we have taught them to learn to do school work—to read, write, spell, do arithmetic, pass tests—we can teach them to live with and around other people in a normal manner. Just as we have had to use different methods to teach school subjects, so we have had to use different methods to teach them how to get along with others. First, we had to be sure they felt physically fit. This was accomplished for some by controlling hypoglycemia and developing alpha waves. For some children, other physical aspects had to be considered. Then they needed to learn how to "change" the emotions like anxiety, fear, discouragement, disappointment, and frustration to such emotions as courage, serenity, determination, and cheerfulness. This cannot be just a byproduct of other teaching. It must be consciously taught. The children at the school-hospital have SCADQUIC as their guide. In fact, they created SCADQUIC. It stands for those characteristics that they are consciously developing. Let me share them with you:

S — stands for Self-esteem. We must teach the children that if they do not think well of themselves, no one else will. They must know their good points, and their bad ones. They know that everyone has strengths and weaknesses. They must learn to have faith in themselves, to become self-confident. They need the help of adults to do this. So often because of their great interest and desire to help, adults inadvertently hinder children. For example, one mother, who has worked diligently with her child's learning disability, did such an excellent job that the boy is now graduating from high school, has passed the college entrance exams and has picked his own field of advanced study. Said Mama, "He is a handicapped child. Will he be able to do it?" Handicapped? By whose standard? How can the boy think well of himself with his parents having this attitude? Or consider the example of parents who are too quick to try to build up the child's confidence by bragging about him. They say things like, "John is such a GOOD driver." Instead of just making a statement, they must emphasize it out of all intelligent proportions. The child gets the message, although it's not the message intended. He understands that he is so inferior that he needs a big buildup to boost his ego. If we would give compliments or praise as convincingly as we give labels, we would help instead of hurt.

C — stands for Courtesy. These children have been the recipients of rudeness, from both children and adults. Much of the rudeness is just thoughtlessness. By the time a parent or teacher has told a child to do something three or four times, the tone of the next telling, which has now become a command, isn't always as polite as it should be. Perhaps the child has frequent recurrences of momentary inability to accept the spoken word. Perhaps he doesn't get the meaning the first few times the instructions are given. By the time he does get the meaning, an exasperated, impatient tone is what he hears. These children have learned to dish out what they have received. They haven't liked the world too much at times or the people in it; they have learned to show it by their tone of voice even more than through words. We must help them learn thoughtfulness for others, which is evidenced by courtesy. Isn't the mature adult the one who puts the good of others above the good of self?

A — stands for Accepting Change. A day, for almost anyone, is made up of many little changes. We can't get into the elevator because it is too full. We can't go down the street because it is closed for repairs. We can't go to lunch right now because we have to take yet another telephone call. We can't serve the soufflé before it falls because Daddy missed his ride home. Little changes can frustrate or can be accepted. Many so-called normal people react negatively to unexpected changes. How much worse it is for these children who have, as a common characteristic, the inability to accept it. It is imperative that parents and teachers help them consciously learn how.

D — stands for Desire of Knowledge. This has been killed or badly stunned in many of our children. Often it is because the information is buried in all those words that are too hard to read or to comprehend when read. Often adults don't read to them for fear that they will always depend on being read to instead of doing the reading themselves. Often we as adults have stopped their search for knowledge by saying, "Can't you keep quiet? Do you always have to be asking questions?" Sometimes we are just too busy to share their discoveries. We say, "Pay attention *here*" when it is over *there* that the child is learning—not necessarily what we want him to learn, but he is learning.

Q — stands for Quietness. This is a quietness of self—a serenity, an ability to to be quiet in the midst of noise, an inner peace, a quietness of tone of voice. The noise pollution is worse than the air pollution. Everyone needs quiet. Our children need it more so.

U — stands for Undivided Attention. Those who react to every stimulus need to learn to give undivided attention to tasks. This is necessary if a child is going into a regular classroom. This is necessary if he is going to keep a job. This is necessary if he is to use the skills we are diligently teaching him.

I — stands for Independence. This is not the independence of the child in dressing himself, feeding himself, or the like. This is independence of "making myself do what I am supposed to do when no one else is around." This is independence in control of emotions, of "doing what I am supposed to do rather than what I want to do." This is an independence that gives the child an ability to think for himself, to not follow blindly what others say, to think through situations and come to meaningful conclusions.

C — stands for Compassion. These children have known troubles. They have needed compassion from others. They need to learn not to give back to the world what it has so often dished out to them but to give back true understanding, true love, and true compassion.

SCADQUIC is a prescription for living. This is as important as a prescription for teaching. This is as important as a prescription from the doctor. We only partly meet the needs of our children with learning disabilities if we do not give them a prescription for living. And the adult who gives the prescription? He must provide the opportunity to learn it—only more so. He must himself be the model—only more so. He must be ready to guide the children—only more so. He must have faith in them—only more so.

NOTES

1. John A. Schindler, *How to Live 365 Days a Year* (New York, N.Y.: Prentice Hall, 1954).

Formal Evaluation of the Effectiveness of Performance Contracting Programs for Learning Disabilities

Lowell A. Seymour*
Barton B. Proger

CONTRACTS BETWEEN PUBLISHERS of educational materials and school systems that consume those materials are increasing in number and there is no let-up in sight.[1] Such contracts assume various forms: some merely provide materials and offer no insurance or guarantee that certain minimum achievement will be produced in the children who use them; others offer a comprehensive package of materials, personnel, consultation, and guarantees. However, no matter what arrangement is reached between the publisher and the school system, there is an implied or stated assumption that *accountability* will prevail. The concept of accountability has become so common among educators that no definitions need be given here.[2] Stated very simply, the term refers to an attempt to evaluate how well certain educational objectives are achieved. Another term that is receiving increased usage in the educational literature is *program evaluation*; indeed, one might consider this term synonymous with accountability.

We have outlined here some aspects of program evaluation that school systems should be aware of as they embark on more and more publisher-school contracts; such considerations are important if we are to insure that the taxpayers get their money's worth. A highly detailed account of program evaluation for the learning disabled has been issued elsewhere and will not be repeated here.[3] That publication also offers a comprehensive review of literature on accountability regardless of whether or not performance contracts are involved in the learning-disabled programs that it evaluates. This paper considers a model for program evaluation of performance-contracting setups for the learning disabled, and a series of operational problems that are associated with such a model. The model presented will have maximum util-

---

Lowell A. Seymour is a research associate with the District 5 Administration Office, Philadelphia, Pennsylvania; Barton B. Proger is the director of dissemination and evaluation for the Pennsylvania Resource and Information Center for Special Education King of Prussia, Pennsylvania.

This paper was partially supported by PRISE, which is a Title III Project funded under the Elementary and Secondary Education Act of 1965. However, no endorsement on the part of PRISE or its funding agency, the U.S. Office of Education, is to be inferred. The opinions expressed herein are solely those of the two authors.

ity in focusing immediately upon performance contracting itself rather than dwelling on a lot of peripheral, technical details. This model thusly becomes an "exportable" commodity that can be used in any performance-contracting operation for the learning disabled.

The word "performance" in the phrase, *performance contracting*, reflects what is to be measured: student achievement. If a commercial enterprise has guaranteed to raise the performance of each child by a specified amount, which in turn determines how much reimbursement the company receives, then an evaluation model is needed. Unfortunately, while a "model" as such, is easy to devise for measurement and research specialists, most people embarking on such a project are unaware of the many pitfalls they will encounter in the process of setting up an evaluation model.

Before the model can be presented, the terminology that is used in it must be clarified. When one talks about formal program evaluation for performance contracts, he is referring to measuring with acceptable testing procedures just how successful the performance contract program has been with *both* individual learning-disabled children and all children as a group. When one looks at the total group of children, he can gauge whether or not the program as a whole was successful in the goals it had set for itself; the changes in individual students allow one to qualify any generalizations from the total group that otherwise might be somewhat shaky with such a highly variegated population. Nonetheless, educators of exceptional children still manage to confuse formal program evaluation with other, more common types of evaluation, such as one that is made by the psychologist when an individual child has been referred for placement. Another mode of evaluation, that is somewhat less common, is a statistical placement strategy for ensuring maximum success for each learning-disabled child.[4]

Once the conceptual details are devised, we can describe existing formal program-evaluation models that are specifically designed for special education. First, however, some general features of formal program-evaluation models are presented in the sense that the original accountability movement intended. Finally, the performance-contracting evaluation model is presented. A concluding section will discuss some typical problems that are encountered by the serious learning-disabilities program evaluator.

The conceptual model for accountability

Even though the accountability movement is still in its infancy, the general theoretical framework for the stream of formal program evaluation models that has arisen in recent years can be traced to the Stufflebeam structure: Context, Input, Process, and Product (CIPP).[5] Rather than review some of the characteristics of the original CIPP model, let us look at one of the many, modern adaptations of the model: the Randall Context, Design, Process, and Product (CDPP) model.[6] Describing the major steps in the CDPP evaluation process, Randall states:

> Context evaluation consists of planning decisions and context information that serves them . . . . Design evaluation entails structuring decisions which depend on design information . . . the objectives need to be specified operationally if possible, and activities

or means of attaining them need to be specified . . . . After a design has been structured and is put on trial, often called the pilot test, restructuring decisions are faced. Restructuring decisions are based on process information . . . . After components of a design have been tested, they can be put together in a program for a product or field test. Since this is the first full-cycle test, the major decisions faced are whether to recycle through another full-scale field test. The information needed, called product information, entails not only evidence about effectiveness in attaining short- and long-range goals, but also effectiveness . . . compared with that of another program or strategy.[7]

The model that is presented at the end of this paper illustrates in greater detail exactly what is meant by this general conceptual framework.

Special education program-evaluation models

Before presenting the detailed model that we recommend for performance contracts, we mention some existing guides to formal program evaluation. These guides do not dwell on models as such, but rather emphasize operational evaluation problems. In this sense, the existing guides should be highly beneficial to anyone who endeavors to engage in accountability. A. Ahr and H. Sims have provided special educators with an entire organizational setup for carrying out program evaluation on a large scale.[8] Many examples from different fields of exceptionality, including learning disabilities, are given. Those interested in organizational patterns of research offices in school systems should refer to E. Mosher.[9] A somewhat less ambitious guide to program evaluation in special education has been presented by W. Meierhenry,[10] and one of the earliest guides was issued by P. Annas and R. Dowd.[11] While not aiming specifically for special education, the Center for Instructional Research and Curriculum Evaluation, along with the Cooperative Educational Research Laboratory, Inc., has produced a similar guide,[12] and finally, another regular-education oriented guide was written by H. Grobman.[13]

A formal evaluation model for performance contract programs

The total evaluation process, including the planning stages, has already been described briefly in connection with the Randall CDPP conceptualization. However, most so-called formal program evaluation models must of necessity be stated in very general terms so as to be applicable to a variety of different situations; the model usually loses meaning and fails to provide direct implications for the program administrator or teacher who is forced to resolve a host of specific problems.[14] Thus, our task now is to present some highly specific guidelines for learning-disabilities educators to follow in order to achieve several evaluation objectives.

First, the reader must be aware of some basic details of performance contracting.[15] If a guaranteed contract is signed by the school district and the commercial publisher, then somehow the company must be made accountable for backing up their guarantee. The school district must somehow arrive at some criterion level of performance to be reached by each child at the end of an academic year if the company is to be reimbursed a stated amount for each child that reaches such a level. Thus, before any thoughts can be given to a formal program evaluation design, the school district must come up with realistic objectives of just how much achievement (or motor performance, or affective reactions) must be evidenced in a given child before the profit incentive is provided to the company. For example, perhaps for a normal child one might expect that his independent level of reading should be raised at least one whole grade level by the end of an academic year's effort by the company. This is fine for the normal child. However, the determination of reasonable objectives for the learning-disabled child is a sticky problem. If such a child has a severe or even moderate degree of specific reading disability, is it still reasonable to expect a year's growth in reading ability even after intensive remediation by the contracting company? Or should the objective be revised downward to 0.6 of a year's growth, or even 0.5? Here, then, is a major hurdle to the implementation of performance contracting for the learning-disabled child: the learning disabilities field is in such a constant state of change and redefinition year by year, and data upon which to make rational decisions such as for determining realistic goals are so noticeably absent, that contract negotiations lose their "straightforwardness."

At any rate, once realistic objectives have been set, the student achievement, upon which the school district's reimbursement to the company depends, must be measured. The minimally acceptable design for measuring change would consist of the administration of both a pretest and a posttest. With this simple measurement paradigm, the evaluators can determine for each child whether or not the company should be reimbursed. Further, the evaluators can gauge the progress of the program as a whole by averaging together the responses of all of the students. If one carries this logic one step more, he can extract additional valuable information if some meaningful classification system is built into the total pretest-posttest design. For example, perhaps the total group of students can be classified at the outset as to their degree of specific reading disability (from a mild through a moderate and into a severe disability) on the basis of some legitimate measure available or taken on all students. With this refinement in the design, the evaluator will be able to detect whether the performance contract package operates differentially for certain categories of children within the total program. For example, the contracting materials might work quite effectively for most children in the mild and moderate categories of specific reading disability but miserably with the severe disability group. These qualifications on the overall success of a contracted instructional program are often left to the "evidence" of heresay or opinion.

At this point in our discussion of evaluation models, the above design would be sufficient to gauge the progress of the program and to determine the extent of the reimbursement. A few words need to be said here about the methodological philosophy implied in the above designs. A very clear distinction must be made in formal program evaluation between judgmental evaluation and monitoring evaluation.[16] The above designs are of a monitoring type in that the success of the overall program can be determined only within the relativistic framework of the children themselves according to predetermined levels of criterion achievement. In this sense, the evaluation is criterion-referenced in nature.[17] The major *deficiency* is in the lack of data-based information on how well the contracted program functions in relation to different methods of instruction (such as traditional, teacher-directed reading activities, or other programed instruction approaches). This line of thought leads one to the final stage of sophistication in a formal program-evaluation design for performance contracts: the judgmental program-evaluation design.

The only way in which one can safely say that the performance contract succeeded in a general way (not in a relativistic way defined by one's own subjective criteria for success) is to compare it directly with some competing instructional approach. An evaluation design that embodies such comparisons would be judgmental in nature. One can literally make the value judgment of whether or not one approach was more successful than the other. That is, the monitoring evaluation designs that are described earlier in this section are descriptive in the sense that one is recording test data and the other records information for each child but only under *one* form of instruction: the performance-contracting approach. However, a judgmental design would collect exactly the *same* data on not only the performance-contracting type of instruction but also more traditional types of instruction and then would allow one to make judgmental inferences about the success of one instructional approach over a competing one. Naturally, the judgmental evaluation design assumes that the school district can allow more than just the performance-contracting type of instruction to operate within the same district but on different children. Such an assumption might be objectionable on the part of community groups that believe all children should be given the same instruction.

One point of confusion among teachers and administrators of learning disabilities programs is that the only "legitimate" program-evaluation designs are of the judgmental type; that is, the monitoring or descriptive designs covered earlier in this section should really not be used. Such reasoning is totally wrong. First, one should not be confused by the use of the terms "monitoring (descriptive) evaluation" and "judgmental evaluation." In statistics, a distinction is usually made between descriptive statistics and inferential statistics, the latter somehow being more refined and useful than the former. When one speaks of monitoring or descriptive program evaluation, he is doing so in a global sense, not in a strict statistical fashion; statistical inferences are still possible with monitoring evaluation with regard to the classification categories embedded within the design. One should also note that when at least two monitoring evaluation designs are placed side by side, they become a judgmental program-evaluation design. There is a whole host of reasons why one would find a great deal of use for monitoring evaluation designs.[18] The one bias in reasoning against which one must be constantly on guard is the assumption that if an evaluator cannot carry out a judgmental design involving various control groups, then he should not even bother with a "mere" descriptive or monitoring design of a one-group-only paradigm. The basic philosophy behind any design is the gathering of data in as scientific a fashion as possible; one might even call this a data-bank type of activity.[19] In this regard, *both* the judgmental design and the monitoring design are ideally suited. The ultimate goal is to make cautious, intelligent decisions that are based upon carefully gathered data.

We have discussed two basic formal program-evaluation designs: monitoring and judgmental. In terms of the original conceptual CDPP model (context, design, process, and product), all but the "process" phase has been described. Process evaluation feedback is crucial because of the flexibility it allows the evaluators and educational programers; this flexibility makes it possible for them to make necessary changes in the middle of a program (in-process) to improve the final educational product. One obvious way in which process feedback can be obtained is to institute the administration of a middle-of-the-year test that is equivalent to the pretests and posttests that are used. This midtesting can be incorporated into either the monitoring designs or the judgmental designs that have already been described.

Other types of in-process feedback can be incorporated. For example, the school district of Philadelphia has begun a computerized process evaluation, data-collection procedure. Various types of key in-process information on the progress of each child throughout the academic year are collected from teachers on specially coded sheets. At fixed points throughout the year these data sheets can be processed by computer to yield various types of analyses; the results in turn can be fed back to administrators and teachers throughout the district. Here is a perfect example of the data-bank philosophy in special education: collect as much information as possible on the progress children make throughout the year at predetermined, uniform intervals. In connection with certain reading program packages bought from commercial publishers, the Philadelphia school district also considers it important to conduct in-process interviews of how teachers feel about the new programs and to conduct observational studies of how the programs *really* function in the classroom settings.

Operational problems and concluding comments

We have attempted to present a realistic program-evaluation accountability model that can be used by any learning-disabilities program, or for that matter, any special education program in general, to gauge how successful their efforts were. The name of the rational educational game is decision-making on a logical information basis. For judging success of perfect contracting, such decision-making with respect to keeping or changing an existing performance contract relies on change in student performance throughout the year. Various agencies have attempted to provide information background to the decision makers upon demand.[20] However, let us stop for a look at accountability and reality.

Most evaluators of programs agree that change in student performance is of primary interest. The model presented here has embodied the concept of change in a rather clear-cut fashion. However, be not deluded! *Regardless* of how one measures change, methodologists will attack his calculations from all angles. There are theoretical difficulties in any approach.[21] Nonetheless, let us assume your professional egos are sufficiently strong to withstand these assaults on your end-of-the-year evaluation reports on the status of the performance-contracting setup in your district. Your problems have just begun, if you are truly committed to accountability.

One of the worst pitfalls the administrative decision-maker could fall into is not to wait until the evaluation of performance contracting is complete. Put yourself in the position of the administrator who has bought a performance contract and is currently in the middle of the academic year. Pretesting has been completed and in-process monitoring is presently being completed. However, the real pay-off criteria will not be available until the posttesting is completed at the end of the year. Yet you have just been asked by the district superintendent to make a decision one way or the other as to whether or not to keep the performance contract for next year. You will not have the complete evaluation picture until the end of the year. If you are the typical administrator, you will forget everything formal evaluation could tell you and rely on those old decision-making stand-bys: the number of smiles on the faces of children and the verbal praise from your favorite teachers and administrative aides. And here is the real tragedy in high-level decision-making: no one can, or perhaps wants to, wait for the verdict to come in. The decision for next year's program is made on a partial, sometimes faulty picture of what's happening now, and the final evaluation report, with all its wealth of implications, is completed at the close of the year and gathers dust on the administrator's bookshelf. Of course, most school districts do not have this problem. They simply don't bother to evaluate programs in a formal way at all; they base their decisions on opinions only. However, those few rare districts that do bother to evaluate at all run into the perennial time-lag problem between the decision and the evaluation. Will the biggest industry in the country always make decisions in this manner? Will the professional school evaluator-researcher always feel like a rather sophisticated but largely ignored professional? One could argue, of course, that even if the school district where a formal evaluation is conducted ignores such findings, at least the evaluation is done and will be available for other districts to examine in the future if they are faced with similar problems. This latter argument does hold some plausibility, but it seems a poor substitute indeed for a legitimate data-based decision-making process.

Let us go on to consider a few other frustrating problems that evaluators of performance contracts for learning-disabilities programs are likely to run into. The learning disabled realm, or any area of special education, differs markedly from that of regular or normal education. In terms of implications for evaluation and testing, this means that the focus must be on the individual child. Group approaches are largely meaningless. Thus, part of the formal program evaluation of the effectiveness of any performance contract for the learning disabled must take individual testing into account in some way. For example, perhaps part of the evaluation design would include the administration of the *Peabody Individual Achievement Test* or the *Illinois Test of Psycholinguistic Abilities.*[22] Fine! But now ask yourself this question, and make sure you provide an honest answer! Just who will administer all the individual achievement tests? One of these tests may well drag on for an hour or more per child. Make sure that time has been released from the usual time schedules of your psychologists or clinicians. Otherwise, as the year progresses, you may see an otherwise beautiful evaluation design falling apart before your eyes.

Another problem may arise that concerns any group measures of achievement that the evaluator feels might be appropriate for learning-disabled children. If one is involved with a large series of learning-disabilities classes, perhaps some type of group testing will become a necessity. (An alternative would be to draw a sample from the total population for intensive individual testing.) In turn, probably not enough testing personnel will be available. Thus, some fast and competent in-service training will be needed to prepare the teachers to carry out their testing legitimately. The main problem one runs into here is cooperation: getting the teachers together, finding enough time to go over all of the instructions, and enlisting the teachers' cooperation to agree to abide by whatever rules the total group comes up with. In the field of education, cooperation is often very difficult to obtain.

Finally, regardless of whether or not you decide to go into performance contracting for your learning-disabilities programs, the general issue of accountability should be examined rather closely before you embark on a full-fledged program evaluation. If you do not have a commitment to making rational decisions on the basis of data and past research, forget it! Formal program evaluation will merely be hypocrisy on your part. The really sad part of all this is that the vast majority of learning-disabilities programs do not engage in formal program evaluation.

At worst, the only testing the children get occurs during the initial psychological evaluation at best, only once during the academic year. Very rarely is change measured. This reflects what has been termed "the failure of evaluation."[23] At present, only token lip-service is being paid to the concept of accountability as we have interpreted it here. Perhaps a few of you recall the huge Educational Research Training Program.[24] Where have all the graduates of this doctoral training gone? Professors of educational research who are working in colleges and doing isolated research studies and a little teaching are necessary, to be sure, but wouldn't it be nice to see a large number of these people enter the real world and try to rig the ongoing learning-disabilities machinery to keep a continuous program-evaluation system in operation to provide continuous data for decision-making. Clearly something has gone wrong with the whole educational-research movement. That movement, when viewed now in somewhat skeptical retrospect, could be interpreted as a rather vague embodiment of the accountability concept before it ever came into vogue. While isolated studies of both semibasic and applied types have increased in quantity and quality as generated out of universities, the real payoff for realistic classroom practice in the field is still rather shabby in appearance.

NOTES

1. R. Schwartz, "USOE and OEO Fund More Than 30 New Projects: Performance Contracts Catch On," *Nations Schools*, 86 (1970), 31-33; R. A. Ehrle, "National Priorities and Performance Contracting," *Educational Technology*, 10, No. 7 (1970), 27-28; J. Morton, "Contract Learning in Texarkana," *Educational Screen and Audiovisual Instruction*, 49, No. 2 (1970), 12-13.

2. S. Elam, "The Age of Accountability Dawns in Texarkana," *Phi Delta Kappan*, 10 (1970), 509-514; Leon M. Lessinger, "Robbing Dr. Peter to 'Pay Paul': Accounting for Our Stewardship of Public Education," *Educational Technology*, 11, No. 1 (1971), 11-14.
3. Barton B. Proger, "Program Evaluation: The Model-Building Game," *Journal of Learning Disabilities*, (in press).
4. B. B. Proger, "Improving Evaluation Procedures in Physical Education Programs for the Learning Disabled: The Neglected Use of Multivariate Techniques." Paper presented at the 7th International ACLD Conference, Philadelphia, Pa.: February 12, 1970.
5. D. L. Stufflebeam, "The Use and Abuse of Title III," *Theory Into Practice*, 6 (1967), 126-133; idem, "Evaluation as Enlightenment for Decision Making," *Improving Educational Assessment and An Inventory of Measures of Affective Behavior*, ed. W. H. Beatty (Washington, D.C.: Association for Supervision and Curriculum Development, NEA, 1969).
6. R. S. Randall, "An Operational Application of the CIPP Model for Evaluation," *Educational Technology*, 9, No. 7 (1969), 40-44.
7. Ibid., 40-42.
8. A. Edward Ahr and Howard D. Sims, *An Evaluation Model for Special Education* (Skokie, Ill.: Priority Innovations, Inc., 1970).
9. Edith K. Mosher, *What About the School Research Office? A Staff Report* (Berkeley, Calif.: Far West Laboratory for Educational Research and Development, 1968).
10. W. C. Meierhenry (ed.), *Planning for the Evaluation of Special Education Programs* (Lincoln, Neb.: Teachers College, The University of Nebraska, 1969).
11. P. A. Annas and R. A. Dowd (eds.), *Guide to Assessment and Evaluation Procedures: The New England Educational Assessment Project*, No. ED 012087 (Washington, D.C.: ERIC Document Reproduction Service, 1966).
12. Center for Instructional Research and Curriculum Evaluation (CIRCE), and the Cooperative Educational Research Laboratory, Inc. (CERLI), "Information Supplement No. 5: Evaluation Kit: Tools and Techniques," *Educational Product Report*, 2 (1969).
13. Hulda Grobman, *Evaluating Activities of Curriculum Projects: A Starting Point* (Chicago, Ill.: Rand McNally, 1968).
14. Proger, "Program Evaluation: The Model-Building Game."
15. Albert V. Mayrhofer, "Factors to Consider in Preparing Performance Contracts for Instruction," *Educational Technology*, 11, No. 1 (1971), 48-51; H. M. Harmes, "Specifying Objectives for Performance Contracts," Ibid., 52-56; George H. Voegel, "A Suggested Scheme for Faculty Commission Pay in Performance Contracting," Ibid., 57-59; W. Frank Johnson, "Performance Contracting with Existing Staff," Ibid., 59-61.
16. Lester Mann and Barton B. Proger, "Achievement Accounting and System Accountability: Their Roles in Urban and Suburban Special Education." Paper presented at the Convention for the Council for Exceptional Children, Miami, Fla., 1971.
17. W. James Popham and T. R. Husek, "Implications of Criterion-Referenced Measurement," *Journal of Educational Measurement*, 6, No. 1 (1969) 1-9; George B. Simon, "Comments on Implications of Criterion Referenced Measurements," *Journal of Educational Measurement*, 6, No. 4 (1969), 259-260.
18. Donald T. Campbell and Julian C. Stanley, "Experimental and Quasi-Experimental Designs for Research on Teaching," *Handbook of Research on Teaching*, ed. N. L. Gage (Chicago, Ill.: Rand McNally, 1963).
19. Gilbert Austin, "State Directors Discussions: Test Scoring and Data Banking," *NCME Measurement News: Official Newsletter of the National Council on Measurement in Education*, 13, No. 3 (1970), 9; John C. Flanagan et al., *The Project TALENT Data Bank for Research in Education and the Behavioral Sciences* (Pittsburgh, Pa.: Project TALENT, University of Pittsburgh and American Institutes for Research, 1965).
20. Proger et al., "Large-Scale, Personalized Information Retrieval of Psychological and Educational Research Findings for School District Decision-Making." Paper presented at the Seventh Annual National Information Retrieval Colloquium, Philadelphia, Pa., May 8, 1970.

21. Chester W. Harris (ed.), *Problems in Measuring Change* (Madison, Wis.: University of Wisconsin Press, 1963); Doris R. Entwisle, "Interactive Effects of Pretesting," *Educational and Psychological Measurement*, 21 (1961), 607-620.
22. For sources of tests mentioned in this article, see Appendix.
23. E. G. Guba, "The Failure of Educational Evaluation," *Educational Technology*, 9, No. 5 (1969), 29-38.
24. Ken Walker, "Training Educational Researchers: For What?" *Educational Researcher*, 20, No. 10 (1969), 1-2, 7.

Madison School Plan

Frank D. Taylor*

THE DECADE OF THE SIXTIES has left special education in ferment. Dissatisfaction with the traditional disability categories as a basis for educational programing is widespread. The specialist approach that has emerged, with reference to teacher training, credentialing, legislation, curriculum, and organization of special classes in the public school, may be contributing to an unnecessary preoccupation with labels. Past efforts to classify, describe, and provide separate educational programs for handicapped students need to be reappraised.

Concern about possible limited effectiveness of traditional curriculum, instructional methods, doubts about the cost-effectiveness and the social-psychological impact of traditional special classes have reached major proportions.[1]

I and my co-investigators have felt that students could be grouped according to their learning deficits, with resource room or a type of learning center remediation and maximum regular classroom integration rather than separated into discreet categories of exceptionality and isolated in separate, self-contained rooms. With this in mind an educational model, the Madison School Plan, was developed and made operational. It provides an instructional program for exceptional children based on their specific learning deficits rather than traditional categories for the handicapped. These efforts were made possible through a California State Department of Education Title VI-B Grant.

The project was directed toward the demonstration and evaluation of a plan for the education of a group of handicapped children who would traditionally be labeled educable mentally retarded, educationally handicapped, learning disabled, visually impaired, and auditorily impaired.

Frank D. Taylor, Ed.D., is director of special services, Santa Monica Unified School District, California.

Dr. Taylor has coauthored a related discussion of the Madison School Plan. See F. M. Hewett, F. D. Taylor, A. A. Artuso, and H. C. Quay, "The Learning Center Concept," Behavior Modification of Learning Disabilities, ed. Robert H. Bradfield (San Rafael, Calif.: Academic Therapy Publications, 1971).

This plan, to be described in detail below, provides for the education of these children in a setting that allows free flow of children between the regular classes and the specialized facility (Learning Center). It permits the elimination of traditional disability grouping for all but administrative purposes and provides an instructional program that is linked to a continuous assessment of those educational variables that operated to hinder the performance of the exceptional child in the regular classroom.

The grouping framework utilized in the Madison School Plan was organized on four levels: Pre-Academic I, Pre-Academic II, Academic I, and Academic II.

Pre-Academic I

The first level is conceived as a largely self-contained class grouping of six to twelve children with behavioral problems that overshadow academic deficits. The students learn to sit still, pay attention, respond appropriately, take turns, follow simple directions, get along with others, and develop the ability to function in a small group. Initially, these students would have been unable to spend any length of productive time in a regular classroom. This setting is designed to bring the overt behavior of the children into line with minimum standards required for learning. Lengthening attention span, encouraging appropriate responses, and developing student-like behavior represent the main focus. In many ways, it is similar to the "Engineered Classroom."[2]

Pre-Academic II

The second level is a small teacher-group setting for four to eight children having readiness academic problems that overshadow academic problems. These students need to receive intense remediation in specific academic areas. Severe deficits in reading or arithmetic are typical of the factors that make it difficult for these students to function in a typical large group setting or a regular classroom. This small group setting provides opportunities to concentrate on primary academic remediation, developing a readiness for participation in larger group settings in terms of oral participation and language emphasis. Flexible assignment between settings within the learning center is stressed, with continuous daily and hourly student assessment emphasized. Students in Pre-Academic II are still on a systematic immediate and frequent reinforcement schedule similar to Pre-Academic I.

Academic I

The third level is a simulated regular classroom setting within the learning center for twelve to twenty-five children who have primary academic problems that can be dealt with in a large teacher-class setting. Students in this setting have the ability to spend increasing amounts of time in the regular classroom and have a readiness for the more traditional system of grading in terms of effort, quality of work, and citizenship. The teacher leads large class type discussions and presents large group lessons in reading, arithmetic, spelling, social studies, and English. Students are grouped within this large setting in the same manner expected by a regular classroom teacher, opportunities for silent, independent study are present. Emphasis is also placed on helping each student with the specific skills needed to increase the amount of time spent in a regular classroom.

Academic II

This setting is the regular classroom in the school, with from twenty-eight to thirty-five students, and it follows the typical public school program. All handicapped students in the program are assigned to one of the Pre-Academic I, Pre-Academic II, or Academic I settings, with those in the latter two groups integrated for varying periods of time in Academic II (the regular classroom).

A daily schedule for all three settings within the learning center is carefully planned to provide individual, independent, and group lessons dependent on student needs. Commercially available materials are utilized, programed instructional techniques employed, and teacher preparation time is kept to a minimum. One of the specific learning center daily schedules is shown in *Figure 1*.

Assessment

The model implies, in essence, that first you assign children to a grouping category, and once this assignment has been made, you zero in on a detailed assessment over a period of time, rather than stopping with just an initial full-scale preplacement assessment, as is often the case in traditional programs.

In order to maintain a continuous assessment of each child's progress and provide data for reassignment to different groupings, two types of procedures are utilized. A checkmark system in Pre-Academic I and II, and a numerical rating system in Academic I and II. The checkmark system involves giving each child a possible ten checkmarks, in the form of alphabet letters, every twenty minutes during the morning.

This system makes it possible to determine the percentage of rating points earned by each student over the week in relation to his readiness for regular class functioning, as well as a profile of pre-academic or academic areas in which he needs to improve. In the Academic I rating system, the teacher gives each student a one-to-five rating in three areas every twenty minutes: effort, quality of work, and citizenship. Weekly percentages reflect the child's functioning in these traditional grading areas. Each regular classroom teacher who has contact with a project child also is asked to provide a weekly rating in these areas for each child. When they consider reassignment for a given child, his progress, or lack of it, as shown in their evaluation data, is carefully reviewed.

Regular Class Integration

At the beginning of the school year, as many of the educationally handicapped children with learning disabilities as possible are assigned to regular classrooms. As students are referred out to the special program because they cannot handle the behavioral and academic demands of the class, an attempt is made to preserve some link with the regular class by having the child return for morning exercises, P.E., music, etc. As they demonstrate academic and/or behavioral improvement, an effort is made to increase their time in

Figure 3
Daily Schedule of Activities in the Learning Center

	Academic I	*Pre-Academic II*	*Pre-Academic I*
8:45	Typical Class Opening Exercises		Direction-following Task
9:00	Reading: Typical large class reading program. Group and individual reading. Basal Readers, SRA, etc.	Reading: Remedial-reading instruction or motivation for story writing / Story writing or remedial follow-up task / Word study. Individual reading, programed material	Reading: Individual Reading / Word Study / Skill Reading
10:00	········Recess·········	········Recess·········	········Recess·········
10:15	Arithmetic: Typical large class program. Discussions. Group and independent work	Arithmetic: Arithmetic instruction. Specific follow-up tasks. Remedial opportunities	Arithmetic: Arithmetic Drill / Instruction / Follow-Up
10:55	Spelling	Language Development and/or Spelling	Language Skills
11:25	········Lunch·········	········Lunch·········	········Lunch·········
12:25	Read to Class	Pre-Academic II students join ←either→ group according to their individual needs	Exploratory: Art, Science, Order, Communication
12:40	Social Studies, English, Art		
1:50	········Recess·········	········Recess·········	········Recess·········
2:00	Physical Education		Opportunities for individualized remedial instruction
2:30	Individual Tutoring		
3:00			

the regular class until optimum placement is reached. The evaluation procedures presented in the last section aid in determining this reassignment. The educable mentally retarded children start in the special program, but early in the school year efforts are made to establish a regular classroom link for them. During the year their progress on the evaluation ratings is noted, and integration is increased whenever possible.

IN SUMMARY, the Madison School Plan, developed over a four-year period, attempts to combine traditional categories of exceptionality along a dimension of readiness for regular classroom functioning and provide education for special types of exceptional children in Pre-Academic I, Pre-Academic II, and Academic I groupings. Assessment and evaluation of the children is based on academic and behavioral functioning, and a major goal of the plan is to increase the amount of time the exceptional child participates in a regular classroom program.

NOTES

1. L. M. Dunn, "Special Education for the Mildly Retarded—Is Much of it Justifiable?" *Exceptional Children*, 35 (1968), 5-22; L. Blackman, "The Dimensions of a Science of Special Education," *Mental Retardation*, 5 (1967), 7-11; L. Connor, "The Heart of the Matter," *Exceptional Children*, 34 (1968), 579; H. C. Quay, "The Facets of Educational Exceptionality: A Conceptual Framework for Assessment Grouping, and Instruction," *Exceptional Children*, 35 (1968), 25.

2. F. M. Hewett, "Educational Engineering with Emotionally Disturbed Children," *Exceptional Children*, (March 1967), 459-467.

Success-Oriented Program: Private Plus Public Schools

Ruth Tofanelli*
Nancy Jo Telford

SUMMIT SCHOOL was founded in September 1968 to fill a known educational need for children with learning disabilities. At the time of its inception, children with learning problems were being recognized by public schools; at the same time parents were being told, "We know the type of program your child needs, but we just don't have it for him. We cannot meet his educational needs right now." The criteria for entrance to our program are two-fold and clear cut: the children must have average or potentially average intelligence and basic emotional soundness. We fully realize that most of the children that are accepted at Summit will have a moderate to severe emotional overlay to their learning problems. However, we are neither staffed for nor do we have the physical setting for handling pre-psychotic or psychotic children. Keeping the school limited to the above population has been our utmost consideration in our initial evaluation of each new student.

Diagnosis for entrance to Summit is made through psychological and neurological examinations. If the findings of these examinations indicate that minimal brain dysfunction and the resultant learning problems are present, the prospective student is brought to Summit for educational testing. It is on the basis of the results of these tests that an individualized program of remediation is prepared for each student, and both short-term and long-range goals are set for the student.

Part of the basic philosophy of our program is that we cannot rehabilitate a child to normalcy by completely removing him from it. Therefore, when a child is accepted at Summit it is on a cooperative basis with his home school. The Summit program is in operation daily from 8:30 to 12:30—4/5 of a legal school day in Illinois—after which time the child is returned to his home school for the afternoon session, the length of which varies according to the districts and schools. Every effort is made to make the afternoon session success-oriented so that the student can begin to regain the respect of his peer group. On the junior high and high school levels, this is comparatively easy because subjects can be selected in which he can meet success and

---

*Ruth Tofanelli is executive director of the Summit School, Dundee, Illinois. Nancy Jo Telford is a teacher on the Summit School staff.

feel comfortable. On the elementary and primary levels, however, this is more difficult and requires greater communication between the special and the classroom teachers. Basically, all we ask is that the receiving teacher accept the child as he is and that she let him perform when and where he can at a success level. Insuring social acceptance by the group is probably one of the most important facets of the afternoon placement.

Our approach to remediation of learning disabilities is interdisciplinary. We have one neurologist on our staff; two others serve as consultants and work closely with us. We feel that it is only by this close communication that a medical program can be intelligently and successfully executed. Forty-five of our fifty-one children are presently on a medical therapy program. Weekly consultations with our neurologists insure that all medications are kept adjusted and effective. Any other use of a drug therapy program would not be considered by Summit.

Our teamwork with the afternoon teachers is a vital part of our success-oriented program. We find that regular classroom teachers are most eager to know and understand the problems of these children and to help in any way they can. The key to the child's success in the afternoon session is the teacher. Her acceptance of this child's problems and limitations is the cue to his peer group to accept him. This same teacher is the ultimate key to success when the student is making the complete transition back to regular school.

Another extremely important aspect of the total program is the work that is done with the parents. In order for the program of the day to be totally effective, it is necessary for each child to also experience the success-oriented life in his home life. Parents are eager to understand their children more fully, and they welcome suggestions on how to handle the child properly at home. Our parent group meets on the first Friday of each month and is well attended. For parents of future enrollees at Summit, attendance at these meetings is mandatory if it is certain that the child is to be accepted. We feel that it is advisable to have consulting doctors, psychologists, and staff members speak to the parents at these meetings in order to help them further understand their children. We are trying to achieve a twenty-four hour success-oriented program without placing the child in a residential setting.

IN THIS PAPER I will discuss the inside workings, the educational plans and goals that we as a staff at Summit use as a working guide for our children. First, I will provide some background concerning the planning and/or defining of the goals, and later, I will conclude with some specific examples that may or may not indicate success. Each child that is accepted at Summit is given an educational test battery that is appropriate to his age and academic level. This, at times, is difficult to accomplish, but fortunately we have a highly trained and competent staff that individually and collectively is able to administer appropriate educational tests and plan an educational program that is geared toward success. As the child works within it, the program is greatly changed and augmented.

We feel that each child, with his clusters of strengths and weaknesses, must be individually understood by his teacher before a program can be initiated or goals can be stated. In this light, each teacher takes the responsibility for her own educational diagnosis, educational planning, and ultimately, for the recommendation concerning the proper time to return the child to the classroom as a full-time student. Stated briefly, the purpose of the educational diagnosis is to initially identify, for the teacher, the major areas of strengths and weaknesses in the auditory, visual, or motor areas. Since a successful educational system must capitalize on the strong input channel, the diagnosis should pinpoint the areas of strength as well as the most efficient channel for output. With this important information kept clearly in mind, and with personal observations that have accrued from the testing situation, our staff members are able to plan an academic program that will fit the needs of each child with an optimum amount of success.

It would be very nice if we could delineate the most efficient learning system—plug in a teaching system and have a perfect positive match. This is not the case and probably never will be. There are other aspects that are very real in either a positive or a negative way. In order for the teacher to be effective with each child, she must consider his real life experiences and must make them an integral part of his program.

EACH MEMBER of the Summit School staff was asked to indicate some general goals that are of paramount importance to him in working with his children. No specification was made as to whether we were concerned with academic, behavioral, or social goals. Ultimately our primary goal for all of the children is to return them to the mainstream of school and life as fully functioning individuals. It is interesting to note that in the citing of the long-term, and occasionally of the short-term goals, no one on the staff mentioned academic levels of achievement. All members of the staff are very concerned with the behavioral and social aspects of these children, the difficult intangibles, which ultimately do separate learning-disabled children from the more average members of their peer group.

As it has been stated by many experts in the field, and as it is experienced daily by our staff members, children who have severe learning disabilities don't develop these disabilities when they begin the first day of school. The symptoms have been there for many years and are greatly compounded when the child enters public school. This is reinforced when we consider some of the important goals that were listed by our primary teacher, who works with children from age seven to nine.

- Foster and maintain the child's self-esteem.
- Encourage self-acceptance and acceptance of others.
- Develop his ability to work in social relationships with others.
- Support him in taking a positive approach, rather than an avoidance reaction toward problem solving and situational changes.

These goals take into consideration the very intangible aspects of personality development and ego structure, which are important to each individual's ability to learn in an efficient and meaningful manner.

As we move along the age line, we find our next group of children who have all had one or two unsuccessful years of school experience. Academically the teacher is secure and knows the level at which to begin successful teaching, but before this can be accomplished, or possibly while it is being accomplished, she must set a goal. Of primary concern is the child's internal environment. He emerges from within himself, rather than from the regulated external conditions. Thus, it is necessary to promote an atmosphere for the child, in which he can develop as an individual person and as a member of a group. There are important stages to be followed, each of which is dependent on the successful mastery of the previous level. Initially, a child needs to have a basic trust in others and himself. This promotes a feeling of autonomy, which, in turn, allows for the development of the individual, which is followed and capped by industry for the task of living. Ego strength is developed through mastery.

As we move along, we find the goals that are set for a group of middle-school children. These are boys who have had more years of school than those mentioned above. They have developed a failure pattern in spite of various *attempts* at remediation. In the case of most of these boys, some attitudes must be changed. These boys must learn to honestly trust the one who is to teach them. If the teacher is to gain their trust, she must deal with them honestly, fairly, firmly, and consistently. It is necessary to develop the individual's ability to accept other members of the class without undue critical remarks and actions. The children must develop an understanding of their need to depend on others, both in their peer group and with adults. We must strengthen and foster emotional maturity so that they will become comfortable about themselves. More specifically, we must allow the level of emotional maturity, as well as the level of achievement, to direct the academic programing. At this point it becomes necessary for the teacher to help the student consider realistic goals for his future adult life.

For those children who are in late middle-school, and for a few who are in early high school, our goals become more academic in order to facilitate their transition into high school. Generally we work toward developing their motivation to learn and work for achievement and accomplishment. Each child needs a structure that encourages his use of good learning skills and habits, his ability to complete tasks, his concentration, and his monitoring of habits. Once again, all the aspects of self-respect and individual worth are considered to be of primary importance in the growth and development of the child. Social, emotional, and intellectual growth are an integral part of each child's program.

Children who are at the high school level have problems that are compounded by years of failure. Before we are able to help these students achieve academic success, we must plan and implement general, more immediate goals. Because our high school program is quite unique, I am including in this paper a detailed description of its five major goals, which has been given in the following verbatim statement from our high school teacher.

GOALS: HIGH SCHOOL LEVEL

Improvement of self-concept: In most cases these students come to Summit feeling discouraged, stupid, and disliked by the world. They frequently react by rejecting the world through escape (drugs), fighting back (delinquency), or withdrawal (social isolation). Until this feeling of rejection has been somewhat alleviated, the child is hard to reach. He totally rejects school and teachers because he thinks that they are the primary cause of his present misery.

Development of positive attitude toward school and teachers: It becomes necessary to develop a warm, personal relationship with each child so that his preconceived notion that teachers are hard, inflexible, and inhuman individuals changes to a realization that teachers are very human and capable of having feelings that are the same as the students', and that teachers have weaknesses too (they love the fact that I don't spell well).

In order to make the concept of school a tolerable one, I try to "throw in" the unexpected as frequently as possible. Sometimes we play pop music all morning while they work; sometimes they have donuts and chocolate milk while I read to them. They are allowed to sit on counters, tables, and the floor during free time. (These unstructured times are in sharp contrast to the highly structured periods of academic skill development.)

Recognition of limitations and desire to improve: Many teens can begin to function positively when they understand that they are not inherently dumb or retarded but that they have very specific difficulties that have interferred with their previous learning. They need to understand that teachers did not formerly know what these problems were, and that is why they haven't been helped. I tell them that I know the problem and that I know how to help them solve it. If I fail to convince a student that he has problems that can be treated, or if I fail to motivate him to make a change in his attitude toward learning, then very little can be accomplished.

Socialization: Most teenagers with learning disabilities are social isolates. The small class-enrollment prevents these students from hiding in the background; they are forced into interaction with the teacher and the other students. They soon come to realize that each student in the class has a problem and thereby has just as much to hide as he does. These students come to be close, almost like a family. They begin to see that they have something to offer the others, such as a sense of humor and friendship. They come to see that while the other students have serious learning problems, they are still very acceptable human beings. They begin to see themselves in the same light. They become more outwardly oriented and willing to give of themselves.

Improvement of parent-child relationships: By the time the learning-disabled child has reached his teens, his parents have become quite frustrated, and the typical teen attitudes and behaviors are thrown on the parents to compound the difficulties. Parents need to know or be reassured that some behaviors are just typical of teens, and that other behaviors may be serious problems that were caused by many years of misunderstanding before the child became a teenager. Parents need someone with whom they can talk, someone who knows their child and is willing to listen. They sometimes need guidance in finding professional family counseling.

WHEN WE CONSIDER the overall significance of the goals mentioned in this paper, a clear, general theme emerges: learning-disabled children must have more than a well-planned academic program. If the need were solely academic, a proper program could easily be devised. Learning is everywhere and everything. It is the generalized aspect of learning that our children do not experience. It is our purpose to provide them with that experience.

An Inner City Program for Children with Learning Disabilities: Problems and Solutions

Lillie Pope*

DURING TIMES when financial deficits command far more public attention than learning deficits do, a unique, economical, and far-reaching program has been instituted for dealing with the problem of learning retardation in the schools and in the community. The fact that this program has been set up in a city hospital, and is independent of the formal school structure, makes it more novel and more effective. In the area serviced by this hospital, there are sixty elementary schools, seven secondary schools, and twelve intermediate schools. The heart of this area is a typical urban slum in which 80 percent of the children suffer from some form of learning retardation. Although the number of children who suffer from specific learning disabilities varies, depending on who provides the diagnoses, there is no disagreement that children in the area are failing to learn at the expected rate, whatever the reasons are for the failures.

Although some special classes are available within the school system for brain-injured children and for emotionally disturbed children, these classes are too few to handle the great number of children who are presented as problems by parents and teachers. In addition, it does not appear that special education in special classes can solve the problem of educating so large a number of the students who fail to learn. By making assistance available within the regular class, and by generally improving the educational picture within the school system, these children can receive very special education in the regular class, and the number of school and mental health problems will be minimized.

The rationale behind setting up a psychoeducational service in a hospital lies precisely in the connection between school problems and mental health. School problems represent severe stress to the child and this stress endangers his mental and emotional health.

The psychoeducational service is committed to a program of primary prevention. By working with the schools, by making specific recommenda-

---

Lillie Pope, Ph.D., is director of the psychoeducational division, psychiatry services, at Coney Island Hospital, Brooklyn, New York.

tions that help alter and improve the environment of the child at the earliest age that he can effectively be reached, it is possible to eliminate or minimize the number of problems with which the mental health service will have to deal at a later time. This is preventive mental health service at its best.

The psychoeducational service, embedded in a mental health service in the hospital, has a small staff: one part-time and three full-time learning-disabilities specialists, and two full-time paraprofessionals. However, the group is surrounded by a complete hospital staff; psychiatrists, social workers, pediatricians, neurologists, and others are available when their services are needed. The core of the psychoeducational service is the Learning Disabilities and Reading Clinic (known as the Learning Clinic), in which children who have not responded to the special services in their schools are tutored twice a week.

If the psychoeducational service were to operate along traditional lines for a hospital service of this kind, professional staff would tutor and serve only sixty to seventy children; paraprofessionals would assist professional staff by serving as liaison with the home and the school, and by escorting children to and from tutorial sessions in those cases in which mothers were too overburdened to carry through on this responsibility themselves. This would be the total service provided to the community by this group, if traditional practice were followed. This plan was rejected.

As plans for this program were being formulated, it seemed apparent that the community could not be served adequately if there were strict adherence to a one-to-one tutorial service. With the magnitude and urgency of the problem, the limited staff, and the number of unanswered questions in the field, it was essential to enlist allies and to get assistance from wherever possible. New ways had to be found for multiplying the effectiveness of the professional staff. To do this, a coordination program was developed.

The Learning Clinic

The psychoeducational team went out into the schools surrounding the hospital to reach the children and their school community most effectively. Although this team concentrated on the schools in the inner city area, it tried to reach as many as possible of all the schools within the hospital's catchment area. In order to be more readily accepted by school staff, they were assured that back-up services for the children with the most difficult problems would be available at the hospital. For this reason, the Learning Disabilities and Reading Clinic was established at the hospital. Here anyone with a relevant problem can come in and ask for a psychoeducational evaluation; for this, the usual geographical boundaries are extended, age limitations are removed, and the individual can be self-referred or referred by parent or school. The focus of the evaluation is on the questions, "Why is this individual not learning? What does he know? What does he need to be taught? How may he best be taught?" Every evaluation culminates in educational and clinical recommendations. The evaluation is sent to the child's guidance counselor and to his classroom teacher. Recommendations are very specific, in the hope that the individual's teacher will be able to implement them as long as the child remains in that class. Sometimes a curriculum modification is suggested, and, at times, special techniques are recommended. Usually, specific materials are suggested, and sometimes, but infrequently, special class placement is indicated as desirable. If the child is awaiting special class placement, it is our hope that the present teacher may still individualize her instruction for this child on the basis of these recommendations so that the child does not merely mark time while he is in that class.

Some children are retained at the clinic for twice-weekly individual tutoring and sometimes for group instruction, if no other comparable services are available for them in the community. Approximately forty children are fortunate enough to receive this tutoring, and for each of these children, the clinic also deals with the school principal, the corrective reading teacher, the attendance teacher, and any other resource person within the school who works with the child. It is hoped that through these contacts school personnel may achieve heightened awareness of psychoeducational approaches, which would benefit other children who present similar learning problems.

Workshops for teachers

Teachers are usually eager to learn about new materials and techniques. They are sometimes uncertain about how to individualize instruction and how to prepare educational prescriptions. Through workshops at the hospital and at the schools, classroom teachers learn how to identify, diagnose, and treat children who have reading and learning problems. Workshop discussions are very concrete and specific. For example, they may center around materials, or the teaching of concepts, or left-right confusion, or visual-perceptual problems. The language of the workshops is simple, and the ambiance is that of colleagues working together on a common problem, rather than that of a clinic team handing down dicta to technicians.

Teachers are shown how to prepare a psychoeducational evaluation. They are shown what skills to look for in the child at each age, and what skills the child needs for the learning task ahead. The teacher is guided in finding the child's deficits, as well as his skills. She is guided in how to identify and use the pathway in which he learns most easily. Teachers are reminded that hearing is only one of the avenues through which people learn and that they must not neglect the other senses in their teaching plans. It is important also to concentrate on the "how-to" of a multisensory approach. Since teaching practice tends to become static, teachers need workshop experience before they can begin to use those materials in the classrooms that give children opportunities to learn through touching and moving, in addition to seeing and hearing. Emphasis is placed on the importance of providing successful experiences for the child, providing for small steps in learning, teaching the child at his level, and limiting distractions for the child who is distractible. Importance is placed on the high expectations the teacher and tutor should have for the child, in eliciting successful learning experiences from him. The repetitiveness and overteaching in the workshop is deliberate and explicit, since it is important to be repetitive and to overteach children who have failed.

Although the major emphases of work with the teachers are on those "puzzling" children who fail to learn at the expected rate, teachers are able to apply what they have learned about the "special" child to their work with the regular group.

Through this work with the teachers and the schools, the clinic team has had an impact on the classroom environment of many children, many of whom have special problems. Although this can make the difference between success and failure, in some cases this is not enough. For some children for whom more help is needed, no appropriate supplementary services are available within the traditional educational structure.

Volunteer tutors

Since there are so many children who need special attention beyond what the schools offer, it became necessary to develop, through the use of volunteers, a corps of trained personnel to supplement the services that are offered by the schools. The school volunteer movement has great potential for providing individual tutorial assistance, and college students and housewives are eager to do this work. However, without special training and on-going consultation, the volunteers' contribution is dissipated; they become "a nice man or lady in the school." They become ineffective, discouraged, and frustrated.

The clinic team can be very helpful in making this large corps effective. Volunteer tutors are trained in five weekly sessions at the hospital, after which time they come in once a month for consultation throughout the remainder of the year. They are free to call for advice at any time. This past year, 400 volunteers were trained to give this service to local schools. Training involved discussions of child development, how children learn, why they fail, and how reading is taught. The meaning of "reading level" was discussed, and related materials were presented. The volunteers were guided in setting up an instructional program for the individual child, and how to work with and supplement the instruction of the classroom teacher. Although the volunteer tutors cannot be expected to be as effective as professionals, they worked with 600 children who would otherwise have had no assistance.

Many of the volunteers are attracted to this work because they have encountered learning problems in their own homes, perhaps with their own children. They are urged, and they pledge not to tutor their own children, but rather to tutor in the schools. Nevertheless, the insight that they gain into the problems of learning, of failure, and of child development, may have a direct impact on their own children and their own families.

In every sense, this is part of our program of prevention of mental health problems through educational intervention.

Paraprofessional training program

In addition to volunteers, use is made of a trained corps of paraprofessionals who are paid through federal funds that are administered by the local school district.[1] Eighteen paraprofessionals work full time under close and intense supervision in six neighborhood schools. They tutor children on a one-to-one basis, four and one-half days weekly, and come into the hospital on Friday for a one-half-day conference. They provide tutorial service for 126 children. Every child's program is carefully prescribed by the clinic team that is working in close cooperation with the school and with the paraprofessional. These paraprofessionals live in the inner city and tutor children in inner city schools. Their sensitivity and dedication are exceptional. Their own academic skills vary, but are entirely adequate to give assistance to children whose reading skills are primitive, and who have not yet learned to love learning.

Training and consultation for the paraprofessionals is very similar in content and quality to that provided for the teaching staff. The assumption is that if the material is presented clearly, each individual will absorb it at his own level. In this situation, again, care is taken to use language that is nontechnical, courteous, and never patronizing. Paraprofessionals have no difficulty following the instructions, and they never feel they are being "talked down to." Some of the subjects that are discussed include: how children learn, and why they fail, and an analysis of the tasks involved in learning to read. It is often useful to try to teach these paraprofessionals a new language, such as Sanskrit, or some other unfamiliar code so that once more, they may experience the difficulties involved in learning to read. They are shown how to use the body alphabet, sanded letters, clay, velvet, and pipe cleaners to teach the letters. Other sessions deal with common problems that arise, such as teaching the child left-to-right sequencing, how to deal with reversals, loss of place, concepts of over and under, before and after.

The paraprofessionals are provided with realistic expectations for the children with whom they work, and are given confidence that the children will learn. They are given very clearly defined responsibilities, as well as "panic buttons." Efforts are made to keep the program from becoming rigid; paraprofessionals are provided with a variety of materials from which they have the latitude to select what is appropriate for individual needs. They have learned to reject books that are too cluttered, too confusing, too advanced for the child with whom they are working, or that introduce too many skills at one time.

Thomas R.—a case study

The story of *Thomas R.* illustrates how one child benefited from these varied services. This case is unusual in that *Thomas* made use of a greater variety of our services than do most other children, although other children have made more dramatic progress.

Thomas, six years and two months of age, was referred by his first-grade teacher to the Learning Clinic because he was not learning, and she could not understand why this was the case. He seemed adequately intelligent, responsive, and well motivated. His mother was concerned since her three older children had not experienced any difficulty in learning to read. *Thomas* was a handsome black boy of average intelligence, with severe visual-perceptual difficulties. His auditory skills were adequate. His performance was marked by restlessness, perseveration, fragmentation, poor organization, and directionality. He knew very few letters, and had no concept of letter sounds. Gross motor development was good. The results of a neurological examination were negative. It was felt that the child's failure to learn was due to specific deficits, which had not responded to the educational program to which he had been exposed. A prescriptive program was planned.

Treatment: Thomas was accepted at the Learning Clinic for tutorial work, which was scheduled twice weekly. Since his mother could not bring him, a paraprofessional escorted him to and from school during school hours. Learning Clinic staff met with the teacher from time to time to discuss *Thomas'* progress; she followed through by providing individual time for *Thomas* whenever possible. He is now making good academic progress in third grade without tutoring, although he is still restless.

Should any further problems arise, he can be provided with extra assistance by the paraprofessional program or by volunteer tutors who contribute their services to that school. In addition, his teacher and his mother are free to call on the Learning Clinic at any time for consultation. Ordinarily, this child would have been doomed to school failure.

By extending our services beyond clinic walls, we have multiplied our effectiveness enormously. With our small staff, we have made the following facilities available to the community:

- The Learning Clinic at the hospital, where 40 children are tutored, and 250 receive psychoeducational evaluations annually.
- A corps of 19 paraprofessionals who tutor 138 children.
- A corps of 400 volunteers who tutor 600 children.
- Workshops, special programs, and ongoing consultation for teachers, guidance counselors, attendance teachers, and other school staff in sixty local schools with whom contact is maintained concerning the children who are receiving service.

Our program has helped to prevent mental health problems by reducing the incidence of learning problems. It is economical and it has tapped new sources of manpower in providing the necessary assistance. With constant growth over the past five years, our service has responded dynamically and flexibly to the needs of the community.

NOTES

1. Lillie Pope, "Blueprint for a Successful Paraprofessional Program," *Negro Educational Review* (April 1971).

SECTION IV

Educational Techniques

Typing Keys for Remediation of Reading and Spelling

Maetta Davis*
Mary Inez Brownlee

IN ABILENE, TEXAS, we are investigating the use of the typewriter as a remedial tool for teaching reading and spelling skills. Our work is based on two hypotheses: (1) that a child with a writing problem may learn to type reasonably well, and (2) that a child may develop a better awareness of the sequence of letters in words as additional channels for language reinforcement are provided.

We attempted to start our language-disabled students in a conventional elementary typing program. Our students, however, were confused by the directions for the assignments. So much print on each page amounted to clutter, and this caused the children to experience figure-ground confusion. The presentation of the keyboard was geared at a pace that moved too rapidly for the children to establish kinesthetic patterns.

It is apparent to us that many language-disabled children need an entirely new and different approach through which they can learn touch-typing. This is the purpose of our simplified, multisensory, developmental approach. It is a special program that was designed to meet special needs. It is so basic that it is being used as a readiness program for children who are in regular typing classes at the junior high school level in our town.

It was necessary for us to analyze the task involved and break it down into basic segments or steps. Each student must be able to master each step before progressing to the next. Developmental reaches are introduced in logical sequence; correct fingering is constantly reinforced and is presented as rapidly as the child can master it, or as slowly as the child requires it to be. Usually about twenty hours of instruction time are required for the child to learn the alphabetic keyboard.

Selected spelling words, mostly sight words, on three hundred drill cards are used instead of the regular typing book. These drill cards are prepared in twenty diminishing sizes of card and of print. The child is taught to *look* at the card, *say* the letter, *listen* to the teacher say it, and *strike* the key

---

Mrs. Maetta Davis and Mrs. Mary Inez Brownlee are resource teachers for the Learning and Language Disabilities Program in the Abilene, Texas, public schools.

simultaneously. Moleskin covers the home position keys to give a point of reference as well as to utilize the sense of *touch*.

The handbook, *Typing Keys for the Remediation of Reading and Spelling*, which is based on this program, is available for teachers and others who may be interested.[1] It gives complete directions for making teacher-prepared materials, and for developing teaching procedures, suggesting ways to modify the basic program to meet the special needs of individuals.

A set of one hundred key cards is used in various combinations for reviewing horizontal and diagonal reaches, for introducing new letters, and for constant alphabet practice. Stress is placed on reinforcement.

Sentence and phrase dictation exercises, without visual cues, are provided as a part of each lesson for auditory learners and for those students who are striving for improvement in this sense modality. This exercise brings out the child's motor reaction to the letter sound as he hears it. The child is directed to look at his typing chart or otherwise to avert his eyes from the typewriter and his hands; the dictation may be programed on tape or cassette, or may be dictated by the teacher to accommodate the individual student or the small group with whom she is working.

Horizontal reaches (asdf   ;lkj and asdfg   ;lkjh) are taught early in the program. We work in toward the center of the keyboard from the outside, which is not the usual left-to-right progression, but a built-in success factor is involved, as fingering becomes easier.

Balance in diagonal reaches is maintained between fingers used on the right and left hands. We use the proximodistal pattern of first fingers (jujm frfv), second fingers (kik,   dedc), third fingers (lol.   swsx), fourth fingers (;p;?   aqaz), and for the extended reaches of the first fingers (hyhn   gtgb).

Most students are achieving at least two grade levels below placement when they are admitted to our learning disability program. Such students are particularly inept in reading and spelling skills. However, in the teaching situation in Abilene, we, as resource teachers, are encouraged to work with supervisors to adapt techniques and select materials that suit the specific needs and interests of our individual students. We do not attempt to teach typing to all the students who are assigned to us. All students would not profit from such instruction as much as they would from using other materials. Another limiting factor is the lack of availability of typewriters for students in elementary school. However, we are finding that the students who are underachieving are the ones who make the most gains in reading and spelling skills as they work with the typewriter.

THIS ACTION RESEARCH STUDY, limited in scope, was conducted on eleven Saturday mornings in the spring of 1969. The experiment was repeated at a reading clinic in the summer of 1970. This program has been used during the past two school terms by several teachers of children who are language disabled or retarded. Thus far, we have compiled data on a limited number of language-disabled students, ages ten to fourteen years. They received typing instruction in addition to and as a part of other remedial help. The matched control group received remedial instruction, but no typewriting instruction. The *Wide Range Achievement Test* was administered as a pre- and posttest.[2] Standard scoring was used in making comparisons. The gain the typists made over the control group members was 2.53 points for spelling, and 2.38 points for reading. We are aware that part of this gain may be attributed to enthusiasm of the children and their teachers for such an innovative program. However, we felt that the results for the summer program were especially gratifying, as the usual slump in reading and spelling skills was alleviated.

Challenge: To Provide Structure

We begin by covering the home position keys with moleskin to give a point of reference to the child, as well as to utilize his tactile sense. The letters that represent the keys that are to be introduced are written directly on the fingers with magic markers; or, if the child objects, the letter is taped around the appropriate finger. The children work against the desk until they establish a kinesthetic pattern. If possible, mistakes are avoided, otherwise they are overlooked or minimized. Writing may be done in the air—no mistakes there! Intensive drill is used to reinforce correct fingering patterns. The child masters the motor processes that are involved in learning to type, much the same way he masters the process of learning to ride a bicycle. Many children find typewriting to be a challenge, but as they become accustomed to the routine of knowing what to expect, they feel secure in the structure of the presentation. Success is a built-in factor, and the child feels confident because he is rewarded in positive ways.

Challenge: Physical Limitations

Exercises are helpful in strengthening fingers and developing control of small hand muscles. We often use certain isometric techniques. Most children gain better control of fingers and hands as they use them and are able to use regular typewriters. If children have small or weak hands, they may do better with portable electric machines. Some children are tense and rigid as they approach the typewriter. Others tire easily. Relaxation techniques, as suggested by B. Godfrey and N. Kephart, are helpful.[3]

Handwriting problems often result from difficulties with laterality, directionality, mixed dominance, handedness, and inability to cross body midline. The difficulties mentioned here are not problems that carry over to typing. Often, as finger control improves from using the typewriter, so does handwriting skill.

One of our right-eyed and left-handed boys has found that he has an advantage when typing. He looks at the cards and charts on the right side of his machine and returns the carriage with his left hand. Another apparent advantage for him is that letters used more frequently, such as *a* and *e* are left-hand reaches.

Other children have motor impairments due to cerebral palsy or other afflictions. Often they can be taught to use correct fingering on electric portable typewriters. Handwriting is often time-consuming and laborious for such children. Their needs are for remedial techniques that meet the levels of maturation, interests, and visual-motor abilities. Typewriting is a special blessing for such a child.

Challenge: To Sequence Letters in Words

Many children develop a greater awareness of sequencing of letters within words as they concentrate on writing words with the typewriter. One of our more severely language-disabled children had an early history of mirror writing. Now that she is in junior high school, she continues to transpose letters in reading and spelling words. Typing seems to help in overcoming this problem, as she concentrates on using reinforcing multisensory cues, especially in naming each letter as she types it. At this stage, she is conscious of every motor response. The goal of this neurological-impress method is to direct practice until the response occurs at the automatic level. This is happening with most of the children as their learning channels are reinforced in this manner.

Challenge: To Build Attention Skills

An example of the acceptance-anxious child, as described by Katrina de Hirsch, is primarily a visual learner with auditory problems. He often reacts impulsively without understanding what is expected of him. The typewriter may appeal to such a child's interest in movement and be a key to developing attending skills. Because the typewriter is something new to him, he may be receptive to directions concerning its use. Sometimes, the added use of sound cues helps this student to attend to the lesson, as well as to reinforce his knowledge of the keyboard. However, other children, who are good visual learners, may be confused by oral instructions. Therefore, the oral dictation exercises should be deleted from the basic program for some children. The child may use supplemental drill cards, or later he may be able to use a typewriting book for additional exercises. As work progresses, many children are able to attend to the immediate typing task before them. Developing the ability to pay attention is a worthwhile goal.

Groups of mentally retarded junior high school students have been taught to type by this developmental method. Many intangible benefits accrue to such students from the typing program. The teachers and the students are highly pleased with their accomplishments. Each child feels successful as he is able to work at his own pace on a different assignment.

Challenge: To Assess Progress

Sometimes a child may manipulate letter discs into place, placing letters of the alphabet in order, then checking his work for accuracy. This may be done on a chart in a bright color to hold the child's attention, a suggestion made by D. J. Johnson and H. R. Myklebust.[5] It is a learning experience for the child to make his own chart—to draw and cut circles, print letters, and locate a position in space for each new letter as it is introduced. At a more advanced level, a student may fill in a small chart of the keyboard, writing letters in order of the presentation pattern of the keys. When he has difficulty with any letter, appropriate key cards and drill cards from the supplemental list may be used for added practice. Using a variety of different words avoids dull repetition when the same practice letter is used again.

As further assessment of progress, we have the child type the alphabet while he is blindfolded. This program places much emphasis on alphabet practice. The child learns to use his left hand to write *abcdefg*; then spaces, and uses his right hand to write *h(ij)klmnop*; spaces again, and uses reaches of both hands to complete the sequence, *qrstuvwxyz.*

Challenge: To Boost Self-Esteem

It is true, especially with these learning-disabled students, that nothing succeeds like success. At the completion of Group 20 (the final step in the sequence of key presentation), the child has learned correct fingering for the entire alphabet, and, also, is able to use strictly auditory cues to type sentences from dictation, such as, "Capital b . . . space . . . e . . . space . . . s . . . t . . . space," and so on for the sentence, "Best bakers are bald," using the letter *b*. Sentences that contain all of the letters of the alphabet may be dictated, such as, "A quick brown fox jumps over the lazy dog." Additional work with Dolch words and sight phrase cards may be provided at this point for students who are not yet ready to go into the regular program.

One language-disabled boy used the typewriter from his elementary principal's office last year as he learned to typewrite. He was challenged by the motor process involved, but mastered it, and now feels better about himself. He also feels pleased this year in junior high school, as he is able to make better grades because he can use the typewriter for homework assignments. Two boys who were classified as mentally retarded used this developmental readiness program before commencing with the regular school curriculum typing book this year. These boys are now typing accurately at the rate of forty-five words per minute. Two years ago the parents of an emotionally disturbed girl bought her an electric portable typewriter and enrolled her in the initial Saturday morning typing sessions. She perseverated in typing, but she experienced immediate success in building up a skill. As she began to succeed in this one area, her attitude improved, and she regained interest in doing her school work. She now has an excellent attitude and is planning for a secretarial career. Some of these other students may never be able to go into a regular typing program with emphasis on speed and timed performance, but each learns to type reasonably accurately, at his own pace. He attains a skill that is useful to him in everyday living.

OUR OBSERVATION through time is that the first hypothesis appears to be substantiated. *A child with a writing problem can learn to type reasonably well.* Typewriting may be the most acceptable way for some children to write. Supervisors, teachers, and the students themselves, are pleased with the results of typewriting as a remedial activity. Parents are enthusiastic and supportive.

The second hypothesis also seems to be substantiated, that is, *as a child learns to type, he does develop a better awareness of the sequence of letters in words.* This, of course, results in increased accuracy in both spelling and word-recognition skills.

Therefore, we submit that typewriting is an effective and innovative way to teach remedial reading and spelling skills. We encourage other educators to explore more fully the use of the typewriter as an instructional remedial tool.

NOTES

1. Maetta Davis, *Typing Keys for Remediation of Reading and Spelling* (San Rafael, Calif.: Academic Therapy Publications. 1971).
2. For sources of tests mentioned in this article, see Appendix.
3. Barbara B. Godfrey and Newell C. Kephart, *Movement Patterns and Motor Education* (New York, N.Y.: Appleton-Century-Crofts, Inc., 1969), pp. 115-116, 281-283.
4. Katrina deHirsch et al., *Predicting Reading Failure* (New York, N.Y.: Harper and Row, Inc., 1966), p. 79.
5. Doris J. Johnson and Helmer R. Myklebust, *Learning Disabilities Educational Principles and Practices* (New York, N.Y.: Grune and Stratton, Inc., 1967), pp. 221-222.

The Nonreading Parallel Curriculum

Douglas E. Wiseman*

PART I: PHILOSOPHY

A BASIC PROBLEM in the public schools is the vast number of children who are unable to profit from the existing school program. Concern for the excessive nonachievement or nonparticipation of able children in our school programs is consuming the time, talents, and energies of our most able educators at all levels. The problem is further complicated by the many categories of children who are nonachievers, such as the learning disabled, the culturally disadvantaged, the poor reader, the slow learner, the emotionally disturbed, the socially maladjusted, and the delinquent. However, these children all share a common denominator: a discrepancy between the demands of the school and the child's ability to respond or achieve at the levels dictated by the school and the greater community.

Special education has assumed much of the responsibility for correcting or remediating the problems of this massive nonachieving group, but with only marginal success. The vast number of these children, however, do not fall within the categories of exceptional or handicapped children and should be dealt with in regular educational programs. Many of these nonachieving children would not attain special education status if preventative educational efforts were attempted on a massive scale in the early educational years of the child. The goal of this panel is to describe a pilot program initiated in the St. Paul Public Schools, Minnesota, to deal with a portion of the nonachieving, nonparticipating school population.

The role of the schools

We have inherited an education model that is no longer responsive to the needs of a broader, more complex community of people. The system of education we have inherited was designed for the intellectually elite, not for the education of the masses. Historically, the early Greeks, Chinese, and Romans educated their elite young with tutors and at the feet of intellectual masters. The less fortunate poor were trained in a vocation by their family or through apprenticeships. Our current educational model began when the as-

---

*Douglas E. Wiseman, Ed.D., is supervisor of Program Development and Evaluation, St. Paul Public Schools, Minnesota.

piring middle class, with its expanding mobility, recognized the importance of education. The Renaissance brought the reawakening of interest in cultural, intellectual, and academic endeavors. The printing press and techniques of producing relatively cheap paper made reading and learning possible for the first time. Books, plays, and poetry became available for all who were capable of learning to read.

Private schools, resembling in many ways the schools of today, were opened to those few who could afford this luxury. The wealthy continued to aspire, the poor continued to perspire. The labor movement in the United States finally broke this tautological cycle, demanding publicly financed schools for all children. As public schools opened, they imitated the structure, goals, and materials of the elite private schools. Those who were unable to achieve in school were absorbed by the trades and agriculture.

But times have changed, and our highly technical, complex world no longer absorbs the uneducated with ease. Until recently, schools have maintained the scholarly goals of the seventeenth century, and have made only token efforts to adapt to children of widely varied abilities, backgrounds, and interests. Now, however, the role of the school is being modified, in breadth, depth, and the types of children being served. In breadth, we have become concerned with such varied programs as vocational education, sex education, cosmetology, and driver training. We have penetrated deeply into the sciences, such as physics, mathematics, microbiology, and cellular biology. We now serve children with many severe handicaps: the deaf, blind, retarded, and gifted.

Despite this apparent change, however, we depend on the means of information-gathering that was employed by our historical brothers—reading. The child with difficulty in reading gradually descends from the robins, to the bluebirds, and finally to the lowly albatrosses. And here, for all practical purposes, education ends and training is substituted. Since the classroom assignments are largely read, the nonachieving child is relegated to handwriting exercises, running errands, and helping the art teacher. He listens to class discussions and lectures, and does not understand them because they are based on a prior reading assignment. And yes, he is given training in remedial reading. But remedial reading, unfortunately, has the goal of improving the child's reading ability only to return him to the regular program, usually as a very marginal performer.

In a society that values perfection and conformity, the nonachieving child is indeed a thorn. Teachers try hard and value success as much as others do. The nonachieving child is a continual reminder of their lack of success, and teachers, like children, must in some way respond or react to continued failure. The teachers' reaction to failure, due in large part to their dominant role and authority, usually results in behavior that demonstrates disapproval of the child. The effect of continued disapproval by a high-status adult on a low-status child is well documented in the literature.

Children generally enter school with a healthy attitude toward the world. They are in the process of benefiting from a massive language and intellectual explosion. Learning is viewed as dynamic and experimental. Five-year-old children have successfully encountered and mastered many complex learning problems in their home and neighborhood. They enter school as flexible, creative, curious, confident, resourceful, persistent, independent individuals, and they usually show a good track record at figuring things out. But then they encounter failure in this adult world and their learning takes a fatal turn. They learn that they must not be wrong, nor uncertain, nor confused. They learn that they must value "right" answers, must conform, must learn strategies to bluff the teachers, to dodge work, fake, cheat, daydream. They learn to live with being bullied, bribed or conned, to be suspicious or anxious, to ignore the environment, or generally, to "turn off." Perhaps, worst of all, they learn to accept and internalize adult evaluation. The old saying, "What you think of me, I'll think of me, and what I think of me, I'll be," becomes an unhappy reality for these children.

We have laid a psychologically destructive foundation that isolates the child from both the adult and peer groups. He must, alone, perceive all, understand all, remember all, and develop a system of strategies, however narrow and undernourished, to deal with his world. Living with ego-reducing experiences each day demands general restructuring and adaption. The passive survive. The aggressive self-destruct. They resort to desperation measures to support their personality structures and individuality. They are never at peace.

WHAT are we to do? How can we turn away from this form of educational genocide? Many efforts have been made to salvage the nonachieving child. Special classes have been introduced to aid him in reading and arithmetic. Special materials have been developed, such as programed materials in reading, arithmetic, spelling, and in some content areas. Some materials have been compiled to directly attack the gaps in the child's learning process. Basal reading series have reduced the level of difficulty for the slower developing children.

Considerable effort has been made in experimentation in grouping, such as heterogeneous or homogeneous, team teaching, departmentalized teaching, and open schools. Diagnostic centers have been developed in some school systems. Highly specialized diagnostic teachers have been trained to evaluate and write educational prescriptions for nonachieving children. Crisis teachers have been placed in schools to help children who are psychologically unfit to cope with the school program. Remedial tutors have been placed in schools. Reading resource teachers and centers have been developed to enhance the regular class reading programs.

Inservice training to upgrade the regular class teacher is receiving greater emphasis in the schools. Unfortunately, inservice training programs in the school provide little in the way of continuity or depth of content. Inservice training generally relies on state or federal funding, so programs are usually sporadic or occur during the summer when many teachers cannot or will not attend. Attendance is also generally of a voluntary nature; subsequently, ineffective teachers often do not choose to attend.

Some secondary schools have begun to emphasize remedial-reading programs. One school reported that fifteen minutes of every academic class hour was devoted to remedial reading.

Noncompulsory attendance is another attempt at making school more meaningful. Teachers get a meaningful message when few children voluntarily attend their class.

Pairing achieving and nonachieving children in school has met with some success. Basically the pairs of children do everything together, including tests, grades, and assignments. Some schools have done away with testing and grading, with the honest belief that you cannot measure what a person knows.

These are just some of many efforts that educators have made to cope with the problems of the nonachieving, nonparticipating student. All are innovative and to some degree successful. But all have a commonality: *they each rely on reading as the principal means of gathering information.* Each works to make the nonachieving child a capable reader in order to help him cope with the existing educational program. In essence, the rationale is that much time and effort is necessary in training before the educational process can be successful.

The child's education seems to halt at his skill level of reading. Arithmetic is largely dependent on reading, as are social studies and science. Most materials that have a given grade level (third-grade arithmetic books, for example), are written at a level commensurate with the reading expectancy level of the grade. Thus, the nonachieving child is restricted in all areas of education.

Perhaps our greatest handicap in contemporary American education is the continued reliance on reading as the primary means of information gathering. If we persist with the idea that content and skills must be presented at the same level, a large minority of our children will remain uneducated. Intellectually capable and active nonachieving children are restricted to the ideational content of their reading grade level. We propose that many children can effectively comprehend material at their intellectual level if it is presented in a medium other than reading.

The role of the school is varied, dealing with informational content and organized bodies of knowledge, developing appreciation for the values and attitudes of our various social institutions, describing our historical heritage and how it relates to us now, amplifying thinking and intellectual facility, and developing the skills needed in such areas as reading, writing, spelling, arithmetic, and vocational training. Nonachieving children are largely restricted to the skill-building role. Yet all of the above educational concerns are important in the development of the thinking, informed citizen. The community looks to the schools to pass on our historical heritage and to prepare our children to be contributing, vital members, much as less complex societies than ours relied on the training that was provided by the family unit, in which they learned the customs and taboos of the society through dance and song. Theirs was a relatively simple task. Ours is a terribly complex task, and in our efforts to do an effective job we neglect the child's general education in favor of skill-building. Our priorities are confused.

Basically, the schools have a major tract system, and curriculum programs for the major tract system are designed to meet the needs of the regular child. By regular, I mean the child who reads at or above grade level.

The child who does not read at his grade level has limited success; consequently, he is placed in a remedial or skill-building program, such as remedial reading, which has as its major goal the upgrading of the child's skills and returning him to regular tract. The results of short-term, intensive remedial training have not been that encouraging. Even with the best remedial training, most nonachieving children cannot hope to compete with children having adequate reading and study skills. Consequently, he remains an educational second-class citizen. He is the one who becomes a drop-out, truant, school disruptor, or delinquent, and he has a high probability of becoming a criminal as an adult. In a highly complex, technological, competitive society, he is ill-equipped to succeed in any meaningful way.

IN AN EFFORT to provide an educational program that would better prepare the nonachiever for a healthy future, a pilot project was initiated at Drew Elementary School, St. Paul Public Schools. The project had as its major purpose educating elementary-level nonachievers by circumventing the traditional reading-based curriculum. Reading, arithmetic, spelling, and handwriting were relegated to a minor role in the overall program. The major theme was educating without reading. The program emphasized informational content, appreciation for the aesthetic, our historical heritage, the values of our social institutions, and it provided rich experiences for creative and productive thinking.

The children selected for the program had very little success in school and suffered from the severe effects of failure. To overcome the failure syndrome, special effort was made to make this new school experience successful, rewarding, and pleasant. Programs were devised that were rich in ideas, interest, and values. Units were devised according to ideas the children could absorb, and not restricted by content materials with restrictive reading vocabularies. Science and social studies units were developed, for example, around relatively complex ecological considerations, including how the various levels of animal life, including humans, are attempting to survive in a changing world. They were shown various examples of how man can no longer tolerate the belief that the ecosystems of the animal are separate and apart from his own life system. The ideational level of the various units was at a much higher level than normally found in second- and third grade classes. In essence, the curriculum content of the gifted was superimposed on the nonachieving child of regular intellectual capacity. The conceptional level of the program was at a much higher level than we had anticipated. We operated under the assumption that "It is as cruel to bore a child as it is to beat him."

Written tests over the curriculum content were eliminated. A problem in most programs oriented to content or organized bodies of knowledge is that they encourage regurgitation-oriented programs. That is to say, the children are expected to memorize the content of the unit in order to pass tests. We felt no compulsion to develop formal tests. The teacher was free, therefore, to operate as a guide rather than a drill master. The goal of the project was a broad, general education. As Robert M. Hutchins has suggested, the object of education is to develop intelligence in terms of adapting to and understanding new situations, and providing an opportunity for the children to invent new means of dealing with them.

The project made liberal use of audiovisual technology in the learning process. Such materials as tape recordings of books and lectures, movie films, slides, film strips, picture books, television, and records were used extensively. Materials were gathered from many sources in the community—elected officials, guest lecturers, professional groups, civic groups, foreign students, medical doctors, nurses, dentists, family friends, and films or slides taken during vacation trips. Once the teacher had the restriction of skill-teaching removed, many ideas for curriculum content were forthcoming.

The discussions of teaching reading, spelling, handwriting, and arithmetic were deliberately left until the end because of the lack of emphasis placed on these skills in the program. Of course they were taught. But each child had only one hour of skill-building per day. The object of the project was to educate children, not prepare them for the rigors of the regular class. Remedial techniques of reading, spelling, and writing were used, and these methods require a developmental, sequential, and systematic application over a long-term period. The teacher felt no pressure to prepare the children for reentry into the regular school program. The goal hopefully would be to teach them to read well by graduation, but no remedial program can guarantee a year-by-year growth increment as dictated by our basal readers.

We hope that by the time they leave the program the children will have sound reading skills that will permit them to successfully compete in the regular program. There is hope, however, that the parallel program will be extended through all the grades, so that the child, upon reentry, will not encounter failure. We felt strongly that attendance was not the major goal of education, but that it was, rather, a sound educational program that permitted success. We must explore many alternatives to the current unacceptable educational programs to provide an educational setting where children can participate successfully—after all, it's their school, too.

The Nonreading Parallel Curriculum

Warren Panushka*

PART II: ADMINISTRATION

WHEN TEACHERS and their principals meet to discuss the problems that exist in their elementary schools, a common concern is for the distressing numbers of hard-to-teach pupils—most frequently males—who have developed failure syndromes by the end of the first grade. What can we do to facilitate their adjustment and achievement?

In our district, we have implemented reading and specific learning disabilities programs, and have made diligent efforts to supply extra assistance in the form of aides, new materials, and smaller class size. The central administration is cognizant of this problem and has continually allocated significantly large sums of money with which to secure additional services and materials.

Unfortunately, these efforts have not met with commensurate results. Teachers, aware of the school's limitations in spite of these efforts, continued to experience the frustrations that resulted from our inability to reach all children. A few teachers have the perception and fortitude to try a drastically different approach—the will to act to resolve a deep and demanding problem. At one of our staff meetings, a member volunteered to take all of the academically unsuccessful pupils from grades two and three whose capabilities fell within the normal range and to develop a program designed specifically for their needs.

The functions of the principal in this situation were boldly clear: (1) give the teacher full support, (2) work with her to conceptualize the problem in detail, (3) establish goals and methods, and (4) find moneys for equipment and materials. We felt it was essential to assure the viability of the effort by securing expertise from specialists in the field and then to develop a plan out of the totality of professional resource information.

During the planning stages of the development of this parallel program, our concern was directed primarily to the particular class and its needs. At this time, we did not perceive that it would have such significant influence

---

Warren Panushka, Ph.D., is a public school principal in St. Paul, Minnesota.

on the regular classes, too, and we did not include this variable in our dialogue.

It was determined that the parallel class should afford the pupils with informational input through media that are not ordinarily found in a self-contained classroom. Boys who cannot read are starved for exciting information, and we felt that their needs and interests could be satisfied by using appropriate supportive audio and visual devices.

Independent study carrels, tape and record listening centers, individual sound-filmstrip viewers, accommodations for individualized use of visual and audio software, many books with tapes, and numerous materials and kits that require the use of neuromotor skills were purchased. The male population dictated an emphasis on science, and many filmstrips that related to science were obtained. Approximately $6,000 was allocated for equipment and materials beyond the sum normally provided in the regular classroom. These were essentially nonrecurring capital outlay expenditures.

A former home economics room was selected as the classroom since it offered adequate storage, running water, and sinks. Ideally, the room should have been fully carpeted to accommodate the activities and noise of a rather permissive climate. In such a program as this, a regular classroom of less than 900 square feet would have imposed undue restrictions on the instructional activities, since a major portion of the space is encumbered by storage and large audio-visual facilities such as the study carrels.

In the second year of the development and extension of the program, an additional class was organized and an additional teacher was employed. Some apprehension was felt by the principal in the selection of a second teacher. However, after several criteria were listed and applied to possible selectees, one young man became prominent; he satisfied the following criteria better than other candidates:

- Authenticity—is he for real? Do pupils believe in him? Is there a mutual feeling of respect?
- Ability to relate well with boys and their disruptive, acting-out behaviors.
- A track record of willingness to devote time beyond expectations of a normal class as well as patience and understanding.
- Promise of possessing or developing an enthusiastic and innovative attitude toward instruction and a willingness to acquire new teaching skills.
- Personal emotional security necessary for flexibility and testing out novel ideas without the frustration that might result from failure.

After considering potential teachers and selecting the additional teacher, it was evident to the principal that every school staff has among its members several teachers who have demonstrated these highly desirable traits.

Active support from the district administration and from the school administrator are of critical importance to the development of any innovative program. The teacher must be able to work in an atmosphere in which other groups (such as parents) and other members of the school staff are aware of the program, its attributes, and its potential effect upon the educational problem. The district administration of St. Paul has always championed, both spiritually and financially, the dedicated teacher who would pioneer. Teacher-aide time was provided by the district office, along with a virtually unlimited amount of money for field trips. Any rational request that was interpreted to the district office was granted.

Colleges and universities in the area demonstrated a high degree of interest in the program, with the result that a large number of student and observer-aides volunteered their free time to gain experience with the pupil population and the unique class. So many observers sought scheduled time that it became necessary to limit their number, which was a function of the principal.

As the program developed during the early stages, it was anticipated that other teachers might become envious and perhaps even hostile about the special provisions, equipment, and materials that were being supplied to the parallel-program teacher. When one staff member is singled out for an enriched teaching situation and the publicity about her emerges, the *esprit* of her peers is sometimes impaired. This possibility was predicted and countered by offering the use of the class resources to other members of the staff when they were not in use. The counsel of the total staff was secured as the result of their experience with pupil candidates. The advantages of placing disruptive hard-to-reach pupils in a different class were also noted: it was beneficial to those pupils, and it was an advantage to regular classrooms.

Several teachers perceived the parallel class as a potential dumping ground for all their problem pupils. This problem was met by establishing a referral priority list based on criteria of analyzed needs. The principal functioned as a buffer in this situation and exercised his prerogatives by determining which pupils were actually selected. Regular classroom enrollments were then balanced where it was indicated that it was appropriate. The practice of the principal who makes policy and announces it to the staff became a tool for circumventing interpersonal teacher conflict.

PARENTAL ATTITUDES posed no practical problem after the program was explained and after parents visited the class. The highest percentages of parents attending group conferences, parent conferences, and other parental functions are from parallel-program classes. Absenteeism of parallel-program pupils is the lowest in the school. These children, formerly dismal achievers and unhappy kids, enjoy their success and show it with happiness on the job. Their parents have written letters to the parallel-program teachers expressing appreciation for the profound changes in their children. They are learning to read better, and their behaviors manifest these personality changes.

In developing this paper, I sought to search out and include the shortcomings of the parallel program as well as its strengths. In all honesty—no shortcomings exist. The minor situations and personal incidents that occur in any school also happen in the parallel-program classes, but with less frequency than in regular classes.

Without this experience, I would have prejudged that serious behavioral incidents would occur more frequently among a group of problem boys who were all in one class. The track record does not bear this out. It just hasn't happened.

The current school year is the second year of experience with the parallel program. In grades two through five, most of the pupils with severe learning problems have been pulled from the regular classrooms. A request to further extend the program to include grades one and six is under present consideration in the district office.

The following generalizations relating to the administration of the program as it is seen by the principal include:

- Even though many teachers may not be able to accept the demands, nor do they have the professional and personal skills for this kind of program, there are sufficient number of teachers who can gain great satisfaction from the challenge and experience and who could extend the program widely.
- The effect of removing parallel-program pupils from regular classes has been salutary both to the parallel-program class and to the regular class. Regular teachers can plan instruction for a narrower range of needs and without the harrassment of disruptive pupils. Regular classroom instruction and climate have improved dramatically.
- There is an almost infinite amount of software needed for a parallel program since regular textbooks cannot be used as they are in a normal situation, but pupils are in a homogeneous arrangement where expensive materials can be channeled to best meet pupil needs.
- The logistics of taping stories, resource booklets, and magazines requires a large-scale action plan. Volunteers from college and high school speech classes can be utilized to record materials on tape. The parallel program has yielded significant results of changed behaviors of subject pupils and observed objective assessment of improvement in reading skills. All pupils demonstrated a new confidence in word-attack skills. All of the pupils showed freedom and ability to attack words by inviting visitors to hear them read. They particularly showed high interest and achievement in knowledge about science concepts and a confident willingness to express and share this knowledge. Previously all of the pupils had demonstrated insecurity and failure-related behavior in the normal classroom situation. Hard data now being secured from a pre- and post-test study will not adequately measure the effective growth of pupils from which our enthusiasm has generated.
- To assess the merit of wider-scale use, the parallel program should be extended vertically to all grades and horizontally to schools in a variety of socioeconomic circumstances to test its effect on populations that are not subject to current investigation.
- The simple removal of troubled pupils from all classes and grouping them together contradicts an old "ism" of educational folklore. Spreading the hard-to-reach children among all teachers including those who cannot deal with them instructionally, or accept them emotionally, no longer makes sense. What is wrong with assigning them to a master teacher who can meet their needs? On the basis of our experience, nothing is wrong with this new approach.

THE PRACTICAL EVIDENCE yielded by almost two years of the non-reading parallel program is concise and significant. Disciplinary problems are virtually nonexistent in this white, target area school where every class has had its share of chaos and unmet needs. Teacher morale is significantly higher, and parallel-program pupils are happy and confident achieving children. The long lines of discipline problems waiting for appropriate action no longer confront the principal. Children in regular classrooms no longer wait for "Joe Problem" to be squared away by the teacher, before getting on with the class or group assignment. Teachers no longer fret over the impossible task of teaching the child who cannot read and therefore learns little. Better teaching is occurring in all classes because the major problems of each class have been grouped homogeneously and assigned to a master teacher. In spite of violations of traditional theory, the practical evidence is in the pudding.

The principal, once a vociferous antagonist of all ideas contrary to "democratized" heterogeneity in class makeup, becomes an ardent believer in the merits of the parallel program. There is nothing wrong with the grouping of children by their individual needs so that their needs may be best met by a master teacher who has been selected for the job. The parallel program makes sense because it works.

The Nonreading Parallel Curriculum

Aina McDaniel*

PART III: CLASSROOM

THE MAIN APPEAL of the nonreading parallel instructional program is to assure success in school. The children who are in this program were chosen because of their failure in reading, academics, and social relationships. In essence, the children were experts in failure; their personalities had been shaped and molded by failure. Disappointments that were experienced in school were carried home, disrupting family relationships that were already unstable. Some of these second- and third-grade children were already known to the police. We reap what we sow.

Success was an unfamiliar experience for these children. The goal of this program was to provide an educational experience that guaranteed success. The subject-content for the program was selected for high interest and relevancy. The interest factor proved to be an easy hurdle. The children seemed to be interested in nearly any topic, as long as they did not have to read to gather the information. Initially, the children were suspicious and frightened, and they approached content tasks with obvious reluctance. This hesitancy disappeared when they were assured that nothing more was expected of them.

The relevancy of the materials and content was a more important consideration. Many topics interest children but priorities must be established, although arbitrarily, to assure that the most relevant content areas are being selected. Many factors influenced the selection of relevant content areas, particularly the availability of materials that were suitable for audio-visual presentation. One important consideration was that content was not restricted because of reading level. The second- and third-grade children were capable of successfully listening to tape recordings of some fifth- and sixth-grade-level books. The children seemed to grasp meaningful ideas from taped presentations, through lectures and from movies that presented relatively difficult subject matter, particularly when the narrative was assisted by visual representations. It was discovered that much of the material that is found in elementary-level libraries was interesting, but had little relevant content.

---

*Aina McDaniel is a teacher in the St. Paul, Minnesota, public schools.

Some of the material was selected solely for pleasure, but most of the material was chosen for the unique and broadening experiences it could provide for the learner.

Another factor that created a problem was the limited availability of volunteers to record the material on tape or make supportive audio-visual materials, such as slides, pictures, movies, and drawings. Initially, the teaching staff attempted to do all the recording and development of materials. The rate at which the child consumed the materials, however, necessitated extra help. Parents, school volunteers, women's organizations, and older children provided the assistance that was needed. The older children provided the most satisfactory source of help, since the children in the class, interestingly, preferred listening to the tapes recorded by them.

The children were taught to use the class audio-visual equipment at an early stage in the program. When a child demonstrated that he was capable of handling himself independently and responsibly, his instruction on how to load and operate the various types of audio-visual equipment began. Each piece of equipment was taught individually, and each child was required to demonstrate his proficiency at handling the machine before he could use it without the supervision of the teacher or an aide. Learning to use the equipment was a highly enticing task, and examples of self-control and "good" behavior were frequently exhibited for the teacher's benefit. The school year was divided into two major portions: the teacher-managed segment, and the independent learning segment.

Teacher-managed segment

The twenty-one children who were enrolled in the parallel program had severe learning and behavior problems. Before their learning problems could be attacked, some inappropriate behavior patterns had to be changed. The children demonstrated many different forms of acting-out behavior, but particularly common behaviors were high anxiety, aggressiveness, poor judgment, poor impulse control, hostility, immaturity, poor attention span, restlessness, and hyperactivity. The first task was to reduce the number of inappropriate behaviors and increase the number of appropriate behaviors. This was accomplished by establishing a well-defined set of behavioral guidelines in a highly structured classroom environment.

Role expectations were immediately clarified. The teacher's role was to teach, help, supervise, and love the children. The children's roles included respecting others in the class, controlling their own behavior, passing judgment on right and wrong behavior, and most of all, learning. The class discussed each type of inappropriate behavior and set the form and the severity of punishments for infractions. In a sense, the class formed a governing constitution, under the guidance of the teacher, for dealing with problems and determining expectancies. This action, of course, did not inhibit behavior patterns that had long since been established, but it did lay an orderly foundation and procedure for dealing with both group and individual problems.

Certain rules were established, and the child who broke these few primary rules learned quickly that they would be strictly enforced. The first rule was based on the promise that adult yelling would be outlawed, which was fine with the children, but certain behavior was expected of them as a consequence for this unfamiliar reward. When the lights in the room were extinguished, all of the children had to return to their seats and remain silent until the lights were turned on again. This rule was established within three days. The second rule was based on the command, "Freeze." At the command, the children were to stop, statue-like, in the position they found themselves. This rule was also internalized quickly.

The children were promised certain liberties for appropriate behaviors. For example, the children had only to catch the eye of the teacher to go to the restroom or to go to another activity when a seat assignment was accomplished. It became very clear to the children that freedom was purchased with controlled behavior. Group conferences with the children were called one or more times a day to discuss class activities and behavior. We discussed what to do about poor behavior. They soon began to identify group and individual problems, and they discussed them with remarkable insight. In frank discussions with each other, they devised techniques that could be used for controlling the various class problems. The class soon internalized the concept that they could control their own behavior. Fights among individuals in the class were dealt with first by separation and a little Band-Aid type of acceptance until cooling down was accomplished, and later, a group conference to discuss the punishment and how the incident could have been avoided, and the culprits sentenced themselves to some minor punishment. The discussion and sentencing occurred long after the fight when each of the participants was relaxed and open-minded.

HUMOR WAS AN INTEGRAL part of the group conference. The punishment was given and taken in good spirit. The punishments that the class devised were remarkably simple and effective, but were often too severe. The teacher had the delightful role of intervening, playing the comfortable role of the benefactor. The "do-nothing place" was a class invention. Each day or so, a spot was designated for those being punished. The "do-nothing place" was simply a location where nothing was to be done—no play, no work, nothing. The "do-nothing place" was also used by those children who were in foul moods and wanted to keep from getting into trouble, or even by those who were tired and needed a moment of rest and quiet.

A token economy was initiated with immediate success. Initially, candy, toys, and free time were used; later, clothing was donated to the class, and the children set prices on each article. They then worked to earn the right to buy the clothing. A play-money system was devised whereby the children were paid for their efforts and fined for their indiscretions. The children set their own fines. The token economy was fun and interesting, but its major contribution was making the children aware of appropriate and inappropriate behaviors. However, social reinforcement was by far the most important and effective reward. Success was the order of the day, and soon the children openly expressed the feeling that school was the greatest place in the world. Attendance, which had been a major problem with these children, improved to the point that even sick children were coming to school.

A tight rein was needed initially, but as the children became accustomed to the new environment, less structure was required. As a child proved himself responsible, freedom was encouraged within prescribed limits. The children had much work assigned to them, but it was individually prescribed and designed to assure success. Sessions of work were kept short and intense. Work was accomplished in small homogeneous groups or individually. Self-correcting assignments were frequent. Periods of short, intensive instruction were alternated with more relaxing, but controlled, activities. As the children learned to cope with their behavior, they were taught how to use the audio-visual materials. Those who had problems had to postpone using the equipment individually until they could control themselves. Learning to use this equipment was a powerful motivating force.

During the teacher-managed segment, diagnostic teaching was possible. Specific behavior problems were noted and academic skills were evaluated, particularly reading, writing, spelling, arithmetic, attending behavior, and attention span. Formal diagnostic tests were not used. Information was gathered on actual performance over several weeks of participation. This information permitted homogeneous grouping and individualized seat work.

The teacher-managed segment was a very difficult and energy-draining period for both the teacher and the pupils. Tears and laughter were shared, but the benefits were well worth the effort.

Independent learning segment

For some children, the independent learning segment overlapped in time with the teacher-managed segment. Those who were capable of responsible independent behavior began working individually or in small groups on the various audio-visual equipment. Those who were not capable of exercising restraint were accorded little free time for independent work. The children working independently were given opportunities to display their new knowledge before their less fortunate classmates and were rewarded with lavish and obvious praise and greater freedom. This became a strong incentive for the recalcitrant few to modify their classroom behavior. As they earned the freedom privilege, they also earned the rewards of meaningful production.

The independent learning period was divided into skill training and content gathering. Each child received one hour each day of skill training, such as phonics, oral reading, silent reading, arithmetic drill, and quantitative reasoning. Part of each hour's skill training was spent with the teacher or aide and the other part was spent doing assignments as seat work. Handwriting, spelling, and reading were taught together using the Orton-Gillingham reading method, which is a highly elemental, sequential, remedial-reading approach.

The children were drilled on recognizing letters and sounds, blending the sounds into words, and learning to spell and write each word they learned. None of the twenty-one children had developed systematic, reliable methods of word attack. The Orton-Gillingham method is designed to gradually develop reliable word-attack skills. It is a highly mechanical approach, which brings in constant review and overlearning of the elements learned.

Reading instruction could not begin where the child was apparently functioning in his basal reader. In almost every case, the children had to have beginning reading instruction so they could unlearn all the poor habits they had acquired up to this time.

The children were more advanced in arithmetic in the sense that they were fairly consistent in arithmetic computation. Quantitative concepts, however, were almost entirely lacking. Time and space concepts, and seeing quantitative relationships were a major problem. The Cuisenaire Rods were introduced to provide the conceptual portion of mathematics. Each child was provided with a set of rods and systematically introduced to the equation form of programing that was suggested. The children learned to develop, compute, and correct equations on their own. As they progressed, the equations were transformed into numbered equations and later into story problems.

The content-gathering portion of the independent learning segment was the most ambitious and rewarding aspect of the project. We noted that when the children visited museums, they were constantly involved in meaningful and joyful learning experiences. The decision was made to try to make the classroom as much like a museum as possible. Initially, this was a very difficult task, but as soon as the fetters of traditional teaching were released, possibilities for an enriched curriculum, without reading, became evident.

THE RICHEST SOURCE of informational content was science, which, as any teacher knows, is usually the most exciting and interesting portion of a child's school day. These second- and third-grade children were no different, and they had the decided advantage of being unrestricted by clumsy and narrowly based second-grade science books. The concepts of science are relatively simple if these concepts are broken down into bite-sized chunks, and not restricted by a limited reading sight vocabulary. The children explored many far-reaching corners of science through tape recordings, video tapes, movies, slides, filmstrips, records, lectures, discussions, and a variety of field trips. Weighty topics, such as astronomy, ecology, living and nonliving categories, overpopulation, rocketry, and the problem of finite natural resources were covered. The children visited the various science museums, conservatories, and planetariums in the Twin Cities. The famous nature author, Sigrid Olson, and the noted nature photographer, Les Blacklock, visited the class and discussed their various interests. Medical personnel, such as medical doctors, dentists, nurses, and medical technicians, were enlisted to teach the "unteachables." Many of the visitors were so intrigued with the class and with what we were attempting to accomplish that they volunteered to return.

Ecology was of particular interest to the class. They learned how man is simply a part of a larger ecosystem and is entirely dependent on the maintenance of this natural chain. They studied the relationships between one-celled animals, insects, reptiles, birds, larger and more complex animal life, and finally, man. The children came to realize that the most destructive animal in the forest is none other than man. They learned that man is systematically destroying his ecosystem with a swollen population, insecticides, industrial pollution, strip mining, excessive lumbering, and poor farming practices, and all of this was taking place without reading!

Social studies became an important part of the curriculum. The ecosystems of nature were compared to the social ecosystems of man, and it became abundantly clear how important we are to each other. Government, when it was taught as a subject, was of little interest to the children, but when it was compared to the various levels of other ecosystems, it became meaningful. The class identified the gross levels of government, starting with the home, the school, the city, the county, the state, and finally the federal government. They visited the state capitol, attended city council meetings, and even met St. Paul's "super-mayor" and other public dignitaries. The class began to recognize the necessity for laws and a disciplined citizenry. They composed letters regarding unanswered questions and directed them to Minnesota senators Hubert H. Humphrey and Walter F. Mondale.

The informational content portion of the program was not restricted to the unit system. Many miscellaneous topics entered the program through situational happenstance. An individual who was employed in rocketry was invited to the class to discuss jet and rocket propulsion through lecture and film. Shopping centers were visited. Greenhouses, libraries, and medical facilities were explored. A major unit on care of the teeth was developed as a result of one trip, including visits from dentists, dental nurses, and dental technicians. Foreign visitors came by to discuss the customs, art, and music of their respective nations.

Appreciation of various art forms was introduced to the class. Professional musicians, artists, and photographers visited the class and demonstrated their various specialties. Art museums were visited and lectures on primitive and modern art forms were greeted enthusiastically. Puppet shows and circuses were also part of the program.

The historical heritage of our nation was also explored. Various social institutions were discussed, and their historical backgrounds were traced. The children studied the various Indian tribes of the local area and visited the historic Fort Snelling. The American "melting pot" concept was also investigated.

Thinking skills were often introduced within the content of the class. Social problems were identified and solutions were explored. In science, for example, the children witnessed a polluted aquarium destroy a fish. They discussed the effects of cigarette smoke on man and watched its effects on a terrarium. The class attempted to generalize value systems of one group to all aspects of life, noting relationships and discrepancies. Cuisenaire Rods were used to promote logical thinking and to note relationships.

Discussions of values and attitudes proved to be of major interest to the children. It seems that children of this age understand very well that relationships with other people are dependent on how we treat one another. We discussed good manners and how to greet visitors, the importance of being a good friend, the difference between friendship and civility, caring for things that do not belong to them, such as the audio-visual equipment, or art work of others, the importance of courtesy toward others, kindness, honesty, and perseverance. Values and attitudes were of great importance to them. And they wanted to learn techniques of good manners and when to use them.

THE RESULTS of the parallel program have been gratifying to the extreme. The children are happy, secure, and productive. The other teachers are now accepting the program. The children are developing sound reading skills, despite the fact that reading is deemphasized. They have adopted a very positive attitude toward school and have lost the suspicion they felt toward teachers and administrators. And they have learned much—all without reading.

Teaching Visual and Auditory Decoding Skills to Learning-Handicapped Children within a Reinforcement System

A. Carol Hartman*
Thomas M. Stephens

A SYSTEMS APPROACH that uses directive teaching procedures has been designed and implemented in the Lancaster, Ohio, city schools with children who had reading difficulties. Primary level children from an attendance area containing a high percentage of low-income families, were randomly assigned to treatment and control groups.

The children who were placed in the treatment groups were systematically tutored within the systems approach. The members of the control groups were tutored in a non-systematic fashion within small groups. Results to date indicate that the treatment group has made reading progress beyond what would have occurred without tutoring. Posttesting and statistical analysis of scores across the two groups have not been completed yet.

Previous program results

The Lancaster, Ohio, city schools typically contains high numbers of elementary-age children who have minimal development in language and cognition. Evaluation of previous projects funded with federal monies clearly indicated that traditional instructional approaches had not resulted in significant academic gains in this attendance area. High teacher-pupil ratios, coupled with standard elementary level instruction, seemed to contribute little to the students' reading progress.

Teacher aides and tutors were placed in first and second-year classrooms to provide more adult direction for selected children. In addition, a language development teacher was made available to teach selected children. Five staff members were employed as tutors. They were at different stages in their professional training, and no one had a college degree, yet. Three of the tutors had no previous teaching experience; one has taught four
tors had no previous teaching experience; one had taught less than a year; and one had taught four years at the elementary level. Only one of the five

---

*A. Carol Hartman is the Title 1 project director for the Lancaster, Ohio, city schools. Thomas M. Stephens, Ed.D., is associated with the Child Study Center of the Ohio State University, Columbus, Ohio. The authors wish to acknowledge the administrative support and teacher cooperation they received from the staff at South Elementary School in Lancaster, Ohio.

taught at the early primary level before coming into the program. The language development teacher was a trained speech therapist with two years experience teaching kindergarten and first-grade children.

During the first year (1969-1970), the tutors were responsible for the reading instruction of those children who encountered the greatest difficulty in skill acquisition. The approach was developmental in nature with emphasis on *readiness* activities. The end of the year evaluation of growth in skills of these pupils was disappointing. Since there were many pupils with rather severe problems, tutors often found themselves trying to work with as many as fifteen children. The result was that little or no impact was possible other than to relieve classroom teachers.

Systematic tutoring

During the 1970-71 academic year, a systematic approach to teaching beginning reading skills that uses a tutorial model was implemented. The major objectives were to increase reading performance of selected primary pupils as measured by criterion-referenced tests and norm-referenced tests in reading, and to demonstrate that minimally trained personnel can provide quality instruction through a systems approach based on a behavioral model.

A secondary objective was to determine if by teaching decoding skills, beginning readers subsequently make greater gains in reading than children taught traditional readiness activities in standard fashion.

The systematic instruction, based on Directive Teaching consists of gathering instructionally relevant information; applying instructional strategies; and evaluating performance.[1] *Figure 1* depicts this system.

Figure 1
Directive Teaching System

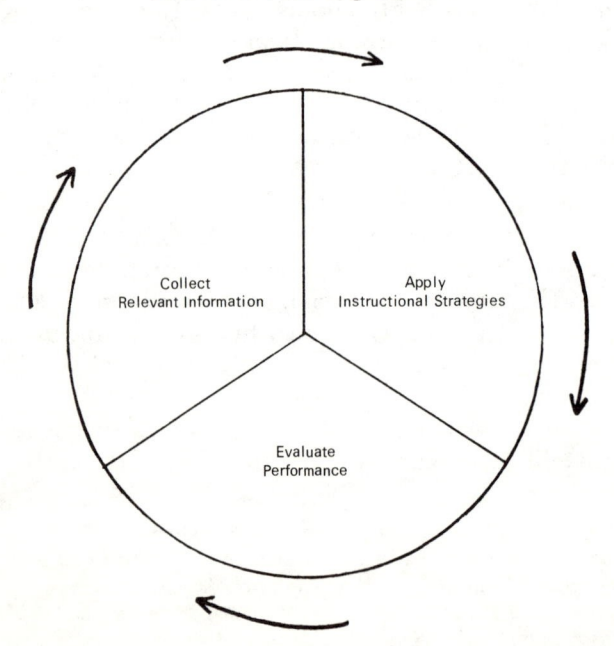

REINFORCEMENT is built into instruction. Tutors emphasize verbal reinforcement by informing children as to the accuracy of their responses and encouraging remarks and gestures. Coupons are also issued and are redeemable for leasing objects from the "toy store."

The tutors' functions consist of five steps:
> Assess child on entry and at the beginning of each skill.
> Select tasks within child's instructional range.
> Apply instruction.
> Evaluate effects of instruction.
> Reassess after criterion is met.

Treatment variables

The following variables were controlled within the treatment groups:

Materials: A set of decoding skills were developed for assessing reading skills. Each skill is accompanied by a criterion referenced test. The skills are keyed to the *Sullivan Program* through Book 7,[2] and the vocabulary is taken from the Sullivan readers through Book 7. Instructions are specific for the tutors and criterion levels must be met before a child goes on to the next task.

Tutors are also provided with directions as to what constitutes readiness for instruction. The following criteria were established:

> Level 1: *Task too difficult*
> Below 70 percent accuracy
> Level 2: *Instructional range*
> Accuracy between 70 to 90 percent
> Level 3: *Mastery*
> Accuracy above 90 percent

Sullivan materials are not available to classroom teachers, which provides control over classroom instruction for treatment groups, without affecting the instruction of members in the control group.

Time: The tutors met with each child for two ten-minute sessions each day. Small kitchen timers are used to insure that the time limits are observed.

Reinforcement schedules: A fixed schedule of reinforcement was used initially. During assessment, pupils received one point for each two minutes work to encourage them to continue and avoid penalizing them for incorrect responses. Points were earned for attending behavior rather than for academic skills. During instruction, a one-to-five schedule was used. The child received one point for every five correct responses that he made. These schedules were modified during the year according to the requirements of the interests of the children and tutors. Children in the treatment groups have access to rewards in the "toy store." Control-group children are not permitted to participate in the toy store activites.

Selection of groups: All children in the first and second-year classes were given the *California Achievement Tests* (CAT) and the *California Mental Maturity Scale* (CMMS) in September.[3] Fifteen children from each of five classes were selected from the total class enrollment. Selection was based on IQ scores and achievement scores in reading (for second-year pupils), one-half year or more below age and grade expectations. Intelligence scores were within an IQ range of 70-110. Names were drawn at random from the fifteen, seven for the treatment group, and three for the language development teacher's group. The remaining names constituted a no-treatment control group for each classroom.

Table 1

Pretest Mean Reading and IQ Scores for Treatment and Language Development Groups

Treatment Groups

Group	Number	M IQ	M Reading
1	7	87	14
2	7	90	21
3	7	91	36
4	7	92	51
5	7	96	19

Language Development Groups

Group	Number	M IQ	M Reading
1	3	98	37
2	3	91	23
3	3	94	47
4	3	98	45
5	3	93	23

Tutorial component: Tutors meet each child individually at a station within the classroom. This area is screened to reduce distractions from on-going classroom activities. Tutorial sessions are scheduled so they do not interrupt the child's regularly scheduled reading instruction.

Each child is assessed on the programed materials to determine entry level skills. At the point where a child fails to meet criterion on a task, instruction is begun. Tutors are responsible for developing teaching strategies for each task. These are then kept in a master file and may be used by other tutors when needed. Each child receives points for attending behavior as well as points for correct responses. Verbal reinforcers, such as, "very good," or "you're working well," are used at a variable rate throughout tutoring sessions.

It was anticipated that more frequent reinforcement would not be necessary since a child would always be working at his appropriate level. However, tutors found that they had to individualize reinforcement for particular children and were given permission to modify the schedules and to note such changes in the child's records.

The coupons or points represent interim rewards. Tutors soon devised a punch card system for ease of administration. Points or punches are accumulated for a week. At a designated time, each treatment group has access to a "toy store" where they turn in their cards to purchase playtime with a toy or game of their choice. Initially, the toys were leased overnight, but the rate of loss was quite high and the system was changed to a play period during the school day.

Control groups: Fifteen children, three from each classroom, receive small group instruction with our language development teacher. These sessions are for approximately twenty-five minutes. The approach is developmental with great stress on language experience charts "read-along" activities, and eventually, into more formal phonics instruction. Reinforcement for these children is verbal, and tangible rewards are given in the form of time-out during instruction for activities of the pupils' choosing. Other children, who are identified but not selected for treatment, receive only the regular classroom reading instruction.

EVALUATION OF THE PROGRAM consists of baseline information collected in September; entry level skills on the criterion-referenced tests and standardized tests to be compared with posttest scores, and progress on the programed tasks. The CAT, alternate forms, will be administered to all pupils in each classroom from which treatment groups were drawn. It is anticipated that evaluation for the first year will show positive, if not, significant gains by the treatment groups.

Gains in reading among children in tutoring groups are already evident. The children being tutored have maintained high interest levels. Periodic reviews of skills that were previously mastered have proven helpful. On some occasions, the tutors seem to become less interested in their teaching, but, the project director's reinforcement tends to raise their interest levels.

NOTES

1. Thomas M. Stephens, *Directive Teaching of Children with Learning and Behavioral Handicaps* (Columbus, Ohio: Charles E. Merrill, 1970).
2. Sullivan Associates, Webster Division (New York, N.Y.: McGraw Hill Book Company, 1968).
3. For sources of tests mentioned in this article, see Appendix.

Judgment-Making Skills: Can They be Developed?

Maurice Kubena*

THINKING *how*, thinking *of*, thinking *up*, thinking *about*, thinking *through*, thinking "seems to be a part of the human equipment."[1] "We have difficulty refraining from making judgments about anything that comes into our view, whether it is a person, a thing, an idea, or a situation."[2] These statements emphasize the fact that judgment making is a very human thing. We are called upon at all hours of the day to make judgments as we interact with our peers, our supervisors, and our subordinates. J. P. Guilford elaborates on the complexities that are involved in judgment making:

> Of all the problems that the average person encounters on a day-to-day basis, those concerned with personal interactions are among the most common. The processes of social living generate numerous problems, little ones and big ones. Coping entails numerous tactical measures of one kind or another. One can develop certain habits and skills for such copings, but they do not cover all contingencies. New kinds of situations continually arise, calling for new modes of coping behavior, and this in turn calls for problem solving.[3]

This paper represents an attempt to deal with *some* of the variables that are involved in a child's development of judgment-making skills. It certainly does not pretend to be a demonstration of complete coverage. It is not clinically clean and neat, and it elaborates few, if any, finished truths, but it does represent some directions in which we are interested in making further explorations. Since we are not going to be dealing in finished truths, I will feel free to make use of a number of "what ifs."

- What if judgment making is not something that is housed in a mysterious black box and cannot be touched, but is something that is made up of a number of subskills.
- What if judgment is not something that can be labeled as being present or absent, but is a group of skills that is present in each of us and, like the *capacity* for *love*, has to be drawn out and encouraged.

Maurice Kubena is educational director of The Brown Schools in Austin, Texas.

- What if some of our students who act impulsively, fail to consider and reflect, make judgments based on the immediacy of satisfaction, move rapidly and randomly, act with little more than "whim or caprice," act without apparent goals, fail to discriminate the relevant and the irrelevant, or act immaturely—what if these are the children who are poor at judgment making.
- What if we can make these children better *thinkers*, more *able* to make good judgments.

Following these suppositions, we come to the final "what ifs" that suggest important implications for the classroom:

- What if judgment making is based on a series of skills that are developmental and learned, and that can be remediated.
- What if developmental programs in these skills could be established.
- What if tests could be constructed that would be similar to the visual-perceptual tests that are currently available, so that judgment-making skills could be fractionalized, tested, and dealt with.
- What if remedial programs could be designed so that instead of going to remedial reading, speech therapy, or psychotherapy, the student could go to remedial judgment classes.

It is recognized that when one breaks up a task such as visual perception or, as in this case, judgment making, there is a possibility that the subskills will not fall into distinct categories with neat boundaries. There are going to be some points at which similar skills touch and overlap. But by breaking the tasks down into logical parts, we are able to point out some testable teaching skills that appear to aid remediation. Some efforts are being made in this direction. In fact, many of the ideas that are presented in this paper come from ideas that were suggested in a kit by L. E. Raths et al., called *Thinking Skills Development Program* and the accompanying book, *Teaching for Thinking: Theory and Application.*[4]

Let's take a look at the need for comprehensive developmental and remedial programs. First of all, I would like to suggest that there are *at least* six subskills that form the framework of good judgment making. A child may be deficient in any one of them and consequently exhibit poor judgment making. The subskills include:

- Observing.
- Classifying.
- Comparing.
- Identifying assumptions.
- Hypothesizing, which includes the generation of possible causes and the generation of consequences.
- Criticizing, which eventually includes the selection of a preferred alternative.

This list is by no means complete, and it is similar to the visual-perceptual subtests in that some skill boundaries are grey; it is difficult to see where one skill ends and another begins.

Let's take a look at a developmental program for judgment-making skills. Such a program would ideally be similar in organizational design to *The Frostig Program for the Development of Visual Perception*.[5] The program as I visualize it would, however, need to continue through high school and should be subject-related as well as skill-related. There are some efforts being made in this direction at the present time. If you follow the works that B. S. Bloom spearheads, you will recognize that much of his thrust is in this direction.[6] The program designed by Raths and his associates provides practice in thinking activities for specific subjects as well as practice in specific skill areas.[7] It appears to me that the kit is not comprehensive, but it is a step in the right direction. If teachers and administrators will study this program, and "try it out," I feel sure that the kit will serve as a springboard for generations of other ideas, activities, and sequences.

A large portion of the efforts that have been made by Bloom and Raths are directed at "providing an opportunity." While these efforts are valiant, it should be recognized that the learning disabled often need more than just the traditional "opportunity." Many of the learning disabled need strong remedial activities. Such a remedial program should have standardized testing instruments so that:

- Individuals and groups can be screened.
- Areas of strengths and weaknesses can be identified.
- Remedial programs can be outlined and applied.

I do not know of any such formal test that is available at this time. However, Bloom and Raths do suggest some possibilities. Also, there are parts of some standardized tests that are presently in use that could be adapted to, or at least provide a standardized setting for the evaluation of some skills. The Similarities and Comprehension subtests of the *Wechsler Intelligence Scale for Children* (WISC) each contain elements that are closely related to the skills that are being discussed in this paper.[8]

The *Thematic Apperception Test* (TAT) could probably be used to analyze skills of observation as well as skills in identifying assumptions and generating hypotheses. If one were to analyze other tests, such as the *Illinois Test of Psycholinguistic Abilities* (ITPA), other subtests could be located that relate to judgment making. Many of the tests for creativity would yield information about the subject's ability to generate alternatives and consequences as well as to criticize systematically.

In the remaining portion of this paper I will discuss each of the six subskills that must be developed in the child if he is to have an adequate judgment-making ability. The definitions for these skills are largely based on Rath's work. It should again be emphasized that these skills are not exclusively separate, nor are they necessarily the only factors that relate to the child's proficiency in this complex thinking process.

Observing

When a person makes an observation, he records all the details of what he sees. In responding to what he sees, he does not have to include his personal opinion. His observation may merely be a report. An analysis of a student's judgment-making style and behavior might reveal that he needs to work on observational skills. If this is so, he would be encouraged to sharpen his skills of observation by observing pictures and objects; eventually he would be asked to describe interactions between several people. Some students may be so poor in making and reporting on their observations that language therapy might be needed. The question the teacher asks would also help students to focus on relevant points of observation.

Later he would be asked to report observations of events in which he participated. Such observations are called for in such programs as Reality Therapy, in which the client is asked: "What are you doing . . . what is it getting you?" When you ask the client or child these types of questions, you are asking him to observe what is happening. You hope he is able to respond at a low anxiety level so that learning can take place.

This gradual progression from the impersonal to the personal is an important part of such a remedial program. At the present time, most of us tend to respond to the crisis situation where observations, in particular, are almost impossible, where anxiety is high, and defenses are even higher. It should be noted that we often label these children as poor in judgment-making because we focus on crisis situations in which poor judgment has been displayed, but we fail to note that these same children, during the course of the day have also made some good judgments. For example, they did select the appropriate color of blouse to wear, or the appropriate coat for the weather condition. Many of the good judgments are not noted and therefore are not rewarded.

Those who feel comfortable using behavior modification techniques can see their potential value when used in these types of activities. Imagine the power that might be unleashed if we began, at least in a remedial program, to recognize and reward all of the good judgments students make each day? Of course, by breaking the judgment-making process down into discrete steps we can also reward the student as he approximates good judgment making.

Classifying

When items are classified, they are put into related groups. It is important to teach the child that in classification, *many* types of groupings are possible. If the student is found to be poor in classification skills, a remedial program could be designed in that direction. Here again, the student would be asked to classify or group objects; later he would move up to situations and events. The student would be asked to remember that *many* types of groupings are possible. Elements of creative thinking are related to this skill. There are many techniques from the field of creativity that can aid in sparking ideas about new groupings. In fact, on the social end of the continuum, Guilford and his associates have recently suggested activities that they call "Reclassification Abilities."[9] In this test, the subject is asked to classify the following social comments in a number of different ways:

1. You get out of here
2. Are you sure
3. What a bore

4. How could you do such a thing
5. Didn't you listen to me
6. I wonder what time it is

No punctuation marks are given to the student so that a slightly open-ended situation exists. Guilford feels that the ability to reclassify is an important part of flexibility. Flexibility, as we all know, is a valuable dimension of a fully functioning individual.

Comparing

Closely related to the classifying skill is the ability to make comparisons. As Raths et al., note in their kit: "When you compare, you are asked to look at two things and tell how they are alike or similar and different."[10] Moving from some simple comparison like dog-cat, the student, in the remedial program, would be expected to move into comparison of two events, two backgrounds, or circumstances, etc., even into a comparison of two feelings.

Identifying assumptions

Practice in looking for and recognizing assumptions might be necessary for some students if their poor judgments could be traced to faulty assumptions. As Raths points out, "In every situation in which a conclusion is drawn, one or more assumptions are being made!"[11] Some children might be poor at separating facts from assumptions. Thus, they may exhibit behaviors that are not consistent with the facts, but *are* consistent with what was assumed. Perhaps training children to look for assumptions will encourage them to be more creative in their thinking, for when the child labels something as an assumption, he is at least recognizing the possibility that what is assumed *might* not be so. This can lead him into seeking creative alternatives.

Hypothesizing

An hypothesis is an attempt to solve a problem. It is a hunch, an explanation, and a solution. Hypothesizing is concerned with both the past and the future; it is an attempt to suggest reasons for something that has happened or for something that is going to happen. A generation of many possible causes as well as many possible alternatives might be included in the process. Many students who are labeled poor at judgment making are, in fact, poor at generating alternatives. When given alternatives, they can select the the appropriate one! Some who are poor in this area act as if they are not aware that alternatives even exist! Not only must several alternatives be generated, but the consequences of each must also be generated.

Principles of creativity can be used to the fullest in this judgment-making skill. A checklist designed to stimulate divergent thought can be used here. Here also the student should be taught to use deferred judgment. In problem-solving situations, it is often necessary to defer judgment so that ideas may be presented without fear of rejection. *Deferred* does not mean that judgment will not occur, but only that it should be postponed. Eventually ideas need to be evaluated, and judgments made. Deferred judgment has been used quite effectively in problem-solving courses and can be used in day-to-day activities, particularly in judgment-making activities.

Criticizing

When the individual tells whether he likes or dislikes an event, an idea, etc., he is making a critical judgment, but it should include more than liking or disliking, because it should contain some reason why. Of course, as one does that, he reveals, he sets up his standard or basis for judgments. The field of creativity has contributed to this area also. Many companies that use creativity principles ask their staff members to think of as many things as possible that can go wrong with a project or an idea. They are also asked to point out what is good. Many ideas are usually generated and many issues are weighed. Perhaps practice in these skills will cause the student to adopt critical behavior as a part of his learning "style," and a formerly inflexible individual might begin to demonstrate that he can consider both sides of an issue before making a judgment. Of course, when criticizing comes to an end, a choice must be made and the choice must be translated into a behavior.

THIS PRESENTATION has discussed only a few of the aspects of judgment making. Many points and dimensions have not been covered. For example, instant or automatic judgments were not discussed. Judgments based on *good-bad*, *like-dislike* dimensions were not fully explored. Judgments based on expressions of tastes, whims, or habits have not been alluded to. The influence of short-term and long-term goals was not discussed at all. The important role that private meanings play was not discussed.[12] It is hoped, however, that some aspects of judgment-making skills have been highlighted, as well as the need for further research into the field, particularly as it applies to the learning disabled.

NOTES

1. Louis E. Raths et al., *Teaching for Thinking: Theory and Application* (Columbus, Ohio: Charles E. Merrill Publishing Company, 1967).
2. Benjamin S. Bloom et al., *Handbook on Formative and Summative Evaluation of Student Learning* (New York, N.Y.: McGraw-Hill Book Company, 1971).
3. J. P. Guilford et al., "Solving Social Problems Creatively," *Journal of Creative Behavior*, 2, No. 3 (1968).
4. Louis E. Raths et al., *Thinking Skills Development Program* (Westchester, Ill.: Benefic Press, 1967); idem, *Teaching for Thinking*.
5. Marianne Frostig and David Horne, *The Frostig Program for the Development of Visual Perception* (Chicago, Ill.: Follett Publishing Company, 1964).
6. Bloom et al., *Handbook*.
7. Raths et al., *Thinking Skills*.
8. For sources of tests mentioned in this article, see Appendix.
9. Guilford et al., "Solving Social Problems."
10. Raths et al., *Thinking Skills*.
11. Ibid.
12. Charles W. Lavaroni, "Humanity," *Dimensions in Early Learning Series* (San Rafael, Calif.: Dimensions Publishing Company, 1970).

Music in Special Education

Vera Moretti*

IN 1962, Martin F. Palmer reported on the effects of music therapy upon neurological disorders.[1] His report was based on an experimental study that was conducted by Paul Nordoff and Clive Robbins, music therapists at the Institute of Logopedics in Wichita, Kansas, who subsequently published their investigations and experiences with this type of therapy.[2] I have studied with Nordoff and Robbins, and from 1964 through 1968 I used their unique approach as a classroom teacher and music therapist with ninety neurologically impaired, institutionalized children. The results were encouraging. For the past three years, Sheila Mermin and I have used this form of music therapy at a state institution in the treatment of severely handicapped residents with communication disorders. The following are the educational and therapeutic goals of this program:

- Speech initiation and language development.
- Ego organization and personality development.
- Behavior modification.
- Motor control.
- Lengthened attention span.
- Memory development.

The purpose of this paper is to help special education teachers become more aware of the possibilities that music as therapy offers in the education of the whole exceptional child. Nordoff and Robbins provide an insightful description of the importance of this kind of therapy:

> The study of the general effects of music in the aphasias of children and adults has been both fascinating and productive for many years. The areas of the brain subserving musical reception and performance are practically invulnerable . . . . In the communicatively handicapped individuals there lies behind their silence a possibility of emergent development. Their musical approach is a way of reaching past the silence to the individual in order to bring him to a potential fulfillment.[3]

Vera Moretti is a music therapist at the Walter E. Fernald State School, Waverly, Massachusetts.

All teaching methods are based on effective communication. When we discuss communication or the lack of it, we usually refer to the ability to verbalize in a given language at a certain level. In music, communication between two human beings has little to do with language as we know and use it. Music is a universal experience. All people can share it. Comparing language to the larger order of communication, Susanne Langer said:

> The fundamental human capacity for response to ordered sound represents a kind of universal human communication system, of which language is a refinement and an elaboration, but of which it can never be a complete expression.[4]

The components of music

Music is form and movement in time and space. It is ordered sound. The three basic elements of music are melody, harmony, and rhythm.

Melody is any succession of single notes in horizontal or progressive association.

Harmony is a balance of rest and unrest, of tension and relaxation. Dissonance in music furnishes an element of movement and progress, and keeps the mind and the imagination of the listener aroused. Consonance in music invites relaxation.

Rhythm is time divided into units of absolutely equal duration. Rhythm is order. The components blend to form an image in time:

> The image of musical art, unlike the stationary creations of the arts of painting, architecture and sculpture, is progressive; as in the art of poetry, the impressions in music succeed each other by progressive motion. Therefore time is absorbed in the expression of musical thought, and it is the province of rhythm to define and regulate the divisions and subdivisions of this passage of time.[5]

Music expands the child's world

The common plight of most special children is isolation and loneliness. Often a handicapped child lives in a state of continuous tension, and is unable to express his emotions in an orderly fashion. Frequently, he is unable to assimilate life's experiences. He may be confused because he fails to interpret them. He has little or no faith in his own capacities. He feels rejected, and he rejects himself. Often, he is unable to communicate his needs, unable to control his inner conflict. The results are well-known manifestations of unacceptable behavior.

In music therapy, the child is encouraged to express all of his emotions without fear. No demands are made on him to acquire skills. In the first individual music therapy session, the child finds a drum and a cymbal in the music room. He is greeted and welcomed with an "hello" song. He may choose to respond vocally or instrumentally. We do not try to influence, modify, or change his initial response. We accept him, follow him into his disturbed inner rhythm, interpret his responses through improvised music, and return to him a musical portrait of himself that he can accept. As Nordoff and Robbins put it, "The child expresses his disturbance rhythmically, the therapist works with it musically."[6] Rhythmic responses develop into challenges to new rhythmic patterns, and a give-and-take may follow. The first signs of musical communication appear, trust and understanding between child and therapist are gradually established, and pleasure and confidence in making music together create an atmosphere of warm expectancy. A happy child wants to learn. At this time, we introduce a simple structure: a greeting song, instrumental or vocal improvisations, and a "goodbye" song. The child's individual responses are encouraged and developed, and, as therapy progresses, a desire to participate in group activities is awakened in the child.

Among children with communication disorders, two basic types of responses, vocal or instrumental, are observable. The child's vocal responses are carried from the heart to the head on the stream of breath. A nonverbal child's response to a sung "hello" may be rhythmic breathing, "h—h." Another child's response may be expressed in the form of crying. When this crying sound is accompanied or interpreted by improvised music, it may become singing in the tonality of the music. Vowel sounds may follow. It has been noted that the choice of vowel sounds often has a specific meaning for very young children. A fearful child may moan and sing an *oo* sound, while a child who is ready to assert himself may express himself with an energetic "e—e—e."

Children who prefer an instrumental response feel their emotions being driven from the heart to the limbs on the waves of blood circulation. These children are energetic and prefer the drum to assist them in establishing the rhythm of the word, or the syllables that are needed for a given word, before they are willing or able to voice it. A child who masters the beating of the basic beat feels satisfied and secure. His breathing pattern may improve and his actions may be executed in a more logical sequence. A child who is struggling to overcome speech or reading difficulties may choose to beat the melodic rhythm. Once the melody has been established, the child may begin to sing as well as beat the rhythm. This is an encouraging experience, and as repetition strengthens memory, singing engages the emotions and pleasure replaces the fear of failure.

The rare child who beats the harmonic rhythm of chordal changes has to concentrate, listen, and be alert at all times during the session. This seems to be a deliberate effort to channel his inherent capabilities, an unusual and interesting way to fight hyperactivity, and a conscious effort to form thoughts, speech, and actions in a logical sequence.

Certain musical intervals can have a great impact on children. For example, the single tone could be described as the "inner voice." The fourth interval is often experienced as the threshold to the outside world. "Hello," "goodbye," and simple commands, such as "sit down," and "come here" are usually voiced in the interval of the fourth. The fifth, the "bugle call," could be experienced as the entrance into, and the acceptance of, the outside world. The octave establishes a balanced relationship between the child and the world.

There are a few children who will not respond to music, and very few who will resist completing an unfinished phrase. Our first verbal response usually comes in the unfinished "good . . ." of the familiar "goodbye" song.

The incomplete phrase compels the child to add the final syllable. Now he belongs and is ready to join in group activities. I agree with J. P. Dobbs that it is essential to offer the children a choice of many varied songs, various moods, and emotions:

> Children must have songs through which they can express their sadness as well as their joy . . . . Songs which are written down to what is considered to be a child's level must be avoided like the plague.[7]

Children sense quality. I feel that the musical works of Nordoff and Robbins contain music of artistic discipline and vitality, and an expressive quality that has never before been realized in compositions for exceptional children. All of their music was composed and written for exceptional children during their work with them. All lyrics belong to the music. *Play Songs, Book 1* and *Book 2*, contain songs that incorporate the rhythmic patterns of speech,[8] and may motivate the children to sing and retain pertinent information before they are able or willing to express the same thoughts in their speech. All of the many daily activities can thus be introduced. Action games can fulfill a variety of valuable functions. Social interactions, with a task to perform and accomplish, can lead the children to an awareness of the world and the people around them, and sustain concentration and interest in the contents of unfolding stories. *Pif-Paf-Poltrie* is an example of such an action game.[9]

Two other works by Nordoff and Robbins are *Fun for Four Drums* and *The Three Bears and Goldilocks*.[10] *Fun for Four Drums* permits a gradual stepping up to proficiency in rhythm recognition and responses. It is a lively, challenging, fun-filled conversation between four drums, which demands each child's full attention. *The Three Bears and Goldilocks* provides an opportunity for a large number of children to participate. There are twenty-three instrumental parts within the grasp of the musical abilities of all children, regardless of their handicaps. The story, songs, and music are delightful, and the children unite in happy, successful work.

AUDITORY INPUT is magnified or even scrambled for many handicapped children. Therefore, the choice of instruments should be partially based on the tone quality and the degree of resonance. Children who are overly sensitive to sound enjoy working with such instruments as xylophones, lyres, psalteries, harps, zithers, and shepherds' pipes. Other children may prefer percussive instruments, such as drums, cymbals, resonator bells, and metallophones.

A. C. Harwood distinguishes four basic childhood temperaments,[11] which may be described musically in the following way:
- A choleric child will usually choose the drum.
- A sanguine-tempered child prefers to "blow his brains out" on a horn or trumpet.
- The melancholy child feels comfortable with a stringed instrument.
- The phlegmatic child can be engaged with a neutral instrument, such as a birdcall.

All musical work should be done with live music. Responses to recorded or taped music become mechanical, and much of the direct involvement is lost. The child experiences deeper involvement with live music because the tempo, pitch, and mood can be changed to meet his individual needs.

Creative results in the classroom

A break in academic work and a release from tension of some classroom activities has long been recognized as necessary and beneficial for children. We felt that creative movement, art, and music could provide more of a release than purely physical activities. We combined art and music, or music and creative movement. The extension of these diversions into classroom and everyday activities assumed many different forms. The following are some examples:

- *Reading* was frightening for many children, and so we invented a game. One child would express his feelings in movements, while the other children selected their instruments and gave a musical interpretation of the moving child's emotions. In this way, the children were "reading" each other, and reading became an exciting adventure.

- *Centering* presents great problems for many children who have learning disabilities. The children in my class composed songs. We called the exercise, Write it—hear it—sing it—own it. Learning to center circles on and between the lines became a melody, and thus, a song. These series of circles became a preliminary exercise to writing and an incentive to learning to write since *a, e, o,* and similar letters could be evolved from circles.

- *Sound—color—symbol development* was the unique idea of a severely handicapped child. One day, Lisa demanded, "Make me some circles and squares." I did this for her and she then colored around the circles with orange and red, and colored around the squares with blue and green. She put a vowel in each circle, and placed a consonant in each square. Lisa said, "Vowels sound hot—consonants sound cool." Lisa found an expression for her feelings about the sounds and structure of language. One could say that she felt the vowels as an inner experience, and the consonants as outside impressions, before she learned to place her letters correctly.

Gina and I worked for many months in an attempt to develop and establish a secure, basic rhythm. The day finally arrived when this child declared, "I don't need your four/four anymore. I am free now—I can do five-seven-five." Gina had found the rhythm of simple haiku.

John hated school. He hated himself, and he hated his fingers: "They always get me in trouble, they never do anything right for me." He would throw a temper tantrum and employ an exquisite vocabulary. One day, I handed him a split brush, paint, and paper, improvised an angry song, "We are angry, very very angry," and from that day on, Johnny would ask for his "angry music" and he would paint his temper tantrum. He developed a fairly stable rhythmic pattern in his behavioral and motor activities, and within a few months, this child could listen and participate in group activities with pleasure and growing confidence.

It is possible and desirable to bring all children together in musical activities if the exceptional children are prepared. As W. Cruickshank states:

> In music do not give him a separate program. If possible bring him into the musical experience of normal children, where the exceptional child can cease to be exceptional.[12]

This, then, is our goal in music therapy for special children.

NOTES

1. Martin F. Palmer, "Effects of a New Type of Music Therapy Upon Neurological Disorders." Paper presented at the Convention of the American Speech and Hearing Association, 1962.
2. Paul Nordoff and Clive Robbins, *Music Therapy for Handicapped Children* (Blauvelt, N.Y.: Rudolph Steiner Publications, 1965), pp. 49-50.
3. Ibid.
4. Susanne Langer, *Philosophy in a New Key* (Boston, Mass.: Harvard University Press, 1951).
5. P. Goetschus, *Tone Relations* (New York, N.Y.: G. Schirmer, Inc., 1931), p. 13.
6. Nordoff and Robbins, *Music Therapy*, p. 43.
7. J. P. Dobbs, *The Slow Learner and Music* (London: Oxford University Press, 1966), pp. 38-39.
8. Paul Nordoff and Clive Robbins, *Play Songs, Book 1* (Bryn Mawr, Pa.: Theodore Presser Company, 1962); idem, *Play Songs, Book 2* (Bryn Mawr, Pa.: Theodore Presser Company, 1968).
9. Paul Nordoff and Clive Robbins, *Pif-Paf-Poltrie* (Bryn Mawr, Pa.: Theodore Presser Company, 1969, revised).
10. Paul Nordoff and Clive Robbins, *Fun for Four Drums* (Bryn Mawr, Pa.: Theodore Presser Company, 1968); idem, *The Three Bears and Goldilocks* (Bryn Mawr, Pa.: Theodore Presser Company, 1966).
11. A. C. Harwood, *The Way of the Child* (London: Rudolf Steiner Press, 1967); idem, *The Recovery of Man in Childhood* (London: Hodder & Stoughton, Ltd., 1958).
12. W. Cruickshank, "Challenge of the Exceptional Child," *Music Education Journal*, 38 (1952), 18-20.

REFERENCES

Alvin, Juliette. *Music for the Handicapped Child*. London: Oxford University Press, 1965.

Benda, C. E. *The Image of Love*. New York, N.Y.: The Free Press of Glencoe, Inc., 1961.

Gaston, E. T. *Music in Therapy*. New York, N.Y.: The Macmillan Company, 1968.

Nordoff, Paul, and Clive Robbins. *Music Therapy in Special Education*. New York, N.Y.: The John Day Company, Inc., 1971.

SECTION V

Language Programs

Processes of Language Development

Sandie Barrie*

IN EVERY AREA of language research, the psycholinguistic approach is currently providing many new and enlightening insights into the nature of language and the various language pathologies. A workable diagnosis of a language problem depends upon a thorough description of the patient's language and language capabilities. When we consider the child who is delayed in language acquisition, we are faced with the problem of pinpointing the process or processes that are responsible for the delay. Although such a diagnostic procedure is crucial to our subsequent approach to the child's problem, we do not yet have procedures that effectively explore the relationships between the various processes of language acquisition.

N. Chomsky provided us with the foundation of a dynamic approach to the study of language.[1] He describes a "generative grammar" as a system of rules that specifies sound-meaning correlations and generates structural units that constitute the language. Such an approach is necessarily analytical, yet it binds the phonological, syntactic, and semantic aspects into a dynamic whole. The concepts of deep structure and surface structure are basic to this psycholinguistic approach. The formulation and understanding of the sentence is due to the processes reflected by the concept of deep structure, but also involves memory and intelligence. The speaker-hearer's knowledge of his language is termed linguistic competence, while his actual use of language (that is, in surface structure form) is termed linguistic performance. If this theory actually mirrors reality, one would expect that competence must be intact in order for the individual to understand and/or produce the surface structure of an utterance.

The purpose of this study was to design a test that would allow for compilation of data illustrating the dynamic relationships between linguistic

---

Sandie Barrie is associated with the Child Development Institute at the University of North Carolina, Chapel Hill.

The author wishes to acknowledge the invaluable advice and guidance given to her by Dr. Clement Brooke, University of Missouri professor of pediatrics and Dr. Jerome Paulker, University of Missouri associate professor of anthropology. In addition, the guidance of Dr. Doris Bradley of the University of North Carolina is sincerely appreciated as well as the continued guidance and stimulating influence of Dr. Patricia Goodding, of the University of Missouri.

processes and, therefore, one that would suggest more effective ways for analyzing the processes of language.

Method

Thirty-six sentences, representing progressively complex transformations and combinations of transformations, made up the Auditory—Syntactical—Sequential Memory Test (ASSM). The sentences were intended to test the short-term retention of an utterance and the comprehension of that utterance. In this way, one aspect of linguistic production, that of imitation, was compared to the understanding of the utterance, which was demonstrated manually.

Rationale

Linguistic performance may be impaired due to: (1) failure to retain the auditory string, and (2) the inability to deal with the complicated ordering that changes deep structure to surface structure (that is, transformations). Psycholinguistic research suggests that if the child can comprehend and retain the linguistic string he will be able to produce it; therefore, if related abilities are within normal limits, he will achieve competency in his language functions. Several processes are involved in the retention and comprehension of linguistic strings:

- Auditory memory span.
- The ability to retain sequential ordering of sounds and sound combinations.[2]

The ability to retain and integrate the syntactical information provided by the sound string.[3]

- The ability to make associations between the linguistic information and life experiences.

The subjects consisted of eleven four-year-olds, five boys and six girls, who were enrolled, or had been enrolled in the University of Missouri Laboratory Nursery School or the Home Economics Pre-School Nursery. The subjects were all white, middle-class children who were judged by their teacher to be functioning within normal limits. Each child was seen for a one-hour session, during which one examiner administered the ASSM and a second examiner administered three short supplementary tests.

Procedure

Repetition Task: A record sheet printed with the sentences and with space for scoring was provided for each child. The subject was first instructed to "Say these words after me." The examiner presented each sentence orally to the subject, and both the stimulus sentence and the subject's repetition of it were recorded on a tape recorder. There was a conscious effort on the part of the examiner to regularize the oral presentation of the stimulus sentences among the subjects. For each sentence the child was scored either correct (+) or incorrect (0) on the left column of his record sheet (*see Figure 1*). Any alteration of the surface structure of the string that could be described as having a basis in deep structure resulted in an incorrect score for that item. Errors included omission of words or inflectional endings of words, modifications of transformations, and substitutions of one in-class word for

Figure 1
Sample Scoring Sheet for the ASSM

(R)			(M)
1.	1.	Mother sits. (simple kernel)	1.
2.	2.	Father and Mother stand up. (conjoining)	2.
3.	3.	Tom walks slowly. (adv)	3.
4.	4.	John, the big boy, goes to the door. (noun of app.)	4.
5.	5.	Father goes out the door with Tom. ("with" + comp.)	5.
6.	6.	John is standing. (be + V + ing)	6.
7.	7.	John hits the table with his hand. ("with" + phrase)	7.
8.	8.	The little boy sits on the chair. (adj.)	8.
9.	9.	The big boy stands up on the chair (adj.)	9.
10.	10.	The boy who is on the bed stands up. (adj. of loc.)	10.
11.	11.	Who stands up? (Wh-Q:subj.)	11.
12.	12.	The boy is sitting by the window. (to be + pred. + adv.)	12.
13.	13.	Is the boy standing? (Q)	13.
14.	14.	The boy isn't standing, is he? (Q:pos.tag)	14.
15.	15.	The boy is sitting by the window, isn't he? (Q:neg.tag)	15.
16.	16.	Mother is doing the cooking. (nominalization)	16.
17.	17.	John gets a chair for Mary ("for" + comp.)	17.
18.	18.	Father is giving the towel to the boy. (gerund phrase)	18.
19.	19.	Mary takes the towel off the table. (separation)	19.
20.	20.	Mother takes the towel from Mary. (separation)	20.
21.	21.	Father sits down, but Mother does not sit down. (neg.)	21.
22.	22.	John goes to the living room. (Nominal comp.)	22.
23.	23.	John sits on the chair or he sits on the floor. ("or" + comp.)	23.
24.	24.	If John is standing he goes to the window. ("if" + comp.)	24.
25.	25.	Everyone stands up but John. (inversion)	25.
26.	26.	Everyone but Mary sits down. (inversion)	26.
27.	27.	Mary goes out the door and John does too. (conj. by "and . . . to")	27.
28.	28.	Mary sits down, and so does John. (conj. by "and so")	28.
29.	29.	The father stands leaning against the table. (part phrase)	29.
30.	30.	Tom goes in the door, and then he goes to the window. (pro. conj.)	30.
31.	31.	John goes to the window and looks out. (conj. deletion)	31.
32.	32.	Father pulls out the chair to sit down. (infinitive)	32.
33.	33.	The small boy goes in the kitchen and goes to the stove and then sits down by the door. (adj./conj./prep.)	33.
34.	34.	After Mother goes to the window she goes to the stove. ("after" + comp.)	34.
35.	35.	The dog goes out the front door and, standing on his hind legs, looks in the window. (adv. phrase/pro. deletion)	35.
36.	36.	The girl goes out the front door and goes around the house and comes in the back door before she sits down on a chair. (pro. deletion/conjoining seq./time order)	36.

another.* The examiner scored the subject's responses during administration of the test and later rechecked the record sheet with the tape.

During the first presentation of the sentences, six dolls were introduced to the subjects and associated with the appropriate names used in the sentences. However, the subjects were not allowed to hold or manipulate the dolls during repetition of the sentences.

Manipulation Task: The second part of the ASSM required the subjects to demonstrate an understanding of each of the thirty-six sentences by correctly manipulating the dolls in a doll house according to a stimulus sentence spoken by the examiner.† The children were instructed to "Make the dolls do what I say." Success (+) or failure (0) was recorded on the right column of the child's record form. In addition, the nature of the manipulation error was noted for each string scored (0).

For both repetition and manipulation tasks the examiner repeated the sentence a second time if it was apparent that the child had not been attending. The rationalization for this procedure is that the test purports to measure short-term memory (auditory) for language from the beginning of the sound string to the completion of the sequence. For this reason, a practice effect was not felt to have been an important factor. If it was the examiner's clinical impression that a subject was not performing typically as the test progressed due to fatigue or distractions, the subject was excluded from the study.

Scoring

Two scores were obtained for each subject. One represents the number of successful repetitions (R), and the second, the number of times the subject successfully demonstrated understanding through doll manipulation (M).

Supplementary tests

A second examiner administered three supplementary tests to each subject; the tests used were *Peabody Picture Vocabulary Test*, *The Metraux Test of Auditory Memory Span* and *Goodenough Draw-a-Man Test*.[4]

Results

Analysis of the data revealed the following:
- The mean (R) score on the ASSM: 20.88.
- The mean (M) score on the ASSM: 29.88.

---

*Errors such as omission of inflectional verb tense endings (when the child demonstrated the ability to produce the inflectional sound in some other context) and substitution of one in-class word for another could be considered surface structure (morphological) manifestations. However, because these errors could actually be caused by "transformational overload," therefore, related to deep structure operations, they were treated as errors for purposes of the binary scoring of this test.

†The six dolls (Mother, Father, John, Tom, Mary, and the dog) were realistic and made of bendable rubber. The dolls, doll furniture, and open-topped doll house were made by Creative Playthings, Inc.

- The correlation between the (R) task scores and the (M) task scores on the ASSM: .3015.
- The t score for correlated mean scores of the (R) task and the mean scores of the (M) task of the ASSM: −4.72. This score indicates a difference between the group means for the (R) task and the (M) task that is significant at the .01 level of confidence.
- Correlations between the ASSM (R) tasks and the Peabody IQ scores: .4865; the Metraux mean score for vowels: .6191; and the Metraux mean score for consonants: .3277; and the Goodenough number scores: .5861.
- The correlation between the ASSM (M) task scores and the Peabody IQ scores: .7042; the Metraux mean score for vowels: .5172; and the Metraux mean score for consonants: .2929; and the Goodenough number scores: .7587.

Statistical computations were done on an Olivetti Underwood Programma 101 desk calculator using programs for Txy Pearson r and t test for correlated means. Further analysis reveals that the ability to manipulate the string was equal or superior to the ability to repeat the string for 35 out of the 36 sentences. For 24 of the 36 items, the totals of the subjects' scores on the two tasks were within 4 points of each other. Scores for the ability to manipulate the string exceeded the scores for the ability to repeat the string by 5 scoring points or more on 12 of the 36 items. On only one item (Figure 1, No. 26) did the ability to repeat the string exceed the ability to manipulate the string.

Discussion

There seems to be an increasing inability to manipulate, as well as to repeat, the strings as they increase in transformational complexity. This is illustrated by the high concentration of errors in items 25-36 in Figure 1. Another apparent concentration of errors of the (R) task for items 11, 13, 14, and 15 occurred partly as an artifact of the children's habit patterns. The children tended to give an answer to the stimulus question rather than to repeat it.

The reversed pattern on item 26, in which ability to repeat the string exceeded the ability to manipulate it, seems to indicate that the subjects had difficulty understanding a sentence in which the predicate had been transformationally deleted in the first part of an inverted sentence conjoined by "but" when "but" means "except." The same pattern was not noted when the deletion was of the second predicate of an inverted sentence, as in item 25.

The low correlation (r=.30) between the (R) and the (M) scores on the ASSM indicates that the two functions (that is, the ability to repeat or imitate a linguistic string and the ability to show understanding of the string manually) may either be two separate abilities or similar abilities developing at different rates.

Subjects who attained high scores on the ASSM generally showed relatively superior abilities on an objective test of receptive vocabulary, on a measure of auditory memory span, and on a very general test of intellectual ability. In addition, the especially high correlation between the Peabody IQ scores and the ASSM (M) task scores is an interesting contrast to the lower correlation between the Peabody IQ scores and ASSM (R) task scores.

Two of the most basic linguistic processes are reflected in the ability to formulate correctly a verbal repetition of the string. The results of this investigation indicate that it is possible to reliably illustrate the dynamic relationships between these processes using a formalized test made up of a progression of transformationally complex sentences. Before a definitive measure can be designed, however, refined investigations on larger numbers of normal, as well as linguistically impaired subjects are necessary. Nevertheless, the results of this study are an encouraging impetus for future attempts to design more sophisticated tests of language development employing the concepts of transformational grammar.

Currently, this author is engaged in studying a specific category of linguistic transformations, conjoining and embedding through temporal links, such as *when*, *while*, *until*, *before*, and *after*, using a revised form of the technique described above. In the revised form, the length of surface structure is carefully controlled (9-10 syllables). In addition, each of the four-time adverb links is used in varying structural relationships (that is, time adverb to constituent sentences), as well as in varying surface structures (semantic). Hopefully, this technique will yield data that, when analyzed, will provide an indication of the subjects' ability to understand and use these particular linguistic relationships.

NOTES

1. N. Chomsky, *Syntactic Structures* (The Hague: Mouton Press, 1957); idem, *Aspects of the Theory of Syntax* (Cambridge, Mass.: The M.I.T. Press, 1965); idem, "The Current Scene in Linguistics: Present Directions," *College English*, 27 (1966), 587-595.
2. A. G. Epstein, "Auditory Memory for Language," *Folia Phoniat.*, 16 (1964), 271-289.
3. P. Menyuk, "Alteration of Rules in Children's Grammar," *Journal of Verbal Learning and Verbal Behavior*, 3 (1964), 480-488; idem, "Comparison of Grammar of Children with Functionally Deviant and Normal Speech," *Journal of Speech and Hearing Disorders*, 7 (1964), 109-121; D. McNeil, "Developmental Psycholinguistics," *The Genesis of Language*, eds. F. Smith and G. A. Miller (Cambridge, Mass.: The M.I.T. Press, 1966); idem, "The Creation of Language by Children," *Psycholinguistic Papers*, eds. J. Lyons and R. J. Wales (Edinburgh, Scotland: Edinburgh University Press, 1967); C. Fraser, V. Bellugi, and R. Brown, "Control of Grammar in Imitation, Comprehension, and Production," *Journal of Verbal Learning and Verbal Behavior*, 2 (1963), 121-135.
4. For sources of tests mentioned in this article, see Appendix.

Neurological Basis of Language in Children

Clement E. Brooke*

THE CHILDREN whose problems are being discussed at this conference are said to have difficulty learning. In the last few years, this group of children has been defined, redefined, and renamed for what appear to be political and administrative reasons, if not by clear diagnostic criteria. The children we study in our clinic at the University of Missouri have been brought to our attention because of their failure to learn well in school. We have concerned ourselves with a detailed assessment of their language in an effort to determine the relationship of language usage to other problems. Clarification of the relationship of specific disorders of language to other learning difficulties might lead to more effective treatment and management.

What do we know of the neurological basis for language? A number of oversimplified statements have been made that were based upon limited experimental and observational data. The data are limited, not because of a lack of effort, but because it is necessary to assemble a massive amount of data before it is possible to form a clear construct of the very complex functions of the central nervous system. Techniques have developed slowly and have depended upon the general development of research technology. Even more important is a dependency upon, and a development from, prior concepts of central nervous system function. The development of attitudes, formulations, and concepts about this fantastically complex set of problems has been slow, and has required the examination of data that has been obtained by very diverse research methods. A useful appreciation of the significance of each bit of data to the formulation of a complex model of function has become essential to progress.

As they are observed in behavior, the anatomical and physiological correlates of central nervous system function are only partially clear. The entrance into the brain of specific sensory information is certainly a complex process, but it is understandable to a degree. When the connections between the central nervous system neurons and the sensory or effector cells are direct, the functions of the central neurons in specific areas can be de-

---

Clement E. Brooke, M.D., is a professor of pediatrics in the School of Medicine at the University of Missouri, Columbia, Missouri.

fined. This is exactly as we should expect it to be. The concept of highly localized and very specific centers for definable brain functions arose as a result of cases in which brain damage was caused by accidents and as a result of experiments with ablation and stimulation.

From here on, the problem becomes more difficult. Those brain functions that involve integration, coordination, or feedback in more complex patterns are not easily assignable to specific localities in the brain. The anatomical location of brain damage in the older child or adult, which results from a direct trauma or from strokes, gives evidence that certain tissue is essential for specific complex functions. Experimental evidence from ablation and stimulation in the experimental animal, even primates, obviously becomes of less direct value as the functions to be measured become more unique to man. The size and extent of accidentally or experimentally produced lesions are impossible to define as accurately as everyone would like them to be. The exact location of neurons, as defined in three dimensions, may vary from one individual to another even though the functioning structures and tracts might bear an almost identical relationship. There is the further possibility that functional structures in different individuals may not bear the same quantitative relationships in what appear to be similar complex actions. Almost all of the well-defined anatomical data has come from cases of older children and adults where one can see the result of damage to a long-established system but not the result of local damage to a developing system. The evidence that we have on the effect of brain lesions on the *development* of speech certainly confirms the general data that exists on localization in the mature organism. However, there is a much greater flexibility in the developing nervous system, which enables it to compensate for damage to certain structures.

As the functions that are being observed become more complex, it becomes necessary to attempt to break them down into discrete, measurable processes. At this level of observation it is apparent that the effects of the the total past history of the subject, the conditions that prevail just preceding the experiment, and even the timing of what appear to be unimportant conditions can result in quite diverse results. Making attempts to reconcile the diversity of results may lead to a new concept of the underlying mechanism, which is sometimes a mechanism that was not even considered when the original model of the behavior being observed was formulated.

The relationship of one set of modulating, integrating functions to another set of similar functions may be looked upon as a third order of complexity. Such relationships are utilized almost constantly in complex learning. The relationship of short-term to long-term memory also must play a regular role in language usage. All of the above-mentioned factors must be related to a series of well-ordered anatomical and biochemical developmental processes, for the anatomy and chemistry of the brain are changing constantly and impressively during infancy and early childhood.

At this point, if one looks for a speech reception or a speech production center, one might expect to find that they are not easily defined or located. The relationship of the temporal lobe cortex to speech and language is now well established; here are located at least some of the necessary neurons for the development of language. However, localization of specific language functions within this region is much less established. It is becoming more apparent that connections between the temporal lobe cortex and the underlying limbic system are involved and that the ability to organize sound perception, relate it to prior experience, and convert it to language is not a function of discrete areas of the temporal lobe cortex alone. The concept of "brain centers" for receptive speech, expressive speech, and language needs to be modified to describe a system of cortical and subcortical relationships rather than a system of highly specific "centers." Such a concept allows for different functions in different parts of the system and also allows for input to the system from other neuronal systems that are less directly involved in the language process.

Functions other than speech are at least partially controlled or modified in this area. Stimulation or injury in an older person may cause any of a multiplicity of language problems, the aphasias in all their variety. Stimulation or injury in the same general area may result in a number of other observable behaviors, such as psychomotor seizures accompanied by characteristic changes in the electroencephalogram, vague feelings, mental confusion, chewing movements, and sometimes behavior that is extremely difficult to ascribe clearly to either *organic* or *psychogenic* causes. The close relationship of the limbic system to the phenomena of arousal and attention is now well established. What at one time looked like a well-organized set of centers for language now appears to have a number of related functions within its circuitry that may affect language but should not be considered a direct part of of its formation.

In the case of the young child, our ability to differentiate among some of the tasks is difficult. The same neurological systems may be utilized in carrying out several functions that we may look upon as having different origins. For example, impairment of an arousal system might obviously affect attention to danger, failure to carry out a sequencing task, or even the conversion of information into long-term memory. In addition, any pathological process that causes "brain damage" may not be confined to discrete areas; indeed, "damage" is more likely not to be discrete. The damage, which in most cases we define by its effects, not by its anatomical location, may be far more extensive than is easily apparent. We ordinarily describe the damage by its observed and measured impairment of functions and not by other lesser changes in function that cannot be distinguished from normal variation. If the damage causes an obvious malfunction of two quite different systems, the distinction is easy enough, but if the two malfunctioning systems are similar or dependent upon each other, great confusion can arise as to the nature of the defect. The susceptibility of brain functions to serious impairment as a result of a pathological process seems to be quite variable. Some brain processes, particularly the newer and most complicated ones, appear to be more vulnerable to damage from anoxia than the older centers that are essential for the maintenance of life. It appears that the process of evolution has been acting for a long time to develop safety factors for critical functions, while the newer functions are still being developed in a flexible but vulnerable manner. The complex of behavioral abnormalities that are often considered to be characteristic indicators of brain damage can be seen in individuals with inborn errors of metabolism in whom all cells are theoretically subject to the harmful effects of the abnormal metabolite. Individuals who appear to have defects of function that are determined on a genetic basis have their abnormalities of function determined by the abnormal production of gene products, which affect developmental or biochemical processes but do not affect behavior directly.

With this kind of a concept of central nervous system function, it is possible to proceed with observations, measurements, and analyses of behaviors that can be related to other behaviors. An inability to understand or produce language as efficiently as others do may affect a child's classroom behavior and interfere with his learning or even thwart an accurate evaluation of what he has learned. However, language dysfunction may be quite distinct from other central nervous system dysfunctions that may interfere with learning. Both problems may be present as a result of diffuse "damage" or as the result of an abnormality of some critical pathway that may be essential to more than one seemingly distinct process.

If one looks at the development of language in young children, it seems apparent that as vocabulary grows, a related ability to use linguistic structures according to the rules that are not formally taught is also developed. As one listens to the speech of some children, who may or may not have other specific learning disabilities, it is also apparent that their speech differs from that of "normal" children. This inefficiency of language use can lead to problems in the classroom, and in *some* children it is associated with other neurological deficits. Our interest lies in determining whether some of the defects that we observe in language use can be ascribed to difficulty in rule use. The study of the defects in language use might lead us to a better understanding of the developmental process or to a realization that defects of language function may be specific for certain kinds of expressions of cognitive functions. At present we cannot postulate that specific linguistic structures and usage have specific neurological pathways or even that they represent corresponding processes. A study of the spontaneous speech of children with language disabilities should provide information that is different from that which emerges from formal tests of vocabulary or of processes that are suggested by existing models. If we can characterize the language of children more effectively by a system that enables us to isolate and examine the process of actual language production, we may be able to determine the nature of the specific neurological processes that go into language production. Only with the clarification of these processes will we be able to say whether a particular child's failure to achieve is due to a communication defect that is distinct from or associated with other defects that are present in central nervous system functioning.

THE CHILDREN examined in this study were not doing well in school according to an informal assessment that was made by the teachers and the school system. A diagnostic category for them is relatively meaningless unless that diagnostic category conveys useful information. Diagnosis may be highly specific and useful in that the term applied gives a listener a reasonably consistent body of knowledge about the *diagnosed*. The information may or may not include etiology. Confusion arises when diagnostic terms cannot be relied upon to describe etiology or when several diagnositc terms are used to describe limited characteristics of individuals. The use of limited diagnostic terms to describe individuals in broader terms or to imply the presence of other characteristics or even the exclusions of other characteristics leads to further confusion. If we are to make progress in studying the selected behavior of children, we must define the characteristics of the children we are studying rather carefully without any implication beyond inclusion or noninclusion in the study.

Analysis of Syntax as a Method of Determining the Linguistic Facility of Individuals

Marvin D. Loflin*
Nancy Barron

MUCH OF THE INFORMATION that is transmitted when individuals communicate is implicit rather than explicit. This paper will elucidate some of the methodological assumptions underlying the linguistic taxonomy that make it possible to compare the speech behavior of learning-disabled children with that of normal children. Learning-disabled children often present bizarre patterns of oral language. Before assistance can be given, in an organized manner, a systematic approach for the analysis of their linguistic facility is necessary. Hence, this discussion will present the assumptions that underlie analyses of this type.

We label the major methodological process *reconstruction.* In its most general sense, reconstruction is the process of adding to messages that which is otherwise not directly observable in the communicating behavior but which is directly predictable by the grammar and context.

We assume that verbal symbols in natural situations of communicative interaction may be divided into three types: phrases, sentences, and discursements. In this study we are excluding phrases and discursements, and concentrating on the ways in which simplex sentences are related to each other within natural sentences. A natural sentence may be composed of one or more simplex sentences. We have further narrowed down our study to center on natural sentences that contain two or more reconstructed simplex sentences.

The discussion that follows elaborates some of the mechanics and details of the reconstruction procedure. Reconstruction proceeds from a transcription of a tape-recorded interview that provides the primary verbal data. (For an account of the transcription process, see Patricia Goodding, "Syntactic Structures Used by Learning-Disabled Children," in this volume, pp. 169-175.) Three kinds of sentences are identified in the transcription: the original natural sentences, fragments, and selected nonverbal communications. All of these are delimited and tagged as sentences in the text.

---

*Marvin D. Loflin, Ph.D., is associate professor of linguistics and chairman, Department of Linguistics, University of Wisconsin, Milwaukee. Nancy Barron, Ph.D., is research associate, Center for Research in Social Behavior, University of Missouri, Columbia.

Natural sentences are sentences in the conventional sense. As given in the transcription, they are in a pre-reconstruction stage of processing and have not been parsed into constituent simplex sentences or reconstructed into fuller forms specifying the implicit information contained within them. They are transcribed in a way that preserves the ordering of the words as they occurred in actual performance.

Sentence fragments are also included in the reconstructed text. A sentence fragment is a sentence that is not fully formed, the missing portions of which are not optionally deletable in normal conversation. An incomplete sentence such as *I want the . . .* is an example of a fragment.

For reconstruction purposes, certain nonverbal behaviors that are public, and are easily provided with a conventionally acceptable semantic interpretation, and that obviously enter the discourse stream, are considered as sentences. Hand-raising, meaning *may I speak*, is an example of nonverbal behavior that is reconstructed.

After these three kinds of sentences are classified within the transcription, we identify simplex sentences within natural sentences. If one conceives of speech as the stringing together of sentences, rather than words, it will facilitate gaining a grasp of the process of determining simplex sentences. For example, take this sentence:

(1) *George made a model airplane and flew it.*

This sentence can be paraphrased as, or means the same as:

(2) *George made a model airplane and George flew a model airplane.*

(The *model airplane* is understood to be the same model airplane in both of its occurrences.) In effect, in terms of its meaning, (1) can be shown to be composed of:

(3) *George made a model airplane.*

and

(4) *George flew a model airplane.*

Thus, (1) is reconstructed with the sentences (3) and (4). The two sentences, (3) and (4), are the simplex sentences that comprise the natural sentence, (1). The simplex sentences of a given natural sentence are all of those sentences reconstructed from that one natural sentence as it occurs in the original transcription. A simplex sentence is a primitive sentential form, irreducible into additional sentences. It consists of one verb unit and one or more noun units. Sentence (1) was reduced to two simplex sentences but the reconstructed simplex sentences given in (3) and (4) are not analyzable into additional sentences.

Reconstruction also presupposes reconstituting into simplex sentences information that is only present implicitly in natural sentences. For example, *you* is implicit in:

(5) *Go home!*

If we go back to sentence (1) we note that *George* is implicit in the second simplex sentence. Grammatical rules make it possible to factor out redundant information in sentences joined with *and*. A great many examples of this kind of grammatical deletion are easily adducible from natural language.

IN GENERAL, the criterion for forming a simplex sentence is the presence of an explicit or implicit verb or verbal. In the reconstruction of the original natural sentence, the words and structures are changed as little as possible. For example, in the following sequence:
    (6) Speaker 1: *Did you take a taxi?*
    (7) Speaker 2: *Yes.*
a sentence is reconstructed for (7). In other words it is assumed that an implicit simplex sentence follows *yes*. The question arises, "What form should the implicitly reconstructed simplex sentence assume?" *Contextual rules* provide the cues for making this determination. First, words already provided by the context, which apparently fit the meaning interpretation one wishes to give the reconstructed sentence, are made a part of the reconstructed sentence. For example, a reconstruction for (7) might be:
    (8) *Yes, (I took a taxi).*
We note that *take*, *a*, and *taxi* were all assimilated into the reconstruction as was the interrogative *did*. (Notice that *take + ed* becomes *took* in an assertion and *take + ed* becomes *did take* in a question.) The process of copying content units and grammatical structures from previously occurring discourse is referred to as *carrying over structure*. The basic criterion is that the relevant sense of the messages exchanged in the give-and-take of communication be reconstructed for each utterance. Taking into consideration the contribution of the context to the ideas that the speaker is encoding or decoding helps the investigator avoid making erroneous assumptions about the communicative competence of the speakers. For example, some people might suggest that Speaker 2, who answered *yes* in (7), couldn't formulate complete sentences because the speaker did not provide the full response, *yes, I took a taxi*, as in (8). However, the context makes it possible to interpret the *yes* response of (7) as the full response of (8). Any normal person who either participated in or was witness to the communicative exchange, (6) and (7), would know what Speaker 2 meant by *yes* and that the *yes* response was appropriate.

The appropriateness of the response with the reconstructed sentence in (8) is easily demonstrated. What if we had reconstructed (8) as:
    (9) *Yes, (I defrosted my refrigerator).*
This response is obviously incongruent with (6). The context carries the meaning implicit in (7). This implicit sense of the utterance is made explicit through reconstruction.

The first step in reconstruction was the identification of natural sentence units, fragments, and selected nonverbal behaviors. The second step was the parsing of natural sentences into full-formed constituent simplex sentences. The third step is that of pairing referents with language pro-forms.

In the discussion of sentence (1) above, examples were provided showing the replacement of *it* with *model airplane*. In the natural sentence (1), that is, the sentence spoken by the informant, the word *it* occurred. In the reconstructed example, (4), the word *it* was replaced with the words *model airplane*. This replacement was made because the words *it* and *model airplane* are assumed to refer to the same real-world object, the model airplane. We display this fact, namely, that *model airplane* and *it* reference the same object, by replacing the word *it* with *model airplane* in our reconstructed text. Making these kinds of real-world/language form equations is a major task of reconstruction.

At the beginning of this paper we stated that our taxonomy was one of sentence types. To this point we have been concerned with discussing some of the assumptions underlying the processing of the transcription into a reconstructed text. Now we will briefly examine the subcategories of the sentence taxonomy, which have been relevant for the study.

IN ORDER TO COMPARE the verbal symbols of learning-disabled children with those of normal children, we must be able to classify each sentence from both groups of children. As we have just described, information present in a communicative event may be categorized loosely into three types. First, it can be *explicit* in the behavioristic sense; that is, semantic information can be overtly present in the communication. Second, it can be *grammatically implicit;* that is, redundant units are deleted according to grammatical rules in a language. It must be remembered that when we say verbal symbols can be grammatically deleted we are viewing the grammatical string from the perspective of our reconstructed sentences. *The converse of reconstruction is deletion.* One way to look upon a grammar is as a set of rules for deleting information from fully formed reconstructed sentences. Third, information can be *contextually implicit* as is illustrated by *yes* in (7), that is, not grammatically implicit, not in the overt message, but inferable from the social or extrasentential context. Our primary concern here is with grammatically implicit information.

Within a natural sentence containing two or more simplex sentences we distinguish three classes of multisentence types: *conjoined sentences, embedded sentences*, and *adjoined sentences*.

In embedding, at least two source simplex sentences are combined so that one source sentence serves a syntactic function within the other. The two source sentences, some parts of which may have identical portions, are in some way altered in the connecting of the two sentences in performance so that one fully formed or self-sufficient (natural) sentence is the outcome of the embedding.

The other two categories (conjoining and adjoining) differ from embedding in that they are associated with connecting links. In conjoining, two or more simplex sentences are joined together by the conjoining links *or, and, but,* or *and/or*. Portions of the simplex sentences comprising a conjoined natural sentence may be identical in the reconstruction and hence may be deleted in the natural sentence. On the other hand, if the simplexes share no subparts the natural sentence may not reflect the results of deletion.

Naturally, conjoined natural sentences may possess different kinds of structures. For every possible different structure-type involving deletion, we must presuppose a related deletion rule for English. For example, for:

(10) *The boys and the girls romped all day*

we might reconstruct (11) and (12) as constituent simplex sentences:

(11) *The boys (romped all day)*

and

(12) *The girls romped all day.*

Because the verb phrase, *romped all day*, has been deleted in (10), we can propose that there is a rule in English that makes it possible to delete identical verb phrases. One of our goals in this research has been to ascertain whether or not learning-disabled and normal children share the same deletion rules. (In this volume, pp. 169-175, see Patricia Goodding, "Syntactic Structures Used by Learning-Disabled Children," for a report that made use of reconstructed texts in comparing learning-disabled and normal children.)

In adjoining, two source sentences are joined by a linking word that exhibits the logical relationships of adjoining links. For this study we isolated ten types of adjoining links:

- Temporal: while, before, as, since, when.
- Causal: because, since, as, for.
- Concessional: though, although.
- Conditional: if, unless, whether, provided, where.
- Purposive: in order to, for.
- Inferential: therefore, as, then.
- Adversative: but, however, nevertheless.
- Additive: and, moreover, furthermore.
- Disjunctive: or, nor, lest.
- Additive/disjunctive: and/or, or (inclusive).

IN SUMMARY, we have presented a brief discussion of a research methodology. The methodology had as its objective the preparation of a reconstructed text in terms of which complex sentence structures from learning-disabled and normal children could be taxonomized for comparison. The taxonomy in terms of which the subsequent analysis took place involved three categories of reconstructed multiple sentence sequences: embedded, conjoined, and adjoined sentences.

Syntactic Structures Used by Learning-Disabled Children

Patricia Goodding*

IN THE ACADEMIC SETTING, the child must be able to use oral language to explain, describe, and narrate a series of ideas in sequence. Even in prereading activities, a child is trained to sequence orally, compare orally, and find spoken language that describes. It is this ability to gain increasingly complex information from oral language and to express increasingly complex information with oral language that is the basis for success in school.

Lack of success in school characterizes children with learning disabilities (LD); an inability to use language efficiently has also been postulated as characteristic of them. To reach an understanding of the reasons for this inefficiency by applying linguistic theory, one must obtain from the child a sample of the sort of language that he might use in a school room. This means that a child must be presented with a stimulus that will require him to reach into his cognitive functioning and find methods of converting these operations into linguistic performances. A study of the linguistic performances that LD children render when they are given the opportunity to express themselves should allow us to make a judgment about their free use of rule-governed behavior.

Procedures

For the purpose of the present study, a representative linguistic corpus was elicited from each of six LD boys; we asked them to formulate language similar to the language that would be required of them in school. Linguistic samples were obtained from six other boys who were the same age and of comparable intelligence but showed no evidence of having difficulties in school. The stimuli that were used to elicit language were the same for the two groups. Sentences were analyzed and compared for the degree of complexity of their linguistic patterns.

The criteria that were established for the purpose of the study were applied to patients who had been diagnosed as LD by a multidiscipline diagnostic team. Positive neurological findings other than soft signs, visual or

---

*Patricia Goodding, Ph.D., is an assistant professor of Pediatrics in the School of Medicine at the University of Missouri, Columbia.

auditory deficits, subnormal intelligence, psychopathology, and cultural or educational deprivation were ruled out as contributors to the child's difficulty.

A second set of criteria was applied to establish the presence of a linguistic deficit. These criteria included a Verbal Scale IQ that was at least fifteen points below Performance Scale IQ as measured by the *Weschler Intelligence Scale for Children* (WISC), reduced language development as reported by parents and assessed by the *Mecham Verbal Language Developmental Scale*, and a judgment of linguistic deficiency, which was made by the speech pathologist.[1]

Six males that met these criteria were chosen for the study. Their ages ranged from nine years, ten months to eleven years, five months; the mean age was ten years, six months. The educational consultant reported that achievement in school subjects was below average for all of the children, even though they had received instruction from the time they were of an appropriate age. None were accomplishing the classwork that is normally expected of children their age, although two were placed in the appropriate grade-level for their ages.

A comparative group of children who had normal intelligence and no language deficits, but who paralleled the LD children in as many ways as possible, was selected. The age limits that were set for the LD children were observed. Normal school achievement was established by school records and teacher judgment. Four of the boys were in the fifth grade, and two were in the sixth grade. None had repeated any grades in school. All of the subjects were considered by their parents to be above average in language development.

The comparative subjects were not allowed to have more than a seven point difference between Verbal and Performance Scale IQs as measured by the WISC. The mean Performance Scale IQ of the LD subjects (113) was equated with the mean Full Scale IQ of the comparative subjects (111). Mean Performance Scale IQs (LD, 113; Comparative, 107) also did not differ significantly. Mean Verbal Scale IQs differed by twenty-six points (LD, 85; Comparative, 111), thus establishing a significant difference in the area of verbal functioning.

Three basic types of speech were elicited: narrative, explanatory, and descriptive. Auditorily and visually presented materials within the expected cognitive development and interest areas, served to elicit the language samples during four separate sessions. The interviewer tape-recorded each child's speech, which was then transcribed into a modified standard orthography.

Grammatically complete sentences were extracted from each individual's script. A sentence was defined as a grammatical form that contains a noun phrase and a verb phrase, the interaction of which produces meaning. Because the purpose of the study was to investigate the complexity of structures used by LD children, only sentences that contained two or more constituent sentences within a natural sentence were chosen for study.

Sentences were analyzed by the process of reconstruction and classified according to the taxonomy that was developed by M. D. Loflin and N.

Barron (see "Analysis of Syntax as a Method of Determining the Linguistic Facility of Individuals," in this volume, pp. 163-167). Each of the 3,943 sentences that were selected for study were designated as "complex" sentences. The remainder of the sentences that were not used for study were designated as "simple" sentences. Occurrences of the linguistic variables in the taxonomy and other relevant variables were established as the bases for comparison of the two groups. The *Mann-Whitney U Test* was applied to determine statistical significance of differences.

Selected sentences and recording time

All of the LD subjects spent a longer time formulating their responses to the stimulus questions than did the members of the comparative group. The comparative group had a total recorded time of ten hours and ten minutes while the LD group had a total time of fourteen hours and seven minutes. In this longer period of time the LD subjects generated more sentences (4,296) than did the comparative subjects (3,580). The comparative subjects, however, generated more complex sentences (2,163) than did the LD subjects (1,780). Statistical significance of this difference was at the .05 level. For the LD group as a whole, 41.4 percent of their sentences were complex, and for the comparative group, 60.4 percent were complex. The statistical significance of this difference was at the .025 level.

The LD children generated fewer complex sentences than did the comparative group. One restriction that became apparent was in the limitation of the number of operations they could successfully complete in order to generate sentences. The LD children were also restricted in the efficiency with which they could perform these limited operations. This was evidenced by the greater amount of time they needed to generate their sentences. The significantly longer time required for sentence generation suggested that a knowledge of linguistic rules may have been present, but many attempts, rejections, alterations, and new beginnings were required before the child could use the rules to generate a sentence.

Consistency of performance

Variability of performance is postulated to be a symptom that is particularly common among children with learning disabilities. This variability was not shown in the session-to-session performances of the LD subjects. The percentage of complex sentences that were generated by the individuals in the LD group was as consistent throughout the four sessions as was that of the individuals in the comparative group.

Certainly the LD subject's numerous attempts and failures before they generated grammatically correct sentences shows some variability in the success of their linguistic performance. However, this is a behavior that remained consistent from session to session. In none of the sessions was sentence generation accomplished with noticeably greater ease than in other sessions. The LD subjects' ability to generate sentences seemed to be at a consistent level when they were presented with the tasks that were developed for this study.

Combinations of constituent sentences

Combinations of constituent sentences within the 3,943 complex sentences were examined in two ways. The first was in terms of numbers of constituent sentences within the complex sentences. The second was in terms of the types of processes that were used to combine the sentences.

For all subjects, sentences that contained only two constituent sentences were most frequently produced. For all subjects, the number of natural sentences in each group decreased as the number of constituent sentences defining the group increased. Few sentences that contained six or more constituent sentences were produced by any of the subjects.

Statistically significant differences between the groups' generation of sentences that contained specific numbers of constituent sentences were shown only for those that contained four or more constituent sentences. In all cases in which a statistical significance was verified, the comparative group generated more sentences.

When percentages were compared, statistically significant group differences were again obtained only when sentences contained four or more constituent sentences; and the higher percentage was generated by the comparative group. However, comparisons produced one difference that was not seen when the number of sentences was considered. When percentages of natural sentences that contained only two constituent sentences were rank ordered for the *Mann-Whitney*, the obtained U barely missed statistical significance at the .05 level. The greater percentage of production of the sentences containing only two constituent sentences was by the LD group. These data indicate that LD children generated a greater percentage of sentences that required only one combining process, although the difference cannot be statistically supported by the method that was chosen for the study.

The LD children seemed to be able to convert representations of two sentences into that of one sentence, but the process of converting representations of three or more sentences into that of one sentence was a task that was too long and involved for their abilities. Combinatory processes operated effectively and frequently over a two-sentence domain, but frequency of operation of these processes decreased over a multisentence domain.

Combinatory processes

If more than two constituent sentences are joined together, more than one process must be used. The same process may be applied more than once, or a combination of processes may be applied. The combinations of processes used to join more than two constituent sentences were examined. Examination of combinations used to join successive numbers of constituent sentences revealed that the LD children used fewer combinations of processes, and they often merely used the conjoining process to add information at the end of their sentences.

In multisentence combinations in which more than one process was used, the LD subjects were unable to use the variety of combinatory processes that the comparative subjects used. The LD subjects formed only a few long sentences, and they did so almost exclusively by using the additive process.

For all of the subjects in the study, a variety of combinatory processes was used if the sentence was short. For the LD children, when the sentences became long, the sophistication of the syntax was not increased. Recursiveness of a previously used rule merely added to the length of the sentence.

Conjoining

All of the subjects in the study used the process of conjoining to combine sentences more often than they used either the embedding or the adjoining process. The comparative group used the conjoining process more times than did the LD group; they also used this process in a greater percentage of their sentences than did the LD group. Although the comparative group used the *and* and *or* mechanisms more often than did the LD group, the percentage of use of these mechanisms was not significantly higher than that of the LD group.

Since all of the subjects made far greater use of the conjoining process than any other process of combining sentences, it seems to be indicated that it is likely to be the easiest way to increase sentence length. The greater use of *and* as a conjoining mechanism suggests that mere addition of information is easier than expressing contrast by conjoining with *or* or *but*. All the subjects in the study chose the *and* mechanism most frequently; the conclusion, however, that this choice was made only because it is easiest is not entirely justified. Perhaps the topics of discussion were not those that elicited the other mechanisms, or perhaps contrast was shown through the use of a process other than the conjoining one.

Deletions

The complexity of the conjoining process is determined by the co-occurrence relationships between sentences and by the deletions that result from the conjoining. The obtained data suggest a hierarchy in the process of deletion.

The differences in the deletions that were made by the two groups depended on the order of the category that was being deleted. Larger and more inclusive segments were deleted more easily. As categories were subcategorized, the process became increasingly complex; and the LD children made these deletions less frequently than did children in the comparative group.

None of the LD subjects deleted determiners (a lower and less inclusive category), although they could delete an entire NP (noun phrase, a higher order and more inclusive category) as well as could the comparative group. No statistically significant difference could be established in respect to the group's abilities to delete an entire VP (verb phrase, a higher order and more inclusive category) but only one of the LD subjects deleted the Object NP (a lower order and less inclusive category, where the Object NP is a constituent of VP).

Deletion of subcategories within larger categories requires the use of rules that make finer differentiations. These rules were not used as frequently, and in some cases not at all, by the LD group.

Embedding

Combining sentences through the use of the embedding process was second to conjoining in the frequency of its use by the subjects in the study. Even though this process was used more frequently by the comparative group, this frequency was not statistically significant in terms of the number of applications of the process, the number of sentences that used the process, or the percentage of sentences that used the process.

The specific embedding mechanisms that were chosen for study were then examined. Members of the comparative group were consistent in a greater frequency of the use of the comparative, the appositive and the *ing* complement. Their greater use of these three mechanisms was statistically significant both in the numbers of sentences that contained the mechanism and in the percentages of sentences in which they chose to use the mechanisms.

The difficulty that is encountered in forming the comparative structure is not with the number of operations that are required for its generation; rather, it appears to be either in the level of cognition that is involved or in the conversion of this cognition to a linguistic operation.

The LD group used the *to* complement in sentences more frequently than did the comparative group, but this greater use was not statistically significant. However, the greater percentage of sentences in which the LD group used the *to* complement reached statistical significance. LD subjects more frequently chose to use the *to* complement than the *ing* complement. The reverse was true for the comparative group. The same contrast was found between the verbal complements that were used by the LD and comparative groups that P. Menyuk reported between younger and older age groups in her developmental studies of normal children.[2]

The use of the verbal complement is determined by the selectional restraints that are imposed on the verb. Many verbs may take the infinitival complement, but they may not take the participial complement. For example, the verbs *have* and *want* were frequently used by subjects in the study as in *You have to learn to float*, and *They want to get the day over with*. Use of the participial complement with either of these verbs, as in *You have learning to float* and *They want getting the day over with* is nongrammatical. Likewise, some verbs may not take the infinitival complement. One subject used the sentence, *He was just worried about them coming back*. If he had said *He was just worried about them to come back*, the sentence would have been nongrammatical. These differences in the use of verbal complements suggest that the LD children were less able to apply rules that observe constraints that are brought about by more subtle properties of controlling the grammatical elements than were the children in the comparative group.

Adjoining

The adjoining process of combining sentences was used least frequently by all subjects. Investigation of the significance of the difference between the groups in their percentage of use of each of the adjoining links revealed a statistically significant difference for use of only two, the causal and the disjunctive. Although the LD group did not generate significantly more sentences in which temporal links were used than did the comparative group, the LD children chose it more frequently than any other adjoining link.

Perhaps the nature of underlying difficulty is the same as that suggested by the use of the conjoining process with the *and* mechanism. Information may be added, and it may be added easily with a link that indicates sequence; but contrast or causality are more difficult because they are based on more advanced cognitive developments or on the conversion of these concepts to linguistic representation.

FOR THE LIMITED POPULATION that was considered in this study, both qualitative and quantitative differences in the complexity of syntax were revealed. The question as to whether the same linguistic rules were used by both groups cannot be answered with an unqualified dichotomous response. Both groups applied many of the same rules, but the comparative group expanded them to a higher level of complexity. Other rules were applied by both groups but more frequently by the comparative group.

The LD children were more restricted in the number of underlying operations they could perform to generate sentences. They used these restricted numbers of operations less efficiently than did the comparative group, as was evidenced by the greater time that was needed for them to generate sentences.

The LD children formed sentences most easily by using the additive process and had more difficulty in showing comparisons and contrasts than did the comparative group. They were able to control time and sequence easily by applying linguistic rules, but had more difficulty in showing causal relationships. They were less able to use the deletions and verbal complements that result from making subtle differentiations in the properties of linguistic elements that govern other elements within the sentence.

The frequently reported variability in performance of children who have learning disabilities did not hold true for the subjects in this study in respect to their generation of complex sentences. During the four sessions, their performances were consistent.

The LD subjects in this study represented a wide degree of linguistic impairment. However, although they were at widely-spaced points on the continuum of linguistic disability, they were a homogeneous group.

NOTES

1. For sources of tests mentioned in this article, see Appendix.
2. Paula Menyuk, *Sentences Children Use* (Cambridge, Mass.: The MIT Press, 1969), pp. 85-87.

REFERENCES

Chomsky, Noam. *Aspects of the Theory of Syntax*. Cambridge, Mass.: The MIT Press, 1969.

Goldstein, Avram. *Biostatistics*. New York, N.Y.: The MacMillan Company, 1964.

Koutsoudas, Andreas. *Writing Transformational Grammars*. New York, N.Y.: McGraw Hill Book Company, 1966.

Loflin, Marvin D., and Nancy Barron, "Reconstructing Classroom Behavior: A Manual," CI-32 of *Technical Classroom Interaction Series*. Columbia, Mo.: Center for Research in Social Behavior, 1970. (Mimeographed.)

Complexity of Spoken Language of Children with Learning Disabilities: Implications for Instruction

Veralee B. Hardin*

THE RESEARCH PROJECT, "Syntactic Structures used by Learning-Disabled Children,"[1] has substantiated, within the limits of the study (six boys between the ages of nine years ten months, and eleven years five months), the existence of frequently observed patterns of language difficulty in learning-disabled (LD) children. Realizing that language difficulties do exist for *these* children, we, as educators, have to make a philosophical choice as we consider language development for the child with learning disabilities. The philosophy that we elect to follow will determine the implications that we can obtain from the above research. We can decide to accept a unique and, what might be considered by some, a less effective means of expression. In other words, we can accept and encourage those means of communication that seem easiest for the LD child to demonstrate and use. Or, we can require a level of spoken language that seems commensurate with the demands of the school setting as it most frequently exists.

Spoken language is the tool that is frequently used to evaluate the acquisition of learning. Certainly, with young children, spoken language provides the most frequently used means of evaluating academic achievements. An educator must determine if children with learning disabilities will continue, despite chronological growth and the accompanying opportunities for instruction, to use language patterns that are not commensurate with the patterns that are required in most school settings. If it is decided that the LD child's language patterns can, in most cases, be improved, the implications that are stated in this article will have meaning.

The research project corroborated certain observations, which have been made by teachers, but which have promptly been ignored. For example, LD subjects spent a longer time formulating spoken responses than did the members of the comparative group. Even when this behavior is observable in the classroom, teachers for various reasons, continue to demand quick responses. Apparently, responding quickly is impossible or, at least, extremely difficult for some LD children. It was encouraging to note that when they

---

*Veralee Hardin, Ed.D., is an associate professor of education and director of the Child Study Clinic at the University of Missouri in Columbia, Missouri.

were given a longer period of time in which to respond, the LD children who were examined in this study generated more sentences than did the children of the comparative group. If teachers can find ways of providing time and if they are willing to allow extra time for response, it would appear that children with learning disabilities can and frequently will generate spoken language.

During this study, however, the children with learning difficulties generated fewer *complex* sentences, regardless of the time that was allowed for response, than did those in the comparative group. Whether or not the complexity of the sentences of the LD children should be of primary concern to a teacher can probably be determined only in relationship to the other needs of the LD child. Since, typically, the LD child is experiencing difficulty with several areas of achievement, priority must be given to those instructional needs that seem most significant to his total development.

The author of the study postulated that one reason the LD children were unable to formulate complex sentences was because they were unable to perform the underlying operations which must be performed before complex sentences can be generated. Perhaps, then, instructional priority should be given to teaching the underlying operations with the assumption that the ability to handle the correlates of language will result in the ability to generate more complex sentences. Obviously, more research must be done before we can describe and define in explicit ways the underlying operations that lead to the ability to formulate complex sentences. Perhaps with this knowledge we can analyze language production and thereby determine the hierarchical development of language in LD children. Unless the underlying correlates are correctly identified, much instructional time will be wasted and the LD child will continue to be frustrated by his lack of success with spoken language.

It has been reported that the LD children in this study made many attempts, rejections, new beginnings, and changes before their sentences were finally generated. Such behavior suggests a trial-and-error approach to language, which is not only time consuming but which also does not necessarily lead to a greater efficiency with language. A study of the reasons that underlie these behaviors might give insight into the most direct route to language complexity for those with learning problems.

FINDINGS FROM THIS STUDY that were specifically related to the language processes of conjoining, embedding, and adjoining seem especially significant. All subjects, both learning disabled and comparative, indicated that conjoining was the easiest way for them to increase the complexity of their language. A teacher who is planning a language program might well be encouraged to stress conjoining initially, since this strength might be used as a step toward the use of embedding and adjoining. This study did, as a matter of fact, indicate a sequence of language difficulty for LD children. Conjoining seemed to be the easiest skill for them to use; embedding appeared as the second most frequently used skill; and adjoining was the process that was used most infrequently.

Since the process of adjoining involves the ability to join sentences with a function word that shows relationships of time, cause, and effect, and makes inferences, it is not surprising that adjoining becomes a difficult process. Many children who have learning problems exhibit noticeable difficulties in understanding relationships. If such concept-skills are lacking, how can the children use the adjoining process in their spoken language? Diagnostic teaching is imperative if we want to determine if the LD child has an understanding of the concepts that underlie the process of adjoining.

The implication from the findings that are related to conjoining, embedding, and adjoining might actually be summarized by stating that the more difficult the concepts are that underlie a process, the less frequently attempts to express it will occur. Some LD children are encountering so much difficulty with concept development that they are not ready to perform linguistic operations. At times, it becomes extremely difficult to determine if a concept is lacking or if the problem lies in translating a known concept into a language pattern. Such a dilemma implies that there is an absolute necessity for a teacher to employ regular, diagnostic-teaching techniques to determine which problems should be attacked, whether they are lack of concept development, difficulty with linguistic performance, or both, and in what order these problems should be attacked.

IN SUMMARY, this study might well be considered one of the pioneer studies in the area of learning disabilities. Many implications for further research seem apparent. To be specific, study should be directed toward the phonological and semantic levels of language. Further study should be directed toward the quality and quantity of the fragments and non-sentences that were used by LD children. Attempts should be made to determine if the language patterns of LD males are the same as the patterns of LD females. Educators have discussed many times, the feasibility of setting up different types of language arts programs for boys and girls who are at beginning school levels because of known differences in their use of language. Perhaps the present study will generate research, which will help us determine if language differences are even more pronounced between boys and girls who have been identified as disabled learners.

Practical implications for educators of children with learning disabilities can also be summarized. By allowing more time for the disabled learner to formulate answers, we provide him with an opportunity to express himself and generate grammatically correct sentences. By realizing that LD children typically respond with short sentences, a teacher can deliberately formulate questions that can be answered with limited language operations. By studying the children regularly, the teacher can use task analysis to determine the point at which underlying competencies break down, and then follow up this study with plans for instructional programs of a hierarchical nature going from concept development to the spoken pattern that will most effectively express the concept.

Such diagnostic teaching should indicate how to assist the children who have learning problems to take sequential steps toward the use of more effective language expression. Above all, this study should dramatize the need for a thorough understanding of the language strengths and deficits of unique groups with learning disabilities. Until we achieve these understandings, we cannot actually implement the most effective and defensible teaching methods.

NOTES

1. See Patricia Goodding, "Syntactic Structures Used by Learning-Disabled Children," in this volume, pp. 169-175.

A Program for Teaching Language to Aphasic Children

Kim Winston[*]

THIS IS A REPORT on one language group that was developed in a speech and hearing clinic for the two-fold purpose of: (1) providing a service for preschool children with specific language problems, and (2) providing a training experience for graduate students in speech pathology. No formal research tools of assessment of before-and-after states, controls, or statistical analysis were used; thus, this is a description of the procedure and content.

The criteria for placement into the group were: (1) normal or near-normal intelligence, (2) essentially normal hearing, vision, and motor abilities, (3) a language problem, and (4) no significant emotional problem as judged by the evaluators.

The group was set up to meet for an hourly session three days a week; each child also received individual therapy on the other two days of the week. The group sessions were held in a large, carpeted room that was equipped with a two-way mirror and a viewing room. The mothers were encouraged from the beginning of the sessions to observe each group and individual session. A meeting was held once a week for the mothers and the therapist to exchange ideas and to discuss the methods and materials used, and the purpose of each. Language development and language problems in general, and discipline and management of their children were also discussed.

These meetings were especially significant to the success of this program since each mother was expected to carry out the specific methods discussed, formally using similar materials at home at least once each day. Therefore, each mother had to become trained as a home therapist. Often the mother was required to work with her child during the individual sessions with the therapist observing her and giving helpful suggestions and corrections. As the program progressed, the mothers became more deeply involved and more knowledgeable about their children's problems, and they offered many helpful suggestions, not only on general management of the

---

[*]*Kim Winston is a speech pathologist at the Cleveland County Guidance Center, in Norman, Oklahoma.*

children but on specific methods for manipulating the materials to introduce or carry over a particular concept.

Each mother was informed that before her child would be placed into the group we would need a commitment from her since she had to shoulder a major portion of the language training. It was felt that a child who had failed to develop language normally, although judged to have essentially intact senses and potential, could not be expected to learn the amount of language he had to learn in two therapy sessions a week without the additional training of a home program.

Although three of the original four children remained when the group terminated some eighteen months later, at least three other children were placed in the group and dropped out because of the mothers' reluctance to commit themselves to such a rigorous involvement.

The ages of the children were from three and one-half years to five and one-half years. Upon entering the class, each child had an expressive noun vocabulary of at least fifty words. Although each child's problem was unique and their performance levels varied for different abilities, it was felt that the group sessions were necessary to provide an interaction between the children and to provide situations to utilize the language learned. Some basic premises were decided upon to act as basic guidelines for the group. These included a very rigid structure in every activity—at least at first—to help control the child's behavior and establish a baseline for learning. Also, since these children were obviously not capable of acquiring language in the normal sense of auditory stimulation from their environment, which included parents, TV, and peers, it was decided that a heavy emphasis would be put upon the visual sense to provide the establishment of auditory skills of receptive language and expressive language. It must be emphasized that this program was begun as an experimental group in an attempt to determine an effective method for developing language in aphasic children; thus, the method was very flexible and was continually altered and revised to meet the needs of the children.

THE BASIC AREAS covered were auditory discrimination and attention, vocabulary building, and visual-perceptual skills. The major emphasis of training was placed on receptive and expressive use of English syntax and morphology, and concepts of cause, effect, and description were gradually utilized.

To increase the children's ability to attend, a routing structure was established. The same task was performed in the opening and closing parts of each session, and the order of presentation of the other tasks remained the same in each session. This approach is not new and unique; it is drawn from various sources including the later steps described in Mildren McGinis' *Aphasic Children.*[1] Again, the emphasis of the program was placed on syntax and morphology, which were introduced through a series of structured steps. It was not assumed that the children would acquire these skills naturally once they had an expressive vocabulary. This was accomplished through teaching the children to read words that could not be readily pictured and teaching them the correct order from left to right. For example, once the child has the concepts of some adjectives that describe such things as color and size, he is taught to read and order an adjective and noun phrase such as *big ball* (ball is pictured), or *blue ball* (both are pictured). Later, sentences are formed, such as *the ball is big* or *the ball is blue*. Each word is printed in small case letters on a separate card, which facilitates the child learning to arrange the words in the correct order. The child first learns to read the cards in response to set questions such as "What color is the ball?" or "What size is the ball?" Gradually, the cards are removed and the child responds appropriately in a set sentence structure to the question. During the clinic sessions and during home therapy sessions, situations were set up or selected to give the child an opportunity to utilize these structures. The children understood at a very early point that a structure rather than a single word response was expected of them. Both the therapists and mothers utilized the same cues, such as "Tell me in a sentence," to elicit the structures from the children during the therapy sessions and in spontaneous situations. Some of the structures that were introduced over the eighteen month period included: the three plural allomorphs and their application; irregular plurals; the three past-tense allomorphs and their applications; irregular past-tense verbs; present-progressive tense; prepositions; opposite concepts such as hot-cold, open-closed; concepts of color and number; subject-verb agreement; all cases of pronouns; demonstrative adjectives; ordering of adjectives such as *two, big, red, balls* (number, size, color, and noun); and future tense. These structures were utilized in teaching cause-effect relationships and description of objects and events. The major concern was whether or not the child could remember the structures he had learned and generalize them into other situations, using different words.

At the termination of the group sessions, one child exhibited normal language behavior, and two others were placed in a public school learning-disabilities class that was geared for auditory and language problems and taught by a speech pathologist. This class was initiated through the efforts of the mothers of these children.

NOTES

1. Mildred A. McGinnis, *Aphasic Children*, (Washington, D.C.: Alexander Graham Bell Association for the Deaf, 1963).

SECTION VI

Early Identification

Early Identification of the Not-So-Specific Learning-Disability Population

Howard S. Adelman*

IN DISCUSSING early identification of potential learning disorders, I wish to make three, brief, general points and then describe the prediction strategy that is being employed in a research project in which I am involved.

1. The population discussed in this paper is that entire group of youngsters who are currently labeled as learning disabled. As an hypothesis, it is suggested that this population of youngsters is heterogeneous, ranging from those who do have major disorders and/or deficits that precipitate learning difficulties, to those whose difficulties are caused, primarily, by classroom programs that are not effectively personalized to accommodate individual differences in development, performance, and motivation.

2. If this hypothesis is accurate, there are definite implications for early identification procedures that are designed to detect this population before the youngsters experience school failure. In particular, it is felt that there are serious limitations with reference to those procedures that are based on a *readiness* or *disordered child* model; that is, procedures that are designed only to assess a youngster's deficiencies with reference to a delimited set of school learning correlates such as perceptual-motor and linguistic skills. Such procedures produce a large number of false-negative and false-positive identifications with reference to subsequent school failure. That is, such early identification procedures do not identify many youngsters whose school learning difficulties are *not* caused by disorders or maturational deficiencies but who subsequently are labeled as learning disabled; in addition, such procedures do identify many of those disordered and/or deficient youngsters who might never be labeled as learning disabled because of their good fortune in being placed in a program that effectively accommodates a wide range of individual differences, and thereby prevents school failure among such youngsters.

---

*Howard S. Adelman, Ph.D., is associate professor, School of Education, University of California, Riverside.

This paper draws upon ideas presented previously in two articles: H. S. Adelman, "The Not-So-Specific Learning Disability Population," Exceptional Children, (March 1971); H. S. Adelman and S. Feshback, "Predicting Reading Failure: Beyond the Readiness Model," Exceptional Children, (January 1971).

3. A viable alternative to the readiness or disordered child model is an interactional model. Such a view emphasizes that a given youngster's success or failure in school is a function of the interaction between his strengths, weaknesses, and limitations and the specific classroom situational factors he encounters, including individual differences among teachers and differing approaches to instruction. Stated differently, this interactional model suggests that learning in school is dependent not only on the characteristics of the *student*, but also on the characteristics of the *classroom* situation to which he is assigned.

With these three points in mind, my colleagues and I have formulated an early identification project.* Basing our formulation on the interactional model, we hypothesize that the greater the discrepancy between a child's skills and behaviors and those required of him in a particular classroom, the greater the likelihood of his failure. As a major implication of this hypothesis, we reason that one effective strategy for predicting failure is to assess the degree to which a kindergarten youngster can successfully cope under representative classroom conditions with tasks that are as similar as possible to those that he will encounter in the first grade. In order to accomplish such an assessment, we are involved in the following:

- Evaluating *in situ* the deficits in, or absence of, school-relevant skills and behaviors, as well as evaluating the presence of interfering behaviors in each kindergarten youngster.
- Evaluating each first-grade classroom program to determine the skills and behaviors that the kindergarten youngster, when he is assigned to that classroom and that teacher, will find critical in coping with relevant tasks.
- Analyzing the discrepancy between the youngster's skills and behaviors and what is being required for success in that first-grade classroom.

A brief description of how these three steps are being implemented should help to clarify this approach to early identification. With reference to the evaluation of the kindergarten children, the specific instrument that is being developed is a rating scale, which consists of items that reflect a recent analysis of the behaviors and skills that first-grade teachers generally require and those behaviors that they will not tolerate during instructional activities. After becoming familiar with the rating-scale items, the kindergarten teachers are asked to observe their pupils carefully over a period covering the last two or three months of the school year. At the end of this time, the teachers rate each child on the items, thereby evaluating the pattern and degree of skills and positive and negative behaviors that the youngster has manifested. (If the kindergarten teaching program does not include activities that require some of the skills and behaviors that are included on the rating scale, then a series of "lessons" are initiated by the teacher so that he is able to rate all items.)

The evaluation of the critical demands of a specific first-grade classroom situation and teacher is, of course, more difficult. We are developing a separate but parallel rating scale, which first-grade teachers can use to rate the

---

*This project is supported by funds from NIMH grant No. MH-16796-01-S1.

skills and behaviors that they view as critical for success in their particular classrooms. We are also developing an observation scale for use by independent judges in an attempt to provide another source of evaluation of the characteristics of these classrooms.

It is our expectation that these kindergarten and first-grade evaluation procedures should yield the following:

- An indication of the skills and behaviors that are critical for succeeding in the first-grade program in a particular classroom, school, and district.
- The level of performance of a particular kindergarten child with regard to these critical skills and behaviors.

These data should permit an analysis of the discrepancy between a specific youngster's skills and behaviors and the requirements for successful first-grade performance. For research purposes, all three levels of discrepancy analyses will be carried out; that is, a separate discrepancy score will be derived from the differences between the ratings given a youngster and the normative rating for the district, the normative rating for a particular school, and the idiosyncratic rating given to the first-grade classroom to which the youngster is assigned.

THE PROCEDURES that have been described here are in their initial stages of development. Nevertheless, it is hoped that the description of these efforts conveys the differences between an early identification approach that is based on a *readiness* or *disordered child* model and one that is based on an *interactional* model.

Before concluding, it is also worth noting that in addition to improving predictive accuracy with regard to school failure, two other benefits can accrue from an approach such as the one that has just been described. First, since the kindergarten evaluation procedures assess aspects of socioemotional functioning, there is an opportunity for a rapid, first-level screening of disturbed children. Secondly, the first-grade evaluations allow for an assessment of the actual demands of the programs in these classrooms, as well as the determination of how closely these demands resemble the first-grade curriculum established by the school district. Thus, it may be seen that the early identification procedures described above assess both the problems of the child and the process by which we teach him, and thereby place concerned professionals in a better position to improve the weaknesses that are in the school system, as well as in the child.

In summary, with regard to the not-so-specific learning disability population, it is emphasized that as less restrictive, early identification models are employed, not only will predictive accuracy be improved, it seems likely that more comprehensive remedial and preventive measures will evolve. At the very least, the investigation of such models should help to expand our knowledge regarding the critical variables that are involved in school failure.

Learning-Disability Children in the Public School Setting

Philip A. Hansen*

IDENTIFICATION of children as Learning Disabled (LD) usually occurs after they have been enrolled for several months, even years, in the formal school setting. Their parents, perhaps, experience forebodings somewhat earlier. Several investigators have examined indices of learning disability in preschool youngsters.[1] However, a record of increasing and inexplicable school failure tends to be the most reliable evidence of learning disability in children.

A recent study by the author has provided new evidence regarding characteristics of LD children and public school programs that are designed to serve them.[2] The study was concerned with LD children in California, where they are designated Educationally Handicapped (EH). In California, a child may be placed in the EH program:

> ... if he has marked learning or behavior disorders or both associated with neurological handicap or emotional disturbance. His disturbance shall not be attributed to mental retardation. The learning or behavior disorder shall be manifest, in part, by specific learning disability. Such learning disabilities may include, but are not limited to, perceptual handicaps, minimal cerebral dysfunction, dyslexia, dyscalculia, dysgraphia, school phobia, hyperkinesis or impulsivity.[3]

Thus, in California, EH (LD) classification is broadly defined, encompassing a variety of diagnostic labels. In like manner, the study revealed a pupil population that was distinctly heterogeneous and that presented a complex chiasma of diagnostic-remedial problems.

The population under study included 253 elementary pupils enrolled in EH programs in fifteen southern California school districts. Sampling procedures ensured representation from a comprehensive range of school district and community conformations. Data described educational, medical, and psychological characteristics of EH pupils, as well as managerial aspects of EH program development.

Philip A. Hansen, Ed.D., is assistant professor, School of Education, San Fernando Valley State College, Northridge, California.

Heterogeneity of pupils

Reports from the professional education staff, and, occasionally, from ancillary community agencies described the sample pupil behaviors in the school setting. Educators reported that most EH pupils (70 percent or more) exhibited faulty production of written symbols, difficulty in attending and concentrating, and an excessive need for attention and reassurance. Fifty percent or more of the sample pupils were seen as displaying faulty perception and distortion of body image, impulsive, immature and/or aggressive behavior, and chronic infractions of school rules. Additional interpretations (30 percent or more of the sample pupils) included speech problems, difficulty in concept formation, poor coordination, a tendency to perseverate, and a tendency to withdraw. Generally, school personnel viewed EH children as lacking competence in language and conceptual skills, which was further complicated by lack of self-control manifested in acting-out behaviors.

Physicians' reports in the study indicated EH children to have had a full range of illnesses and accidents. Trauma experienced by EH children, however, usually involved central nervous system (CNS) and respiratory functions more often than other body systems. Illnesses or accidents involving CNS functions were reported for some 20 percent of the sample pupils. Seven percent had medical histories of respiratory illness. Other forms of illness or injury were reported less frequently. Seventy-one pupils (28 percent) received prescribed medication on a continuing basis. CNS sedation and tranquilization were most frequently prescribed, followed in order by CNS stimulants. Both drug forms were frequently prescribed for use in combination. Medical characteristics of EH children tended to support the possibility of a close correlation between physical problems and learning disabilities.

Psychologists reported that the sample pupils exhibited normally distributed intelligence, truncated at the lower IQ levels due to the legal exclusion of mentally retarded children from EH programs. The discrepancy between the sample pupils' academic achievement and mental ability was equivalent to two years and two school grades. As a result of their psychometric findings, psychologists reported EH pupils to lack the intellectual, emotional, and social maturity necessary for success in the regular school program.

EH (LD) children in California were found to be an heterogeneous group defying precise definition. While similar to their "normal" peers in most respects, EH children simply exhibited more confounding and divergent qualities than could be tolerated in the traditional classroom setting.

Interdisciplinary confusion

As inferred earlier, California's EH programs were designed to implement effective remedial programs without particular reference to diagnostic or etiological classification. To assure wise educational planning for this heterogeneous population, a multidisciplinary approach was encouraged by legislative and administrative action. Education, medicine, and psychology as well as ancillary pupil welfare services were involved. Identification of LD children by interprofessional committees has not appeared to be a particularly efficacious process.

Data reported in this study suggested that interpretations of the sample pupil characteristics underwent mutation during multidisciplinary consideration. Medical and psychological specialists reported that two-thirds of the sample pupils evidenced either "hard" or "soft" neurologic signs of minimal brain dysfunction. Prior to placement of the pupils in EH programs, however, these data were reinterpreted through multidisciplinary action to indicate emotional disturbance. Further, educational planning and prescription were not enhanced by the multidisciplinary process. Prescribed interventions tended to be few in number and to be broad statements lacking specificity and detail (for example, "remedial instruction in a small class setting"). Teachers of EH children reported that the sample pupil response to the remediation program was generally below expectation. The evidence suggests, therefore, that LD children in the formal school setting are continuing to baffle the experts, and that innovative program development as a result of multidisciplinary effort has yet to occur.

AS A NATION, we are committed to programs of remediation for LD children who are already enrolled in our schools. Beyond this, we are seeking to identify and help LD children before their entry into the formal academic milieu. These are impressive goals. Their achievement will require new effort and direction. Based upon evidence contained in this study, the following two recommendations appear warranted:

- Affirmative definitions of learning disabilities must be postulated. We cannot describe LD phenomena by explaining what it is not. Effective special education programs cannot emerge by taxonomical default.

- The quality of the multidisciplinary process must be improved. Professionals from various disciplines seeking to help LD children are working side-by-side with great diligence and little communication. Physicians are understood by other physicians, psychologists by other psychologists, and educators by other educators. Professional insularity must be declared obsolete.

Based upon the "track record" of public education's service to LD children, alternative procedures must be considered. Perhaps early identification is one answer—before learning disability problems become magnified in the school setting.

NOTES

1. B. Keogh (ed.), "Early Identification of Children with Potential Learning Problems," *Journal of Special Education*, 4, No. 3 (1970), 307-365, A. Tessier, "Early Identification of EH Children: Prediction and Prevention?", *California State Federation Council for Exceptional Children*, 20 (1970), 8-12.

2. P. Hansen, "Educationally Handicapped Programs in Selected School Districts of Southern California." Unpublished doctoral dissertation, University of California at Los Angeles, 1970; idem, "Children Called E.H.", *California State Federation Council for Exceptional Children*, 20 (1970), 5-8.

3. State of California, *California Administrative Code, Title 5, Education, Article 3, Section 2320* (Sacramento, Calif.: Department of General Services, Documents Section, 1970).

REFERENCES

Hansen, P. "Where Have All the Labels Gone?" *Proceedings of the Claremont Conference*, 1971. (In Press).

Some Questions About Early Identification

Barbara K. Keogh*

IN A DISCUSSION of the early identification of learning problems, the key word is *potential*. The inclusion of this term provides us with a sharp focus and a new dimension. That dimension involves the possibility of *prediction*. In most cases, identification implies that a condition is recognized after the fact; that is, we identify or recognize that the child has visual problems, or an orthopedic condition, or is not developing at the usual rate. Obviously, in each case the condition that is being identified is already evident. It is also obvious that the earlier the condition is recognized, the sooner the therapeutic or remedial program can be started, and this is advantageous because it occurs at a time when the young child is in a stage of developmental plasticity. This kind of early intervention can often prevent the development of secondary, confounding problems. In such cases, the remedial program follows directly from the nature of the already known condition and is directed specifically at that condition.

However, when we consider early identification of children with learning problems, especially the identification of children with *potential* learning problems, we are talking about recognition of a condition that is not yet there, but which we fear may develop. In this sense, we are more accurately speaking of *prediction* rather than identification of school success or failure. Parents, teachers, and clinicians agree that many serious and long-lasting learning disorders might have been prevented—or at least minimized—if the problems had been recognized earlier and if therapeutic efforts had been started sooner. There is considerable enthusiasm for the establishment of screening programs for children who are in kindergarten or who are just about to enter elementary school; such identification may serve to prevent the development of the failure attitudes and the motivational and self-concept disturbances that are so often associated with learning disabilities.

We are seeking, then, ways to identify, that is, predict, which children are likely to have school learning problems later, and to design appropriate preventive programs for them. On the surface, the goal seems obvious and

---

*Barbara K. Keogh, Ph.D., is associate professor in the Program in Special Education, University of California, Los Angeles.

the endeavor clearly positive. However, given the present state of knowledge in regard to learning disabilities, and the limitations of psychological tests, it might be suggested that a note of caution needs to be observed in the enthusiasm we have for early identification.

Some of the complexities involved in the prediction of potential learning problems, which I have described more fully elsewhere,[1] deserve consideration here:

- What are the outcome goals against which we make our predictions? Good grades—success in a college prep program—enthusiasm for school and learning—positive adjustment to school?

- What early signs or behaviors have predictive validity for later development and achievement? Rate of physical growth—perceptual organization—language—sociability?

- How early is early? If screening at age five is helpful, what about screening at age four, or age three?

- What about the possibility of setting up an expectancy of failure, a "self-fulfilling prophecy" that is already in effect at the time of school entrance?

- Is it realistic or wise to base a prediction almost wholly on the characteristics of the child when we consider the fact that success and failure in learning are so clearly a function of interaction between the child and his environment or setting?

The problem of early identification presents us with hazards as well as benefits. Before we implement across-the-board programs of testing for early identification, we should carefully consider such questions as those that have been mentioned above. We must seek answers that will maximize the positive and minimize the negative aspects of the child's potential.

NOTES

1. B. K. Keogh (ed.), "Early Identification of Children with Potential Learning Problems," *Journal of Special Education*, 4, No. 3 (1970), 307-363.

Early Identification: A Diagnostic Dilemma

Annette Tessier*

IF YOU WERE ASKED to predict which children among those at the preschool or kindergarten levels would have learning problems later in their school experience, what would you look for? The many different replies to this question by various types of professionals who are concerned with early education may partly explain the wide range of conceptions and, perhaps, misconceptions that surround this problem. This dilemma is understandable, especially when we consider that the viewpoints and research on early child development also vary widely. At this point we have many questions and few answers concerning the developmental processes of the early years and their effect on later achievement, but perhaps we can begin to make inferences and draw implications from research findings that may give clues to the early factors that facilitate or inhibit learning behaviors.

There is general agreement among professionals that most serious learning problems do not develop suddenly or capriciously. B. K. Keogh has noted that many children with learning disorders are reported to have long and consistent histories of various kinds.[1] In the early years, measures that often define potential learning problems are generally based on developmental histories, such as physical and psychological examinations. In spite of the use of extensive diagnostic procedures, large numbers of children slip by unnoticed. Perhaps we have relied too heavily on tests and scales without having a clear understanding of how developmental behaviors relate to later learning.

One of the continuous concerns of those who work with young children is how to predict the child's future development on the basis of his past and present behaviors and experience. We are interested in cause-effect relationships between early manifestation and later development. Unfortunately, few reliable predictors have been substantiated.[2] We need to expand our thinking and look at the factors that might suggest other ways to consider the problem. For an in-depth consideration of the predictive variables in major growth areas, the reader is referred to Keogh's "Early Identification of Children with Potential Learning Problems."[3]

---

*Annette Tessier, Ed.D., is assistant professor, Department of Special Education, California State College, Los Angeles.

In a search for predictive factors in the area of cognitive and language development, M. Faust points out that we assume that the "trait" resides in the child.[4] Situational determinants, such as home or classroom experiences, tend to be overlooked, so that the burden of cause lies within the child. An example of this type of concern is manifested by the teacher who continually has to reprimand a child for his inattentiveness. This puts the burden on the child. An important question arises here. Is inattentiveness a deficiency in the child, or could it be that the materials presented by the teacher are inappropriate and uninteresting to this child? Faust suggests that predictability of learning problems would improve if we accounted for such situational variables and studied the behavior that results from the interaction between the individual and the situation in which he is expected to learn. In this regard, other questions arise:

- Are the child's deficits the cause of his learning disabilities?
- Are the child's problems due to the situation in which he must learn?
- Is it the interaction of these two factors that contributes to his problem?

Another factor that we often fail to consider is related to the predictive validity of the behavioral measures that are used in the preschool years. We often use IQ scores to predict the child's future achievement behavior, and even his potential scores on future achievement tests, yet IQ scores that are measured in early years have low correlations to later IQ assessments.[5] B. Bloom's reanalysis of longitudinal studies of intellectual development shows clearly that the stability of IQ measurements increases with chronological age.[6] He concludes that intelligence is a developmental concept, and that the rate of intellectual development is most rapid during the early years of life. Environmental effects on IQ are most likely to take place before the age of eight and probably have the greatest impact during the first five years. The fact that the child is experiencing dynamic changes in these important early years should give us cause to pause and reflect on *all* aspects of development during that period.

K. Wedell's investigations in perceptual-motor development indicate that very little work has been done in tracing the consequences of early individual differences in perceptual functioning on later social competencies or educational attainments.[7] In spite of this, we still look for perceptual-motor deficits during the early years and attempt to make predictions that are based on our findings. Wedell noted in his review that the preschool child's success on perceptual-motor "readiness" tasks was generally predictive of his future *success* in learning the basic educational skills, but he also noted that *failure* was not predictive. That is, children who failed might or might not make progress. This finding may not be too surprising when we consider (1) the variety of ways in which children compensate for their educational difficulties, and (2) the variations in the teacher's skills that foster such compensation.

IT APPEARS THAT there are a number of differential variables that are related to acceleration or retardation in early development. Findings in several studies indicate that some of these individual variables seem more characteristic of boys than of girls. Therefore, it would seem that this area of investigation might offer valuable clues to learning differences, especially since more boys than girls are identified as learning disabled. A review of present research findings demonstrates the presence of sex differences in such areas as achievement behavior, learning, problem solving, language development, and IQ correlates.[8] For example, the extensive studies reported by J. Kagan and H. A. Moss showed the relative stability of achievement behavior from the preschool to the school years for both boys and girls, but particularly for girls.[9] A report by H. W. Stevenson and his associates on learning behavior of boys and girls in grades three to seven indicated that performance on learning tasks was much more highly related to IQ for girls than it was for boys.[10] The boys' performances on these tasks seemed more closely related to variables other than IQ than were the performances for girls on the same task. Stevenson's analysis of the paired associate learning task indicated that immediate orientation to a task was highly related to school grades for boys, but not for girls. Immediate ability to concentrate or to attend may be a very significant variable in a boy's ability to achieve in most school environments. In addition, the teachers' ratings of pupils on the "hardworking" trait was significantly related to performance on most of the diverse learning tasks for boys, but "hardworking" bore almost no relationship to the performance of girls on these tasks. Results from these studies and others would seem to indicate that motivational variables might differentiate good learners from poor learners—when the subjects are boys. N. Bayley's longitudinal data on behavioral correlates of IQ suggests that two to three years of age may be a "critical period" for boys because their IQ gains and losses around that time seem highly related to emotional factors. Bayley stated that "Emotional factors operating at this time may serve to depress or to enhance the abilities of many children, primarily boys.[11]

Differential variables that are related to the sex of the child are among the most important factors to consider when arranging appropriate environments for learning. J. Call, in his consideration of biological and behavioral differences, recommends that girls and boys should be measured for different skills and functions.[12] These studies of sex differences would seem to hold promise for future investigation in prediction as well as prevention of learning disabilities. In discussing individual differences and learning in children, L. J. Cronbach said, "While in principle a unique instructional diet could be matched to (individual) intellectual metabolism ... it will be a long time before we have adequately validated rules that take into account even a half-dozen differential variables."[13]

IN THE LIGHT of these complexities of early identification, we need to reevaluate and expand our traditional approaches to assessment in relation to the preschool years. There is no doubt that efforts to develop scales and criteria for early identification are extremely important. However, we must also increase our awareness of the relevant individual differences and situational variables that influence present as well as later achievements, and we must design an educational environment that will most effectively take the child from where he is to where he needs to go.

NOTES

1. B. K. Keogh (ed.), "Early Identification of Children with Potential Learning Problems," *Journal of Special Education*, 4, No. 3 (1970), 307-365.
2. Ibid.
3. Ibid.
4. M. Faust, "Cognitive and Language Factors," in Keogh (ed.), "Early Identification," pp. 335-346.
5. N. Bayley, "Behavioral Correlates of Mental Growth: Birth to 36 Years," *American Psychologist*, 23 (1968), 1-17.
6. B. Bloom, *Stability and Change in Human Characteristics* (New York, N.Y.: John Wiley and Sons, 1964).
7. K. Wedell, "Perceptuo-Motor Factors," in Keogh (ed.), "Early Identification," pp. 323-331.
8. Faust, "Cognitive and Language Factors."
9. J. Kagan and H. A. Moss, *Birth to Maturity: A Study in Psychological Development* (New York, N.Y.: John Wiley and Sons, 1962).
10. H. W. Stevenson et al., "Interrelations and Correlates of Children's Learning and Problem Solving," *Monographs of the Society for Research and Child Development*, 33, No. 7, Whole No. 123 (1968).
11. Bayley, "Behavioral Correlates," p. 16.
12. J. Call, "Emotional-Social Factors," in Keogh (ed.), "Early Identification," pp. 349-356.
13. L. J. Cronbach, "How Can Instruction Be Adapted to Individual Differences?", *Learning and Individual Differences*, ed. R. M. Gange (Columbus, Ohio: Charles E. Merill, 1967), p. 37.

SECTION VII

The Adolescent

Personality and Reading Retardation in Junior High School Students

D. Bruce Bell*
Franklin D. Lewis
Robert P. Anderson

SINCE IT IS generally agreed that learning disorders are *symptoms*,[1] diagnosis of underlying conditions usually precedes any remediation effort. For example, R. Rabinovitch postulated that reading deficits could be explained by deficiencies in one or more of the following areas:[2]

- General intelligence.
- Specific capacities.
- Developmental readiness.
- Emotional freedom to learn.
- Motivation.
- Past opportunities for learning.

D. B. Bell and F. D. Lewis studied selected variables in five of these six areas to determine which types of problems most reliably differentiated between adequate and inadequate readers in the junior high school age group.[3] No measures of developmental readiness were used because of the students' ages.

The findings regarding the effects of intelligence, motor skills, and social status have been reported previously.[4] In reporting data on motivation and personality, Bell, Lewis and R. P. Anderson employed Rabinovitch's definition of reading deficiency, which holds intelligence constant.[5] However, the data have not been previously analyzed in terms of the relationship between the child's reading performance and his age or grade placement. The purpose

---

*D. Bruce Bell, Ph.D., is a research analyst for the Social Security Administration, Washington, D.C. Franklin D. Lewis, Ph.D., is chief psychologist at the Ouachita Regional Mental Health Center, Hot Springs, Arkansas. Robert P. Anderson, Ph.D., is professor of psychology, Texas Technological University, Lubbock, Texas.

The cooperation of the Beaumont Independent School District, Beaumont, Texas, in furnishing the facilities and students for this research, is gratefully acknowledged by the authors.

of the present study was to examine the personality data in this practical context.

PROCEDURES

The sample of 100 students, which has been described in detail in previous reports,[6] consisted of apparently normal junior high school boys, selected to meet the requirements of a 2 x 2 analysis of variance design; 50 percent were black (drawn from one junior high), and 50 percent were white (drawn from a second school). Half were reading within six months of what was expected for their ages (the average readers), and half were two or more years below that level (the inadequate readers). Thus each of the four groups consisted of twenty-five students.

The measure of personality was the *Jr.-Sr. High School Personality Questionnaire* (HSPQ), by R. B. Cattell and H. Beloff,[7] which yields fourteen personality "factors." It was group administered, and the items were read to the students so as not to penalize those students whose reading level was below that demanded by the test. The reading criterion was computed as an average of the Reading Comprehension and Vocabulary subtests of the *Iowa Tests of Basic Skills*. These scores were taken from the students' school records.

RESULTS AND DISCUSSIONS

Table 1 shows the results of the 2 x 2 analysis of variance: the mean sten scores obtained by each of the four groups, and the levels of significance between the means.

Racial group differences

Significant racial differences occurred on five of the fourteen HSPQ measures: Factors B, F, I, J, and O. On the basis of these findings, the black students, as a group, appear to be (1) more concrete in their thinking, (2) more sober, (3) more tender-minded, (4) more doubting, and (5) more placid than the white students.

The fact that the black students obtained significantly lower scores on Factor B (Concrete vs. Abstract) might seem to indicate that the black students were less intelligent. However, this was not the case. The scores of the two groups on the *Wechsler Intelligence Scale for Children* (WISC) were not significantly different; moreover, Factor B failed to correlate significantly with any of WISC scales. Among the alternative explanations that might be suggested for the differences among the races on this variable, D. H. Ecroyd's observation seems the most pertinent.[8] He found that blacks who are living in ghettos communicate in a language substantially different from standard English. Therefore, the blacks may have done poorly on the items in Factor B because of linguistic rather than intellectual difficulties.

The black students appeared more sober on the HSPQ, as represented by lower scores on Factor F (Sober vs. Happy-Go-Lucky), and in their behavior in the presence of the examiners. According to R. B. Cattell and M. Cattell,[9] Factor F measures a fixed trait that represents, in this study, a stable difference, which may be associated with the relatively higher standing

Table 1

Mean HSPQ Scores for the Two Races and the Two Reading Groups (N=100) and the Level of Significance Associated with the Analysis of Variance

Variable	Racial Group Caucasian	Negro	Level	Reading Group Adequate	Inadequate	Level
Reserved vs Outgoing (Factor A)	5.44*	5.18		4.98	5.64	
Concrete vs Abstract (B)	5.26	4.52	.05	5.14	4.64	
Easily Upset vs Calm (C)	4.80	5.42		4.84	5.38	
Phlegmatic vs Excitable (D)	6.04	5.56		6.18	5.42	
Obedient vs Assertive (E)	5.70	5.64		5.70	5.64	
Sober vs Happy-Go-Lucky (F)	5.56	4.54	.05	4.90	5.20	
Expedient vs Conscientious (G)	5.36	5.94		6.02	5.28	
Shy vs Venturesome (H)	5.14	5.06		4.74	5.46	.05
Tough vs Tender-minded (I)	5.98	7.10	.01	6.32	6.76	
Vigorous vs Doubting (J)	5.28	6.26	.05	5.80	5.74	
Placid vs Apprehensive (O)	5.94	4.96	.05	5.82	5.08	
Group Dependent vs Self-Sufficient (Q_2)	5.66	6.26		6.02	5.90	
Undisciplined vs Controlled (Q_3)	5.24	5.72		5.96	5.00	.01
Relaxed vs Tense (Q_4)	5.78	5.06		5.68	5.16	

*Low scores are associated with the verbal description on the left end of the continuum, whereas high scores are associated with the verbal description on the right.

of the black students within their school.* However, the seriousness may also be, in part, a function of the use of white examiners.[10]

The black readers had a higher mean score on Factor I (Tough vs. Tender-minded), which suggests that they tend to be dependent, overprotected, sensitive, and to have somatic complaints.[11] Since the black students were achieving at or above school norms despite cultural and environmental handicaps, the finding of indications of "stress" may suggest that the black readers are paying a "price" for their academic success.

As a group, the black readers tended to be somewhat more individualistic (higher mean scores on Factor J—Vigorous vs. Doubting). Individuals with lower scores on this continuum tend to participate vigorously in group activities; those with higher scores do not.

Another significant racial difference became evident in Factor O (Placid vs. Apprehensive). Although both groups appear within the average range on this scale, the black students seem to be slightly more placid, self-assured, or confident in their relationships with others, while the white students tend to be more apprehensive or worried.

The picture emerges of the black student who is concrete, very serious, somewhat anxious, and a "loner." He appears to be somewhat more self-assured in his position than his white counterparts. Although none of the racial differences were related to reading when measured against national norms, they may be in part a function of differences in the relative academic achievement of the two groups. The relationship could be more fully understood if the study were replicated drawing samples from all three levels (high, middle, and low) of both local schools.

Reading group differences

Table 1 also reveals two significant differences between the reading groups (Factors H and Q_3). There were no significant interactions between reading and racial groups on any of the fourteen variables.

Factor H (Shy vs. Venturesome) is analogous to the introversion-extroversion concept. The venturesome end of the continuum, which characterized the retarded readers, is associated with activity, overt interest in the opposite sex, impulsiveness, and frivolousness. Since Cattell believes that Factor H is constitutionally determined,[12] the impulsiveness seen in this measure may be the same impulsiveness which S. D. Clements and J. E. Peters observed in minimally brain-damaged retarded readers.[13] Such children may be unable to inhibit hyperkinetic behavior and to assume the quiet, passive behavior which M. D. Jenkinson believes is necessary for the

---

*In order to test whether differences in "past opportunities to learn" were important to reading (see Rabinovitch, "Dyslexia: Psychiatric Considerations," in NOTES), the two schools chosen for the study were quite different in the average achievement of their students. That is, whereas the predominantly Caucasian school had a building norm indistinguishable from the national one, the predominantly Negro school was producing students who read, on the average, two years below national norm. Consequently, the black students who were only reading on an "average" level nationally were in the top 10 percent of their classes locally. Likewise, the inadequately reading blacks were achieving about what was expected in a school two years below national norms.

development of reading skills.[14] The association between venturesomeness and inadequate reading could also be the result of an interaction between the hyperkinetic, driven behavior and the social consequences of such behavior. That is, the children may find that such actions have an attention-getting payoff, and inadvertent reinforcement may make the behavior even more enduring. Regardless of its origin, distractable behavior reduces the opportunity for learning and practicing reading skills.

The retarded readers also obtained lower scores on Factor Q_3 (Undisciplined vs. Controlled). Such scores have been found to be associated with a lack of discipline and self-regard, uncontrolled emotionality, excitability, a rejection of cultural demands, acting out behavior, and juvenile delinquency.[15] Low self-concept among white retarded readers has been observed by others,[16] as has rejection of cultural demands.[17] Again, it is difficult to ascertain whether lack of discipline is responsible for the reading difficulty,[18] or is a reactive adjustment to it.[19]

The significant point is that retarded readers manifest the same personality characteristics on the HSPQ that have been noted by parents, teachers, and physicians. Therefore, this test might be used in conjunction with remediation efforts. Children who have abnormally high scores on Factors H and Q_3 might require psychological as well as educational intervention for improvement of their reading skills. The prevalence of these two characteristics in the group of retarded readers in the present study seems to indicate that they are common in most retarded readers. Practitioners would thus do well to avoid reinforcing these self-defeating traits in their students.

NOTES

1. B. Bateman, "Learning Disorders," *Journal of Educational Research*, 36 (1966), 93-119.
2. R. Rabinovitch, "Dyslexia: Psychiatric Considerations," *Reading Disability: Progress and Research Needs in Dyslexia*, ed. J. Money (Baltimore, Md.: Johns Hopkins Press, 1962).
3. D. B. Bell, "The Motivational and Personality Factors in Reading Retardation Among Two Racial Groups of Adolescent Males." Unpublished doctoral dissertation (Lubbock, Tex.: Texas Technological University, 1969); F. D. Lewis, "Motor Abilities as Related to Reading Retardation in Two Male Racial Groups of Adolescents." Unpublished doctoral dissertation (Lubbock, Tex.: Texas Technological University, 1969).
4. F. D. Lewis, D. B. Bell, and R. P. Anderson, "Relationship of Motor Proficiency and Reading Retardation," *Perceptual and Motor Skills*, 31 (1970), 395-401; idem, "Reading Retardation: A Bi-racial Comparison," *Journal of Reading*, 13 (1970), 433-436, and 474-478.
5. D. B. Bell, F. D. Lewis, and R. P. Anderson, "Personality, Motivation, and Reading: A Factor Analytic Study." Paper presented at Southwestern Psychological Association Annual Meeting, St. Louis, Mo., April, 1970; R. Rabinovitch, "Reading and Learning Disabilities," *American Handbook of Psychiatry*, ed. S. Arieti (New York, N.Y.: Basic Books, 1959).
6. Lewis, Bell, and Anderson, "Relationship of Motor Proficiency and Reading Retardation"; idem, "Reading Retardation: A Bi-racial Comparison"; Bell, Lewis, and Anderson, "Personality, Motivation, and Reading."
7. For sources of tests mentioned in this article, see Appendix.
8. D. H. Ecroyd, "Negro Children and Language Arts," *Reading Teacher*, 21 (1968), 624-629.

9. R. B. Cattell, and M. Cattell, *Handbook for the Jr.-Sr. High School Personality Questionaire*, (Champaign, Ill: Institute of Personality and Ability Testing, 1969).

10. O. Klienberg, "Negro-White Differences in Intelligence Test Performances: A New Look at an Old Problem," *Education and Social Crisis*, eds. E. T. Leach, R. Fulton, and W. E. Gardner (New York, N.Y.: John Wiley and Sons, 1967).

11. Cattell and Cattell, *Handbook for the HSPQ*.

12. R. B. Cattell, *Personality and Motivation Structure and Measurement* (Yonkers-on-Hudson, N.Y.: World Book Company, 1957).

13. S. D. Clements and J. E. Peters, "Minimal Brain Dysfunctions in the School-Age Child," *Archives of General Psychiatry*, 6 (1962), 17-29.

14. M. D. Jenkinson, "The Roles of Motivation in Reading," *Meeting Individual Differences in Reading*, ed. H. A. Robinson (Chicago, Ill.: University of Chicago, 1964).

15. R. B. Cattell, and H. Beloff, *Jr.-Sr. High School Personality Questionaire* (Champaign, Ill.: Institute of Personality and Ability Testing, 1962).

16. R. F. Spincola, "An Investigation into Seven Correlates of Reading Achievement Including the Self-Concept." Unpublished doctoral dissertation (Tallahassee, Fla.: Florida State University, 1960); J. M. Paulo, "Character and Causes of Retardation and Reading Among Pupils of the 7th and 8th Grades," *Elementary School Journal*, (1963), 35-43.

17. G. D. Spache, "Personality Patterns of Retarded Readers," *Journal of Education Research*, 50 (1957), 461-469; R. M. Strang, "The Relation of Guidance to Teaching of Reading," *Personnel and Guidance Journal*, 44 (1966), 831-836.

18. A. A. Fabian, "Reading Disability: An Index of Pathology," *American Journal of Orthopsychiatry*, 25 (1955), 319-329.

19. R. P. Anderson, "The Basis of Underachievement, Neurological or Psychological?" *Elementary School Guidance and Counseling*, 2 (1968) 212-221.

Bridging the Achievement Gap in Negative Learning Adolescents

Kathleen McDonnell*

BY THE TIME an adolescent youngster with learning disabilities reaches the junior high school level, he has acquired a tremendous amount of knowledge. Depending on his receptivity and the opportunities that have been afforded by his environment, he has probably accepted any or all of the following ideas about himself:
- He is stupid—he is not able to learn as everyone else learns.
- He is lazy—he is not able to work hard enough to keep up with his peers.
- He is worthless—he causes much trouble for everyone.
- He is too dumb to learn anything anyway, so there is no use in trying.

Defeat follows him from one grade level to the next. Unless this cycle of negative learning is interrupted, the youngster frequently reinforces his low opinion of himself by giving up the struggle and dropping out of school or by getting into trouble with the police; another youngster may merely continue to widen the achievement gap over the years until it eventually defies all attempts at closure.

The learning disabilities program at Hopkins junior high school, San Jose, California, has found a way to successfully interrupt this negative learning pattern and affect resultant gains in academic achievement and social skills. Twenty-five children, ages twelve to sixteen, were enrolled in the Hopkins program. Their parents provided daily transportation to and from their regular schools for the one to three hours that they attended the clinic. The youngsters were selected from four junior high schools and two senior high schools by the Fremont Unified School District Screening Committee. Selections were based on recommendations made by the children's school psychologists.

They attended Hopkins clinic in groups of two to eleven. There were thirteen children from the seventh grade, six children from the eighth grade,

---

Miss Kathleen McDonnell is coordinator for the Learning Disabilities Laboratory at San Jose State College, California.

five children from the ninth grade, and one child was from the tenth grade. The group was comprised of twenty-one boys and four girls.

Initial test indications

The youngsters' initial scores on the *Wide Range Achievement Test* (WRAT) indicated the following:[1]
- Reading ranged from the first-grade level to the ninth-grade level.
- Spelling ranged from the first-grade level to the sixth-grade level.
- Arithmetic ranged from the third-grade level to the seventh-grade level.

Educational handicaps included poor spatial orientation, language deficits, visual-motor problems, and inadequate social skills. Four of the children were receiving medication. Two children were receiving group therapy outside of the district. Eleven of the boys had histories of behavioral problems ranging from fighting on the school grounds to annoying their classroom teachers with "talking out" behavior and rudeness.

The Hopkins clinic staff consisted of two, full-time certified teachers, a man and woman team. The portable classroom that housed the clinic was divided into learning areas that were separated by bookshelves. These areas were equipped with tables and chairs. Regular student desks were made available to those children who preferred them. The room was carpeted and located next to the driveway to provide ready access to the parents who transported the children.

A close-up of the clinic's approach

When a youngster entered the program, the clinician held an individual conference with the child and his parents for the purpose of acquainting them with the program and with the learning clinicians. Later, one of the clinicians held a second conference with each youngster to discuss his learning problems, establish goals for training, and to plan remediation based on the child's strengths and weaknesses. Individual assignments for each day were written on four-by-six-inch index cards that were attached to the child's work-folder and were reviewed with the child each day. The youngster was encouraged to evaluate his own performance on the tasks and to report incidences of transfer of learning that he noted in his performance in the regular class and at home.

The materials used for training included the *Herr Visual and Auditory Perceptual Training* books, the *Michigan Tracking Program*, Postman's English books, the *Reading in High-Gear* series, the *ITA Reading* series, the *Webster Classroom Reading Kit*, *Botel's Spelling-Writing Series*, *Irving Mathematics Series*,[2] and math and spelling games, among others. The program also included extensive work in movement exploration, which progressed to actual team sports.

The children were discouraged from feeling sorry for themselves and were encouraged to make use of their strong areas in order to develop their weak ones. Considerable emphasis was placed on developing a good sense of humor. The staff promoted group discussion of problems that the youngsters encountered. The children were allowed to move about the room and work with partners or in teams as long as they did not disturb anyone else who was working. Children who worked better while music was playing were permitted to listen to the record player.

The psychology of points

The children were assigned points based on their individual level of daily performance. Each point was equal to one minute of free time, and points were redeemable on Fridays. This enabled the children to accumulate enough points by the end of the week to finish a chess game or request special individual help on a regular class project or test. Behavioral points were assigned separately and were in addition to work points. Behavioral points were designed to encourage the children's social skills and work habits. A shy child might be given points for joining in a group activity. An aggressive child might be given points for helping another child with an assignment. Each child who remained on the "Behavior Honor Roll" for three weeks in succession received a letter of commendation, which was sent to his parents and the principal of his school. Frequently, this was the first good report the child had received, and it went a long way towards building a new image for him.

Youngsters who earned both behavioral and work points were allowed the highly motivating distinction of being a "teacher assistant." This permitted the youngster to help another child with some area of learning. A boy reading on a third-grade level might help a boy who was reading on a second-grade level. One of the boys who was reading on a first-grade level taught another boy how to play chess. Every child was able to help someone else learn something.

Effects of the clinic program

The children attended the Hopkins clinic for seven months, excluding testing and vacation time. Final test results on the WRAT were:
- Reading ranged from the third-grade level to the tenth-grade level.
- Spelling ranged from the second-grade level to the sixth-grade level.
- Arithmetic ranged from the third-grade level to the ninth-grade level.

The most noticeable gains were those reported by the children's classroom teachers. The teachers were asked to indicate in writing, in their own words, what changes, if any, they had seen in the children's performances in the regular classroom. All of the teachers who responded indicated obvious improvement in the following areas:
- Motivation
- Willingness to try
- Study habits
- Behavior
- Ability to get along with other children

The principals of the children's regular schools reported a significant decrease in the number of times these children were seen in their offices. In all except one case, none of the youngsters had been in serious trouble at school since entering the program.

From our viewpoint, as learning clinicians, the greatest gain noted was in the attitude toward self-image. Each child had a new picture of himself as a person of worth, and as such, the child would not allow himself to accept anything less than his best effort.

Nine of the children were returned to full-time regular classrooms at the end of the year. One of our boys reported his progress to us in these words: "My English teacher is really pretty nice. I didn't like her before I came to the clinic, but she's changed a lot." The English teacher reported this boy's progress to us in this way: "Frank used to be a real problem. Now he tries everything, even when it isn't easy for him. He's really a nice boy. I can't get over how much he's changed!"

The negative learning cycle was broken, and the achievement gap was beginning to close.

NOTES

1. For sources of tests mentioned in this article, see Appendix.
2. For sources of materials mentioned in this article, see References.

REFERENCES

Adler, Irving. *Mathematics Series*. New York, N.Y.: Golden Press, 1969.

Botel, Morton, et al. *Spelling and Writing Patterns Series*. Chicago, Ill. Follett Publishing Company, 1968.

Geake, Robert. R., and Donald E. Smith. *Michigan Tracking Program*. Ann Arbor, Mich.: Ann Arbor Publishers, 1962.

Herr, Selma E. *Perceptual Communications Skills Series*. Los Angeles, Calif.: Instructional Materials and Equipment Distributors, 1969.

Kottmeyer, William and K. Ware. *Webster Classroom Reading Clinic-10X*. Manchester, Mo.: Webster Division, McGraw-Hill Book Company, 1967.

Pittman, Sir James. *ITA Breakthrough Series*. New York, N.Y.: ITA Publications, 1967.

Postman, Neil, Harold Morine, and Greta Morine. *Discovering Your Language*. New York, N.Y.: Holt, Rinehart and Winston, Inc., 1967.

Wollman, Myron. *Reading in High-Gear*. Chicago, Ill.: Science Research Associates, Inc., 1965.

Learning-Disabled Children at the Secondary Level: Educational Programing in Perspective

J. Gerald Minskoff*

IN OUR NATION'S public schools, there are two levels of education that have received only minimal attention: preschool and secondary education for children with learning disabilities. In recent years, however, there has been a growing attempt to provide relevant preschool education for the young, handicapped child through (1) activities of national legislation, such as The Handicapped Children's Early Education Assistance Act of 1968, (2) modification of state and local codes, such as Connecticut's Public Act, No. 627, and (3) initiation of Headstart Programs. Generally, our current knowledge indicates that enhancing the childs' readiness and providing him with early stimulation and care leads to a more successful and integrative life, both in school and afterwards. As a result, many significant innovations have been fostered in preschool education. However, there have been few attempts at providing relevant educational services for older learning-disabled children.

Traditionally, special education has focused on the middle-age range of children with learning disabilities. We know that it is during this period of time that these children's problems become too blatant to be ignored. Typically, they have been placed in special classes or given special remedial teaching while continuing in their regular classes.

When learning-disabled children go on to junior or senior high school, such special education services are often discontinued, although they are still needed. In some cases, learning-disabled children at the secondary level are given existing services that do not fit their needs; a learning-disabled child of average intelligence may be placed in a class for the mentally retarded, or a child with a severe reading disability may be given a heavy dosage of industrial arts. Realistic planning and programing have suffered because of the slowness and general confusion that permeates educators' and administrators' approaches to providing appropriate services. Obviously, we must recognize that minimal modification of the school day is often not enough.

---

*J. Gerald Minskoff is professor of education at Southern Connecticut State College, New Haven.

Furthermore, the usual methods and models of remedial reading or rigid, special class programing are not the answer.

The time for action is overdue. We must now create specific programs for learning-disabled children at the secondary level. We need to apply here the same force, motivation, and attention we have begun to muster in meeting the needs of the young child. However, before appropriate programs can be started, educators must first conceptualize the nature and purposes of these programs. This discussion is an attempt to stimulate such conceptualization. I have no way of providing definitive answers here; rather, I can only hope that this discussion will open up some further dialogue on this topic.

It is safe to say that no one kind of curriculum is best for all learning-disabled children at the preschool, elementary, or secondary levels. Children differ in their learning patterns and characteristics. Therefore, one type of curriculum cannot and should not be designated to meet the needs of all learning-disabled children.

THREE CURRICULUMS FOR THE LEARNING DISABLED

I would like to suggest that there are at least three methods or curricular approaches that might benefit many children with learning disabilities. These approaches recognize that, among these children, there are many different kinds of learning problems. At the risk of generalizing, let us assume a continuum of curriculums that ranges from one point with maximum special considerations, *Curriculum A*, to another point with minimal special considerations, *Curriculum C*.

Curriculum A — Sheltered Workshop Approach

The types of children who might best profit from this curriculum are (1) those who are severely learning disabled *and* emotionally disturbed, and (2) those who have a severe disability in social functioning, such as children who cannot "read the signs" of social interaction and have acquired little, if any, social knowledge. Although many such children have IQ's that measure above the retarded level, their observable behavior often appears to be retarded. At the elementary level, these children were probably placed in special classes for the learning disabled, emotionally disturbed, or mentally retarded.

Curriculum A would be *analogous* to a sheltered workshop but not necessarily the same as a sheltered workshop environment. These two types of children need a highly structured, but more simplified and less stressful environment than is needed by other children. Training in social learning that is related to a job and general functioning in the adult world would be given in such subjects as, how to act during a job interview, and what to do if a co-worker makes fun of you. In addition, there would be training for specific types of jobs that these children might eventually be expected to hold. It is important to recognize that if they are not provided with such a curriculum, these children might possibly never hold a job.

Curriculum B — Vocational Education

Children receiving training in this group would be of average intelligence but would not have potential for college. They would be children who do not have social problems, who get along fairly well, and who *can* learn at a rate, quantity, and level that is superior to that of the children in *Curriculum A*. However, they might have learning disabilities in perceptual or academic areas, which have not been ameliorated. Here again, we must suit our objectives for each child according to his strengths. Examples of children who need this curriculum would be a sixteen-year-old boy who reads at the second-grade level, or a seventeen-year-old girl who has a severe auditory perception problem.

The essence of this curriculum is to fit each child's learning characteristics to specific types of jobs and functions. The child would be trained for jobs that interest him and that would use his strengths and aptitudes. For example, the sixteen-year-old boy who has a severe reading disability might be trained in a trade or a set of skills that require little reading. The seventeen-year-old girl, who has the auditory perception problem might be trained as a file clerk or in some similar occupation that requires little use of auditory abilities.

Curriculum C — Precollege

The children receiving training at this end of the continuum would probably be intellectually superior to the previous two groups of children, yet they would still have learning disabilities. However, these disabilities may not be extreme, and the child may have developed ways of compensating. Furthermore, such disabilities might even be ameliorated. Here, we have the child who may even have appropriate perceptions about his own disability but who has not quite overcome the problem by the time he has reached adolescence or young adulthood. Examples of children requiring this curriculum might be a boy with an IQ of 135 who reads extremely slowly because he says each word to himself, or a boy with an IQ of 150 who has a visual-perception problem.

The curriculum for such children would be the regular precollege course. However, their areas of weaknesses would be taken into consideration and circumvented. For example, the boy who reads extremely slowly would not be given timed assignments or tests, while the boy with the visual-perception problem would be steered away from such courses as geometry and geography.

Generally, once the three curriculums are set, it is necessary to determine which learning-disabled child is to receive which curriculum. Obviously, the use of the IQ alone is not sufficient. It is necessary to determine a child's pattern of strengths and weaknesses in such areas as social integration, language, reading, problem solving, perception, motor skills, and arithmetic. Obtaining such a profile on a learning-disabled child is often difficult; nevertheless, it is absolutely necessary for effective educational programing at any level.

ROLE OF REMEDIATION AT THE SECONDARY LEVEL

Presumably, the philosophy underlying most programs for learning-disabled children at the preschool and the elementary levels is to work intensively on the child's disabilities while teaching through his abilities. This philosophy is appropriate for children below the secondary level, but it may not be appropriate for children at the secondary level. Most learning-disabled children at the secondary level will be in school for only two or three more years. Therefore, *time* becomes a major consideration in determining the role of remediation in a secondary curriculum. There may not be time to try to remediate a child's learning disability *and* build in the necessary skills and knowledge, which he needs to function after he leaves school. Another consideration in determining the role of remediation is that it becomes increasingly more difficult to remediate a child's learning disability as he grows older. This is due to at least two factors: (1) the great amount of prerequisite learning, which must be mastered by the older learning-disabled child, and (2) the emotional overtones often associated with the learning problem that make remediation more difficult. Therefore, when faced with the choice of concentrating on remediation of learning disabilities or direct input of knowledge through intact areas, it is necessary to choose the latter as the major point of emphasis in a secondary curriculum. Perhaps in the next five to ten years our educational technology and multimedia resources will enable us to provide the necessary remediation and compensation simultaneously.

In order to develop the learning-disabled child's knowledge, we must utilize the advanced technology that is available for use in other areas of special and regular education. For example, the adolescent with learning disabilities could benefit from training that utilizes accelerated tapes that are used for the blind, or film loops and movies for input of textbook data, or tape recorders for classroom lectures and discussions. The traditional textbook and test-taking approaches of many secondary schools cannot always be successfully used with learning-disabled children. Creative changes that allow for maximum mastery of information must be implemented.

In this discussion I have not mentioned specific logistics for instituting secondary programs for the learning-disabled. The following are a few of the logistical variables:

- The enlightenment of public school administrators about the needs of older learning-disabled children.
- Training teachers in the specific types of curriculums or in just one type of curriculum.
- Integration of the special curriculums into the high school setting.
- Alteration of the standard requirements for graduation of the learning-disabled child.

These matters only become important after the purposes, nature, and philosophy of secondary curriculums are fully conceptualized. Coping with the "here and now" problem requires a compensatory type of education for children who are moving rapidly into adulthood. The best methods for combining compensation with remediation need to be brought clearly into focus as a high educational priority. We are far from this goal, but we are beginning to aim in the right direction.

SECTION VIII

Teacher Training

Teacher Certification in Learning Disabilities

Harold J. McGrady*
Margaret Atchison

THE FIELD OF LEARNING DISABILITIES has grown so rapidly within the past few years that there has been little time for self-appraisal. It is now time to step back and say, "What kinds of standards are we setting for ourselves?" Any profession that can truly regard itself as a profession must have an adequate and appropriate set of standards for its members to meet. This may be the one characteristic that makes an occupation qualify as a profession—the establishment and maintenance of standards of conduct, ethics, and qualifications for competence. It is to the latter that we will address ourselves.

Qualifications for competence are typically represented in some form of certification, issued by some formal organization considered to have the appropriate authority. Our concern in this presentation will be with teacher certification in the field of learning disabilities. That it is needed has been established. A professional needs to be more than "just interested" in or "dedicated" to his field; he must have developed a series of competencies to perform his responsibilities. We cannot survive as a profession with just "dedicated incompetents." We must have dedication *and* competence.

Are we satisfied that in the U.S. today we have standards, guidelines, and safeguards that guarantee that the teachers who teach children with learning disabilities are qualified to do so? Let us see what the picture is.

In order to determine certification standards for teaching children with learning disabilities throughout the U.S., letters were sent to each of the fifty states and the District of Columbia requesting information regarding the current status of the states' requirements. These letters were sent in April and June of 1970. The response was unanimous, so that the data we will discuss are complete. For this we thank the representatives in the various states who provided us with their then-current regulations. We must point out now that many states were in periods of change regarding their certification stand-

---

*Harold J. McGrady, Ph.D., is director of the Learning Disabilities Program, Department of Communicative Disorders, Northwestern University, Evanston, Illinois. Mrs. Margaret Atchison is currently a doctoral student in Learning Disabilities at Northwestern University.

ards. Therefore, our analysis will not reflect the exact status of teacher certification in learning disabilities as of this moment, rather its status as of nine-twelve months ago. However, it does indicate some important trends. In cases where a state noted that changes were being made, we have considered that in our analysis.

In reviewing the information obtained, it is obvious that uniformity of certification requirements for teaching children with learning disabilities is noticeably absent. An attempt to organize the present data revealed the following four major categories for teaching certification:

- Seven states require only a provisional or standard state-approved teaching certificate.
- Four states require some coursework in addition to an approved teaching certificate.
- Nine states require a special education teaching certificate.
- Twenty-two states require a specific special education certificate, which can be further organized into these three specific areas:
    1. Four states require certification in teaching the physically handicapped.
    2. Two states require dual certification in teaching the emotionally disturbed and learning disabled.
    3. Sixteen states require certification in specific learning disabilities.

At the time of our survey, seven states required that prospective teachers in learning disabilities meet the certification standards for a provisional or standard teaching certificate. In some instances this alone suffices to teach learning-disabled children. There are many variations on this theme, however. One state allows a regularly certified teacher to teach in the field of learning disabilities if she simply provides a letter stating the intent to accumulate several hours of credit in the area of special education; another state will employ teachers for learning-disabled children if they "demonstrate a sincere interest in the field" and have done extensive reading in the area. One state favors teachers with strong elementary education backgrounds, but prefers those with some training in remedial reading. There are some states that require coursework in special education in addition to the regular teacher's certificate. In most instances, it is stipulated that the special education courses be in the learning disabilities area.

Some states have opted for broad general training in special education. This may or may not include specific course work in learning disabilities. Altogether, the requirements of twenty states fit into our first three categories—general education, general education plus coursework in special education, or special education in a broad sense.

There are twenty-two states that certify teachers specifically in learning disabilities (LD). These, too, represent a spectrum, largely influenced by a variety of notions about what the field of learning disabilities really is. For example, some states certify for specific learning disabilities under the category of physically handicapped, indicating a tie to the neurological nature of LD; some states have built their certification for LD in close tie with certification for emotional disturbance or behavior disorders, but the predominant number of states in this category are certifying LD as a totally separate area of special education (sixteen states). There are, of course, some states with no formal programs for learning disabilities.

It can be seen from an overall view of certification for LD in the U.S. that it is patchwork. Requirements vary significantly among states, ranging from specific course sequences to very unstructured requirements. If we were to examine requirements for amounts and types of practical experience, graduate versus undergraduate training, uniformity of theory and practice, and other important qualitative controls, we would again see extreme variations.

The primary intent of this survey was to obtain data regarding certification requirements in the area of learning disabilities throughout the U.S. Our interest, however, was not limited to quantifying and classifying the information but sought to draw from the data some implications for the education of the learning-disabled child, as currently defined by the U.S. Office of Education.

Although certification requirements are not uniform throughout the country, a majority of states are funding programs for the learning-disabled child and have adopted frames of reference operating on that definition. However, it should be noted that a well-defined classification system is not consistent from state to state despite a general concurrence on such a definition of the learning-disabled child. Howard Adelman, of the University of California, has stated this very well: "Despite all that has been written about children with learning disabilities in the last several years, neither the nature nor the heterogeneity which exists in this population has been widely discussed in the literature."[1] In training and certifying teachers of LD children, this heterogeneity must be taken into consideration.

WE HAVE NOTED that the educational needs of the learning-disabled child have been recognized. Individuals who are aware of these children's particular educational needs realize that they cannot function maximally in a learning situation governed by traditional teaching methods. Alternative techniques are fundamental to their achievement. Yet individuals teaching in some learning-disability programs throughout the U.S. at this time are required only to meet the standards for a general education certificate, standards which themselves are often under scrutiny. Our assumption is that teachers prepared for general education have mastered those skills and competencies necessary for successful teaching in a regular classroom—but are not necessarily qualified as learning-disability specialists. If it is accepted that the learning-disabled child requires alternatives in instruction, can it be assumed that alternatives can be offered by teachers trained in traditional teacher-education programs? Programs implemented under general education certification should be appraised to determine if some children with learning disabilities can be offered an alternative approach to learning in the regular classroom setting.

Another caution regarding programs in this category of certification may be a tendency to meet the learning-disabled child's educational needs through a tutorial approach rather than diagnostic or clinical teaching. Tutorial situations may be effective if we accept the premise that "if he doesn't get it—try again." All too often, however, children who have not mastered the requisite skills to progress through our education system have been retained.

One might argue at this point that suitable learning situations can and do exist without benefit of a specially trained learning-disabilities teacher. However, we must question if it is possible to abstract from principles for teaching the "normal" child, the necessary techniques specifically applicable to a variety of learning disabilities. And, if indeed, teachers with such skills do exist, can we generalize that all teachers trained in a similar manner have this capability?

What about certification in other areas of special education? Would a general education background be sufficient to qualify a teacher to work with the mentally retarded, with the deaf, or with the physically handicapped? If we answer this question negatively, then can we exempt the area of teaching children with learning disabilities from specific training criteria?

Another category under which certification for learning disabilities is offered is special education. Persons certified under the criteria established in this category are qualified to operate in all areas of special education. Certification for learning disabilities through this channel may be appropriate if it can be demonstrated that areas of exceptionality are not mutually exclusive. However, establishing separate categories of special education, such as mentally retarded, emotionally disturbed, and learning disabled, may be considered in contradiction to a general special education certification. Differentiating educational needs should presuppose a need for differential teacher-training and certification.

The following questions might be raised regarding certification in "special education":

- To what extent can an overview be considered sufficient preparation in developing teacher competencies in a specific area of exceptionality?
- Assuming that a field experience is provided in the training program, how applicable is that experience from another area of exceptionality to learning disability?
- Might it not be more realistic to train for a variety of areas, recognizing that learning-disability classrooms are not limited in the types of problems presented? This is the primary argument for broad special education certification and training.

CERTIFICATION for teaching learning-disability children is also offered in the areas of teaching the emotionally disturbed and the socially maladjusted. Recognizing that many children with learning disabilities have concomitant behavior disorders, teachers proposing to enter the field of learning disabilities do need to develop some competency in the areas of social and emotional adjustment of children. However, it is questionable that training for learning disabilities should be limited to the scope of emotional problems. It is probably an erroneous assumption that *all* learning-disabled children present emotional disorders to such an extent that teacher training should be restricted solely to that area of exceptionality. There is also confusion in some instances as to whether the behavior disturbance is the cause or the effect of the learning disability. Concentration in developing competency in handling emotional problems will tend to direct attention to problems other than in the area of learning. Therefore, with such concentration, you have no longer provided a suitable alternative for teaching the learning-disabled child.

Although we recommend specific certification for the learning disabilities field, we recognize the need for familiarity and competency in handling behavior problems that may accompany a learning disability. However, this training can be kept in appropriate perspective to the needs of the learning-disabled child, and training may be accomplished within the framework of a learning-disabilities program.

It is obvious that we have not as yet developed consistent certification standards for LD in the U.S. If we are to develop appropriate certification for teachers of children with learning disabilities, this certification must correlate with what teachers are expected to do. Let us look briefly at a summary of what the roles and functions of the LD teacher have been construed to be (as per the 1969 Tucson Conference on LD):

- Assessment
    1. Observational skills.
    2. Testing skills.
    3. Interpretative skills.
- Program planning and implementation (use of available resources: people and materials)
    1. Basic instructional skills (individualize).
    2. Curriculum skills (develop, select, adapt, apply, and evaluate methods and materials for academic skills and sensory, perceptual, motoric, cognitive, language, social, and emotional functions).
    3. Classroom management skills.
    4. Interpersonal skills.

Several conclusions seem warranted. If a person is to be competent in all of the tasks mentioned, he requires *comprehensive* training. We cannot expect superficial inservice or preservice training to accomplish this level of comprehension, since "one workshop does not a learning-disabilities teacher make," nor does one course, nor does extensive reading (formal or informal) To be competently trained, one needs accompanying practical experiences, a preceptor, for example, and competent supervision of teaching. In essence, we must insure that comprehensive, integrated training is given to prospective learning-disabilities teachers.

We are not currently meeting this need. Although we would not want our appendix removed by someone who has just had a short course in appendectomy, we are often willing to place untrained, partially trained, or poorly trained persons in positions dealing with our children. Something must be done about this on a national level. We sincerely hope that the burden of any reforms or improvement will be taken up by the appropriate professional organizations. The learning-disabilities field is in need of quality control.

NOTES

1. Howard Adelman, "The Not So Specific Learning Disability Population," *Exceptional Children,* 37, No. 7 (March 1971), 528-533.

Description of a Secondary SLD Teacher-Training Program and its Clientele

Shirley Pearl*

THE EDUCATIONAL Professional Development Act (EPDAB2), a federally funded program, was designed to train twenty people with bachelors' degrees to become secondary learning-disability (SLD) teachers. The project was jointly sponsored by the St. Paul public schools, the University of Minnesota, and the Minnesota Department of Public Instruction. Upon successful completion of this nine-month training program, the trainees became certified SLD teachers by the Minnesota Department of Public Instruction.

The goals of this project were twofold: to attempt successful intervention with secondary students who displayed serious learning difficulties, and to train graduates with bachelors' degrees to be effective SLD teachers.

The twenty trainees, who were selected jointly by the special education staff of the University of Minnesota and the St. Paul public schools, received intensive instruction during the first half of the training program and actual teaching experience during the second half of the program.

There were two separate training situations during the first half of the program, which began on September 3, 1969 and concluded on January 22, 1970. Both training situations took place in classrooms at Como junior high school in St. Paul. The initial instruction, provided by both the St. Paul public school staff and university professors, consisted of lectures, sensitization experiences, demonstrations, and field trips. Later, instruction was a simulated tutorial situation for each trainee working separately with two different Como junior high school students, designated by the staff as secondary learning-disabled. The twenty trainees met daily with forty SLD students from November 10, 1969 to January 22, 1970. Thus, each trainee had two SLD students: one student who was seen for an hour in the morning, and another student who was seen for an hour in the afternoon. The remainder of the day was spent in direct instruction with university professors in remedial academics, curriculum preparation, and in feedback sessions from super-

---

Shirley Pearl directs the Behavior Learning Center of the St. Paul public schools in Minnesota. The author expresses her appreciation to Pat Will, special education teacher, for tabulating the data and preparing the graphs that appear in this article.

visors who were observing the trainees during their tutoring sessions. During the nine months of the program, the trainees were taking regular graduate courses on campus at the university.

During the second half of the training program, that began on January 26, 1970 and concluded on May 22nd, the nineteen trainees (one student had dropped out of the program because of illness) were placed in eight secondary schools in St. Paul, which service approximately 285 secondary learning-disabled students. Three of these schools were high schools, and the trainees were sent in teams of two, three, and four. The eight schools were a mixture of inner-city, fringe area, middle-class, and upper-middle class schools. Trainee placement preferences were assigned whenever possible but the staff placed at least one assertive trainee in each of the eight schools.

In the schools to which they were assigned, the trainees assisted in screening the students. They did all the testing, and made the final selection of students whom they judged were most severely learning-disabled. The school counselor and classroom teachers made referrals to the trainees, which was based on a checklist of characteristics of the SLD student that was provided for each teacher. Trainees examined the standardized achievement test scores of students who were in the lowest 10 percent of their class in reading comprehension or vocabulary, hunting for discrepancies between verbal and quantitative measures. On-the-job testing in the diagnosis of reading disabilities was supervised by a university professor in each of the eight schools.

Each trainee taught a maximum of fifteen SLD pupils weekly, teaching half-days from 8:30 a.m. to 12:30 daily. Trainees were given three classes and one preparation period daily. Group sessions on Thursday and Friday afternoons continued throughout the remainder of the training program to provide cohesion and short-courses in areas of immediate concern to the trainees.

SUPERVISION OF TRAINEES was provided by the coordinator of the project, two doctoral candidates in educational psychology, and a staff member, all provided by the University of Minnesota. One of these supervisors was extremely competent in the area of curriculum production, vocabulary development, language experience and reading comprehension for secondary students. The other was competent in the area of behavior management techniques ranging from counseling techniques, contingency contracting to token-economy approaches. The third person was competent in the area of task analysis and the development of instructional objectives. These three people and the coordinator visited the eight schools regularly, then met weekly with a professor of teacher-supervision at the university to discuss the progress of the trainees and ways of improving supervision and instruction. Ideas for short courses and consultants emerged from these supervisory meetings in order to provide trainees with specialized techniques or demonstrations with their students. It was found that most trainees needed additional help in managing behavior of disruptive students, individualizing instruction for each member of the class, keeping the kinesthetic modality in their teaching, involving students and their interests and concerns in curriculum offerings, keeping the learning tasks relevant and varied, yet integrated, and developing activities and games to use in reinforcing rote skills. Short courses were provided in all of these areas.

Trainees submitted weekly progress reports to their principal and to the project coordinator. This was to keep the principal informed of what they were doing and what specific difficulties and successes they were encountering. It also gave the coordinator and her supervisors a quick overview of the week's activities in each of the eight schools. In addition, the coordinator sent out weekly newsletters that shared the events at other schools with the trainees and the supervisors' reactions to the ongoing instruction. Facts and announcements were also dispersed through this weekly newsletter.

Trainees were asked to gather pre- and post-data on their fifteen students using the Jastak *Wide Range Achievement Test* (WRAT)[1] for word recognition scores. In addition, they were asked to fill out a form that requested a description of the kinds of children, the kinds of learning blocks, the kinds of instructional materials used, and the kinds of progress that they subjectively felt their students made. The purpose of gathering such data was more for the purpose of training the trainee than for the evaluation of pupil progress. It was assumed that not much pupil progress could be objectively measured by the trainee, but the need to have data to use when planning instructional objectives for each pupil and making budgetary priorities and requests to the principal was highly relevant and very possible. Nonetheless, an examination of the data provided by the trainees about their pupils revealed some interesting information.

Characteristics of the secondary SLD pupil

What kinds of students were labeled as SLD in the secondary schools of St. Paul, a school system where previously no secondary SLD services had been offered?

With a total SLD population of 214 students, 162 were boys and 52 were girls. The average level of retardation in reading before instruction was 4.3 grades below school placement. After instruction the average level was 2.6 grades below placement. Instruction was offered to these students for one hour daily, five days a week, for approximately three months.

Table 1 indicates that out of the 184 students, only sixty were described as learning disabled with no other characteristics by their SLD teachers. On the other hand, ninety-one students were seen as slow learners, underachievers, or emotionally disturbed rather than as learning disabled. Thirty-eight adolescents were seen as learning disabled and emotionally disturbed and/or educationally disadvantaged.

These SLD trainees judged ninety-eight of the 184 students as learning disabled with or without other identifying characteristics such as emotional disturbances and cultural disadvantages. On the other hand, the trainees felt that they were working with ninety-six students who were not learning disabled at all. Probably most interesting is the high number of slow learners and underachievers who found their way into these pioneer secondary SLD classes. Even though all of these 184 children appeared to the trainees as SLD according to intake testing procedures, by the end of three months they no longer seemed so. These are the kinds of students whose instruc-

Table 1
**Kinds of Secondary Students Labeled
as Learning Disabled by Trainees**

N	Kind
60	Learning disabled
38	Slow learner but not learning disabled.
23	Underachiever but not learning disabled.
20	Emotionally disturbed but not learning disabled.
15	Learning disabled + emotionally disturbed.
12	Learning disabled + culturally disadvantaged.
11	Learning disabled + emotionally disturbed + culturally disadvantaged.
5	Mentally retarded but not learning disabled.
184	Total

tional needs are believed to be met adequately by the regular school program. These data suggest otherwise.

We asked these teacher trainees to consider the kinds of learning blocks that they believed inhibited pupil learning. *Table 2* reports their judgments.

Table 2
**Blocks to Learning as Judged
by SLD Teacher Trainees**

N	Kind of Learning Block
73	Poor memory retention.
72	Poor auditory discrimination.
54	Poor attending to any task.
50	Chronic absenteeism.
47	Poor visual discrimination.
26	Inability to blend letter sounds.
25	Inability to make sound-letter associations.
20	Poor sensory-motor coordination.

Most students were perceived as having more than one learning block. Poor memory retention could be attributed to hopelessness on the part of the learner or not caring enough to remember. It could also be a function of poor habit training or it could be a neurological dysfunction. Poor attending to any task was seen by most trainees as a deficit in the ability of the student to organize himself for learning. Chronic absenteeism was greatest in the three high school populations. We were alarmingly surprised to find so many junior and senior high school students having trouble with such basic phonic elements of reading as the ability to recognize letter sounds. These adolescents seemed more like the truly "battered learning-disabled child" found in the elementary schools.

Kinds of SLD instruction in the eight secondary schools

The greatest emphasis of the training program was on remedial academics, especially in the area of reading and particularly, for the "battered" learning-disabled child. Less time was spent on working with highly disturbed adolescents or developing a remedial reading and social studies program, directly teaching work-study skills or strengthening cognitive functions.

Particularly, our four trainees who were placed in the three senior high schools, found it necessary to place primary emphasis on various kinds of concept development activities and on teaching work-study skills. Short courses were offered to our trainees in these areas. But the trainees themselves offered much creativity in setting up SLD programs that were markedly different from the junior high programs.

In Harding senior high school, a white, middle-class school, where most of the forty students in the SLD classes had at least minimal mechanical reading skills, the two trainees paid more attention to communication skills, developing critical thinking and creating awareness of the social and political environment surrounding them. The unit approach, team teaching, audio-visual aids and field trips were used extensively. The teachers were actively encouraging their students to become curriculum producers rather than passive curriculum consumers. Thus, an activity-centered classroom including a curriculum production corner was devised. As many as sixteen students received instruction at the same time. The teachers saw themselves as resource people or guides to learning. Some large group instruction was offered followed by guided group interaction. Students then worked individually on different aspects of the same task while the two teachers walked around the room, offering assistance. The two trainees in this school seemed to have evolved a highly appropriate curriculum for their students in the two months during which their program was in operation.

In Washington senior high school, a mixed, lower socio-economic level school, located on the fringes of the inner city, there were more students with profound reading disabilities. Thus, more extensive use was made of the *Orton-Gillingham-Stillman* remedial reading method stressed by the training program.[2] An extensive reading program was offered including both remedial books and a "hooked-on-books" approach. One of the two teachers placed much emphasis on the teaching of cognitive skills such as problem solving, spatial-time relationships, and listening skills. A work-study skills class was offered on Fridays to anyone who wished to attend and a spelling lab was made available twice a week. The students were described as highly motivated by their teacher trainees, and they expressed gratitude for having a program designed to meet their instructional needs.

The third senior high school was an affluent, predominantly white school, and there were remarkably few learning-disabled students. Consequently, the neighboring junior high school was included in the program. Again, few disabled readers were found. Instead, more emotionally disturbed and underachieving youngsters were referred to the trainees. The trainees involved felt reluctant and ill-prepared to handle any but severely disabled readers. As a result, they did not include in their program those children with the kinds of cognitive and work-study skills problems who were included in the other two senior high school programs. Thus, these two trainees worked with significantly fewer children and used mostly the *Orton-Gillingham-Stillman* method coupled with an extensive reading program using *Stone Readers* and the *Readers' Digest Series*.[3]

Another teaching team was utilized in one of the five junior high schools. This, too, had a predominantly affluent, college-bound population. An activity-centered approach, utilizing a wide variety of audio-visual equipment was used by the two trainees along with a heavy emphasis on the *Orton-Gillingham-Stillman* reading method. In addition, field trips and cognitive skill development were used to a lesser extent along with an extended reading program. Both trainees worked together in the same room, sometimes teaming up but usually working individually with a group of about five youngsters each.

Probably the most severely reading-disabled youngsters were found in Mechanics' Art junior high school, which is an inner-city school. Four trainees were placed in this school. A heavy emphasis was placed on remedial academics and an extensive reading program. No teaming up was done, and each teacher worked with his own group. However, much consultation among the four trainees did occur. These adolescents showed the greatest reading gains. The program lasted longer than those at the other schools. Identification of SLD students was no problem here. Thus, more time could be spent on getting started and getting a well-defined program into operation.

Another inner-city junior high school, also with a team of four trainees, had more difficulty in meeting the needs of their readily defined students. These trainees overloaded themselves with children, started the program too soon, and left themselves little time to prepare and communicate among themselves. Thus, they felt more isolated than those at most of the other schools. The administration was more rigid, making it difficult for them to shift students, go on field trips or engage in experimental methods. Two trainees made extensive use of the *Orton-Gillingham-Stillman* method as their primary teaching tool. One trainee had a largely cognitive skill-development approach, using a unit approach and spending much time on concept and vocabulary development. The other teacher had difficulty finding a method of choice with his highly disruptive, reading-deficient youngsters.

An unusual problem developed at Como junior high school, the school that had hosted our training program. The forty children who had been saturated with twenty caring adults and their supervisors suddenly found themselves having to share the three trainees who remained. Some students dropped out of the program. Others stopped trying. Each teacher operated in isolation from the rest. Ironically, this group showed the least amount of reading gain. The major emphasis was on remedial reading.

It seemed to the supervisory staff that those trainees who either worked together in the same room or who had excellent communication among themselves within their school, developed the most relevant, creative and flexible programs that met the needs of their students. Those trainees who were operating in isolation from one another seemed to be most restrictive in their teaching, and tended to follow the training model too closely.

Growth in reading after SLD instruction

All trainees were asked to subjectively estimate the progress of their students during the three-month instructional period.

Table 3

Progress of SLD Pupils as Reported by Trainees

N	Kind of Progress
80	Good but "spotty" progress.
68	Making "some progress."
52	Excellent progress.
14	No progress.

A comparison of WRAT reading scores for the 214 students indicated that ten students made no reported gains whereas 204 made gains of three months to five years improvement. *Table 4* provides the WRAT scores.

Table 4

Growth in WRAT Reading Achievement by Years (N = 214)

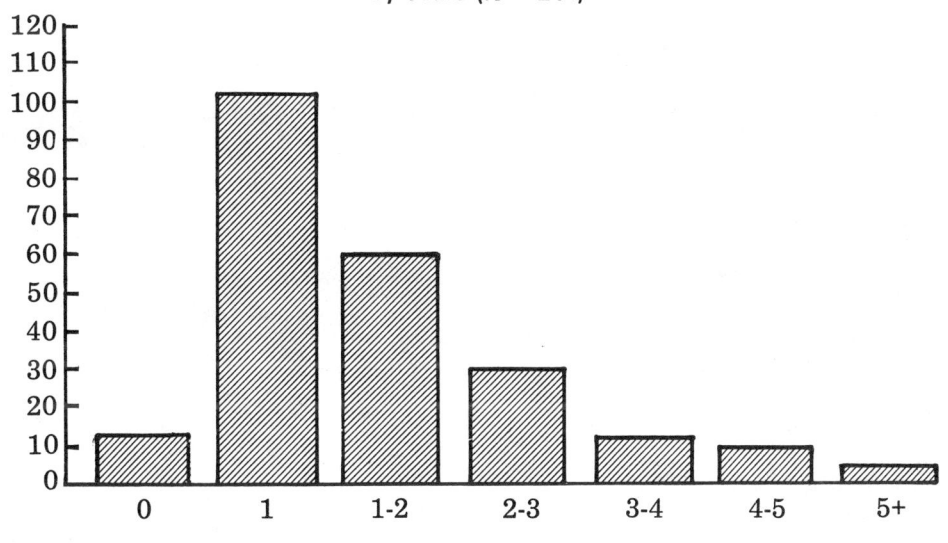

NOTES

1. For sources of tests mentioned in this article, see Appendix.
2. Anna Gillingham and Bessie Stillman, *Remedial Training for Children with Specific Disability in Reading, Spelling, and Penmanship*, 7th edition (Cambridge, Mass.: Educators Publishing Service, 1960).
3. Clarence R. Stone et al., *New Practice Readers* (New York, N.Y.: McGraw-Hill Book Company, Inc., 1962); Reader's Digest Educational Division Editors, *Reader's Digest Original Reading Skill Builders* (Pleasantville, N.Y.: Reader's Digest, 1968).

Teacher Training in the Public Schools

Carole Post*

THE PURPOSE of this presentation is to discuss a unique post-baccalaureate teacher-training program that prepares teachers to become level learning-disability specialists. A critical analysis of the program is best served by comparing it to a more conventional teacher-training program.

Since I have received educational training in two different institutions, under two very different types of programs, I can compare and contrast these programs, delineating the positive and negative aspects of each, as I see them; my purpose lies in the possibility of improving future programs. All of my observations are limited to my personal experiences, and should not be generalized as universal.

I received my undergraduate degree in elementary education at the State University of New York at Oneonta. At the time, Oneonta was specifically a teacher-training college that specialized in elementary education. It was a very traditional program in which all degree courses were predetermined upon entrance into the program, with very little allowance for electives; theory was taught during the first three years in complete isolation from student teaching, which was done in the fourth year. Student teaching consisted of two different all day assignments, which lasted a half-semester each. While I was student teaching, it often occurred to me that the only contact I had with the college was during a monthly hour-long observation, which was performed by my supervisor, and two seminar days at the college. I feel the entire structure was an inadequate preparation for a teaching career.

While student teaching, I floundered without support, ideas or positive instructor-models to follow. The models that I did have to follow were authoritarian, impersonal, and non-creative — in short, they were the kind of teachers that I did not want to emulate and their type of approach was one that was not advocated by the university, since creativity and meeting individual differences were stressed in our training.

---

*Carole Post is a special learning disability teacher in the St. Paul public schools, Minnesota.

During the first three years of preparation for student teaching, I was unmotivated by my educational theory courses — in fact, I thought at the time that they were composed of irrelevant busy-work, not because they *were* worthless, but because I was not applying them to any concrete experiences and because I had never taught children. Not only did I not learn the theory I needed; I didn't learn the curriculum skills either. I must admit that I did not know how to teach reading when I accepted a third grade teaching job. That year I did a lot of scrambling to learn what I needed to know.

Something seems drastically wrong with the system when you end up learning teaching skills *after* the completion of your training, rather than during it. Perhaps the most unfortunate factor is the inefficient use of the educational specialists at the university level. What actually happens is that students are with the people who can be most helpful at the wrong time. It's during the first year of independent teaching, when you are faced with the realities and responsibilities of total classroom management that you need the advice and aid of the experts. I taught in an elementary school in Indiana where there were no consultants, no specialists, no classroom demonstrations, no sharing of ideas, no curriculum planning and development, and the principal had never taught in an elementary classroom. When I needed ideas or assistance with problems there was no one available who could provide possible solutions or methods. This situation did not make sense to me.

It also appears not to have made sense to the developers of the Educational Professional Development Act's (EPDA) SLD teacher-training program in which I was involved last year. The purpose of the program was to educate and train a group of twenty graduate-level students to become state department certified specialists in secondary special learning disabilities. The emphasis was two-fold: (1) to train remedial tutors, and (2) to begin developing alternative programs for nonreading children in the secondary schools. The structure of the program set it apart and enabled it to serve as a vehicle for the integration of educational theories, methods and lay opinions effecting actual practical results in the school.

The span of time between September 1969 and May 1970 was separated into three different subdivisions:

SELF-CONTAINED CLASS

THEORY AND PHILOSOPHY OF REMEDIAL EDUCATION

Differential diagnosis, differential treatment-screening and in-depth diagnosis.
General concepts—IQ, MA, intelligence, deviant learning.
Introduction to evaluation.
Introduction to teaching methods.

UNIVERSITY COURSEWORK

Lecture and discussion: teaching techniques and behavior management two and one-half hours daily.
Working with children two hours daily.
University coursework.
Evaluation—by supervisors.

TEACHER TRAINING

PRACTICUM IN SCHOOLS
ESTABLISHED SLD PROGRAMS IN SECONDARY SCHOOLS.
UNIVERSITY COURSEWORK.
EVALUATION:
By supervisors on the job.
Formal evaluation—tests and techniques of teaching.

THE SELF-CONTAINED CLASS was the first period of the training, during which the twenty students met all day with two team-teaching instructors. It afforded us an intensive, in-depth orientation to the theory and philosophy of remedial education. We covered the topics of differential diagnosis, differential treatment, screening and diagnosis procedures, general concepts of IQ, mental age, intelligence, and deviant learning processes, and an introduction to evaluation and teaching methods. The second phase was a continuation of the self-contained class for lecture and discussion for two and one-half hours per day and two hours per day of individual tutoring. When we worked with the children, we worked under the direct supervision of our instructors. Because of the intensity of the supervision, we received instant feedback about our progress; at the same time our instructors were getting feedback as to the effectiveness of their instruction. In some instances, this proved to be an eye-opener. It also reinforced the idea that adults learn best in the same manner as children — through repetitition, reinforcement, concrete demonstration, and trial and error. The teacher trainers had to know how to teach children themselves, because it was often necessary to demonstrate the use of materials when the feedback indicated that the trainees had not understood the initial, auditory instructions. This type of on-the-scene immediate feedback and interchange is nonexistent in the traditional teacher-training programs where the professor lectures through his prescribed curriculum, tests whether or not the student can rephrase the book, and never sees the mutilated results that often occur when the student begins to work in the classroom. This program allowed for a spiralling effect of learning where information goes from instructor to student, back to instructor, to student, instructor, student, climbing higher and higher until a new level of learning is achieved by everyone involved.

During the first two phases of the EPDAB2 program, we took university courses in the area of learning disabilities in addition to what we learned in our self-contained classroom. Since the communication lines were so open during the day, we were often able to discuss, analyze and integrate ideas we had heard in lectures at the university. This opportunity gave continuity to the total program and affected all of us in reaching a higher level of learning.

The third subdivision was a practicum in the schools. SLD programs were established in secondary schools in St. Paul, with teams of three and four trainees per school. We received teacher referrals, screened them, individually diagnosed the children, and set up schedules to treat a maximum of fifteen children each. During this time we were treated as professional, skilled people by our instructors, and yet, we were given continual professional support and guidance by a highly specialized team of supervisors. Rather than relying on one supervisor, who would occasionally drop in for an observation, we had assistance from an educational psychologist, a reading expert, an experienced SLD teacher, and our program instructor. The supervision was in the form of observations, written reports, discussions, concrete suggestions for improvement, problem sessions, idea trading brain-storming sessions, and workshops.

An important concept of the entire program is the gradual readiness approach to instruction. We progressed slowly from observation, to teaching a small group. All the while we had supportive supervision from instructors who were responsive to our needs and who taught with the philosophy that our success or failure with materials and methods just might be directly related to their effectiveness as teachers. This kind of sensitivity is not characteristic of university courses where insulation from reality takes a heavy toll on educational training institutions.

By having our practicum during the day and our university courses in the evening, student teaching and the courses that are designed to prepare one for it were not isolated and dealt with separately. All relevant theories, methods, and curriculum were integrated, tried out immediately, and refined, used as is, or discarded accordingly. I felt the courses I was taking at the university were meaningful because I could relate them to something real.

The key is that we learned by doing. There is an ancient Chinese proverb which states: "I hear and I forget, I see and I remember, I do and I understand." I think this is just as relevant a concept in instruction on the college level as it is with preschoolers. The simplest and most effective way of teaching an abstract idea is through concrete involvement. And there was something very concrete about the sense of immediacy and urgency that comes from facing, each day, fifteen teenagers with histories of recalcitrance or overt behavioral problems or unexplained inability to learn at school. Knowing that we had to teach right away, tomorrow, and the next day, and the next week, made us understand that this was the time to learn how to do it and how to do it correctly. We were motivated by urgent relevance and it worked.

AFTER SPENDING one year out in the field, I have also found that I am thoroughly familiar with the existing materials in the SLD field. This is the result of not only being exposed to what was available, but actually using and experimenting with these materials. As students, we were given permission to use the Special Education Instructional Materials Center owned and operated by the St. Paul public schools. Access to this facility meant that we could thoroughly familiarize ourselves with the newest materials as well as those that were already in use in the schools.

The group cohesiveness and support which developed should also be considered a positive aspect of the program. Because we were twenty people involved in exactly the same program, facing the same problems at the same time, much group learning and sharing took place; we benefitted from each others' mistakes and triumphs, and were able to get practical advice from someone else who was tackling the same problems. We formed study groups to pool and extend our knowledge, and most importantly, we were able to combine our many differing viewpoints for better problem solving ability.

Most problems are only difficult to solve because we neglect to look at them in a new way. In other words, we develop a *mind set* which does not allow us to look objectively at the problem. An example of this *mind set* at work can be seen in finding the solution to the following story question:

> *A man and his son were in an automobile accident. The man was killed and his son was brought to the hospital in critical condition. When he was brought into the operating room, the surgeon looked at him and said, "That's my son." What relation was the surgeon to the boy?*
> (Answer — It was his mother.)

Do you see what point of view can do to complicate the solution of a simple problem? Group problem solving sometimes helps cut through some of that subjectivity.

Within our group, an atmosphere of experimentation was fostered. Perhaps it was because the children we worked with were not responding to traditional instruction, perhaps it was a result of the way in which we were being taught. I tend to think it was a combination of both factors. Throughout our program, we were presented with many divergent and often conflicting theories of learning and teaching, since we received instruction from many people of differing backgrounds and philosophies. This gave us a more objective view of what we were attempting to do in the classroom, and developed within us a sense of "if at first you don't succeed, try, try again" either with a modification or a change. We drew continually and immediately upon the theory we learned at the university to find which ideas or approaches worked best for us.

In addition to the growth we made as teachers, it is possible that as a group, we had some impact on influencing change in the schools by offering a special service and by infiltrating the teacher and administrative ranks and spreading ideas and attitudes, as well as some possible solutions.

However, this aspect of the program could have been improved upon. As an SLD resource teacher, I need preparation for going directly into classrooms and attempting to make an impact on teacher attitudes and methods of teaching. This was discussed as an important aspect of our work in the schools, and yet, we never became involved in this area during the training. We should have had an opportunity to analyze the problem, develop some guidelines for approach, and actually try them out in regular classrooms.

Last year while I was a trainee, I felt that more contact with in-service SLD teachers would have resulted in improved education for us as well as the SLD teachers; my conviction about this is even stronger this year, now that I am an SLD teacher. I would welcome an opportunity to learn what the new trainees are learning and share what I have learned in a direct interchange with them. Perhaps the reason we did not do much of this last year was because we were being trained for junior and senior high school, and St. Paul had only elementary SLD people at that time. However, after working this year at the elementary level, I find that after the initial gearing downward I made within the curriculum and my approach to it, I am still using much of what I used last year, and I think the gearing down would have helped me last year. There is a tendency for teachers to set expectancies at a level commensurate with the size of the junior and senior high schoolers, while in reality, most of the SLD teenagers are academically, emotionally, and behaviorally *little kids*, even though they want to be treated like *big kids*. They need time, successful experiences, some consistency in their world, and much skill development before they can operate on a level with their peers.

Perhaps one of the best preparations I had for teaching junior high SLD children was my elementary background, and specifically, two years of teaching nine and ten year olds (some of whom operated on a higher social, emotional, and academic level than the fourteen- and fifteen-year-old SLD children with whom I worked).

Having elementary classroom teaching experience before becoming an SLD teacher has two major benefits. First, it helps to put your expectancies for academic achievement in perspective, and secondly, it provides a common ground for communication between the SLD resource teacher and the classroom teachers she would like to influence. It is much easier to identify with someone who has had similar experiences, and the suggestions for change may seem more credible.

THERE IS ALSO another side to this coin. It is good for the SLD teacher to have classroom experience—it is just as good for the classroom teacher to have experience with remedial tutoring techniques so that she is better equipped to handle special problems in the regular class. This relates back to the idea of a gradual readiness approach to teaching teachers how to teach. Too often, a teacher does not meet the individual needs of her pupils because her experience has only been group teaching.

I feel that a program like EPDAB2, if it were integrated within a larger undergraduate teacher-training program, would produce considerably more sensitive and capable classroom teachers as well as SLD teachers, if it followed the existing structure, and added experience in a large classroom practicum at the end of the year. There would then be four major subdivisions of gradual readiness training; the last would be a regular classroom internship.

> Self-contained class — lecture, discussion, observation.
> Self-contained class — tutoring one child.
> Practicum in schools — small group teaching.
> Practicum in schools — large class teaching.

I do not mean to imply that one year of intensive on-the-job training, similar to EPDAB2, is all we need to train competent teachers in undergraduate school. There is more to teaching than learning a specific skill or teaching method. No matter what specialization is pursued, one must have a wide exposure to areas of existing knowledge, in theory and practice in order to first, realize how much we don't know and be willing to learn with our pupils; and secondly, become capable of guiding the childrens' search for knowledge, thirdly, to competently respond to their differences and similarities as learners and as people; and finally, to be able to integrate our area with the rest of the world.

Consider how relativity physics can be better understood in terms of the relativity of people's dress, or physical beauty, or even meanings of words like *cool* or *bad*. Most academic areas can and should be integrated, and a teacher must be able to help a child understand how his studies fit in the total picture, and how it relates to him personally. For this reason, a program such as EPDAB2 by itself, is not enough to fully prepare a teacher to meet all the needs of all the children, nor is it enough to meet all the needs of all the teachers in training.

A major drawback of the program was caused by the lack of alternatives and orientation to what we would actually be learning to teach. Most of us didn't even really know what SLD meant, let alone what would be expected of us on the job, and since this program was one of a kind, there was no available option for transfer if we decided we didn't like being an SLD teacher. There were several members of the group who felt misplaced when teaching beginning reading and spelling. The effective teacher is one who not only knows the methodology, but honestly thinks what he is teaching is important, enjoys doing what he's doing and can communicate this feeling to his students.

Considering the many positive aspects of the program, perhaps the shortcomings could be overlooked if the concept of the EPDAB2 program were integrated into a wider teacher education curriculum. Given a four year college course in education, one possible curriculum arrangement might be as follows:

- Allow one year of liberal arts education for the student to familiarize himself with existing bodies of knowledge as he becomes familiar with the possibilities available to him in higher education.

- Follow this general year with one year of exposure to many different areas of teaching which do exist or will exist in the public schools where he will teach. At this time, broad areas which pertain to both elementary and secondary education such as the inner city classroom, or programs for the slow learner, or community resources as a classroom extension could be explored in depth in terms of, (1) pertinent theories, (2) the implementation of these theories as observed in the schools, and (3) an analytic approach to comparing and contrasting several programs or classes in the hope of finding successful common denominators as well as figuring out why one method worked well in one place and not in another. This year would be an overview of the existing possibilities of the elementary and secondary public school system and should include an examination of programs involved with children of all abilities, ages and backgrounds.

- The third year could parallel the EPDAB2 program offering in-service training and instruction in the specific area chosen by the future teacher. The choice to specialize, therefore, would only be made after the students know the many available areas within the schools.

- Finally, the last year would be reserved for electives. By this time, the student has been trained in the area of his choice, knows what he individually needs to know in order to better teach in this area, and is really the only one who can decide what gap needs to be filled in or what knowledge he could use to help him teach in his area. There should be no restrictions placed upon subject matter or college department. If he is going to be an English teacher and feels he needs to know about relativity, then the opportunity should be made available. Some people will decide to work toward a refined specialization, some will decide to broaden their base. This choice should remain with the student. We need all kinds of teachers and all kinds of methods because we have all kinds of kids who learn in all kinds of ways.

In this model, the third year would encompass the positive aspects of our training program, while eliminating some of the negatives. Better interaction could be developed between in-service teachers and the trainees, enhancing the experience of both groups; the trainees would be exposed to many different teaching roles and would consequently become capable of competently choosing their specialization accordingly; prospective teachers would have a general, broad base of knowledge to support their specialization (and I classify regular, classroom teaching as a specialty); all classifications of teachers would share a common, experiential awareness of each other's roles. Wouldn't this help to promote closer working ties between teachers and subsequently develop a more integrated school program through open communication lines?

IF WE WANT to successfully incorporate new approaches to teaching in the public schools, in order to bring new materials and methods to the children, then we had better start teaching the teachers in the same way that we want them to teach. Let's provide a model for instruction which they can follow by using a gradual readiness approach, developing a total program continuity, motivating by relevance, teaching through concrete experience, providing an atmosphere of experimentation, and initiating a learning spiral. Perhaps teachers do tend to teach the way they have learned.

SECTION IX

Research from Allied Fields

Vision and Learning Disabilities: Part I

Curtis D. Benton, Jr.*

ONE OF THE FIRST things that is recommended by a school teacher or sought for by the parent of a child with a learning disability is an eye examination. If the child is taken to a busy ophthalmologist who has no interest in dyslexia or reading problems, the parents will most certainly hear a statement such as, "Your child's eyes are fine; they have nothing to do with his reading problem." Far removed from this extreme could be the response of some very active optometrist who might tell the parents of this same child, "Your child has a developmental vision problem; he needs bifocal glasses and perceptual-motor visual training in my office twice a week at a cost of $450.00 for the first three months."

There is much we don't know about vision and learning disability and much basic research needs to be done, but according to the current consensus of informed opinions among ophthalmologists researching this field, the facts lie somewhere between the above two extremes. Here is what we feel is true—today:

1. Learning problems are not related to impaired visual acuity. In children with very poor vision the use of special optical aids and special educational materials may impose some restrictions, but learning is usually otherwise normal.

2. Errors of refraction are not a significant factor in learning disability in children. There is definite observation that in this group of school children, hyperopia (farsightedness) is less prevalent than in good readers. The practice of prescribing weak-plus lenses in the form of reading glasses or bifocals should be curtailed. There is no physiological justification for such glasses. They are sometimes prescribed by harassed ophthalmologists who feel they are being pressured into doing something to satisfy the frustrated parents of these children. The glasses usually find their way to the dresser drawer after a few weeks. I have also seen similar glasses prescribed by well-intentioned optometrists who have either measured a weakness of accommodation or observed that the child could read better in his office when +0.50

---

*Curtis D. Benton, Jr., M.D., ophthalmologist, serves on the advisory board, Broward Reading Academy, Fort Lauderdale, Florida.

spheres were held before the two eyes. Again, the glasses are worn only as long as the parents' patience lasts, since they must constantly remind the child to wear them.

When the eye doctor examines dyslexic children, he should be aware of the pitfalls that stem from two causes: (1) the unreliability of accommodative measurements in children, and (2) the Hawthorne effect of holding lenses before the eyes. A ten-year-old child with ten diopters of accommodation may exhibit no more than half that amount on a test if he isn't motivated or free from anxiety. It's very impressive to watch how much better a boy will read a paragraph from his school book when a doctor encourages him to perform while looking through trial lenses. The response is purely psychological and not dependent on the glasses, and the examiner must be very careful not to let himself be deluded otherwise.

The prescribing of corrective lenses for children with learning disabilities should follow the same rules as are followed when prescribing for children without learning disabilities, with the exception that correction of borderline refractive errors may properly be a part of the overall treatment of dyslexic children. In any event, simple glasses weaker than +1.00 diopter of hyperopia or +0.75 diopter of astigmatism should never be prescribed for these youngsters. If accommodation is thought to be inadequate (and such a circumstance is extremely rare in children), it should be corrected with accommodative exercises and not made worse by lenses that are intended to relieve accommodative effort.

The Hawthorne effect of spectacle lenses was checked in another way recently. We were able to induce immediate improvement in reading in twenty-six dyslexic children by fitting them with prescriptionless contact lenses. We made tape recordings of their reading before and immediately after insertion of the lenses. Almost without exception the children read with more certainty and fewer mistakes or hesitations. The parents were thrilled. The youngsters wore the lenses for a few weeks, then stopped on their own volition.

3. Manifest strabismus, whether esotropia or exotropia, has nothing to do with reading retardation. I reviewed the record of 117 of my own squint patients and found only two conditions that seemed to interfere with a child's maximum reading potential. They were intermittent exotropia with a troublesome phoria at near point and small angle esotropia with a slight degree of fusion, or rapid alternation at near point. Surgical correction, orthoptics, and glasses—with or without prisms as indicated—were often helpful in the overall management of these children's reading problems. This has also been observed by Dr. E. A. Dunlap of New York.

4. Convergence insufficiency is a common finding in dyslexic children. I found it in 22 percent of 2,000 cases as compared to 4 percent or 5 percent in children without learning problems. This is not the cause of their reading problem, but it does contribute to difficulty in sustained reading and should be corrected. It responds quickly to standard convergence exercises.

5. Optometrists interested in reading problems often report finding abnormalities in ocular rotations in their dyslexic patients. They speak of a child moving the head rather than the eyes when visually pursuing a moving

target, of erratic visual pursuit movements, of inability or difficulty in crossing the midline, of overshoot or undershoot in fixation.

In the absence of genuine neurological disorders of the ocular-muscle nerve supply, these tests only show the extreme variability of children in responding to unfamiliar tests. I have reexamined many children previously seen by developmental vision specialists, and I have never been able to observe what I considered to be abnormalities of ocular pursuit movements.

Eye-fixation movements in reading have been studied photographically. Many regressions and irregularities are found in dyslexic patients, but with careful study it can be seen that these abnormalities are caused by uncertainty of recognition or comprehension of the test words rather than defects of eye movements.

Many children are put through time-consuming exercises of ocular rotations—with eyes closed, eyes open, clockwise, counterclockwise, following swinging objects, and locating fixed objects. All these manipulations are a waste of time and money and serve no useful purpose in reading remediation.

6. Eye dominance has been considered an important factor in reading problems. A variance from strict homolaterality of eye, hand, and foot occurs with considerable frequency in children with learning disabilities. I found either crossed or mixed dominance in 75 percent of 2,000 dyslexic children. I treated 1,000 of these children with occlusion or atropinization of the eye that should have been nondominant. Although most of these children improved in their reading during the one-year observation period, subsequent tests and research experiments proved that treatment of the dominance was not the real cause of the improvement. Here again, the Hawthorne effect was operative.

We must conclude that problems of dominance and laterality are common manifestations of the dyslexia syndrome, but are not causative factors in most cases. I still encounter a few cases, however, where correction of crossed or mixed dominance is an important part of the total treatment program. These patients constitute less than 10 percent of the total.

7. Visual perception tests have received a lot of attention. Whether one uses the Frostig, The Winter Haven materials, or a similar test with younger children, or the Bender Visual-Motor Gestalt with the slightly older children,[1] about half the retarded readers will exhibit deficiencies. Although exercises and training for perception and perceptual-motor skills have been devised and administered with considerable enthusiasm (and expense), there is no supportable evidence that such activities are beneficial in reading remediation.

If a visual perception problem does exist, this can be important information for the child's teacher. The avenues of auditory and kinesthetic input become vital routes of learning to read for children with a weakness of visual perception.

DYSLEXIA IS THUS not really an eye problem or a vision problem or a perception problem, but this does not mean that the eye specialist cannot or should not supervise the treatment of children with learning disabilities. However, he cannot properly treat such children without help from the educator and one or more medical specialists. Many of these children need neurological evaluation. A large percentage of them need medication to control hyperactivity and distractability. Nearly all need specialized educational help. Thus, when an eye specialist chooses to captain such a team, he must realize that he is assuming a broader role than his basic training has equipped him for and that he must be willing to broaden his own education to fit the job he has chosen to perform.

NOTES

1. For sources of tests mentioned in this article, see Appendix.

Vision and Learning Disabilities: Part II

Irving J. Peiser*

THE LITERATURE that relates vision to learning disabilities is, at the present time, inconsistent, contradictory, and confusing. This is understandable in the face of the semantic jungle that surrounds the terms *vision* and *learning disabilities*. For the purpose of this discussion, vision is defined as *the individual's ability to react to and interact with his environment on the basis of information received through the eyes.* It is necessary to distinguish between eyesight, or visual acuity, and the above definition of vision. Eyesight is the sensory ability of the eye to distinguish small detail at both far and near, and is only one of the components of vision. Vision, on the other hand, is a cognitive act that enables us to look at an object and not only identify it, but determine its location, its size, its distance from the observer, its rate of movement, its texture, its smell, and everything else that can be determined by visual inspection. This involves the matching of visual stimuli with information from other sensory modalities: audition, touch, kinesthesia, taste, and smell.

This definition of vision as an information-processing modality involves far more than merely seeing a clear contour (20/20 acuity or eyesight). The concept that vision consists solely of 20/20 eyesight and healthy eyes was postulated more than one hundred years ago and is pitifully out of date in an atomic age.

In order to show the relationship between vision and learning disabilities, it is necessary to also define the latter term. R. M. Wold defines learning disability as follows:

> A child, usually a boy, whose performance in the languary arts (e.g. reading, spelling) is significantly below his grade placement and general intelligence. He does not exhibit any measurable neurological defect; loss of visual or auditory acuity, mental retardation, cerebral palsy or other obvious defect. In the academic environment, he has a defective capacity for acquiring at a normal time, through the general curriculum, a proficiency in reading,

---

*Irving J. Peiser, O.D., optometrist, is chairman of the Illinois Optometric Association, Forum on Vision and Reading, Chicago, Illinois.

spelling, etc., corresponding to his general ability even with proper instructions, intact senses and normal motivation. He shows one or more of such "soft" neurological signs as: time disorientation, right-left disorientation, impaired motor control, perseveration, perceptual-motor deficit, visuo-motor deficit, hyperkinesis (motor and/or visual) impulsivity, short attention span, mixed laterality, impaired directionality, abnormal reading and writing posture, impaired two-point discrimination, and by late grade three, behavior or emotional problems. Psychometric testing yields a typical wide scattering of the subtest scores even though the average score is in the normal or above, intellectual range. The disability is neuro-psycho-physiological in nature and affects the integrative abilities and not the acuity or "pure" perceptual processes.[1]

VISUAL ABILITIES INVOLVED IN LEARNING TO READ

In this paper, *reading* is used as if it were synonymous to *learning*, inasmuch as reading ability is the basis for all academic learning, with the possible exception of arithmetic computation.

At the very outset, it is important to note that there is an extremely low correlation between refractive error (optical distortions of the eye: nearsightedness, farsightedness, astigmatism) and success in beginning reading.[2] Other end-organ visual functions play a small role at this stage. These functions include accommodation (focusing), convergence (turning both eyes inward to see at near), and fusion (two-eyed seeing).[3]

In beginning reading the child has to "break the code," and must make the visual-verbal match.[4] In other words, he has to match the appearance of the printed form of the word to its sound, and give the vocal equivalent. During the child's first five years of life, all of his language experience is strictly oral; there is no reading or writing involved. When he enters first grade, he has to be able to make an intersensory shift from audition to vision. The visual skills involved at this stage of learning are visual directional awareness, visual form-perception, intersensory integration, and eye-hand coordination.

Visual directional awareness

Awareness of visual directionality is obviously essential in all academic learning, simply because letters and numbers are oriented in our culture on a left-to-right basis. In order for a child to appreciate visual directional differences, he has to establish a set of internal visual coordinates in his own body: up and down, left and right, front and back. A child learns these directional coordinates through awareness of his body image,[5] his general self-directed movement,[6] and by relating his eye posture with his general body kinesthesia.[7]

During the child's preschool years, he generally ignores directional differences in favor of establishing form constancy. Thus, a table is a table whether he views it from the right, left, front, back, top, or bottom. To be sure, the retinal images are different, but the perceived image is still that of a table. D. Alexander and J. Money refer to this as the *law of object constancy*.[8] Letters and numbers violate this law. For example, the only basic visual difference between b and d, p and q, u and n, N and Z, M and W, 6 and 9, is simply that of directional orientation.

The child who reverses letters and words (*was* for *saw*, *on* for *no*) has not developed his visual directional skills to the point where he is sure of his own internal body coordinates.[9] On this basis, he develops visual directionality through proper awareness of eye posture. This involves total body posture information, kinesthetic awareness, and feedback from the proprioceptive receptors in the external eye muscles.[10]

Much has been written about the role of dominance in reversals,[11] but N. Flax points out that eye dominance is not a factor in reversals.[12] While the right arm and right leg are controlled by the left cerebral hemisphere and vice versa, *each* eye sends half its information to *each* hemisphere in the brain. Thus, all of the information to the individual's left is transmitted to the right side of the brain and all of the information to his right is transmitted to the left side of his brain.

Visual form-perception

Visual form-perception is the next visual skill involved in early reading,[13] since letters obviously consist of shapes. Although adults can readily identify forms and tend to think that this skill is spontaneous and natural, visual form-perception is nonetheless learned.[14] The child's first concept of form develops in infancy when he becomes aware of the boundary of his crib. Later, when he begins to crawl, his movement may be blocked by a wall. The discontinuities in his surroundings teach him an awareness of shape because he feels the movement of his body in relation to the borders of the shape. At this stage of his development, tactile form is more meaningful than visual form. As he grows, the child becomes able to substitute eye movements in place of actual body or hand movements in perceiving the contour of the shape. Accordingly, his eye movements recall his body movements, and this in turn enables him to recall the feel and contour of the object that he is seeing.[15] As the child continues to grow, he no longer needs to move his eyes around the borders of the shape, and the process of recall takes place instantly.

Intersensory integration

Making the match between audition and vision was mentioned earlier in conjunction with "breaking the code" for beginning reading. At birth there is a reflex movement of the infant's eyes toward bright light.[16] This movement of the eyes is executed, on an involuntary level, by the same external eye muscles that he will use in later life to selectively aim his eyes. There is also a reflex association between sound and sight, which causes the infant to aim his eyes at a loud noise. Finally, there are reflex connections between eye movements and body position. In fact, about 20 percent of the retinal fibers go to the postural system of the body. These reflex associations between the various sensory-motor systems set the stage for learning through intersensory equivalents. On this basis, the infant is provided with a reflex mechanism to match visual, auditory, kinesthetic, tactile, olfactory, taste, and postural data.

As the child grows and develops, he passes through two stages in this intersensory matching process. The first stage is to match one sensory modality *with* another so that he can substitute one *for* the other. For example, the first time he sees a rubber ball it means nothing to him. Only by repeatedly tasting, squeezing, smelling, and lifting the ball, will he be able to look at it and realize all of its characteristics without having to use the other sensory systems to reinforce vision. The second stage of visual development is to override these reflex associations so that vision can ultimately substitute for other modalities.[17] Thus, even though the teacher's writing isn't the brightest visual stimulus in the room, nor is her voice necessarily the loudest noise in the room, the child nonetheless must selectively attend to the task at hand without the reinforcement of other sensory systems such as touch and kinesthesia. According to H. Birch and L. Belmont, retarded readers were significantly less able to make judgments of auditory-visual equivalence than were normal readers.[18]

As the child's visual perception becomes more sophisticated, his need for multisensory stimuli decreases and vision can now supersede all of the other sensory systems as the primary learning modality. The short attention span and the hyperkinesis of the learning-disabled child are frequently due to the persistence of an immature level of visual control. This is especially evident in American classrooms, where teaching is based upon the hierarchical development of the sensory systems within which vision is dominant.[19]

Eye-hand coordination

The final visual skill in beginning learning is eye-hand coordination. In the preschool child, it is quite normal for tactile and kinesthetic cues to reinforce eye aiming (hands guiding the eyes).[20] At about the time the child starts school, developmentally he should shift the relationship so that the eyes lead the hands. Failure to make this developmental shift is often the reason for poor handwriting. It may also explain the child's need to continue using his finger as a guide to steer his eyes in reading. It should be noted that while the above skills are discussed singly, they certainly have to function simultaneously if the child is to become an effective learner.

Those visual abilities that are necessary for beginning reading are not likely to be identified on the basis of examining the child for eye health, visual acuity, or corrective lens findings. These skills, or the lack of them, will be found only on investigation of the development of vision, with special emphasis on form perception, directionality, eye-hand coordination, and the intersensory match between vision and the other sensory modalities. An examination that does not include these areas of investigation will likely result in the "underdiagnostic" statement that "nothing is wrong with this child's eyes."

VISUAL SKILLS INVOLVED IN EFFICIENT READING

Once the child has learned to read in grades one and two, visual factors other than the ones listed above must come in to play for smooth, sustained learning performance.[21] To explain this, let us consider reading as a task that includes a wide spectrum of skills with different demands made at diferent levels of the spectrum. For example, the first-grader who is just learning to read has a very different learning problem from that of the college student with grade "A" potential but who is barely passing. The first-grade child is exposed to very large print; the words are well isolated on the page, and he is expected to pay visual attention for only a few moments at a time. The primary objective here is not necessarily to understand the concept behind the word, but to transform a visual symbol into a vocal equivalent. The college student, on the other hand, has to look at appreciably smaller print that is arranged in sentences and embedded in paragraphs and pages of similar print. He is expected to sustain his attention for long periods of time, and his primary objective is to derive information from the printed page and to understand the conceptual thinking of the writer. Considering this, is it any wonder that so much confusion exists when we try to ascertain the role of visual function in learning?

Now let us consider those visual abilities required for sustained, meaningful learning.

Binocular (two-eyed) problems

Nothing in the literature is more confusing than descriptions of the role of binocular (two-eyed) vision in learning disabilities.[22] In grades one and two, binocular vision plays a very small role in effective visual performance because the print is isolated and demands the child's attention for short periods of time only. Accordingly, binocular fusion problems (integration by the brain of the two ocular images) have very little effect on the initial skills that are necessary in learning to read. However, in the third or fourth grade, there is an abrupt reduction in print size in textbooks, and on this level, binocular vision problems can be a significant factor in reading. Poor binocular vision can cause words to run together, can result in fatigue, carelessness, omissions (especially of short words, such as *to*, *a*, *as*, *in*, and *on*), and a great loss of comprehension.

Because of the reaction of the visual system to stress, a paradox exists here. It is apparently better to be completely one-eyed than inefficiently two-eyed. Of course, it is best to be able to use the two eyes easily and efficiently at all times, for maximum visual performance. Because of this paradox in binocular vision, many one-eyed children (those who have a turned eye or one amblyopic eye) apparently have no difficulty with the two-dimensional reading task. On the other hand, a child who cannot use his two eyes easily as a team, but has to expend energy to do this, may be expected to have less energy available for the learning task. As a consequence, his performance may suffer.

On this basis, many people erroneously conclude that binocular vision has little to do with impaired reading performance in grade three or higher, because the greater degrees of binocular impairment have a lesser impact on academic learning.[23] If binocular vision screening instruments (Telebinocular, Ortho-Rater, or Titmus screeners) are used to identify children with binocular vision problems that affect learning, the cases most in need of attention are those who just fail to pass, rather than those who grossly fail. The gross failures on binocular vision screening instruments do, in fact, need clinical attention but not necessarily for learning problems.

Accommodation (eye focusing)

Another visual skill that frequently interferes with efficient reading for meaning is accommodation, or eye-focus ability. The assumption is generally made that this function is intact in all people until they reach their forties, but this is refuted by the fact that many young children cannot adequately maintain clear, close vision. If vision is considered as a link in the processing of data from the printed page, there is the possibility that reading inefficiency may result from poor focus ability. This problem by itself will not prevent a child from initially learning to read, since the print is large and the attention demands are low.

When prolonged reading is attempted, children and young adults with accommodative problems may experience discomfort (headaches, eyes burning), poor comprehension, and inaccurate reading long before they report that the print becomes blurred. The problem of accommodation is further complicated by the fact that this function is mediated by the involuntary nervous system, and can be influenced by endocrine and emotional (stress) changes in the child or adult. Fortunately, accommodative difficulties in young people frequently respond very well to low-powered convex lenses, which are generally prescribed in bifocal form.

It should be noted in passing that accommodative function cannot be assessed if the examination is done under cycloplegic eye drops. These drops temporarily paralyze the focus mechanism and prevent an evaluation of its flexibility.

Eye movements and convergence

The ability to aim, move, and converge the eyes (turn both eyes inward to look at near) is a basic requirement in tracking a line of print. There is a complicated control problem involved in this, since six muscles are attached to the outside of each eye that are responsible for eye movements. These muscles surround the eye in a complex fashion and are of different lengths, diameters, and strengths. To further complicate matters, there are three pairs of cranial nerves that control the action of the twelve eye muscles, and the effectiveness of these muscles depends on the eye's direction of gaze. Moreover, the eye does not move about a fixed center of rotation, but actually moves slightly sideways and forward and back as it rotates.

These muscles are controlled by the voluntary nervous system and must aim the eyes precisely when they look from far to near and back again. Failure to properly aim the eyes will result in miscopying (even though acuity is good) and loss of place.

When the child looks at the printed page, two oculomotor (eye-movement) conditions are required. First is the ability to converge both eyes so that they both aim exactly at the same place. This requires a high degree of precision because the eyes must converge at a line whose thickness is that of the letter *i*. The second condition is that the eyes must make small, precise movements (called saccadic fixations) along the line of print. Failure to do this will result in loss of place, skipping of lines, omissions, and poor comprehension.

The situation is further complicated by the relationship that exists between accommodation and convergence. While either system, tested independently, may function well, there must be a good relationship between both systems for efficient learning.[24] Both eyes must focus precisely at the point of convergence. This linkage between accommodation and convergence is the only place in the body where the voluntary and the involuntary nervous systems must work in concert. Failure to do this will not by itself cause learning disabilities, but it can explain the performance of those children who begin well in the lower grades but who decline academically in the higher grades. Problems between accommodation and convergence can cause headaches, eye discomfort, fatigue, poor comprehension, blurring of print, and avoidance of reading.

IMPORTANCE OF PROPER DIAGNOSIS

The preceding visual functions of binocular performance, accomodation, eye movements, convergence, and the accommodation-convergence relationship are generally referred to as *end-organ* functions, which are in contrast to the central visual skills of directionality, form perception, intersensory integration, and eye-hand coordination. In general, end-organ visual skills play a much greater role in reading and learning *efficiency* than they do in the basic aspects of *learning* to read. Discussing these skills one at a time is at best rather artificial, for in reality, all these visual functions are quite interrelated with one another and with other sensory and motor systems.

Any child with a learning problem should be referred for a complete evaluation of his vision. A word of caution must be mentioned in the use of the word *vision*. It is for this reason that vision was defined at the beginning of this paper. Despite this definition, semantic confusion will continue to exist because many educators, psychologists, pediatricians, and others equate vision solely with end-organ defects (acuity). On the other hand, many optomotrists consider a model of vision as one that incorporates the perceptual, developmental, and integrative aspects along with the end-organ functions of acuity, fixation, accommodation, convergence, and fusion.[25] What complicates the diagnosis of the learning-disabled child?

Diagnosis is another confusing area because of the many labels that we give this child. R. L. Clemmens points out that the diagnosis is invariably couched in the language of the examining professional (educational, neurological, or psychiatric).[26] Wold lists ninety-two separate terms that are used in describing children with learning disabilities.[27] These terms include *brain damaged, perceptually handicapped, dyslexia, hyperkinetic syndrome, psychic blindness, strephosymbolia,* and *underachiever,* to name just a few. To add further confusion to the problem, the choice of label is often a matter of geography. In California, for example, the official educational term seems to be *neurologically handicapped*, while in New York or New Jersey this same child is labeled *brain-injured*. If this child moves to Indiana, his diagnosis is changed to *perceptual handicap*. In Alabama he would be called *aphasoid*, and in Illinois, *learning disabled*. R. C. Wunderlich broadly states that "brain injury means any interference with the functioning of the brain . . . due to an environmental or emotional . . . effect."[28]

Professionals appear to be so busy labeling the learning-disabled child that they seem unable to provide much help for him. F. Rappaport states that "diagnosis without realistic plans for implementation is diagnosis in a vacuum,"[29] while S. A. Cohen questions "how many of your diagnosticians can treat children?"[30] I wonder if the clinician's diagnosis would be different if he had to apply it? Diagnosis and treatment should be combined to help the child. Reviewing the literature, Wold states that thirty papers are written on diagnosis for every one paper that is written on remediation.[31]

OPTOMETRIC VISION THERAPY

What can be done to alleviate the visual problems of the child with learning disabilities? Since vision, as it is defined and explained in this paper, is the primary sensory modality for learning, is it not logical that procedures for enhancing visual performance may be effective in teaching the child the prelearning skills? Optometric vision training is a remedial therapy that is designed to teach the child the proper use of his visual mechanism so that he can effectively respond to standard academic teaching procedures.

These classroom teaching techniques assume that the child's visual development is sufficiently mature to enable him to process visual stimuli (words in his book or on the chalkboard) and immediately integrate them with auditory or verbal stimuli (oral instructions). Furthermore, the assumption is made that the child can do this with a minimum of reinforcement from tactile or kinesthetic cues.[32] Estimates vary widely (from 7 to 20 percent) as to the number of children who cannot respond to standard teaching. Many of these children have major problems in visual development.

Optometric vision therapy is designed to overcome these problems. This type of vision training goes far beyond orthoptic training, in which the patient looks at a target in a stereoscope and by means of some herculean mental effort, is asked to fuse, or bring together, two separate images, one seen by each eye.

Optometric vision therapy is NOT "eye exercises."[33] It does not consist solely of eye-movement training and eye-hand coordination. Therapy procedures involve the use of postural and vestibular information to establish visual direction.[34] Gross motor and balance activities are used to develop the proper internal coordinate system to give correct spatial direction to stimuli received by the eyes. Integration of kinesthetic, auditory, and tactile data with visual data is taught in order for the child to achieve intersensory equivalence and to encode from one sensory modality to another. Form perception is taught kinesthetically, tactilely, and visually. Visual memory is stressed. This type of vision training has been practiced by some optometric clinicians for more than thirty years.[35]

Much controversy appears to surround the value of this type of training. Work by D. D. Durrell, M. W. Morgan, S. O. Richardson, and R. C. Wunderlich has shown the value of perceptual-motor training in helping school achievement.[36] Durrell divided 540 first-grade pupils into four homogeneous groups. Each group was given ten minutes of daily training for four months as follows: Group 1, auditory training; Group 2, visual; Group 3, auditory and visual; Group 4, no training (control group). When the groups were evaluated at the end of four months, their reading scores were: Group 1 (auditory) 75.7 percent; Group 2 (visual) 85.0 percent, Group 3 (auditory and visual) 93.4 percent; Group 4 (control) 59.4 percent. Morgan, in her study of third and fourth graders who had taken visual therapy, found statistically significant improvement (.001 level of confidence) in the following areas: self-image, scholastic performance, speech patterns, and perception of rotated letters. In addition to these controlled studies, a large body of optometric clinicians who use these vision-training techniques find that their young patients are better able to achieve in school with consequent improved self-image and reduction of behavior problems that result from frustrations in school.

DESPITE THE IMPORTANCE of adequate visual development in learning, it would be presumptuous to assert that this is the sole factor. In evaluating reasons for a child's learning disabilities, consideration must be given to other variables, such as home environment, experiential background, motivation to learn, genetic "grey matter," general physical health and development, and good teaching techniques. In the final analysis, there must be complete interdisciplinary cooperation between all of the professions concerned with this child's future: education, psychology, optometry, pediatrics, neurology, speech therapy, and others.

By combining the perceptual-motor approach with help for the other variables listed above, optometric clinicians have been remarkably successful in helping learning-disabled children to achieve.[37] Ideally, developmental diagnosis and therapy should start very early in life, rather than serve as a court of last resort after all else has failed.

NOTES

1. Robert M. Wold (ed.), *Visual and Perceptual Aspects of the Achieving and Underachieving Child* (Seattle, Wash.: Special Child Publications, 1969).
2. Charles Huelsman, "Some Recent Research on Visual Problems in Reading," *American Journal of Optometry and Archives of the American Academy of Optometry* (November 1958); Ralph Rychener and Jean Robinson, "Reading Disabilities and the Ophthalmologist, "*American Academy of Ophthalmology and Otolaryngology, Transactions* (November-December 1948).
3. Nathan Flax, "Problems in Relating Visual Function to Reading Disorder," *American Journal of Optometry and Archives of the American Academy of Optometry* (May 1970).
4. Herbert G. Birch, "Dyslexia and the Maturation of Visual Function," *Reading Disability*, ed. John Money (Baltimore, Md.: Johns Hopkins Press, 1962).
5. M. L. J. Abercrombie, "The Body Image," *Developmental Medicine and Child Neurology*, 6 (1964); Duane Alexander and John Money, "Reading Disability and the Problem of Direction Sense," *The Reading Teacher*, 20, No. 5 (February 1967); N. Dale Bryant, "Characteristics of Dyslexia and Their Remedial Implication," *Exceptional Children*, 31, No. 4 (December 1965), 197.
6. Richard Held, "Plasticity in Sensory-Motor Systems," *Scientific American* (November 1965).

7. Arnold Gesell and Catherine Amatruda, *Developmental Diagnosis* (New York, N.Y.: Hoeber, 1947).
8. Alexander and Money, "Reading Disability and the Problem of Direction Sense."
9. Ibid; Bryant, "Characteristics of Dyslexia."
10. Bryant, "Characteristics of Dyslexia"; A. Gesell, F. Ilg, and G. Bullis, *Vision—Its Development in Infant and Child* (New York, N.Y.: Hoeber, 1949).
11. L. Belmont and H. Birch, "Lateral Dominance and Right-Left Awareness in Normal Children," *Child Development*, 34 (1963), 268.
12. Nathan Flax, "The Clinical Significance of Dominance," *American Journal of Optometry and Archives of the American Academy of Optometry* (September 1966).
13. Jean Turner Goins, "Visual Perceptual Abilities and Early Reading Progress," *Supplementary Educational Monograph No. 87* (Chicago, Ill.: University of Chicago Press, February, 1958); George D. Spache, *Reading in the Elementary School* (Boston, Mass.: Allyn and Bacon, Inc., 1964).
14. N. C. Kephart, "Visual Behavior of the Retarded Child," *American Journal of Optometry and Archives of the American Academy of Optometry* (March 1958).
15. A. V. Zaporozhets, "The Development of Perception in the Preschool Child," in *European Research in Cognitive Development, Monographs of the Society for Research in Child Development*, 30, No. 2 (1965) 82-101.
16. Gesell, Ilg, and Bullis, *"Vision—Its Development in Infant and Child."*
17. Ibid.
18. H. Birch and L. Belmont, "Auditory Visual Integration in Normal and Retarded Readers," *American Journal of Orthopsychiatry*, 34, No. 5 (October 1964).
19. Birch, "Dyslexia and the Maturation of Visual Function."
20. Gesell and Amatruda, *Developmental Diagnosis*.
21. Flax, "Problems in Relating Visual Function to Reading Disorder."
22. Ibid; Nathan Flax, "Visual Function in Dyslexia," *American Journal of Optometry and Archives of the American Academy of Optometry* (September 1968).
23. Wold, *Visual and Perceptual Aspects*.
24. Earl A. Taylor, "The Spans: Perception, Apprehension and Recognition," *American Journal of Ophthalmology*, 44, No. 4 (October 1957).
25. G. N. Getman, "Vision, Perception and Learning in the 1970s." Paper presented to the 1970 White House Conference on Children, December 1970; Robert Wold, "Vision and Hearing," *Journal of Optometric Vision Therapy*, 1, No. 4 (December 1970), 3-6.
26. Raymond L. Clemmens, "Obscure Causes of School Failure—A Pediatric Viewpoint." Paper presented at the 42nd Annual Conference of the Council for Exceptional Children, Chicago, April 3, 1964.
27. Wold, *Visual and Perceptual Aspects*.
28. Ray C. Wunderlich, *Kids, Brains and Learning* (St. Petersburg, Fla.: Johnny Reads, Inc., 1970).
29. Florence Rappaport, "Etiology and Identification: The Parental Merry-Go-Round," *1967 Convocation on Children and Young Adults with Learning Disabilities* (Pittsburgh, Pa.: Home for Crippled Children, 1967).
30. S. Alan Cohen, "Diagnosis and Etiology or Operation Overthink," *1967 Convocation on Children and Young Adults with Learning Disabilities* (Pittsburgh, Pa.: Home for Crippled Children, 1967).
31. Wold, *Visual and Perceptual Aspects*.
32. Kephart, "Visual Behavior of the Retarded Child."
33. Lawrence MacDonald, "A Programmed Approach to Vision Training," *Optometric Extension Program Papers*, (October 1962—September 1965); Robert A. Kraskin, "Vision Training in Action," ibid. (October 1965—September 1967); Ralph E. Schrock, "Optometric Training in Action," ibid. (October 1968—September 1970); A. M. Skeffington, "Clinical Optometry in Theory and Practice," ibid. (1928—Present).

34. Alexander and Money, "Reading Disability and the Problem of Direction Sense"; Bryant, "Characteristics of Dyslexia."
35. Skeffington, "Clinical Optometry in Theory and Practice."
36. Donald D. Durrell and Helen A. Murphy, "The Auditory Discrimination Factor in Reading Readiness and Reading Disability," *Education* (May 1953); Mavis Welch Morgan, "The Effect of Visual-Perceptual Training Upon Subsequent Scholastic Progress of Children with Specific Visual Disabilities." Unpublished master's thesis (Reno, Nev.: University of Nevada, 1966); Sylvia O. Richardson, M.D., "Learning Disorders and The Pre-School Child," *New Jersey Education Association Review*, 41, No. 6 (February 1968); Wunderlich, *Kids, Brains and Learning*.
37. Wold, *Visual and Perceptual Aspects*.

Cerebral Stimulants for Children with Learning Disorders

Hunter H. Comly*

IN LATE June, 1970, the *Washington Post* published an article that misrepresented the use of medication among Omaha school children. Misquoting a physician's estimate of the incidence of learning disability led to implications that 10 percent of the children were being drugged on a "mass medication basis" and that coercion by *the school system* was being used to enforce conformity. A Nebraska politician, seizing the chance to polarize and further confuse the blacks, accused the school board president of abetting a plot to experiment on deprived children like guinea pigs, drugging them into submission, and thereby continuing their enslavement by the "Establishment." A widely syndicated columnist sensationalized the information, fanned the flames of suspicion, referred to physicians as "speed merchants" and "dope pushers" who, by "biochemical mediation" put the "cop and the concentration camp inside the pill and the pill inside the kid." A New Jersey congressman, of the House Government Operations Committee, presided at the "Right to Privacy" inquiry that investigated the use of drugs on grammar school children. Early in February, 1971, a widely read authority on how children learn and how children fail displayed in blushing color for the nation's breakfast TV audience his "instant reaction of outrage when someone blew the lid off this in Omaha."

The mass communication media make misinformation instantly available. Now even cool heads, rattled by the shrill alarms, contribute further to the alarm and confusion.

Responsible child experts have, with justification, after viewing shoddy, understaffed, institutional programs for retarded and disturbed children, protested the wholesale use of drugs. Objections regarding drug use with children range from the soundly reasoned (by varying degrees) to the paranoid and absurd. Unfortunately, the outcome of reasoned discussions rarely makes the big headlines as much as do the politically inspired shrieks of protest.

---

*Hunter H. Comly, M.D., is associate professor of child psychiatry, State Psychopathic Hospital, Iowa City, Iowa.

It seems appropriate to review the clinical and behavioral features of children with minimal brain dysfunction syndromes that may call for medication. This paper will narrow the focus to a report of a double-blind assessment of the use of cerebral stimulants with forty children suffering minimal brain dysfunction whose behavior was rated by classroom teachers. It will also report on the observations of parents of 197 comparable children who took such medication over an extended period.

In both groups to be reviewed, the "chief complaints" varied. Some of the children were referred by the juvenile court workers as firesetters, shoplifters, truants from school, or incorrigibles. Doctors were consulted regarding such matters as the children's nightmares, headaches, excessive crying, and vomiting, or because they were too fat, too tired, or wet or soiled themselves, or seemed accident-prone. Schools referred children who were forgetful, daydreamy, clumsy, noisy, disruptive, overactive, or failing academically despite good mental abilities as indicated by IQ tests.

The complete psychiatric clinic examination very frequently brought puzzling clinical pictures into a more comprehensible focus, as similarities in history, and in physical, psychiatric, and psychological test findings emerged: over 70 percent of the children had been exposed to one or more unusual hazards before, during, or just after birth. The histories indicated their immature nervous tissues had been subjected to the devitalizing effect of such events as maternal toxemia, malnutrition and anemia, or diabetes, placental detachment, premature birth, episodes of jaundice, asphyxia, bleeding, or dehydration, or by serious viral and bacterial infections.

Closer examination of the behavioral histories revealed the presence of unusual developmental patterns, such as underactivity or overactivity, clumsiness, accident-proneness, delayed and/or disordered speech, disturbed sleep patterns, inattentiveness to relevant stimuli (such as pain, cold, or fatigue), peculiarly concrete and confused thinking, perseverative activities, poor penmanship, poor arithmetic, and poor reading abilities, inappropriate excitability, and erratic and group-disruptive behavior. Such behavior patterns were also observed during the *psychiatric, physical, and psychological examinations.*

DOUBLE-BLIND STUDY OF AMPHETAMINE VERSUS PLACEBO
EFFECTS ON MINIMAL CEREBRAL DYSFUNCTION CHILDREN

Method

School social workers referred fifty-seven overactive children from five to eleven years of age. School authorities granted permission to oblige the classroom teacher to rate the child's behavior using the *Fels Rating Scale of Classroom Behavior* twelve times over a six-week period.[1] Forty-eight of the children were included in the study, and the ratings carried out by the classroom teacher were, for the most part, satisfactory. Pupil absences and other unavoidable circumstances resulted in only forty cases being included for data evaluation.

All the parents who were invited to participate (after the child had been examined) agreed to do so. The parents were given six marked and dated envelopes, each of which contained seven capsules. The sustained release capsules contained either 5, 10 or 15 mg. of dextroamphetamine or (though identical otherwise in appearance) an inert substance that served as a placebo. Directions for drug administration were simple. The parent was to give the child one capsule before breakfast daily for six weeks beginning on an assigned date.

The order in which the drug and placebo were given was random within four different patterns. The three drug weeks were, of necessity, consecutive. That is, the child would get 5 mg. daily the first week, 10 daily the second, and 15 daily the third, and receive the placebos through weeks four, five, and six. That is, the dosages of active drug might be given the first three weeks and none the last three of the experimental period (5, 10, 15, 0, 0, 0). Three alternative patterns were 0, 5, 10, 15, 0, 0, or 0, 0, 5, 10, 15, 0, or 0, 0, 0, 5, 10, 15. Thus neither the parents (who administered the medication), the children, the classroom teachers, nor the data analyst knew when or how much medication was being given. The psychiatrist knew at all times, but the record key was not revealed to the data analyst until the scores had been obtained from the ratings and a guess was made as to when active drugs were received by the children. Thus, the double-blind arrangement for data evaluations was strictly followed. The classroom teacher was given a package of materials including the *Fels Rating Scale of Classroom Behavior*, instruction sheets, and twelve data sheets for recording their ratings. The ratings were mailed to the data analyst. From the rating data sheets, a score was mathematically derived, such that the higher the total score, the poorer the child's overall classroom adjustment; conversely, the lower the score, the better the child's classroom adjustment.

Results

After each of the six weeks was scored for each child, a total score for the three medication weeks and the three placebo weeks was obtained. These "drug weeks" and "placebo weeks" totals were then totalled and the mean calculated for all forty children. The mean score for the 120 (that is, 40 times 3) "placebo weeks" was 172.7. The mean score for the 120 "drug weeks" was 142.3. These scores proved that the children were "better behaved," that is, less disruptive of the classroom and less burdensome to the teacher, while receiving medication. The level of confidence was beyond .001. Thirty-one of the forty children had better scores while receiving medication, and the average improvement (drop) in score was 42.4 points. Of the nine children whose scores were poorer while receiving medication, the average lack of improvement (elevation) score was only 10.6 points. This suggests that if the medicine helped, it helped considerably, and that if it failed to help, the increase in score was only one-fourth as much as the decrease in the score if improvement occurred. The greatest individual improvement in score was a drop of 96 points whereas the greatest score difference reflecting worsened behavior in a child was an elevation of only 22 points.

It was concluded that this study supported much of the previously published clinical work that showed the beneficial effects of dextroamphetamine on the behavior of children with minimal brain dysfunction and that the medication effects were superior to those effects that might have come about as a result of the special attention the child received in the clinic and in the school and from the placebo effects of the capsules per se.

PARENT RATINGS OF BEHAVIORAL CHANGES IN 197 CHILDREN RECEIVING CEREBRAL STIMULANTS

One hundred ninety-seven children with minimal brain dysfunction were followed from 1 to 65 months, using a detailed questionnaire. The frequency of occurrence and the changes in 48 different relevant signs and symptoms were assessed. At the time of the survey, 49 percent of the dextroamphetamine cases were still taking the drug after an average of 16½ months. Fifty-nine percent of the methylphenidate (Ritalin) cases were using their medication after a mean duration of 13.7 months. Twenty-six percent of the 197 children had been excluded from school for varying periods because of poor behavior. *Table 1* shows the effects of cerebral stimulants on *school performance* of children with brain dysfunction as rated by their parents. *Table 2* reflects the effects of cerebral stimulants on the *behavior* of the same children as rated by their parents. Both tables show the percent that were improved minus the percent that were worse, and in each case figures are given separately for both medications. The effectiveness of dextroamphetamine so closely approximates that of methylphenidate that one confirms the other.

The only items on which parental ratings indicated cerebral stimulants typically had an adverse effect on children were in difficulty in going to sleep and in the weight of underweight children.

Of 107 youngsters rated as having difficulty in going to sleep, 27 improved on methylphenidate but 52 became worse. Of 22 rated as having difficulty in going to sleep, 5 improved on dextroamphetamine and 10 became worse.

Of 71 youngsters who were considered too thin, 8 improved on methylphenidate and 20 became worse. Of 20 considered too thin, 4 improved on dextroamphetamine and 1 was rated worse. Of 32 youngsters considered too heavy, 17 were rated as improved on methylphenidate and none became worse. Of 5 considered too heavy, 2 improved on dextroamphetamine, and 1 was judged to have become worse.

Those items on which there was not a net improvement of at least 20 percent on methylphenidate are not included in the table. These are: frequent urination, daytime wetting of pants, bedwetting, frequent headaches, excessive sweating while sleeping, sluggishness and underactivity, tendency to stay indoors too much, tendency to stay indoors too little, and association with undesirable friends. A number of these items have such a low frequency in this group as to preclude a 20 percent improvement rate.

Discussion

Eighty-six percent of the parents indicated that the total clinical experience of diagnosis, testing, interpretation, and observation of medication effects enabled them to more clearly define the difficulties so that they could understand that the "learning and/or behavior problems weren't just due to our or the teacher's mistakes." The average number of professional man-hours of time per case was seven.

In the double-blind placebo study that is reported here, it is clear that dextroamphetamine produced an effect superior to that of the placebo. J. F. McDermott reported a peculiar "placebo effect" encountered in the use of dextroamphetamine in the hyperactive child.[2] Medication instructions had been misinterpreted and medication was discontinued, yet the boy's dramatic improvement in school performance—both academically and behaviorally—held up for six months despite his exposure to continued marital difficulties in the home. The family attributed the improvement to Dexedrine. McDermott believed that the pills gave the boy the dose of "strength" that he needed, and that his enhanced confidence permitted him to not worry about how well he was doing in spelling or baseball. At first glance it seems difficult to understand how these short-acting drugs can seemingly have a continuing beneficial effect on some children after they are no longer being used, while other similar patients have immediate recurrence of symptoms. If one will consider the enormous number of variables involved in the production of symptoms and the complexities of the setting in which the symptoms are expressed, this becomes somewhat more understandable. It is a great help to the family to realize that the child's difficulties do not flow from simple, willful disobedience, or from a "double dip" in "original sin," etc. Each child, when first seen, could be understood to be traversing a very rough road. His "shock absorbers" are simply not up to the tasks (some of these children have been thrown completely off the "road to learning" or the "highway of life"). Just as a car might traverse a smooth highway very adequately, even though its shock absorbers are defective, a child may be able to get along in some situations quite well, but he may lose control seriously when his particular defective servomechanisms are called upon to function. Quite often we learned of the parents and school making great efforts to create new arrangements and expectations that would be analogous to smoothing the road out considerably.

In J. G. Millichap's excellent review article, the superiority of cerebral stimulants both the placebo and to other psychoactive drugs was confirmed.[3] He suggested that they be given for only four to eight weeks and then stopped to see if behavioral difficulties recurred. The experience reflected in the series of cases that are reported here suggests that it is feasible and may be safe to give the drugs daily, if necessary, for over a year. Many of the children took them regularly for two to four years. Subsequent experience in the past seven years has so far confirmed the safety of this approach with this particular group of children as well as several hundred similar ones. I have not, in twenty-five years, learned of a child for whom I have prescribed cerebral stimulants who became dependent on or habituated to these drugs. On the contrary, the children must often be reminded to take their medications. Forgetfulness of routine acts is a very common problem in these children, and this fact usually results in an occasional morning or afternoon when the child is not being aided by the drug. Parents and teachers usually have

Table 1

Effects of Cerebral Stimulants on School Performance of Children with Brain Dysfunction
(as rated by parents)

Changes in Children on Cerebral Stimulants
162 Children on Methylphenidate (Ritalin)

	No Rating	Never a Problem	Much Better	Better	No Change	Worse	Much Worse
School behavior							
Citizenship, conduct, or deportment grades	28	11	66	41	13	2	1
Academic subjects							
Reading	24	13	40	56	21	5	3
Spelling	24	13	40	55	21	4	5
Handwriting	23	6	42	50	31	4	6
Arithmetic	31	7	33	54	29	2	6

Net Improvement on Cerebral Stimulants

	162 Children on Methylphenidate (Ritalin) % Better minus % Worse	35 Children on Dextroamphetamine (Dexedrine) % Better minus % Worse
Citizenship, conduct, or deportment grades	64	49
Reading	54	49
Spelling	53	31
Handwriting	51	37
Arithmetic	49	26

Table 2
Effects of Cerebral Stimulants on Behavior of Children with Brain Dysfunction
(as rated by parents)

	Net Improvement on Cerebral Stimulants	
	162 Children on Methylphenidate (Ritalin)	35 Children on Dextroamphetamine (Dexedrine)
	% Better minus % Worse	% Better minus % Worse
Listening and following directions	65	60
Span of attention	65	41
Overactivity	58	63
Getting along in play groups	57	49
Tendency to become wild and overexcited easily	51	63
Enjoying quiet hobbies (model building, stamp collecting, table games)	49	43
Using a plan to find things (TV guide, dictionary, index, etc.)	46	51
Accepting disappointments	45	34
Sympathy or feeling for others	40	26
Cleaning up his own messes	38	40
Enthusiasm for life	36	34
Restless, purposeless jerks of body	34	20
Stubbornness	33	23
Reaction to teasing	33	20
Automatic habits (flushing toilet, zipping, buttoning, switching lights off, replacing tools, etc.)	33	17
Spilling and breaking things	30	37
Tendency to hurt or bruise self often	28	26
Speech	27	23
Coming home from play or school on time	26	20
Self-centeredness	26	31
Tendency to misplace or lose things frequently	25	29
Knowing when he is cold, tired, or in pain	23	23
Forgetting what he wants to say	23	17
Frequent bad dreams	22	29

little difficulty in noticing deficient controls or functions and can confirm that a dose was overlooked.

In a recent study by L. Pope, it has been shown that a distinction can be made between hyperactivity and restlessness in children with minimal brain dysfunction (MBD).[4] While the total motor activity level of the children did not differ from that of normal controls, their restlessness was significantly greater. Other refined studies of so-called hyperactive children in a free-play situation, where their total activity is accurately measured with an actometer, indicate that after the child has been given cerebral stimulants his total activity in a free-play situation actually increases. In our experience, about 20 percent of the MBD children are lethargic and underactive. They are daydreamy, "quiet" wigglers with patterns of historical and clinical findings that are similar, and they are also aided to a comparable degree by cerebral stimulants; the improvement includes a clear increase in their motor activity. I think it is unfortunate that so much attention has been paid to hyperactivity. This inaccurate designation has come to be a glib cliché that has been seized upon by imaginative writers and politicians who have contributed to the weaving of a rather dangerous myth as mentioned above. *Hyperactivity* is a word of mixed parentage in which a Greek prefix meaning *over* has been added to a Latin root. Actually, the Greek prefix *dys*, which means *bad*, is perhaps more appropriate than *hyper*. Clearly, cerebral stimulants seem to improve the problem of *dys*activity rather than *hyper*activity. In our experience, a much more universal finding in children with MBD is confusion. They may write or read backwards, draw pictures upside down, get *before* and *after* mixed up in telling time. Confusion is likely to show up as concrete thinking, poor short-term memory, perseverative thoughts, poor speech and action, and faulty discrimination in many learning and social situations. If the headlines would reflect the point that the MBD children are confused and dysactive, and that after medication they are less confused but actually more active in free-play situations, it would be harder for the political opportunists to leap to the false conclusions that sensationalize the instant media messages.

THIS STUDY lends support to the view that the cerebral stimulants enhance the functioning of the higher critical faculties that are probably mediated by the cerebral cortex or by those portions of the brain that are more recent products of evolutionary development. The data viewed from this point of view seems less mysterious, and the so-called paradoxical effect seems more in keeping with common sense.

The disruptive child who has repeatedly interfered with the teacher's job satisfactions and his classmates' learning is very understandably a target for anger. It is very tempting to expose the daydreaming or distractible child to his classmates' ridicule and laughter by calling upon him when it is certain that he will not know the answer or what has been said. The child who is repeatedly jolted into this kind of reality contact readily becomes clownish. He attempts to produce class laughter that is *with him* when *he chooses* rather than be the object of laughter that occurs when the teacher chooses. He thereby becomes an active agent rather than a passive victim. The awkward or forgetful child is often momentarily helpless; he spills, loses, tears, messes, or drops, and even if not scolded, he is painfully reminded of his weaknesses. The accidental misdeed (which proves such a sharp reminder of his helplessness) may lead the child to "pretend" that he is in charge of himself; that is, he may even loudly assert that he did it on purpose, and this he does mainly to deny his sense of fragility. Unfortunately, these common defenses of clowning and apparent defiance are often misunderstood, and various punishments are used, which produce a vicious circle and a more intense sense of alienation in the child.

When the dedicated teacher who has patiently applied all her skills and energy to aid a wiggly, clownish, noisy, defiant child, senses a sudden improvement in the child after he takes a little pill, it is understandable that she may react by saying "I can't believe it's the same child," or "To think that a little pill can cause that much change. It's got to be magic." Such commonly heard statements reflect a struggle to cope intellectually and rationally with data that doesn't fit the teacher's fundamental views of the learning process, or even of the basic "nature of man."

It is unfortunate when a teacher responds overtly to the child or parent with guilt or anxiety—often expressed as oversolicitude and openly voiced misgivings about using drugs. Teachers, as well as parents, do not want children to grow up "depending on a crutch." Yet they have to accept the fact, as do doctors, that there are many kinds of human weakness and growth irregularities that respond well to temporary (or even permanent) support. We don't think of *glasses* or orthodontic *braces* as "crutches." Unfortunately, there are many conditions for which long-term aids are essential (convulsive disorders and hormone deficiencies, to name only two).

Fortunately, most children who are helped with cerebral stimulants are able to exert increasingly better self-control as they approach full adult size and are able to take on adult-like responsibilities. The cerebral stimulants rather often seem to cause responses similar to the effect on the adult—with increased sleep problems, jittery feelings, irritability, and appetite suppression as the child becomes an adolescent.

There are, however, many adolescents who profit from the support of cerebral stimulants; this is not because they are dependent upon or addicted to the drug, but because they still show a cluster of handicaps that interferes with social and learning abilities.

NOTES

1. For sources of tests mentioned in this article, see Appendix.
2. J. F. McDermott, "A Specific Placebo Effect Encountered in the Use of Dexedrine in a Hyperactive Child," *American Journal of Psychology*, 121 (March 1965), 923-924.
3. J. G. Millichap, "Drugs in the Management of Hyperkinetic and Perceptally Handicapped Children," *Journal of the American Medical Association*, 206, No. 7 (November 11, 1968), 1527-30.
4. L. Pope, "Motor Activity in Brain Injured Children, *American Journal of Orthopsychiatry*, 40, No. 5 (October 1970), 783-793.

Reading Achievement as a Function of Maturity, Diet, and Manipulation of Chronic States of High Arousal

George von Hilsheimer*

IN THE SEVEN YEAR PERIOD that ended in June 1970, we had seen one resident population of 527 adolescents for periods of three months to five years. The average stay was eighteen months. Their histories listed severe learning disabilities, school failures, social maladjustments, delinquencies, and psychoses as well as other emotional disorders.

Until June of 1966, this population had been enrolled in a program that was based on the models evolved by A. Aichorn, H. Lane and D. Wills.[1] Reduction of stress in the group was sought by removing them from common behaviors of adults, establishment of a democratic existential subculture in which adults and children are political peers, and in which a great deal of behavior that is ordinarily regarded as punishable by schools such as, language, dress, and attendance was ignored. Limits were set either by a democratic meeting (not a psychodynamic or emotion-centered therapy group), or by frank admission that there was a breakdown of democratic procedures and the naked use of arbitrary adult force.

This program, known as Summerlane School, was based on a number of the following assumptions:

- Children learn to fail from adults, or from other children who have learned failing patterns from adults.

- Much childish failure is caused by adults who make inappropriate demands on the children.

- All children, and all organisms for that matter, have a basic posture of growth and development and strongly move towards the achievement of power and control.

- Most core skills regarded as essential for middle class Americans in the twentieth century will be learned without instruction by the child, if highly visible adults spend a great deal of time with children in organic or "natural" settings, rather than institutional and formal ways.

---

*George von Hilsheimer, a Brethren minister, is superintendent of the Green Valley School Psychiatric Hospital in Orange City, Florida.

- Democratic decision making is a precise tool that should be used not merely for making decisions, but also for shaping values, behavior and identity; it must be seriously, consistently, and primarily the goal of adults who are working with children to reinforce democratic behaviors in every possible way.

Our initial results at Summerlane School were impressive. In a population that included drug addicts, psychotics, delinquents, and others, our five-year follow-up success rate has been in excess of 90 percent for more than 100 children, some of whom were in residence for as short a time as three months. Our intuitive and clinical impressions in this initial study were that the children who reach our "behavioral sink" were all very much alike:[2]

- They seemed immature, physically, behaviorally, and in perceptual and learning abilities.
- They seemed chronically tense.
- They seemed to exhibit episodic confusion, fatigue, and disorientation.
- They all preferred soft, easily digested, sweet, primarily carbohydrate food; consequently, they all seemed in need of energy and yet ate a non-energy producing diet.
- They were always bored.
- Technically speaking, they were chronically in high states of physiological arousal, that is, low basal skin resistance, but with high variability in that low range; fast and shallow respiration, variable blood pressure, fast and variable pulse rates, and desynchronous, fast, low amplitude brain waves.

Maturity

It seems condescending to rehearse the concept of maturity and development for a literate audience who is concerned with children who do not learn readily. Unfortunately, it seems necessary. I have frequently heard platform attacks, usually in the form of asides, in particular attacking Gesell, Ilg, and Ames. For example, I listened with no little astonishment at the University of Hartford to Marianne Frostig who casually stated, "Oh, the Gesell people made up an ideal scheme and forced children into it; no one takes their data very seriously; there is a very serious question about its validity." I know of no such serious study, and I would be most interested in any study which might emerge from the commercially very successful Frostig program that shows the kind of readily described and replicated assessments and programs that are published by the Gesell Institute and others that are concerned with very large numbers of children.

One of the more incredible attacks on the *concept* of maturity decried a "growing tendency to ascribe delayed language ability to immaturity," and complained that the "concept is not capable of operationally precise definition because in organized behavior, immaturity is only representative of a phase of growth in which the organism has not arrived at full development."[3]

These incredible assertions are utterly unsupported by evidence or the literature. The statement that any *term* is incapable of operationally precise definition boggles the mind. One wonders what that writer thinks when he tries to comprehend, if ever he does, a biochemical vector, or any other process in science. I cannot think of any area in science in which "mere" phases of dynamic processes are not the subject of investigation.

Teachers and parents are usually familiar with the developmental concepts that were yielded by research done at the Gesell Institute and was substantially supported by other American psychologists.[4] S. M. Ervin, D. McCarthy, D. McNeill, and D. I. Slobin have shown that verbal behavior follows similarly consistent patterns of development and maturation.[5] For example, *no* and *don't* appear before *yes* and *do* in all cultures and language groups. *He* and *it* are used by the growing child before *I* and *me*. All of these authorities are in substantial agreement on how speech development may be accelerated or retarded. Other things being equal, speech develops earlier and better:

- The healthier and better fed the child is.
- The more intelligent the child is, although slow speech development is not necessarily a sign of low intelligence.
- The more adults who are in daily contact with the child.
- When the child relates more to adults than to children.
- The greater the number of playmates.
- The greater the exposure to verbal materials.
- The higher the social class of the family; indications emerge around the end of the first eighteen months of life.
- After the first year, speech develops more so in girls than in boys, and the difference grows larger with age.
- Speech defects, with the exception of lisping, are more frequent in boys than in girls and the difference grows greater with age.
- If the child is in a normal home and not in an institution where speech development is slower than it is in even the poorest of normal homes.
- The fewer the number of siblings.
- If the child is learning only one language.

A. S. Aslanov, A. R. Luria, B. B. Anan'ev, C. H. Waddington and D. E. Berlyne have provided an exceptionally elegant series of research, which demonstrates the operational development of maturity through genetic transactions, environmental transactions, brain growth, interaction between motor and verbal factors and the development of epistemic organization, curiosity, play, and novelty.[6] E. Zigler and A. R. Luria have particularly related this work to the problems of learning dysfunctions.[7]

Luria told children to put a quoit on a dowel, which they readily did. Later he ordered them to stop, after they had begun the movement. Quite young children could not stop. When asked to stop they intensified the placement of the quoit on the dowel. If he offered them a reward for stopping they intensified the movement even more, but they could not stop. Slightly older children could readily stop the placement after they had begun. Luria then asked the children to switch from one dowel to another, after the placement had begun. The same events occurred. It is easy to see that the interaction between verbal and motor factors develops or matures. Luria taught children to squeeze a rubber bulb with their right hands when they saw a red circle on a grey background, and with their left hands when they saw a green circle on a yellow background. Once the child had learned the task, Luria switched the backgrounds. The children did not notice and continued squeezing the bulbs in response to the red circle or the green circle. If he told the children to change in accordance with the background the children who were from age three to about five years old could not do it. Children who were older than five generally could. If, however, he used a red airplane and a green airplane and then gave semantic content to the signals such as, squeeze with your right hand when you see the yellow background because the plane can fly since the sun is out, and with the left when it is grey because the plane can't fly since it is raining, then the younger children could relate to the background. Each of these simple tasks is related to the age and development of the child. Luria has further shown that retarded individuals and brain injured individuals are very much like young children in this verbal/motor interaction.

A. D. Pick recently surveyed these issues and drew conclusions that support W. W. Lewis' findings that reading interventions for failing or young children do not seem to be supported by careful studies.[8] In fact, they often seem harmful. Maturation seems to control, both in children recapitulating the average time schedule and in those widely separated from the mean. D. Elkin very strongly supports this point of view in assessing the recent fad of academically oriented preschool programs.[9] R. A. Freeman's survey of compensatory education programs yields even more compelling evidence that instruction, even when elaborate, individualized, and well funded, does not seem to yield improved reading or other skills even in quite deficient groups of poor children where one would expect regression effects to have some formal "improvement" effect.[10]

Arousal

It is well known that continuous deprivation, of almost any kind, causes individuals to appear to be younger than undeprived people of the same age. Stress and boredom are forms of deprivation, which prolong immaturity. Children who are simply removed from violent families and placed in quiet and supportive normal home situations will enjoy startling physical growth after six months or so of relief.

Arousal seems very closely to approximate much of the characteristic behavior of infants and young children. Infants spend an enormous amount of time in sleep, and the largest portion of this sleep is in REM or rapid eye movement sleep. During this REM time the brain is very active, with low amplitude, high frequency brain waves, intracranial blood pressure and temperature are high and variable, and the eyes and face are very active. Inundation with noise, boredom, stress, and trauma seem characteristically to produce similar brain phenomenon with bursts of hyperactive behavior alternating with flaccid, atonal, bored and inactive "tune-out" behavior.[12]

The arousal pattern, which is controlled by the sympathetic nervous system, richly interacts with the hormonal system.[12] Anxiety-producing events can produce chronic endocrine imbalance, and endocrine imbalance can produce all of the physiological and subjective attributes of anxiety or arousal. Chronic states of high arousal seen in children are generally called hyperkinetic, and can be reduced by drugs which produce arousal and hyperactivity in normal individuals.[13] There are data which suggest that children who fail at reading show abnormal EEGs, which are characteristic of chronic high arousal.[14] Our own data support this suggestion. In general, the behavioral effects of chronic high arousal in children seem quite consistent with the phases of development that L. B. Ames called "disequilibrium."[15]

Our experience, in 1966, led us to conclude that most of the children who were sent to us, despite their being accompanied by a fantastic variety of referring "diagnoses," were quite similar. In a much larger group of children, M. Klapper and W. Neff found no objective differences among children who were labeled with various dysfunctions.[16] A survey of professionals who were working with hyperkinetic children found practically the same similarities that we report.[17]

Using dexedrine and ritalin to reduce arousal

We selected twenty-three members of our population who were distinguished by the following characteristics:

- A history of drug abuse excluding any who were limited to marijuana or hashish smoking.
- Sleep disorders.
- Clinical evidence of subictal neuroses, or paradoxical brain activity as evidenced by sporadic hyperkinesis, functional narcolepsy, extremely deviant rate of eye blinks or discrete, irregular bursts of eyeblinks, clinical impressions of fogginess, sleepiness, sporadic discontiguous interaction with the environment (petit mal) without psychotic elements, and individuals showing sleep spindles during waking EEGs.

Reading disabilities, or inconsistencies in repeated tests of reading achievement, or mountainous profiles in reading ability subtests with discrepancies at least as great as fifty percentile ranks.

THESE TWENTY-THREE STUDENTS, who range in ages from thirteen to twenty, and included seven girls and sixteen boys, were matched according to reading ability, age, social status, IQ, thirteen points of history, gender, and fifteen points of social interaction with twenty-three controls. Neither group differed in the treatment it received, or the social structures that were set up in their schools. The control group members were given placebos, which were drawn from envelopes distributed by a nurse to the aide. The nurse knew only that the two groups received medication from alpha or beta bottles of dextroamphetamine or ritalin. Therefore, neither the distributing nurse, nor the aide who was giving the medications, nor the group itself, knew that placebos were being given, or which group received the placebos. Since this group was quite sophisticated about drugs and their appearance they did know that the drugs were psychic energizers. A third control group was matched from the previous history of the school, since the total population could not produce three well matched groups at one time. This routine was continued for nine months. Four months following the routine the protocols for academic achievement and reading skills were inspected with the following outcome:

On the *Iowa Silent Reading Test* the active drug group improved a total of 8.4 percentile points over the placebo group, and 7.6 percentile points more than the historical control group.[18] The average distribution of high and low percentile ranks on the subtests among the active drug group was 15.8 points as compared to 22.3 points in the placebo group and 23.9 points in the historical control group after the same period of time. *Iowa Tests of Educational Development* showed a similar significant difference in improvement. Although we have not been able to continue formal academic testing of this group of twenty-three students, it is clear that substantially superior results in changing behavior have continued since out of the twenty-three only two have returned to drug usage, and neither of these two became involved to a degree that involved medical or police intervention. Moreover, of the two relapses, neither has subsequently abused *speed* or other elevating drugs.

A methodological problem is the question of regression, since it may be assumed that the group that formerly used drugs very likely did have intellectual deficits as a by-product and continuing problem; however, the regression effect would ordinarily be expected to migrate toward norms and not show significant improvement above norms of control groups; moreover, the historical control group was matched for drug abuse. All of the groups are well above their age norms in reading ability.

Since dextroamphetamine sulphate and other energizing drugs are seldom used with adolescents, we suggest that this small study invites further investigation of the utility of these drugs for the enhancement and acceleration of other interventions.

Diet

The literature that regards the effects of malnutrition and diets that are low in protein and the vitamin B complex is extensive.[19] We early determined that the gross states that are observed in migrant farm children had correlates in middle class children, and evolved routines for across the board interventions in this regard.[20] Unfortunately, this means that our evidence does not meet the criteria of manipulating one variable only, nor of double or triple blind control, but must rely on previous history control, clinical results and predictability for evidence. We have offered substantially different diets in two different centers, without making other changes in the program; however, the most useful data we can provide are that adolescents who were ranked by the staff and their peers as having greatly improved, or as becoming milder problems, tended spontaneously to choose a better diet than their more troublesome but similar peers. From the clinical point of view, our data indicate that we have improved our discharge time rate from an average of twenty-four months, to an average of eight months with the major change in procedures being a substantial reduction of sugars and carbohydrates in the diet, an increase in B vitamins in organic foods, and an addition of very high doses of vitamins to difficult cases, or cases with laboratory verification of low blood sugar or dysinsulinism, which would indicate a functional, or stress causes dysfunction of the adrenals.

Desensitization

A well established technique in behavior therapy is desensitization; it has been modified in our schools.[21] Hierarchies of picture slides are shown to the student while he is monitored by a digital GSR meter. Slides are organized both for specific phobic material, namely, mothers, and for more abstract concepts, such as social closeness, death, exhibitionism. If the galvanic skin response is downward (less resistance) when the slide is shown, the slide remains on until recovery and a slight elevation. It is then changed. No relaxation instructions are given. Sessions last about thirty minutes.

The most interesting data we have produced with this technique to date comes from a small group of severely emotionally ill children all of whom were transferred from long hospitalizations for psychoses, and exhibited concomitant learning deficits and apparent perceptual and learning dysfunctions. The technique, as developed by us in collaboration with D. Quirk of the Clarke Institute of Psychiatry, can be automated, which eliminates the therapist effect, or can be administered by other students, aides and technicians who have no conceptualization of the re-education rationale. In our center it is known by the acronym SCARS and generally is called "testing" by the lab technicians and the students. Thirteen individuals for whom no other educational intervention has been attempted in our setting have received naive technician-monitored routines. We simply used all of the slide trays in our catalog in numerical order. If we base our expectations on earlier experience, we would expect failure with these individuals, or that it would take from three to five years for the democratic existential milieu to function well enough for the student to be able to live independently. Our first result was that we eliminated a formerly consistent area of failure — the long-term hospitalization of the schizophrenic child. Secondly, we have been able to bring the range of re-education time down to one to three years. The last third of this residence has clearly become devoted to formal academic acceleration and not to emotional, perceptual, or behavioral reeducation. Thirdly, we have been able to corroborate earlier clinical impressions that reading skills seem to be a function that is inversely related to the severity of chronic long-term arousal, which appeared unrelated to external events. As the physiological variables normalized, the perceptual liabilities receded, the ability for switching and other motor/verbal tasks improved, and scores on standard reading and achievement tests improved.

We are now sufficiently satisfied with the utility of desensitization so that it is routinely utilized in our centers. We are also attempting a deconditioning program and are using this as the sole intervention in an attempt to improve reading and testing abilities for a group of black students. The preliminary results are gratifying.

Sleep therapy

Six years ago, some comments that were made by a Russian psychologist led us to attempt sleep therapy. This involved putting the patient to sleep for a very long period of time, ranging from three to eight days, by chemical means. This procedure used to have a wide and reportedly successful use in America.[22] Following the Russian model, we used a "sleep cocktail," which consists of small amounts of a large number of soporifics that are primarily derived from natural alkaloids, or we used substances which work through the mid-brain and do not interfere with dream time. We have used this technique as a last resort for highly resistant individuals, who frequently have extensive diffuse brain dysfunction, who are usually in a crisis state, sometimes following a long chain of crimes with complete disregard for consequences. The evidence indicates that a ten or twelve-hour night of uninterrupted sleep, combined with a pattern of waking every three hours during the day, and strenuous exercise, is quite safe.

We have seen some very disordered individuals emerge from this procedure in a manageable, quiet, alert and functioning state, which enabled them to learn. Unfortunately, our data here are entirely clinical. We have been surprised at the paucity of research that has been done in this area, when we consider the uniformly excellent data that have emerged from the USSR.

This is not a procedure that is applicable in a setting that lacks medical supervision and intensive nursing. Some of the results did suggest to us the idea of applying the concept of electrosleep. A review of the literature convinced us that electrosleep was generally a misnomer. The electrosleep theory postulates that the hynogenic tract can be driven, either by apparently direct stimulation of the cortex via various electrodes placed on the scalp or eyelids, or by induction through the application of weak, unusual, repetitive stimuli in which habituation or suggestion leads to sleep. The evidence seemed overwhelming that what was usually done in the name of electrosleep was really habituation, or the building up of generalized inhibition in the brain. We began a study which utilized electrodes that were placed on the fingers or the toes, and delivered an electric stimulus that was just above the threshold of sensitivity, far below the pain threshold, at pulses from five to twelve per second.

Thirty subjects were randomly selected for this study from a population of seventy-three adolescents. Every other one was assigned to electrotreatment and every other one to sham treatment in which electrodes were placed on the fingers and toes and the switches were adjusted, but dead batteries occupied the instrument. The Inhibitron (Humanitas Systems) produced sleep in eight of the fifteen experimental subjects, and strongly reduced the physiological symptoms of arousal such a pulse rate, blood pressure, low BSR, and low pain threshold in all of the subjects. In six of the control subjects good reduction of physiological symptoms occured, but only one subject regularly went into sound sleep.

THE INHIBITRON was applied in the nurse's office during normal working hours, and no attempt was made to create a sleep-conducive atmosphere. Traffic, noise levels, and light levels remained normal. The subjects were placed in a reclining chair. We found that all of the experimental subjects except two reported that their evening sleep was much improved after each daily session of habituation or so called electrosleep. The six controls who obtained physiological relief from the sham treatment also reported better sleep as did two who showed no physiological change. These results are consistent with placebo studies. The nurse did not know which of the machines was supplied with an active battery, but was merely told to use the black machine on some subjects and the white machine on other subjects. Unfortunately, the nurse was familiar with the goals of electrosleep and the treatment was generally known as "shock therapy" even though it is painless.

In seven of our experimental subjects sleep was induced so deeply that mild shock did not produce awakening, nor did pin pricks or pain that was produced by pressure points. These subjects all seemed to be characterized by exceptionally high arousal levels, but had no hyperactive or acting out behavior, and had a high degree of subjective dysphoria and anxiety.

This study was continued for four months. At the end of this time we found that the experimental group had improved on reading and academic achievement scores by an average of 11.3 percent greater than the control group. The subjects that were most responsive to the treatment, as was evidenced by sound sleep, or strong physiological variations achieved the greatest improvement, as did the placebo responsive group among the controls. The two resistant subjects actually showed a decline in formal testing scores. These findings are consistent with P. London's suggestion that tests may measure nothing more than a person's reaction to instruction or authority *per se* and that suggestible pupils are very likely to make higher scores on any test than pupils who score, immediately before the test, as being less suggestible or contrasuggestible.[23]

A more impressive finding was that the highly dysphoric individuals, who ordinarily seemed quite hostile and negative though passive, not only gained sleep and reduction of stress, but also improved substantially on measures of perceptual ability and field dependency, as well as in reading.

We are now investigating an electrosleep device, SEDAC (Reiter Scientific) which does seem to require head placement of the electrodes, and directly induces sleep or unconsciousness in every subject. Preliminary data indicate that an even more powerful intervention is available. Theory, of course, would indicate that strobe lights, metronomes or any light, repetitive, unusual stimuli would achieve much the same effect as the Inhibitron.

Implications

Investigation of the related literature indicates that chronic high arousal and immaturity are similar, or even related. The developing child seems to go through periodic phases of disequilibrium in which the physiological attributes of high arousal are seen as well in the loss of social and other skills. In a sense, it is as if our children were frozen at one of the disequilibrium phases—in skills, behavior, and perceptual and physiological measures. It is also clear that these stresses can be mediated through the endocrine system, or by a closed endocrine-allergy-nervous-system dysfunction that seems to be self-regenerating.[24]

It is also clear that specific learning disabilities can become functions of the operations of stress, chronic arousal, endocrine imbalance, and allergic responses as well as by immaturity or undeveloped nervous-system-interconnectivity. For example, all but one per cent of the adolescents we have seen seem to have a parietal lobe, particularly a lower parietal lobe dysfunction. The functions of spatial orientation, complex grammatical statements, and arithmetic all seem to be controlled by the parietal lobe and all of these skills are impaired in our students.[25] Since our adolescents also seem to have poor body image and poor ability to orient themselves in space, functions that are also controlled by the parietal area a highly specific higher nervous system factor seems to be dysfunctioning.[26] It seems clear that this dysfunction can be corrected through emotional reconditioning, relief of chronic stress, maturation, achieving endocrine homeostasis, direct inhibition of the nervous system, enhancing cortical functioning by energizing drugs, or reduction of biological stress by reduction of allergic responses.[27]

Epistemological considerations and caveats

Biological solutions seem to us to be simpler than complex psychic "therapies". Simple interventions seem scientifically more elegant than heroic measures. Therapeutic or educational conservation strongly urges the ruthless application of the law of parsimony, or Ockham's Razor (entities should not needlessly be multiplied, or the simpler explanation is more likely to be the more accurate).

If diet, energizing drugs, deconditioning of phobias, inhibition of the nervous system or simply removing stressing artifacts in the social life of the child while waiting for maturity to develop can all improve specific, formal academic skills without any academic training, it is clear that Piaget is correct in saying that not only may it be a waste of time to teach a young child grammar, it may be harmful.[28] Instruction, itself, may be the simple explanation for the negative findings of Lewis, Pick and Freeman that expensive, complex and individualized special education does not seem to work for retarded, failing, and disadvantaged pupils.[29] It may be normal to read poorly. It may be normal to read much better than average. It is possible that either condition is abnormal. By taking the child to asylum or refuge, we may allow spontaneous development or "cure" to emerge. By seeking the more simple, and more likely causes of dyskinesis we may minimize the cost, time, and probable side effects of our interventions. It is clear that the common school, and the common special programs are highly artificial, and highly unsuccessful enterprises may harm the child. There is certainly no evidence that we have any instructional means that substantially improve the verbal or reading skills of any individual over any reasonable period of time, such as six years. The only methods we do know that enhance reading skills are social, political, and biological in nature.

This is not to say that "experts" evaluate many programs as successful. This is not to say that enormous sums of money are not spent on programs and institutions in the face of compelling evidence of their inadequacy and harmfulness. John Pierce recently testified that the publishers of "*Effective Listening*" sent Bell Labs a "long, strongly worded letter, urging (Bell) not to publish (their) findings. They said that casting doubt on the course's effectiveness would be unfair to the people to whom it had been sold,[30] the people who had taken it and the 'experts' who had praised it."

Two careful studies had shown *"Effective Listening"* to be utterly useless.[31] A panel of high school principals demonstrated a minus .72 correlation between their evaluations of the effectiveness of samples of programed instruction, while graduate education students were equally as poor in evaluating teaching material.[32] "Evaluation" is simply magic.

Summary

A preliminary program attempting merely to remove social and institutional stresses from failing adolescents demonstrated both successful results and confirmation of other research showing a high congruence among the behaviors, perceptual abilities and biological status of children bearing divergent histories and multiple diagnostic labels. The similarities converge in immaturity and chronic high arousal or the biological effects of long periods of stress.

Attempts to accelerate cortical maturity by psychic energizing drugs proved not only to be safe, but in a triple blind study, proved significantly superior to the placebo, or no treatment. Reading ability was significantly enhanced.

Enrichment of the diet by reduction of sugars and carbohydrates and increasing protein and vitamin B rich foods seemed to significantly reduce the time that was required for residential reeducation. These findings were not subject to a placebo or a double blind control.

Desensitization, or deconditioning for a broad spectrum of specific and abstract phobias both enabled the center to succeed with a previously intractable category of students, and significantly to reduce the time that was required for residential reeducation.

Relaxation training, and sleep improvement through habituation or inhibition induced by mild, repetitive, painless electric stimulation proved to be superior to a placebo in a double blind study, both for sleep and relaxation, and for reading achievement.

This group of studies demonstrated the interaction between a higher nervous system factor (body image, spatial relationships, complex grammatical statements and arithmetic), an apparently very specific learning disorder based on the parietal lobe of the cortex, and the sympathetic nervous system as well as the endocrine and immunological mechanisms.

The studies tend to show that an apparent dysfunction in a higher nervous system factor can be directly attacked by chemotherapy, or indirectly, by spinal reflex reconditioning, general systemic improvement through diet and improvement of autokinesis or biological self-regulation, or by general systemic relaxation through induction of apparent general inhibition in the central nervous system by electric stimulation.

In each of these studies, significant improvement in reading achievement was demonstrated over controls, past history of the individuals, and common reportage in the literature.

It is suggested that research be directed towards regulation of the dynamic homeostasis of the entire biological system as a means of correcting specific learning disabilities. This study tends to confirm the findings of other researchers that instruction is not the intervention of choice for specific learning dysfunctions, but that biological regulation, and maturation may be sufficient, as well as necessary.

NOTES

1. A. Aichhorn, *A Wayward Youth* (New York, N.Y.: The Viking Press, Inc., 1935); H. Lane, *Talks to Parents and Teachers* (London, England: George Allen & Unwin, Ltd., 1928); D. Wills, *Throw Away Thy Rod* (London, England: Victor Gollancz, Ltd., 1960).

2. G. von Hilsheimer, "Summerhill: A Radical Approach to Education," *Values for a Changing America*, ed. H. Huss (Philadelphia, Pa.: University of Pennsylvania Press, 1965), pp. 59-75; idem, "Humanistic Values in Special Education," panel presentation at the 43rd International Conference for the Council of Exceptional Children, Portland, Oregon, 1965; idem, *Children in Trouble* (Orange City, Fla.: Humanitas Curriculum, 1966); idem, "Children, Schools and Utopias," *This Magazine is About Schools*, 1, No. 2 (1966), 23-27.

3. R. Cohn, "The Role of Immaturity in Reading Disabilities," *Journal of Learning Disabilities*, 3, No. 2 (1970), 13-14.

4. A. Gesell et al., *The First Five Years of Life* (New York, N.Y.: Harper & Brothers, 1940); idem, *The Child from Five to Ten* (New York, N.Y.: Harper & Brothers, 1946); F. L. Ilg and L. B. Ames, *School Readiness: Behavior Tests Used at the Gesell Institute* (New York, N.Y.: Harper & Row, Inc., 1965); R. G. Barker et al., *Child Behavior and Development* (New York, N.Y.: McGraw Hill Publishing Co., Inc., 1943); L. Carmichael (ed.), *Manual of Child Psychology* (New York, N.Y.: John Wiley & Sons, Inc., 1946); W. E. Martin and C. B. Stendler, *Child Behavior and Development* (New York, N.Y.: Harcourt, Brace & World, Inc., 1959).

5. S. M. Ervin, "Structures in Children's Language," *Proceedings* (Washington, D.C.: International Congress of Psychology, 1963); D. McCarthy, "Language Development in Children," *Manual of Child Psychology*, ed. L. Carmichael (New York, N.Y.: John Wiley & Sons, Inc., 1946) pp. 476-581; D. McNeill and D. I. Slobin, "How Does a Child Learn to Talk?", Symposium, American Association for the Advancement of Science, Annual Meeting, 1965.

6. A. S. Aslanov, "Certain Characteristics of the Joint Activity of the First and Second Signalling Systems in the Course of Late Sequelae of Closed Brain Traumata," *Works of the Institute of Higher Nervous Activity: Pathopsychological Series*, 5 (1963), 186-201; A. R. Luria, *The Role of Speech in the Regulation of Normal and Abnormal Behavior* (New York, N.Y.: Liverright Publishing Corp., 1961); idem, *Handbook of Mental Deficiency*, ed. N. R. Ellis (New York, N.Y.: McGraw Hill Publishing Co., Inc., 1963), pp. 134-158; idem, *Restoration of Function After Brain Injury* (New York, N.Y.: The Macmillan Co., 1963); B. B. Anan'ev, "Problemy Pedagogicheskoi Antropologii (Problems of Educational Anthropology)," Sovetskaya Pedagogika, 5 (1966), 27-37; C. H. Waddington, *The Strategy of Genes* (London, England: George Allen & Unwin, Ltd., 1957); D. E. Berlyne, "Curiosity and Exploration," *Science*, 153, No. 3731 (1966), 25-40.

7. E. Zigler, "Familial Mental Retardation," *Science*, 155 (1967), 292-298. Luria, *The Role of Speech*; idem, *Handbook of Mental Deficiency*; idem, *Restoration of Function*.

8. A. D. Pick, "Some Basic Perceptual Processes in Reading," *Young Children*, 25, No. 3 (1970), 162-181; W. W. Lewis, "Continuity and Intervention in Emotional Disturbance: A Review," *Exceptional Children*, 31, No. 9 (1965), 465-475.

9. D. Elkin, "The Case for the Academic Preschool: Fact or Fiction?" *Young Children*, 25, No. 3 (1970), 132-140.

10. R. A. Freeman, "The Alchemists in Our Public Schools," *Human Learning*, Monograph No. 11 (1970).

11. R. Lynn, *Attention, Arousal and the Orientation Reaction* (New York, N.Y. Pergamon Press, 1966); Berlyne, "Curiosity and Exploration."

12. S. Levine, "Hormones and Conditioning," *Nebraska Symposium on Motivation*, ed. W. J. Arnold (Lincoln, Nebraska: University of Nebraska Press, 1969), 85-101.
13. Knights and Hinton, "The Effects of Methyphenidate (Ritalin) on the Motor Skills and Behavior of Children with Learning Problems," *Journal of Nervous and Mental Disorders*, 148, No. 6 (1960); C. Bradley, "Behavior of Children Receiving Benzedrine," *American Journal of Psychiatry*, 94, No. 577 (1937); idem, "Benzedrine and Dexedrine in the Treatment of Childrens' Behavior Disorders," *Pediatrics*, 5, No. 24 (1950); J. G. Millichap, "Drugs in Management of Hyperkinetic and Perceptually Handicapped Children," *Journal of the American Medical Association*, 206, No. 7 (1968) 1527-1530.
14. D. Tuller, "EEG's of Children Who Fail in Reading," *Exceptional Children* (May 1966), 637.
15. L. B. Ames, *Child Care and Development* (Philadelphia, Pa.: J. B. Lippincott Company, 1970).
16. M. Klapper and W. Neff, *Vocational Readiness for Young Disabled Students in New York City: A Three-Year Interim Report* (Albany, N.Y.: Division of Vocational Rehabilitation, 1966).
17. J. Schrager et al., "The Hyperkinetic Child: Some Consensually Validated Behavioral Correlates," *Exceptional Children* (May 1966), 635-637.
18. For sources of tests mentioned in this article, see Appendix.
19. M. S. Read, *Malnutrition and Learning* (Washington, D.C.: National Institute of Health, 1970).
20. G. von Hilsheimer et al., "Some Considerations on the Use of Megavitamin Therapy," *Schizophrenia* (March 1971).
21. J. Wolpe, *Psychotherapy by Reciprocal Inhibition* (Stanford, Calif.: Stanford University Press, 1958); A. Bandura, *Principles of Behavior Modification* (New York, N.Y.: Holt, Rinehart and Winston, Inc., 1969); A. J. Yates, *Behavioral Therapy* (New York, N.Y.: John Wiley and Sons, Inc., 1970).
22. R. L. Williams and W. B. Webb, *Sleep Therapy* (Springfield, Ill.: Charles C Thomas, 1966).
23. P. London, M. Connant, and G. C. Davison, "More Hypnosis in the Unhypnotizable: Effects of Hypnosis and Exhortation on Rote Learning," *Journal of Personality*, 34 No. 1 (1966), 71-79.
24. M. B. Campbell, "Neurological Allergy," *Review of Allergy*, 22 (1968), 80-89.
25. Luria, *The Role of Speech*; idem, *Handbook of Mental Deficiency*; idem, *Restoration of Function*.
26. G. von Bonin, "Functional Neuro-Anatomy," *Nervous System*, ed. F. H. Netter (Chicago, Ill.: CIBA, 1962), pp. 57-77.
27. S. D. Klotz, "Putting Medicine into the 'Medical Model'," *Human Learning*, Monograph No. 9 (1969); Campbell, *Neurological Allergy*.
28. J. Piaget, "A Conversation," *Psychology Today*, 3, No. 12 (1970), 25-32.
29. Lewis, "Continuity and Intervention"; Pick, "Some Basic Perceptual Processes"; Freeman, "The Alchemists."
30. J. R. Pierce, "Real Science for Real Problems," *Analog*, 87, No. 2 (1971), 34-56.
31. H. W. Gustafson and H. A. Shoemaker, "An Evaluation of the Efficiency of the Instructional Program, 'Effective Listening'," Paper presented at A.E.R.A., Division C, February 1968; P. C. Ross and H. A. Shoemaker, "An Evaluation of Listening Training Against Job Relevant Criteria," *Journal of the National Society for Programmed Instruction*, 8, No. 4 (1969), 14-18.
32. E. Z. Rothkopf, "Some Observations on Predicting Instructional Effectiveness by Simple Inspection," *Journal of the National Society for Programmed Instruction*, 2 (1963), 19-20; S. Meyer-Markle, "It Figgers," *Journal of the National Society for Programmed Instruction*, 4 (1965), 4-5.

Making the Child Accessible for Teaching-Learning: The Role of the Internist and Allergist in Learning Disabilities

S. D. Klotz*

IN A PREVIOUS COMMUNICATION, which was presented in 1969, a study was made of 222 adolescents who were treated at the Green Valley School, Orange City, Florida, during a five-year period ending June 30, 1968. It was found that the usual medical workup that accompanied these adolescents when they were admitted to this school, consisted only of a general physical examination concerning the absence of communicable disease, and the adequacy of the heart and lungs, along with a blood count and urinalysis. The director of the school, Rev. George von Hilsheimer, and his staff, have become so well oriented to the potential hazards of physical disability upon behavior that they have developed a high index of suspicion and consequently referred many of their children to me for further medical evaluation.

Surprisingly, in spite of the previous medical clearance, a great deal of medical pathology was uncovered in these students that was of great value in the remediation of their behavioral symptoms. One hundred ninety-one of them were clinically diagnosed as allergic, with behavioral implication reported by their nonmedical and paramedical staff. Of the total group, 117 students were clinically diagnosed as hypoglycemics. One adolescent had a Cushing Syndrome, secondary to an adrenal tumor, the removal of which helped in the subsequent management of this individual's behavioral problem. Others had thyroid imbalance, simple iron deficiency, and other nutritional deficiency states, the discovery of which helped in the management of their behavioral problems. Many of them had been living under strongly stressful conditions, which affect their physiologic functions, particularly those involving endocrine and metabolic systems. It will be the purpose of this discussion to:

- Present several case reports that illustrate our findings.
- Point out how teachers can assist physicians in determining the need for biologic assessment.
- Discuss how and under what conditions, physiologic derangements can affect behavioral symptoms.

---

*S. D. Klotz, M.D., is senior physician at the Par Avenue Clinic, Orlando, Florida.

- Describe the medical means that we have used to correct these derangements, including hypoglycemic diets, and allergic desensitization.
- Discuss the use of energizing drugs for hyperreactive children and nonreaders.

CASE REPORTS

Case 1

A. G.: This case is presented underlying how the staff became alerted and converted, and also to illustrate that learning disabilities are not static but do occur in adults. This person was a mature woman in her early thirties with a high IQ, functioning in a superior capacity as a mass spectrometrist and micropaleontologist. Subsequently she became a behavior technician at the Green Valley School. She was an outgoing and highly social individual with great leadership skills; in the course of two years, she very slowly became withdrawn, apathetic, and photophobic (she actually painted her office dead black). A number of problems appeared: marital problems; increasing inability to function professionally; diminished ability at typing and writing; almost complete cessation of reading; subjective anxiety; dysphoria; many reversals in typing, writing, and accumulation of tabulated data; confusion; and lethargy with sporadic hyperactivity and chronic indigestion. The medical findings indicated that she was allergic to tomatoes in all forms, and to pork. She obtained a complete remission of all symptoms within three months after the elimination of these substances from her diet. There was a minor return of the symptoms after three years, during which time several new food allergies had developed; subsequent remission of her symptoms once again followed the elimination of these substances from her diet.

Case 2

J. W., a fifteen-year-old boy, was admitted after a long history of incorrigible delinquency; he was first adjudicated a delinquent at the age of five, as a fire setter, thief, and runaway. Diagnosed as illiterate, with classic perceptual dysfunctioning of dyslexia, and a high performance IQ, his history showed a classic sequence of counseling, with psychotherapy at a residential psychoanalytic center, and continuing deterioration. Medical findings revealed the presence of hypoglycemia and severe allergies. He developed strong reactions to early hyposensitization. On the first dose of his injection material he responded so strongly to the antigen mixture that he developed anaphylactic shock producing tachycardia, blotched skin, difficulty in breathing, etc. Such experiences were underlined to the nonmedical staff at the school, since it convinced them that these difficult, incorrigible children *are* biologically sick!

Case 3

J. R., a twelve-year-old boy, was admitted after a long history of severe learning disabilities, with unmanageable behavior, such as fire setting and tantrums. He was considered untestable for academic skills. Medical review revealed hypoglycemia, which was severe, not only in him but in his entire family. He received diet management, medical, vitamin, and mineral support, and adrenal cortex extract. The boy was discharged to a special day-school after one semester, which lasted from September through February, and returned to public school where he became an A-B student within one year.

It is interesting to note that, in this case, the boy's father's severe alcoholism has been controlled by following the hypoglycemic diet with medical-vitamin support, and that he is now effectively employed as a vice-president of a large commercial bank. It is also important to point out that just three years ago this family had to travel 180 miles to obtain a five-hour glucose tolerance test, despite the fact that the mother is well organized, rather compulsive, and had quite thoroughly inventoried all medical facilities in a wealthy area of our state.

Case 4

S. R., a sixteen-year-old boy, was admitted from Cook County jail, after having been discharged from Cook County General Hospital psychiatric division as not psychotic but character disordered; therefore, he was considered inaccessible to psychotherapy. He had an arrest record for assaulting officers, glue sniffing, and multiple offenses. He manifested classic psychopathic features with dyscalculia (specific learning disability for calculation), extremely uneven reading performance but a high IQ, and a saw-tooth achievement profile peaking at 99th percentile in four of nine subtests on the *Iowa Tests of Basic Skills*.[1] The patient had a glucose reading of twenty-five milligrams on the third hour of the glucose tolerance test, which resulted in marked weakness, sweating, and faintness. It was demonstrated that by eating a high sugar diet, his insulin (in response to this) overreacted, and his homeostatic mechanisms, which were thus being abnormally controlled, caused a drop below his normal level of blood sugar, and this produced symptoms that altered his general behavior pattern.

Extensive allergies were noted; they appeared subclinical because of the predominance of his mental symptoms. He was placed on hyposensitization therapy and a hypoglycemic diet. He was discharged to outpatient care after two and one-half years, and carried as a conditional failure due to semicontrolled drug remissions. However, his achievement profile smoothed to the upper 90th percentile ranks in all subtests. He obtained a superior rank as a high school graduate and has been employed constantly in the two years since discharge, with no further interreaction with the law or mental health facilities. He has had six months of continued dietary supervision under the supervision of an M.D. Followup has been covert.

Case 5

H. N., a twenty-year-old male, was admitted after being discharged as untreatable after five years in Menninger's Children's Division. The diagnosis was severe schizophrenia. He had chronic daytime enuresis with no willingness to admit that his behavior constituted a problem. He was considered to be academically untestable; his IQ values were regarded as worthless by psychologists, but were potentially high based on intuitive reading of the Rorschach *Psychodiagnostic Plates*. Physical findings revealed that he had a chronic constriction of the urethra, and chronic kidney and bladder infection. With correction of these problems, control of his daytime enuresis was obtained without further verbal therapy. He also revealed severe allergies; hyposensitization therapy was started and is still proceeding. His severe phobias were treated primarily by desensitization as described by Wolpe and as modified by Quirk, and by assertion training as directed by the Rev. von Hilsheimer.[2]

This boy is now beginning his third year of residency and is completely oriented in time and space; he shows no residua of schizophrenia but shows some deficits that are due to long institutionalization and psychotherapy. The staff confidently expects his discharge and graduation within one year. He has an achievement profile in the upper 60th percentile, and a high average IQ.

Case 6

A. E. F., a fourteen-year-old boy, was admitted from Devereaux School custodial care; he was considered to be untestable, very shy, withdrawn, but responsive to gentle support. He was diagnosed as subclinical cretin, given thyroid extract, and has been discharged after six months, fully restored to functioning with some of his educational defects remedied.

Non-goitrous cretinism is ten to twenty times more common than sporadic familial goitrous hypothyroidism. Symptoms that lead one to suspect this condition include physical lethargy and tiredness, disinclination to accomplish simple tasks previously well within the person's capacity, cold intolerance, poor eating habits, and constipation. Physical findings included muscular weakness, thickened dry skin, abdominal distension, and anemia. The carbohydrate metabolism is affected, resulting from poor absorption of glucose from the gastrointestinal tract. As a result, there is increased body fat and hypoglycemia. Muscle cramps, constipation, and weight increase may thereby result. The usual laboratory tests may give low normal values or contradictory results. When the values are below normal, there is no problem in making the diagnosis. In children, a delay in growth and skeletal development may be noted by X-ray examinations.

Asher stated that myxedema is the most important, least known, and one of the most frequently missed causes of organic psychoses.[3] Psychoses of various types may develop with patients having bizarre delusions of persecution.

Case 7

P. N. K., a five-year-old boy, had a history of never having slept with regularity, irritability since birth, constant crying with daily rages, uncontrollable behavior, and slow development with concomitant social retardation and extreme dependence on the parents. His sister, who was six months old, showed no evidence of having difficulties and was a remarkably sweet baby with whom the mother had no difficulty. *P. N. K.* was under chronic high arousal with characteristic perceptual liabilities, high muscular tension, and chronic self-generating anxiety. It was also apparent that no pathology was present in the ordinary life of the family except for the chronic fatigue and tension created by the behavior of the child.

The child was seen by his local pediatrician, who had prescribed a regular dose of phenobarbital, which had afforded some ephemeral relief with concomitant exacerbation during the following day. It was our feeling that the child presented an example of a chronic brain syndrome manifested by irritability, sleeplessness, and overarousal, and that the system was self-regenerating because of the apparent absence of sleep and cortical inhibition. The child was given fifteen milligrams of Dexadrine spansule daily, which afforded positive relief but with subsequent regression within six months. Five milligrams of Ritalin q.i.d. was then ordered and effected complete reduction of the presenting problems. Progression of normal development was attained.

The child was reassessed one and one-half years later and determined to be well controlled by medication with subsequent accelerated development. He reads fluently, began spontaneously to enjoy friendships with other children and has successfully enjoyed nursery school experiences. It is absolutely apparent, however, that the chronic brain syndrome persists and that supportive medication is indicated. Diet control for borderline hypoglycemia is continuing along with complete allergic screening with particular attention being paid to masked food allergies that might be contributing to his neurologic problem.

Case 8

J. K., age 14, experienced a severe personality change and school failure with no biologic findings reported. Her mother is an R.N., and she had her daughter seen by many specialists including psychiatrists and endocrinologists. Screening revealed an 18-percent eosinophilia in her blood count, along with an elevation of alkaline phosphotase and very severe allergic reactions to testing, although there were no apparent clinical symptoms or complaints.

Case 9

J. A. B., a fifteen-year-old girl, was admitted after undergoing a sharp and sudden personality change from an outgoing, scholastically superior, diving and gymnastic champion, to an incorrigible drug user, running and sexually promiscuous girl who had gained 150 pounds, from an average of 90 to an average of 240 in just over six months before admission. Her father was a psychoanalyst. A review of the hypotheses was investigated, tests were done and redone, and the final medical findings were negative. No biologic dysfunction could be demonstrated, and no direct behavioral therapy was accomplished. The child was graduated with a superior rank in home economics, showed a substantial weight reduction, but is still obese, has good tone and flexibility, and a year from graduation has been well employed as a school steward and dietician. She is married and lives with her in-laws, and apparently maintains a very happy adjustment with them. She has taught her mother-in-law many basic homemaking skills, such as making home-ground flour, making bread, knitting, crocheting, and planning a superior diet. This case is included to show that we do not know everything, and after a thorough and painstaking biologic inventory has given a clear bill of health, it may be that all the child needs is TLC, good instruction, and a democratic milieu.

THE TEACHER can help by observing the child's actions as carefully as possible, noting his classroom behavior, whether the child is restless, overactive, excitable, inattentive, shows difficulty in concentrating, seems to be overly sensitive, daydreams, is sulky, is moody, has temper outbursts, disturbs others, and shows other behavioral problem activities. He should be aware of whether or not these behaviors occur following meals, or just before meals, to see if there is any relationship to food allergies or possible hypoglycemic states. It is also important to note how the child does in group participation and whether he teases, interferes with other children's activities, gets along with the opposite or same sex, and whether he wants to lead or retreat. Observations should be made in relation to the child's academic performance, whether his reaction to the teacher is demanding, submissive, defiant, anxious to please, or cooperative. Other things to note are, what type of achiever he is, and whether he has poor verbal, reading, writing, or comprehension skills, Lastly, health and personal habits, such as vision, hearing, right, left, or mixed handedness, whether he rubs his nose or if his nose seems blocked, whether he coughs or wheezes, shows shortness of breath, or seems to be fatigued should be noted. Such observations, plus a high index of suspicion of the fact that these children are under chronic stressful situations, can be an indication that they may be suffering from hypoglycemia, allergies, or endocrine disturbances, whether they are subclinical or not. If so, it would be worthwhile to bring these facts to the attention of the parents with suggestions and advice for further medical diagnoses in these categories.

Teachers are and will be called upon more frequently to help disease investigators evaluate the effects of drugs upon the pupils' behavior patterns, by performing double-blind studies, and evaluating the effects of drugs versus placebos.

At least 85 percent of the children at the school have nutritional deficiencies when they arrive. Many have "allergic" manifestations, which are frequently masked, but do affect their perception and vitality. Most of them have been living under strongly stressful conditions, which affect their physiologic functions, particularly those which involve their endocrine and metabolic systems.

The effects of endocrines on human behavior have been well documented; both excesses and deficiencies can alter the mental and nervous functions of the individual.

RECENT BIOCHEMICAL studies on a cellular level have and will uncover many new and exciting vistas on the modus operandi of disease. Most tissues have receptor endings that regulate their activities. These end organs are controlled by the autonomic nervous system. They are both alpha and beta sympathetic receptors. Activity is regulated by cyclic AMP or $3'5'$-adenosinemonophosphate, which triggers all hormonal action on a cellular level. This in turn is controlled by the activity of a cell membrane-bound enzyme, adenyl cyclase.

The hypothalamus is the head or brain-regulating center for the autonomic system. Stress affects this primary regulator. In this way, it may stimulate or deplete the body's immunologic defense reactions. Experimenters, using an avoidance-learning-situation model, were able to cause hypertrophy of the adrenals in animals, hypotrophy of spleens with decreased white cells, pseudoestrous, increased susceptibilities to such viruses as herpes, cox sachie, etc., delayed rejection of skin grafts and increased susceptibility to acute passive anaphylaxes. Stress can produce a rise in the 19S gamma globulins.

Destruction of the dorsal hypothalamic site leads to the suppression of complement-fixing antibodies with a prolonged retention of antigen in the blood.

The Soviet workers have been able to condition antibody response and produce an anamnestic antibody increase without antigen.

Nervous stimulation in conjunction with antigen administration enhances the antibody response. Thus, in this way psychosocial phenomena may modify immune processes by way of the central nervous system mechanisms.

Hypoglycemia, which follows glucose intake, is usually caused by failure of the adrenocorticosteroids to inhibit insulin activity and influence the rate of insulin catabolism. A fall of the glucose level results in the activation of the hypothalamic-pituitary-adrenal system. This central nervous system, especially the hypothalamus, activates the pituitary, which in turn activates the adrenal response. In pituitary failure there is no response to insulin administration, even though the rate of blood glucose fall would be sufficient to produce an adrenal response with an intact pituitary.

AS WE KNOW, the human organism, and particularly the nervous system, operates for the most part on glucose which must be supplied by the blood in the appropriate concentration. The adrenal cortex through its glucose steroids plays a major role in regulating this concentration. It is felt by many observers that functional hypoglycemia is not a true hyper-insulinism except in the rare case of pancreatic adenoma, but is due to a failure of the glucose steroids to antagonize or catabolize insulin, associated with a hypoadrenal cortical state. The symptoms of hypoglycemia depend upon the degree of the rate of glucose, along with the acuteness and clinicity of its presence. The acute and early symptoms are similar to those seen after the administration of epinephrine, that is, fainting, tremulousness, emotional disturbances, excessive perspiration, chilliness, circumoral numbness and pallor, hunger, apprehension, paresthesia, palpitation, hand tremors, and degrees of mental cloudiness. As the hypoglycemia progresses and becomes more chronic a variety of symptoms such as headache, difficulty in concentration, disorientation, mental confusion, dizziness, faintness, diplopia, and coldness of the extremities may develop. The patient may be unable to walk, or may even stagger; he may be depressed, restless, and maniacal. In severe hypoglycemia, muscle twitching and generalized convulsions may be followed by retrograde amnesia and unconsciousness.

Electrolyte disturbances can alter behavior. Stress of any type augments potassium excretion by the kidneys, because of the mobilization of electrolytes from tissue cells and by sodium retention. The clinical state of potassium depletion results in weakness or paralysis if severe, with tetanic contractions of hands and legs, muscular weakness and parasthesias. The respiratory muscles are particularly susceptible with development of signs of dyspnea, cyanosis and respiratory failure. Magnesium electrolytes play a role in enzymatic functions and other physiologic processes. Hypermagnesia results in lethargy and coma. Hypomagnesia, which must be considered in all patients with malnutrition, may produce bizarre tremors, athetotic and choreiform movements of the extremities.

NEUROLOGICAL SYNDROMES that are due to allergic hypersensitivity have been documented many times. There have been case reports describing, after the ingestion of certain foods, where individuals have developed symptoms simulating such neurological syndromes as myasthenia gravis, spinal cord syndrome, and psychomotor epilepsy. Recent observations suggest that allergic and immunological mechanisms are important in several organic neurological diseases. Since P. Basso and A. M. Goltman separately observed recurrent cerebral edema due to food allergies,[4] there has been no doubt that allergic reactions can occur in the central nervous system. Symptoms frequently reported as due to allergy are some of the headaches, migraines, and convulsions that are usually caused by foods or drugs. The convulsions may be of the petit mal or even grand mal types.

The allergic-tension-fatigue syndrome can be seen in children of all ages and also adults. It may be easily overlooked if one is not aware that it can exist. Clues suggesting its presence are as follows:

- A pale and sallow complexion, although blood tests reveal no anemia.
- Eyes having dark circles with puffiness of skin about the eyelids.
- The child looks irritable, listless, and tired even though he has had a full night's sleep.
- The parents are concerned about his sluggishness, drowsiness, and lack of interest in both play and school work.
- There is irritability, peevishness, unhappiness, and unpredictable behavior.

The severity of the symptoms of fatigue and nervousness vary with the individual. Occasionally there may be more severe neurologic and psychologic signs and symptoms, including paresthesia, facial tics, severe personality disturbances, and even psychotic behavior. Alternating types of symptoms are characteristic. Sleepiness on the one hand, yet insomnia on the other hand, sluggish thinking, difficulty in concentration, inability to be pleased, and general unhappiness. The symptoms can best be divided into those of:

- Motor tension—hyperkinesis manifested by hyperactivity, restlessness, clumsiness, poor manual behavior, and the inability to relax.
- Sensory tension manifested by irritability, insomnia, photophobia, and hypersensitivity.
- Motor fatigue as manifested by aches and tiredness.
- Sensory fatigue as manifested by sluggishness and torpor.

- Less common mental and nervous symptoms may be mental depression, feeling of unreality, bizarre and irrational behavior, paranoid ideas, inability to concentrate, nervous tics and paresthesia.

The above nervous system symptoms may be associated with other systemic manifestations such as increased salivation, sweating, abdominal pain, headache and enuresis.

Certain drugs, particularly psychotherapeutic medicines that behavior problem patients may be on, can cause neurologic symptoms. The tranquilizers, particularly the phenothiazines, reserpine, and steroids, can cause convulsive disorders, Parkinsonism and psychoses.

Ever present chemical agents in our surroundings are often the unrecognized causes of clinical entities that are frequently seen by the allergist, since the reactions to chemical susceptibility may closely resemble the symptoms induced by allergens, and are present in many allergic individuals. Many of the reactive chemicals that contaminate our air, water, and food are derivatives of or are prepared from hydrocarbons of common genesis—coal, petroleum and natural gas. The victim of chemical susceptibility becomes sick from often-repeated exposure to relatively small amounts of materials in "non-toxic" doses that have no apparent effect on other nonsusceptible people who are similarly exposed.

The amount of additives that are derived from coal-tar products that are present in pills, foods, candies, bakery products, soaps, and preservatives is amazing, and most of them are unlabeled.

HOW CAN WE determine if the patient may be suffering from a physical ailment that is producing or aggravating the behavior disorder? As I mentioned earlier one can, by exercising a high index of suspicion along with an awareness that the symptoms may be due to medical disorders other than a primary behavioral disturbance in the classic sense, become aware of physiological roots to behavior problems.

When indicated, the medical workup should evaluate the thyroid function, including a Protein Bound Iodine test (PBI), Triiodothyronine test (T_3), or radioactive thyroid uptake. Electrolyte determinations of potassium, chlorides, sodium, calcium, and magnesium may be indicated. When symptoms are suggestive of problems, an oral five-hour glucose-tolerance test should be done to look for functional hypoglycemia. If symptoms are provoked before the five-hour period is up, the test should be discontinued, and the patient given food. Sometimes an afternoon glucose-tolerance test may pick up a reactive hypoglycemia more easily. When an allergic evaluation is indicated, skin tests for inhalant and food sensitivities may be performed. Food skin tests are not 100-percent reliable and occasionally one uses food elimination diets or provocative food tests. Frequently, twenty-four-hour urinary collections for seventeen-Ketogenic and seventeen-Hydroxycortiosteroid levels should be done.

When an impaired glucose tolerance curve or one which produces hypoglycemia symptoms is found, the patient is put on a diet that is relatively high in protein, and devoid of concentrated carbohydrates and added sugar.

The patient is encouraged to snack frequently during the day and at times during the night. Foods allowed are meats, fish, and shellfish, dairy products (eggs, milk, butter and cheese); milk between meals, milk, cheese, and/or butter and saltines before retiring; salted nuts, peanut butter, protein bread, Sanka, weak tea, sugar-free sodas, soybeans and soybean products. Foods to be avoided are potatoes, corn, macaroni, spaghetti, rice, pie, cake, pastry, sugar, candies, dates and raisins, cola and other sweet soft drinks, coffee, strong tea, and all hot and cold cereals.

When patients are discovered to be allergic to inhalants, a program of hyposensitization injections to those inhalants is started. Definite food allergies are eliminated. Rarely in this day of abundance are attempts at food desensitization made, but occasionally we have done so for a particularly important food item in the patient's diet.

Not to be omitted is the fact that genetic and enzymatic defects may also play an important role in some individuals. Dr. William Philpott, a consultant psychiatrist at the Green Valley School, has found patients with schizophrenic syndromes to show galactose and gluten intolerances, which he feels may be present not only in infants and early childhood, but in later childhood and adolescence, and perhaps may even be carried into adulthood. This area certainly deserves more intensive investigation in the future.

In conclusion, we have found that the medical program is of importance in the restoration and maintenance of body homeostasis, as reflected by stabilizing the nutritional, hormonal and nervous functions of the body. We like to use the holistic approach—that of the entire individual in his environmental milieu, both internal and external, with all its social implications. However, we must emphasize that these individuals still need proper counseling to guide them in their social adjustment. This cannot happen too easily, if at all, unless normal physical homeostasis has been achieved.

NOTES

1. For sources of tests mentioned in this article, see Appendix.
2. J. Wolpe, *The Practice of Behavior Therapy* (New York, N.Y.: Pergamon Press, 1970; D. Quirk, "An Automated Desensitization," paper presented at the annual meeting of the Association for the Advancement of Behavior Therapy, September 1971.
3. R. Asher, "Myxoedematous Madness," *British Medical Journal*, 2 (1971), 555-562.
4. P. Basso, "Angioneurotic Edema of the Brain," *Medical Clinicians of North America*, 16 (September 1932); A. M. Goltman, "Mechanism of Migraine," *Journal of Allergy*, 7 (1936).

Biobehavioral Psychiatry and Learning Disabilities

William H. Philpott*

STARTING IN THE 1950s in the field of psychiatry, there was a great upsurge in the frequency of the discovery of agents that are capable of influencing emotion. Agents that altered tension and mood were studied in detail. These studies did lead us to a greater understanding of what some of the chemical abnormalities are that occur in the central nervous system during these disturbed emotional states. Paralleling these studies were studies that were being made by biochemists who were endeavoring to discover chemical abnormalities that influence the central nervous system such as, deficiencies, inborn errors in metabolism, and toxins, in an effort to discover a rational treatment for these abnormalities. This research did not reach clinical proportions until the 1960s. We are now at the stage where we are making clinical application of information that is coming from biochemistry, relative to the significance of inborn errors in metabolism, toxic states, and nutritional deficiency states. We are also looking into the possibility of managing some of these states through the reduction of some nutrients, additions of nutrients beyond the usual amount for other states, and the correction of toxins by withdrawing or tying them up.[1]

At the same time that the chemical revolution was occuring in psychiatry, there was an upsurge in the application of experimental psychology to the practice of psychiatry. For many years, our main preoccupation in psychiatry had been within a psychoanalytic frame of reference based on the widely accepted theory of repression and its associated concept of *unconscious mind*. Answers were sought as to how the symptom represented the symbolic expression of repressed material and what interpersonal and sociologic stresses were causing the repression of unacceptable ideas and emotions. Speculations were the accepted order of the day. These speculations were readily believed and incorporated into clinical practice without the application of double blind studies, or other objective proof that these formulas produced the speculated results.

William H. Philpott, M.D. is a psychiatrist currently serving as the assistant medical director for the Fuller Memorial Sanitarium in Attleboro, Massachusetts.

Starting in the late 1950s, some principles of learning, applicable to psychiatry, were introduced.[2] These principles had been worked out over an extended period of years in the experimental psychology laboratories and followed specific laws that govern learning.

This insistence on following established laws has increased the efficiency of the psychotherapeutic process of behavioral change. The charm of speculation has lost its hold. Only that which demonstrated its efficiency remained interesting and applicable. When new methods demonstrated new efficiencies they were readily adopted because this was the goal and the new order of the day.

The introduction of double blind studies proved to considerably sharpen the tools of psychiatry. The double blind study found its first application in the area of megavitamin doses of B^3 and vitamin C for the schizophrenic personality. Before this long-term study was completed, it had also been profitably applied to a number of studies of the newly developing tranquilizers and antidepressants. Along the same line, psychotherapy under the newly developing behaviorism, was insisting on observable therapeutic results.

What is biobehaviorism?

It has rapidly become evident that behaviorism as it was developing from the source of experimental psychology was not in itself complete. It was equally obvious that the newly developing contributions from biochemistry were also not complete. The human body is a bag of chemicals but it is also a bag of learned responses, and responses may be stimulus evoked as well as chemically evoked. The fact that each response has its chemistry was becoming better understood. Early behaviorism had been defined as that body of information that comes from experimental psychology and relates itself specifically to learned responses: Yates had more broadly defined behaviorism as encompassing not only the contributions of experimental psychology of learning but also that of physiological psychology.[3] In this sense, behaviorism could be defined from a biobehavioral viewpoint. Since this involves separate bodies of information coming from biochemistry and physiological psychology, I have labelled the combination of these two as *biobehavioral psychiatry*.

THE FIRST THRUST towards the understanding of the chemistry of emotional reactions was especially applied to the schizophrenic reaction and its related schizoid state. It is also becoming increasingly evident that unbalanced chemistries exist in the neurotic, in the personality disordered, and often in the character disordered, though of somewhat different quality than in the schizophrenic. What relationship do these disordered chemistries have to the process of learning and to the resultant educational and social handicaps?

The following observations and conclusions have been drawn from approximately four hundred patients over a four-year period. These observations were begun in a private psychiatric practice with the run-of-the-mill type patient who comes to a general psychiatrist; many of them were neurotic and had personality disorders. Some of the later observations were made at Fuller Memorial Sanitarium with a more concentrated group of schizophrenics and alcoholics, and only a few neurotics. Another source of information was the Green Valley School in Orange City, Florida, where the students are essentially social and educational failures. These observations were made by adding the following items to the standard psychiatric examination:

- A chemical survey of blood, urine, and hair to determine the essential mineral and vitamin deficiencies and toxins.
- An activated six-hour glucose tolerance test for the study of possible hypoglycemia.
- Measurement of the co-factors Nicotinamide Adenine Dinucleotide (NAD) and Adenosine Triphosphate (ATP).

In addition to clinical observations, these tests have been used as a guide to discovering the significance of vitamin, mineral, and protein supplements. At the same time the patients were being treated biochemically for demonstrated deficiencies and defects; they were also treated with behavioral psychotherapeutic techniques that placed special emphasis on the direction of behavioral drills based on the concept that the basic building block of learning is that of excitation of the central nervous system.

Observations about chemistry

Occasionally a normal or near-normal chemistry will be found in a person who is neurotic or has a personality disorder. However, I have never found a normal chemistry in a schizophrenic patient; I have only found gross abnormalities on the chemical survey of a schizophrenic. I have had the opportunity of surveying an entire family where a parent is a schizophrenic, and it is very common to find the same abnormalities in a fair percentage of the children as was demonstrated in the parent. The schizophrenic and schizoid chemical profile is on this order: ATP deficiency approaches 100 percent. The majority have NAD deficiency. The majority have a symptom-producing relative hypoglycemia on an activated six-hour glucose tolerance test. About 50 percent have achlorhydria, and a similar percentage of schizophrenic patients have galactosemia. About one-third have a high alkaline phosphatase and a smaller percentage have B_{12} and folic acid deficiency. Calcium and magnesium deficiencies are found in small percentages, calcium is usually more deficient than magnesium. Thiamine deficiency is found in only a very small amount as tested by the pyruvic acid test. Urine studies for salt-dumping, involving testing on the first day with no extra salt and on the second day with ten grams salt reveal that the majority of schizophrenics have salt-dumping. Hair studies of the essential minerals reveal that sodium is the most consistently deficient mineral and that potassium is the second. The potassium-sodium ratios are inverted with sodium lower than it should be in relationship to potassium. There usually are other deficiencies but these are inconsistent and often involve manganese, magnesium, calcium, and iron. Almost all schizophrenics have an excessive amount of copper. Persons who manifest neuroses, personality disorders, and character disorders reveal some of the same deficiencies but not in such a high percentage. Relative hypoglycemia runs quite high in the neurotics and seems to be the abnormality that occurs most consistently in neurotic patients.

Observations about learning

C. L. Hull's drive-reduction reinforcement theory has served as a profitable guide for the direction of behavioral practices and has become the backbone of present day behaviorism.[4] The practice of systematic desensitization, during which the person is taught to relax and reapproach the feared situation through imagery, is useful in many conditions where anxiety is prominent. Aversion employs a high-level stimulus of sufficient intensity to block a response and is useful in treating many obsessive-compulsive, characterological and mood symptoms. Anticipatory avoidance, in which the energy of anticipated avoidance is tied to a corrective response, is also quite a useful tool. Rehearsal of planned responses in which the person selects stimulus situations where unadaptive responses are usually automatically performed, are helped through planned rehearsals of corrective responses under the same set of circumstances. These planned responses can be placed on a tape recorder and frequently rehearsed while the subject is in a relaxed state.

The implanting of electrodes effected the discovery that drive-reduction is not a necessary part of the learning process and that arousal of the central nervous system at an optimum level appears to be the basic building block of all learning.[5] An increasing number of neurophysiologists and experimental psychologists agree that an optimum arousal of the central nervous system is the central motivation of learning.[6] Using this format, a framework of practices that follow this rule have been made. Carbon-dioxide (CO_2) excitation, in which imagery of adaptive responses, such as pleasure responses, can be used to train out depressive responses. The CO_2 stimulus can also be made sufficiently high by using a rapid rise to 50 percent to inhibit an image so that by placing an anxiety type unadaptive image in the mind, it can be inhibited by a rapid rise to 50 percent CO_2. This occurs usually within about fifteen seconds and it has been shown to have a powerful training effect in inhibiting the unadaptive response. Therefore, about 10 percent CO_2 can be used for the excitation of adaptive responses and 50 percent CO_2 can be used for the inhibition of unadaptive responses. Obsessive compulsive responses that are not based on anxiety are not readily relieved by the technique of rapid rise in CO_2, but do respond to an approach response of a corrective opposite using then the rapid rise in CO_2. For some people, nitrous oxide (N_2O) at 50 percent increases the excitation capacity of the CO_2, improving the imagery and the affect, and reducing any concern of hyperventilation produced by the CO_2. It also prevents any concern about hyperventilation when using 50 percent CO_2. The use of nitrous oxide also offers the advantage that in the hypertensive patient it will nearly always prevent hypertension from occurring as a result of the CO_2. This use of CO_2 and nitrous oxide has proved to be a powerful training tool, both for excitation of adaptive responses and inhibition of unadaptive responses.

A similar method has been developed that uses the stroboscope and a diffuse screen. Using 8-10 waves per second, the brain is driven toward relaxation. Using 18-22 waves per second frequency effects an increase in a person's ability to visualize a vivid, colorful, activated, eidetic image. It takes a bit of practice to use the stroboscope whereas carbon-dioxide and nitrous oxide can produce the same results with a higher rate of frequency, and less learning is required of the patient for the imagery to occur. Using the 18-22 waves per second frequency, adaptive responses can be increased by visualizing these responses. If an unadaptive image is placed in the mind, this can be inhibited by either increasing the frequency, and holding the breath, or suddenly switching to an incompatible frequency, such as 3- per second spike and wave.

Most unadaptive responses are learned; few characterological responses can be characterized as being due to a lack of learning. It does not matter whether responses begin with a disturbed chemistry or as a response to environmental stimuli. The end result is still a learned response if that response is repeatedly evoked. Some of the most tenacious overlearned responses have been initiated by disturbed chemistry, which has produced a state of neuronal excitation, which creates tenacious learning. Some of the most severely phobic patients have learned their phobias when they were hypoglycemic, and the intensity of the response was markedly magnified by the associated state of alkalosis with its increased acetylcholine (ACTH) level. There are also other factors observable when the general energy system is lowered and the specific sensory inputs may be more excitable. States of toxicity, deficiency, and central nervous system allergy are also potent in creating an irritative excitation of the central nervous system capable of training in unadaptive responses.[7]

What is a neurosis?

Viewed from an endocrinological standpoint, neuroses and similar states can be characterized as being caused by an underproduction of adrenal-cortical hormones with its accompanying marked increase of sensory inputs and, at the same time, an increase in ACTH with its symptom of clinging to the response. It has been demonstrated by experimentation that adrenal-cortical hormones have desensitizing value and even anesthetic value. Therefore, they are needed in optimum supply for the process of unlearning unadaptive responses. It has also been established that in the presence of high ACTH, unlearning of unadaptive responses does not occur; instead, there is a clinging to these responses.[8]

The chemical survey would give the indications that the neurotic person is in a state of lowered adrenal-cortical efficiency as manifested by a symptom-producing relative hypoglycemia based, to a great degree, on low glucocorticoids and a parallel salt-dumping, which is based on low mineralosteroids. This should not be considered necessarily low in terms of normals but low in terms of the stress state of the organism at the time, and therefore the deficiency is relative not absolute, but nevertheless has the same effect as if it were an absolute deficiency. It is the natural state of affairs if the adrenal-cortical hormones are not in adequate supply to meet the state of stress, the pituitary produces ACTH in an effort to increase adrenal-cortical function. Therefore, we find the neurotic and many personality disorders in the chemical state, which we could call *stress decompensation*, thus producing the oversensitiveness of response due to low adrenal-cortical function and the clinging to the response due to high ACTH. It seems apparent that the neurosis does not exist until the state of decompensation exists. Any symptoms that develop based on high level stimuli in a healthy organism soon tend to be trained out by such processes as the desensitizing value of dreaming, which is a perfect natural setup for desensitization. During the relaxed state of sleep, the dream life reviews the anxieties and thus trains out the overlearned anxiety responses. After the decompensated stress state occurs, then a neurosis is in evidence. Any chemical defects that are caused either by means of inherited chemical defects, nutritional deficiencies, allergies of the central nervous system or toxins, are going to make it easier for this decompensated stress state to occur. Therefore, these are important items even in a neurosis.

What is a psychosis?

A psychosis gives evidence of the same stress decompensation as the neurosis, only usually to a more severe extent, and there are more obvious evidences of toxins that are distorting to perceptions or activating to the neuronal system so that there is autonomous visualizations, such as hallucinations. These interferences with optimum neuronal function, as seen in both the neurosis and psychosis, reduce the learning capacity and therefore become the basis of many problems centering around children with learning disabilities.

What is the significance of a deficiency in adenosine triphosphate (ATP)? Adenosine triphosphate is the central substance from which energy is derived.[9] Glucose can only be used after being phosphorylated from ATP. Peptides can only be metabolized in the presence of adequate ATP. This is important in view of the evidence that gluten, with its peptides, seems to be handled poorly by the schizophrenic and the schizoid patient.[10] Synaptic junction activity is dependent on adequate ATP. ATP serves as a reservoir for detoxification and in the presence of an inadequate ATP a toxic state will develop. Also, in the presence of toxins, ATP will be reduced and this may well be one of the sources of decreased ATP in the schizophrenic. It is hard to know which comes first—the state of toxicity with lowered ATP, or low ATP with a resultant toxicity. Low ATP can also be a reflection of either inborn errors in metabolic function or of a particular nutritional state, since ATP is made from B-complex vitamins, essential amino acids, phospholipids, and is catalyzed by magnesium. Therefore, deficiencies in any of these, or inborn errors in relationship to any of these, could produce ATP deficiency.

Nicotinamide Adenine Dinucleotide (NAD) deficiency can be the result of either lack of B[3] or lack of B[6] plus tryptophan since these all serve as precursors for NAD. NAD has a key control over carbohydrate metabolism. Hypoglycemia would be anticipated in a person who has had an NAD deficiency and is shown to be very much related on the lab tests. Since B[3] is a precursor to NAD, NAD deficiency can then be taken as evidence of a B[3] deficiency. In most people, megavitamin doses of B[3] will raise NAD in a few weeks or months. In the cases where NAD is not raised, these patients simply do not become well. It does not hold that in the cases where NAD becomes normal, the patient will be well because of this single factor. It seems to be an established fact that schizophrenia is characterized by its multiple defects. If NAD raises to normal and the person does not become well, then other factors must be sought as being responsible for the patient's illness, such as galactosemia or other inborn errors, which leave the patient toxic, or cerebral allergies or exogenous sources of toxins. In the face of NAD deficiency, a wrong chain in the amine-aldehyde acid pathway occurs that produces a morphine-like substance (tetrahydropapaveroline) which, of course, has addictive qualities. Certain chemicals, such as chloral hydrate or alcohol, markedly enhance the production of this toxin in the face of NAD deficiency.[11]

The significance of achlorhydria would be on this order—that B[12] would be less apt to be used. The normal intestinal flora of acidolphilous would die and this would rob the body of one natural source of B-complex vitamins and vitamin K, which is produced by these bacteria. In addition, there would be the result of the toxins that are produced by the putrefactive bacteria with their thyroid-depressing effect,[12] and other symptoms such as headache, which is produced by the high ammonia levels, and the other possible discomforts such as diarrhea or constipation. In all, there would be somewhat of a malabsorption problem. For these reasons, it is best to feed the emotionally disturbed patient acidolphilous bacteria to help correct the situation.

It is obviously a sound medical practice to supplement any demonstrated deficiencies either of the essential minerals, vitamins, or proteins. Experimental work has demonstrated that B-complex deficiencies can literally drive a person crazy and the same is true of mineral deficiency, such as calcium or magnesium.

WHAT IS THE ROLE OF SODIUM AND POTASSIUM? This becomes an important question in view of the consistent deficiency that is observed in many subjects. Both sodium and potassium are needed in the production of the energy-producing substances such as NAD and ATP.[13] Therefore, when these are found to be deficient, they need to be supplemented. The hair test has been demonstrated to be the best way to determine this deficiency. Tissues, such as the hair, will demonstrate what is occurring on a long-range basis, whereas blood samples fluctuate considerably and on any given day may appear to be normal, and yet the overall picture is that of being abnormally low.

Most emotionally disturbed subjects have their greatest problems under states of stress. Since this is true, then it is best to run our tests for deficiencies when the body is under a state of stress. For this reason, a six-hour glucose tolerance test (GTT) was devised to be administered under states of stress. First the subject is given a high glucose meal the night before the test, and after the fourth hourly blood sample is drawn, the subject runs in place for five minutes to produce bodily stress. After the fifth blood sample has been drawn, the subject hyperventilates for three minutes for its stress-producing value. It is customary for many subjects to reveal their hypoglycemia at this time. Many patients drop ten points, but occasionally some drop even forty, fifty, or even sixty points, with massive symptom-production of reactions such as headache or shaking, weakness, faintness, or breaking out in a sweat, hunger, or nausea. Depression, tension and agitation, and apprehension also are produced. By stress activating the glucose tolerance test, many patients reveal a hypoglycemia that otherwise is not revealed. Some have observed that there are those neuresthenic patients who are helped with a high protein, low carbohydrate, frequent feeding diet, even though they did not show evidence of hypoglycemia on the GTT.[14] However, if the test is stress activated, these subjects do reveal hypoglycemia. When tested in this way, the majority of emotionally disturbed patients do reveal a symptom-producing hypoglycemia. This could simply be characterized as an indication of their chemically defective state. These defects, in terms of inborn errors of metabolism, nutritional deficiencies, malabsorption syndromes, endogenous or exogenous toxic states, various allergies and especially corn allergy, hyperinsulinism produced by a pancreatic response to galactosemia and rarely an insulinonia, must still be fathomed in order to properly handle the case. However, since we do understand that hypoglycemia is present, then methods can be developed, which will aid in the relief of these symptoms by giving a moderately high protein, moderately low carbohydrate, sugar-free, caffeine-free, alcohol-free, specifically allergic-free for each patient, preferably tobacco-free, frequent feeding diet so that many of these symptoms can be helped. Sometimes it is best to add the adrenal Cortical Extract during a stabilizing period.[15] A salt supplement is often necessary because of the associated salt-dumping and evidence of low sodium on the hair test.

The subject of the correct utilization of vitamin C need not be speculative. By loading the patient with 3,000 or more milligrams t.i.d. of vitamin C, then testing a twenty-four hour urine sample, one can discover how much vitamin C it takes before this person spills vitamin C in the urine. Some neurotic patients will use anything from 1,000 to 3,000-4,000 milligrams of vitamin C. Often schizophrenic patients are much higher in their utilization of vitamin C. It is important to supply the amount of vitamin C that is utilized by that specific person because otherwise he is in a state of vitamin C deficiency, which serves as a handicap for adrenal cortical function. Vitamin C is readily absorbed by toxins and is therefore used as a detoxicant, so if toxins are present, vitamin C is quickly absorbed leaving the person in a state of vitamin C deficiency. It is not wise to assume that adequate vitamin C can be obtained in food, especially in citric fruit juices. It is unwise to take more than 250 cc. of a citric juice in the course of twenty-four hours, since citric acid ties with magnesium and depletes the body of its magnesium store.[16]

Intolerance to milk is being demonstrated in many patients. There are three sources of this intolerance. The first is the lack of lactase. This is especially noted in celiac disease and it has been found that milk should not be used by the celiac case due to the lack of lactase. It seems there are many who are not celiac cases who still lack this lactase. Doctors Theodore Bayless, M.D., and Shi-Shung Huang, M.D., have reported that 10 percent of white people and 70 percent of black people cannot use milk due to this lack of lactase.[17] When lactase is not in optimum supply, then fermentation of lactic acid, which is absorbed into the blood and produces a state of anxiety.[18] It has been demonstrated that lactase infusion can, in certain people, precipitate states of anxiety.[19]

Another important reason for an intolerance to milk is the condition called galactosemia. This inborn metabolic error is a problem of the liver and it is said to be a deficiency of the enzyme galactose-1-uridyl transferase resulting in the accumulation of galactose-1-phosphate, which is the transfer of galactose to glucose. ATP is also necessary for this process and therefore is likely quite important in view of the demonstrated ATP deficiency. Since a normal liver metabolism is demanded for the transfer of galactose into glucose, also other states, such as the alcoholic cirrhosis, would be important in the production of high galactose levels. Heretofore, galactose had been thought of as a rare entity. However, recently I have been surveying my patients and find this to be running 30 to 50 percent. Most of these patients are schizophrenic. Therefore, it appears that galactosemia may turn out to be a very important source of toxins to the mentally defective and the schizophrenic patient, and some neurotics. I have observed that there seems to be a characteristic of obsessive-compulsiveness, as well as intense agitation in these galactosemics. If the galactosemia occurs early in life, it will stunt the growth.

A third reason for milk intolerance is allergy. Milk allergy is high on the list of foods that produce allergic reactions. These may be nasal stuffiness, nausea, vomiting, a sense of chilliness, mild to severe shaking, epigastric distress and even diarrhea, or a cerebral allergic reaction with the production of any emotional reaction, which you can imagine.

The chemical survey outlined here was formulated with the idea of finding out why the emotionally disturbed subject had reduced energy. It has gradually led to the examination of inborn errors of metabolism. It is now considered that there are approximately 100 known inborn errors of metabolism. I believe that more extensive surveys should be conducted in an effort to screen these inborn errors of metabolism. This is especially true since in the schizophrenic and similar states because multiple deficiencies seem to be the order of the day, and they can only be detected by a screening process for multiple inborn errors as well as a screen for evident deficiencies.

ALLERGY OF THE CENTRAL NERVOUS SYSTEM is assuming increasing importance.[20] It is evident that the central nervous system can serve as the specific allergic shock organ without other evidence of allergy being manifested. Dr. S. Klotz's observations of allergic reactions in the students at Green Valley School also emphasizes the importance of allergy in the social and educational failure group.[21] Tension or fatigue, hyperactivity or hypoactivity, elation or depression are basic responses in central nervous system allergy. Specific mental symptoms will depend on the area of the brain that is affected by the swelling and toxicity, which is produced by the allergic reaction. These can produce any of the numerous emotional reactions of which the central nervous system is capable. Headaches and seizures can also be produced by allergy. The most common offenders are the most commonly used foods such as cereal grains, corn, milk, eggs, etc. These reactions are so frequent that it is imperative that an examination of cerebral allergy, especially of commonly used foods, be a part of the chemical survey. The most satisfactory methods of examination are by deliberate food testing and provocative food testing,* while carefully observing the patient's behavior.[22] Allergic reactions are a type of unadaptive response that is produced by a chemically defective organism. The more defective the chemistry, the more we can anticipate allergic reactions.

The megavitamin therapy, as so ably tested and demonstrated to have value by Abram Hoffer and Humphrey Osmond,[23] does seem to have a specific value in one sense in that NAD deficiency is demonstrated in a high percentage of schizophrenic patients and a high utilization of ascorbic acid is also demonstrated. Therefore, the combination of B^3 in the form of Niacin or Niacinomide and ascorbic acid is in order, in some cases filling a specific need and in other cases at least serving in a non-specific way as part of an antistress program, which helps the person handle the toxins although he is not specifically handling the inborn errors and allergies. As these inborn errors are isolated and altered, usually through nutritional means of providing an adequate supply of the specific B-complex vitamin, essential amino acid, phospholipid, or essential mineral, or withdrawing the offending agent, we will undoubtedly find that the megavitamin doses will be considerably reduced as we develop an understanding of the total picture of the metabolism of the patient. For example, there would not be the great demand for the large amounts of vitamin C, once the toxins are handled. There would not be the great need for the antistress value of B^3 once the defects are handled.

The side-effects of megavitamin therapy have not been very severe, and are usually of such a nature that there is an indication that the vitamin dosage should be reduced, such as, if nausea were in evidence, the amount of B^3 would be reduced. There has occurred one case of kidney stones that was associated with the Niacin therapy. This, undoubtedly, was due to a specific chemical state of that particular patient, since no other subjects out of the many thousands given B^3 have resulted in kidney stones. This case was quickly detected and resulted in no injury to the patient. It would seem logical to run frequent uric acid studies and keep the megavitamin doses at a level so that normal uric acid is not exceeded. If this state of affairs exists, it will show as a high uric acid level, even though the problem is not really a rise in uric acid but a rise in metabolites of B^3 produced by the liver, which show on the uric acid test as uric acid. But in a more refined test, this proves not to be uric acid but rather metabolites of B^3. It should be observed that the side effects of megavitamin therapy have been infinitely less than those produced by any of the tranquilizers or antidepressants.

What is the relationship between a high carbohydrate diet and a protein deficient diet and emotional reactions? It has been observed that in protein

---

*A description of how to do deliberate food testing, how to keep a food symptom diary, and information about individual laboratories that can do particular testing procedures is available to any interested person by writing directly to the author.

deficient states the subject is irritable and overactive.[24] It really is quite impossible to separate a high carbohydrate intake from a low protein intake, because the two go hand-in-hand. When one is present, the other is present. A high carbohydrate intake is also irritating to the nervous system in that it produces a state of deficiency of proteins, vitamins, and minerals, which eventually result in hypoglycemia with its set of symptoms. In addition, other irritating factors of a less-than-optimum protein intake and the learning difficulties resulting from that low protein intake also occur.

A high protein diet is not without possible problems. Allergic foods are frequently protein foods. A person will become worse if the increase in protein foods includes foods to which the person is allergic. Having surveyed for allergies can be helpful in preventing this problem. Also new allergies can develop when a food is increased in its frequency of use. Keeping a food and symptom diary can help spot these deficiencies. Frequently used food tends to have delayed reactions (addictions) ranging from three to twenty hours after eating the food. When a food has not been eaten for four days then the reaction usually occurs within a range of fifteen minutes to one and one-half hours. Sometimes allergic foods can be tolerated if used in the form of one small serving with no greater frequency than every six days.

EMOTIONAL REACTIONS ARE STATES OF STRESS. It does not matter whether this begins with inborn errors and the resultant deficiencies and toxins, or nutritional deficiencies, allergic reactions, or from excessive environmental stimuli with its resultant excessive need of nutritional intake and thus secondarily producing a deficiency state. Since emotional reactions are states of stress, it is important that a basic principle of treatment of emotional reactions start with an antistress program. Thus, the moderately high protein, low carbohydrate, frequent feeding diet with an adequate amount of the antistress factor of the B-complex vitamins and essential minerals is recommended. This can best be handled by understanding, as nearly as possible, the evidence of these deficiencies rather than treating them with a shotgun approach. The deficiencies are best handled by specifically knowing what those deficiencies are and supplementing according to these demonstrated needs. This testing also serves to give direction to therapy, by indicating when correction occurs, and when the supplement needs to be altered.

Emotional reactions are not just states of stress. Emotional reactions are also learned responses and are subject to the laws of learning and unlearning as long as the organism is in a reasonable state of chemical homeostasis. First of all by providing this reasonable homeostatic state, the learning of new adaptive responses and the unlearning of unadaptive responses can proceed with reasonable stability. I first attempted to treat schizophrenic patients with behavioral therapy, along with tranquilizers. I found a considerable degree of success. However, the relapse rate was disappointing. With the more rational biobehavioral approach, the relapse rate has been considerably reduced. The training of corrective responses is just as necessary as before. We should not depend on a correction of chemistry to completely correct symptoms, especially in a psychotic patient, a markedly phobic patient, or an obsessive-compulsive patient, because they may be so tenaciously learned that unless specific retraining techniques are used there will not be as adequate a recovery as is possible.

We might characterize the entrance of behaviorism into the field of psychotherapy as the entrance of an efficiency expert into the system. Under these circumstances, the motivational force behind the psychotherapy becomes the efficiency itself of symptom change rather than a philosophical curiosity of repressed material, which emerges as a symbolic expression.

Many practices with increased efficiency have resulted from the adopttion of practices that are based on the reinforcement theory of drive reduction. There appears to be developing a new focus with a simpler but keener format for the erection of practices based on the evidence that optimal excitation of the central nervous system is the basic motivational building block of learning. With this concept, new responses can be learned by providing the central nervous system excitation while this corrective response is coached. Unadaptive responses can be unlearned by providing an energy threshold, which will either not produce the response while the stimulus is met, or will block the response while the stimulus is met. The therapist becomes a manipulator of energy thresholds. Viewed in this respect, he sees himself as being in need of an organism with an energy homeostatic capacity that is capable of these energy shifts and without some unadaptive chemically driven energy threshold. It becomes important to understand the approach areas of the brain and the avoidance areas of the brain.[25] The avoidance areas of the brain are in operation when energy thresholds are too low, as well as when energy thresholds are too high. There is an optimum level of energy threshold at which approach areas function. Avoidance and approach areas do not operate at the same time. It is important to know how these areas can be evoked and tied with responses for approach on the one hand, and avoidance on the other, depending on the need as a subject meets any specific stimulus. The approach areas of the brain can be activated by such a technique as relaxation, also they can be activated by small amounts of carbon dioxide, or driving the brain with a stroboscope to produce the alpha rhythm. Aversive areas of the brain can be activated through sensory inputs such as high level stimuli that are capable of blocking imagery or producing pain.

How can we produce a response interference without pain that serves the purpose of training out unadaptive responses, yet does not give the subject a sense of discomfort. This has been worked out by the use of a combination of nitrous oxide and CO_2. In most cases, CO_2 of either one or two breaths of 50 percent, or a rapid rise from 10 percent to 50 percent CO_2 will produce such a result. Since CO_2 itself has an inhibiting effect on pain, this is not an uncomfortable procedure. There are a small number of subjects who become concerned by the rapid breathing. This concern is usually trained out by approaching the use of CO_2 on a piecemeal basis, which desensitizes them to this concern. However, there still remains a small number who have such a concern. This can be handled by giving nitrous oxide 50 percent along with the CO_2. The drill is on this order—starting with 50 percent nitrous oxide, 10 percent CO_2, and 40 percent O_2 for one minute, then placing in the mind an unadaptive response and changing the CO_2 to 50 percent, the nitrous to 25 percent, and the O_2 to 25 percent the image leaves within 15-30 seconds with good training effect of inhibiting the unadaptive response. Thus, a painless response interference method with a high efficiency value has been developed.

A stroboscope with a diffused screen can be used both to aid in relaxation by setting the flickering light at 8-10 flashes per second, or can be used to increase vivid activated imagery by setting it at 18-22 flashes per second. This is not as efficient as the CO_2-nitrous oxide technique simply because it requires more experience to learn how to make use of this. It also does not automatically brighten the affect as much as CO_2-nitrous oxide. However, it is a bit easier in its application and does not require medical supervision. For this reason, it may turn out to be applied in a larger number of cases.

The production, either by CO_2-nitrous oxide or by the stroboscope, of an activated eidetic image should have considerable significance in that such an activation would increase memory, producing a rapid learning technique. Also picturing is a compositing of information and therefore has the quality of creativity. Putting the available information into a composite with correcting and problem-solving value may also prove to be the essence of insight. It could be spoken of as operational insight in which the solution, out of available information, has now been discovered, and through the use of imagery the solution can be practiced ahead of time, making it easier to apply in life's situations.

THE MIND AND THE BODY function as a unit. For many years, psychiatry has placed too much emphasis on thinking as though thinking was the all-powerful agent in changing physiology. Only recently have we been obtaining glimpses of understanding physiology in terms of inborn errors of metabolism, deficiency states, endogenous and exogenous toxins, central nervous system allergic responses, and how these can be altered to favorably influence emotional responses and increase the efficiency of the function of the central nervous system in such areas as learning. Only by widely surveying inborn errors of metabolism, toxic states, endocrine disturbances, and allergic reactions, are we able to arrive at a clinically significant methodology for favorably altering mental states through physiological understanding and treatment.

Behaviorism, associated with biochemistry, is bringing to us an increased efficiency in training out unadaptive responses and training in adaptive responses. No longer do we simply ask the question, "Is this person in conflict?", without also asking the question, "Why is this person excessively irritable?"

Based on present concepts of how learning occurs due to excitation of the central nervous system tied with a response, the therapist can become an engineer—manipulating the organism so as to either produce a learning of responses through contiguity of excitation tied with a response or reverse the process and produce a blocking of the response through either low or high thresholds of energy and through contiguity produce unlearning of responses.

The utilization of activated imagery through either the chemical means of carbon dioxide and nitrous oxide, or the driving effect of the stroboscope, are proving to be techniques of high subject acceptance and high efficiency rates both for training in adaptive responses and training out unadaptive responses.

NOTES

1. Abram Hoffer, "Biochemistry of Nicotonic Acid and Nicotinamide," *Psychosomatics*, 8 (1967), 95-100; idem, "Nicotinamide Adenine Dinucleotide (NAD) as a Treatment for Schizophrenia," *Journal of Psychopharmocology*, 1 (1966), 79-92; Linus Pauling, (ed.), *Orthomolecular Psychiatry* (Washington, D.C.: American Association for the Advancement of Science, 1968).
2. Joseph Wolpe, *Psychotherapy by Reciprocal Inhibition* (Stanford, Calif.: Stanford University Press, 1958), pp. 12-13, 166-172; idem, *The Practice of Behavior Therapy* (New York, N.Y.: Pergamon Press, 1969), pp. 91-149; Aubrey J. Yates, *Behavior Therapy* (New York, N.Y.: John Wiley & Sons, Inc., 1970).
3. Yates, *Behavior Therapy*.
4. C. L. Hull (ed.), *Principles of Behavior* (New York, N.Y.: D. Appleton and Company, 1943); Wolpe, *Psychotherapy*.
5. Robert W. Doty, "Conditioned Reflexes Formed and Evoked by Brain Stimulation," *Electrical Stimulation of the Brain*, ed. Daniel E. Sheer (Austin, Texas: University of Texas Press, 1961).
6. D. E. Berlyne, "The Reward-Value of Indifferent Stimulation," *Reinforcement and Behavior*, ed. Jack T. Tapp (New York, N.Y.: Academic Press, Inc., 1969), pp. 178-214.
7. Frederic Speer, *Allergy of the Nervous System* (Springfield, Ill.: Charles C Thomas, 1970).
8. Seymour Levine, "Hormones and Conditioning," *Nebraska Symposium on Motivation*, ed. William J. Arnold (Lincoln, Neb.: University of Nebraska Press, 1968).
9. Martin Rubin, personal communication with author, Washington Reference Laboratory, Washington, D.C., 1971.
10. F. C. Dohan, "Cereals and Schizophrenia, Data and Hypothesis," *Acta. Psychiat. Scand.* 42, No. 125 (1966); F. C. Dohan, J. Grasberger, H. Johnson, and A. W. Arbegast, "Cereal-Free Diet in Relapsed Schizophrenics," *Federal Proceedings*, 27, No. 2 (1968).
11. Virginia E. Davis, and Michael J. Walsh, "A Possible Biochemical Mechanism for the Addiction Liability of Certain Sedative-Hypnotic Drugs," paper presented at the conference of the Society of Biochemical Psychiatry, San Francisco, Calif., May 10, 1970.
12. John J. Miller, personal communication with author, biochemist, West Chicago, Ill., 1971.
13. Ibid.
14. Harvey A. McGehee (ed.) et al, "Hypoglycemia," *The Principles and Practices of Medicine* (New York, N.Y.: Appleton-Century-Crofts, Inc., 1968).
15. John W. Tintera, "Stabilizing Homeostasis in the Recovered Alcoholic through Endocrine Therapy: Evaluation of the Hypoglycemic Factor," *Journal of the American Geriatric Society*, 14 (1966), 126-148.
16. John J. Miller, personal communication with author, biochemist, West Chicago, Ill., 1971.
17. Douglas Sandberg, personal communication with author, associate professor and co-director, Clinical Research Center, University of Miami, Florida, 1971.
18. Ibid.
19. F. N. Pitts, and J. N. McClure, "Lactate Metabolism in Anxiety Neurosis," *New England Journal of Medicine*, 277, (1967), 1329.

20. Frederic Speer, *Allergy of the Nervous System*.
21. Saul D. Klotz, M.D., personal communication with author, Par Avenue Clinic, Orlando, Florida, 1971.
22. Marshall Mandell, M.D., personal communication with author, allergist, Norwalk, Connecticut, 1971.
23. Abram Hoffer, and Humphrey Osmond, *How to Live Schizophrenia* (New Hyde Park, N.Y.: University Books, Inc., 1966).
24. Bacon Chow, "Malnutrition and IQ," *New Scientist*, 33 (1966), 72.
25. D. E. Berlyne, "Arousal and Reinforcement," *Nebraska Symposium on Motivation*, ed. David Levine (Lincoln, Neb.: University of Nebraska Press, 1967), 1-110; idem, "The Reward Value of Indifferent Stimulation."

APPENDIX

Appendix

Sources of all tests mentioned in the Proceedings *articles are included in this Appendix. For the reader's convenience, the tests are listed in alphabetical order by title.*

BENDER VISUAL-MOTOR GESTALT TEST FOR CHILDREN. Aileen Clawson. Beverly Hills, Calif.: Western Psychological Services, 1962.

CALIFORNIA ACHIEVEMENT TESTS. Ernest W. Teigs and Willis W. Clark. Monterey, Calif.: California Test Bureau, 1957.

CALIFORNIA MENTAL MATURITY SCALE. Elizabeth T. Sullivan, Willis W. Clark and Ernest W. Teigs. Monterey, Calif.: California Test Bureau, 1962.

FELS RATING SCALE OF CLASSROOM BEHAVIOR. David Fels. Los Angeles, Calif.: Unpublished, but available through the author, Director of Research, Los Angeles County schools.

THE FROSTIG PROGRAM FOR THE DEVELOPMENT OF VISUAL PERCEPTION (Teacher's Guide.) Marianne Frostig and David Horne. Chicago, Ill.: Folett Publishing Company, 1964.

GATES MacGINITIE READING TESTS. Arthur I. Gates and Walter H. MacGinitie. New York, N.Y.: Teacher's College Press, Columbia University, 1965.

GOODENOUGH INTELLIGENCE TEST. Florence Goodenough. Yonkers, N.Y.: World Book Company, 1926.

ILLINOIS TEST OF PSYCHOLINGUISTIC ABILITIES. Samuel A. Kirk, James J. McCarthy, and Winifred Kirk (Examiner's Manual.) Urbana, Ill.: University of Illinois Press, 1961, revised 1968.

IOWA SILENT READING TESTS. H. A. Greene, A. N. Jorgensen, and V. H. Kelley. New York, N.Y.: Harcourt, Brace, and World, Inc., 1927-56.

IOWA TESTS OF BASIC SKILLS. E. F. Lindquist and A. N. Hieronymus, et al. Dallas, Tex.: Haughton Mifflin Company, 1964.

IOWA TESTS OF EDUCATIONAL DEVELOPMENT. E. F. Lindquist, et al. Chicago, Ill.: Science Research Associates, Inc., 1942-59.

JUNIOR-SENIOR HIGH SCHOOL PERSONALITY QUESTIONNAIRE. R. B. Catell and H. Beloff. Champaign, Ill.: Institute of Personality and Ability Testing, 1962.

MANN-WHITNEY U. TEST. Avram Goldstein. *Biostatistics*. New York, N.Y.: The MacMillan Company, 1964, pp. 55-59.

METRAUX TEST OF AUDITORY MEMORY SPAN. Ruth Metraux. "Auditory Memory Span for Speech Sounds: Norms for Children," *Journal of Speech and Hearing Disorders*, 9 (1944), 31-38.

PEABODY PICTURE VOCABULARY TEST. Lloyd M. Dunn. Minneapolis, Minn.: American Guidance Service, Inc., 1959.

PERCEPTUAL FORMS (Teacher's Manual). Winter Haven Lions Publication Committee. Winter Haven, Fla.: Starr Press, 1963.

PSYCHODIAGNOSTIC PLATES. Hermann Rorschach and Hans Huber. New York, N.Y.: Grune and Stratton, Inc., 1921-54.

THEMATIC APPERCEPTION TEST. Leopold Bellak. New York, N.Y. Psychological Corporation, 1943.

VERBAL LANGUAGE DEVELOPMENT SCALE. Merlin J. Mecham. Minneapolis, Minn.: Educational Test Bureau, 1958-59.

WECHSLER INTELLIGENCE SCALE FOR CHILDREN (WISC). David I. Wechsler. New York, N.Y.: Psychological Corporation, 1949.

WIDE RANGE ACHIEVEMENT TEST. J. F. Jastak, S. W. Bijou, and S. R. Jastak. Wilmington, Del.: Guidance Associates, 1965.

DISCHARGED
MAR 16 1984

NOV 23 1981

~~NOV 25 1991~~

DISCHARGED

NOV 1 1 1980

DISCHARGED

DISCHARGED

OCT 3 0 1991

NOV 1 8 1991

NOV 2 6 1991